The Lesser Gods of the Sahara

CASS SERIES: HISTORY AND SOCIETY IN THE ISLAMIC WORLD
ISSN 1466-9390
Series Editors: Anoushiravan Ehteshami and George Joffé

Contemporary events in the Islamic world dominate the headlines and emphasise the crises of the Middle East and North Africa, yet the Islamic world is far larger and more varied than we realise. Current affairs there too mask the underlying trends and values that have, over time, created a fascinating and complex world. This new series is intended to reveal that other Islamic reality by looking at its history and society over the ages. It will also reach far further, bringing in Central Asia and the Far East as part of a cultural space sharing common values and beliefs but at the same time manifesting a vast diversity of experience and social order.

1. *French Military Rule in Morocco: Colonialism and its Consequences*
   by Moshe Gershovich

2. *Tribe and Society in Rural Morocco*
   by David M. Hart

3. *The Walled Arab City in Literature, Architecture and History:*
   The Living Medina in the Maghrib
   edited by Susan Slyomovics

4. *North Africa, Islam and the Mediterranean World:*
   From the Almoravids to the Algerian War
   edited by Julia Clancy-Smith

5. *Technology, Tradition and Survival:*
   Aspects of Material Culture in the Middle East and Central Asia
   edited by Richard Tapper and Keith McLachlan

6. *Nation, Society and Culture in North Africa*
   edited by James McDougall

The Lesser Gods of the Sahara

Social Change and Contested Terrain
amongst the Tuareg of Algeria

Jeremy Keenan

FRANK CASS
LONDON • PORTLAND, OR

First published in 2004 in Great Britain by
FRANK CASS PUBLISHERS
Crown House, 47 Chase Side, London N14 5BP

and in the United States of America by
FRANK CASS PUBLISHERS
c/o ISBS, 920 NE 58th Avenue, Suite 300
Portland, Oregon 97213-3786

Website: www.frankcass.com

Copyright © 2004 Frank Cass & Co. Ltd.

British Cataloguing in Publication Data

Keenan, Jeremy, 1945–
 The lesser gods of the Sahara : social change and contested terrain amongst the Tuareg of Algeria. – (Cass series. History and society in the Islamic world)
 1.Tuaregs – Algeria – Social life and customs – 20th century
 2.Tuaregs – Algeria – Social conditions – 20th century
 3.Tuaregs – Algeria – Politics and government – 20th century
 4.Women, Tuareg – Algeria – Social conditions – 20th century
 5.Algeria – Politics and government
 I.Title II.The Journal of North African Studies
 305.8'933065

ISBN 0 7146 5410 8
ISBN 0 7146 8410 4
ISSN 1466 9390

Library of Congress Cataloging-in-Publication data

Keenan, Jeremy, 1945-
 The lesser gods of the Sahara : social change and contested terrain amongst the Tuareg of Algeria / Jeremy Keenan.
  p. cm. – (Cass series—history and society in the Islamic world)
 Includes bibliographical references and index.
 ISBN 0-7146-5410-8 (cloth) – ISBN 0-7146-8410-4 (pbk.)
 1. Tuaregs–History. 2. Tuaregs–Ethnic identity. 3. Tuaregs–Social life and customs. 4. Social change–Algeria. 5. Cultural Protection–Algeria. 6. Algeria–Colonization. 7. Algeria–Race relations. 8. Algeria–Politics and government. I. Title. II. Series.
 DT283.6.T83K414 2004
 305.89'33065'009045–dc22   2003021311

This group of studies first appeared in a Special Issue on
'The Lesser Gods of the Sahara: Social Change and Contested Terrain amongst the Tuareg of Algeria' of *The Journal of North African Studies* (ISSN 1362 9387) 8/3–4 (Autumn–Winter 2003).

All rights reserved. No part of this publication may be reproduced, stored in or introduced into a retrieval system, or transmitted, in any form or by any means, electronic, mechanical, photocopying, recording or otherwise, without the prior written permission of the publisher of this book.

Printed in Great Britain by Antony Rowe Ltd., Chippenham, Wiltshire

Contents

Foreword — vii

Glossary — ix

Introduction: Indigenous Rights and a Future Politic amongst Algeria's Tuareg after Forty Years of Independence — 1

From Tit (1902) to Tahilahi (2002): A Reconsideration of the Impact of and Resistance to French Pacification and Colonial Rule by the Tuareg of Algeria (the Northern Tuareg) — 27

Ethnicity, Regionalism and Political Stability in Algeria's *Grand Sud* — 67

Dressing for the Occasion: Changes in the Symbolic Meanings of the Tuareg Veil — 97

The End of the Matriline? The Changing Roles of Women and Descent amongst the Algerian Tuareg — 121

The Last Nomads: Nomadism amongst the Tuareg of Ahaggar (Algerian Sahara) — 163

The Lesser Gods of the Sahara — 193

Contested Terrain: Tourism, Environment and Security in Algeria's Extreme South — 226

Bibliography — 266

Abstracts — 274

Index — 279

Foreword

Algeria has been the focus of public attention for many years, beginning with the cancellation by the military of national legislative elections in January 1992; elections that would have seen the first-ever Islamist political party come to national-level power in the Arab world. That interrupted democratic process was immediately followed by a civil war that continues until today in which an estimated 200,000 people have been killed, often brutally, by a combination of Islamic militants, rogue and regular elements within the armed forces, and opportunistic criminal groups. During this same period Berberists living in Kabylia in northern Algeria have been demanding expanded political, cultural and economic rights, with an increased militancy that has frequently degenerated into violent clashes with the authorities, some of which have resulted in the deaths of innocent civilians.

Throughout all of this chaos and bloodshed, Algeria's Saharan region seems to have escaped untouched, safeguarded by physical distance, a severe climate and the character, lifestyle and traditions of the Tuareg, the 'blue-veiled warriors of the Sahara'. However mythical this latter characterisation may have been, fuelled in part by 'orientalist' depictions provided by French colonialists following France's occupation of Algeria in 1830, the region's placidity was severely shattered in early 2003 when 32 European tourists were abducted by presumed Islamic militants deep in the Algerian Sahara. Although the hostage crisis was finally resolved peacefully more than six months later with all but one abductee returning home safely, the Saharan region and its people, especially the Tuareg, could no longer escape the political turbulence and social violence engulfing the rest of the country. Yet, in the process, one myth about the Tuareg was too readily substituted for another. Idealised as mysterious, exotic 'blue men' in orientalist literature, now the Tuareg were being viewed as 'terrorists' undistinguished from Algerians living in the north who were engaged in radical behaviour, whether in the name of political Islam or greater Berber rights.

It is within this cauldron of paradoxes and confusion that Jeremy Keenan's *The Lesser Gods of the Sahara* brings historical light, intellectual acuity, factual accuracy and enormous personal empathy to provide the reader with what is undoubtedly the most comprehensive and even-handed treatment of the Tuareg people of Algeria ever produced. Keenan has been studying the Algerian Tuareg for over 40 years, involving extensive fieldwork, interviews, surveys and personal encounters, along with a mastery of the existing literature on the subject. Using a multidisciplinary perspective, Keenan incorporates 'thick' anthropological description with contemporary political analysis, providing in the process substantial insights not only about the Tuareg but also about Algerian political, social and economic life more broadly.

Each section of his study tackles an important dimension of Tuareg existence, including clarifying once and for all such common misperceptions of the Tuareg as their fidelity to the Algerian state (they are loyal citizens, although critics of its undemocratic practices), their political ties to their Berberist brethren in the north (they do not share the same political agenda as Kabyle activists), their desire to establish a Tuareg homeland encompassing fellow Tuareg in Niger and Mali (the Algerian Tuareg make no common cause with Tuareg in the south who have never been fully integrated into the post-colonial state and thus suffer continued economic deprivation and political marginalisation), and their indifference or even opposition to tourism in the southern Sahara region (the Tuareg oppose the exploitative type of mass tourism and *tourisme sauvage* of the kind that led to the 2003 hostage crisis, tourism which often results in ecological degradation, cultural looting and economic distortion).

In all these dimensions Jeremy Keenan has brought scholarly passion and human compassion to his subject, expressed in elegant prose which will attract both the specialist on the subject as well as the lay reader. In shattering the myths of the past, Keenan has produced an insightful study of profound significance that will long endure and hopefully result in a new consciousness about a people and a region that are increasingly being incorporated into the modern world, with all the misgivings and tribulations such a process involves.

John P. Entelis
New York City
October 2003

Glossary

[Tk] Tamahak; [Ar] Arabic; [Fr] French.

aballag [Tk] – a form of tribute.
Adrar-n-Iforas [Tk] – the mountainous area of northern Mali.
ag [Tk] – son of (e.g. Mokhtar ag Bahedi) (see *ult*).
agedellehouf [Tk] – lower part of the veil (see *tagelmoust, chech*).
agg ettebel [Tk] – to be in line of succession (lit. son of the drum).
Aguh-en-tehle [Tk] – vassal descent group of the Kel Ahaggar, traditionally attached to the drum group (*ettebel*) of the noble Kel Rela.
Ahaggar (pl. Ihaggaren) [Tk] – mountainous region in the extreme south of Algeria and home of the Kel Ahaggar Tuareg. The plural, Ihaggaren, designates the noble class in Ahaggar.
ahal [Tk] – social gathering at night.
aheg [Tk] – to raid.
Ahl Azzi [Ar] (Kel Rezzi [Tk]) – the Ahl Azzi (known as Kel Rezzi) were Arab nomads with religious status from the Tuat and Tidikelt regions who married into and settled among the Tuareg of Ahaggar.
Ahl el Litham [Ar] – people of the veil (see El Molathemine).
Aïr [Tk] – mountainous region of northern Niger, traditionally inhabited by the Kel Aïr.
Ait Lowayan [Tk] – vassal descent group of the Kel Ahaggar, traditionally attached to the drum group (*ettebel*) of the noble Kel Rela.
Ajjer [Tk] – Ajjer (Azdjer) is the region to the immediate north-east of Ahaggar, known as the Tassili-n-Ajjer. Traditionally inhabited by the Kel Ajjer Tuareg.
alechcho [Tk] – veil (see *chech*).
Algerie Française [Fr] – the cry of many of the French colonialists in Algeria who wanted to keep Algeria as part of France.
amacheg/amajeg [Tk] – term used by Tuareg in Niger and Mali to designate themselves. Its equivalent in Ahaggar is *imuhagh* (see *imuhagh*).
amaoual-oua-n-afella [Tk] – part of the veil that forms turban covering forehead.
Amazigh – the *Amazigh* peoples are the indigenous population of the Maghrib. Often known as the Berbers. The Tuareg belong to the *Amazigh* peoples.
Amenukal [Tk] – The title of the supreme chief of the Kel Ahaggar. The office of Amenukal ceased to exist in Ahaggar in 1974 on the death of the last incumbent. The drum (*ettebel*), which symbolized the *Amenukal*'s authority, was transferred from his camp to the offices of the Commune of Tamanrasset.
amrar (pl. *amraren*) [Tk] – chief, headman, old man, husband, kinsmen of ascending generations, etc.

anagad [Tk] – veiling.
anet ma [Tk] – mother's brother (an important kinsman in all Tuareg groups).
ariwan [Tk] – small camp.
Armée de Libération Nationale – Algeria's national army prior to Independence in 1962. From 1962 onwards it was named the *Armée Nationale Populaire*.
Armée Nationale Populaire – Algeria's army after 1962.
arouri [Tk] – back, father's family.
Association des Agences de Tourisme Wilaya de Tamanrasset (ATAWT) – association of travel agencies (mostly Tuareg) in the *wilaya* of Tamanrasset. At the forefront of the struggle for a more environmentally sustainable form of tourism in Algeria's Sahara (see UNATA).
Atakor [Tk] – the central mountains of Ahaggar. Traditionally the territory of the Dag Rali, rising to just under 10,000 feet in Mount Tahat, the highest mountain in Algeria.
azalay/azli [Tk] – the move of the wife (and children) to the husband's camp (see *ariwan*), from the verb *azli*, meaning to separate.
Berbers – the indigenous peoples of the Maghrib, known as *Amazigh*.
bidonville [Fr] – shanty-town (lit. suburbs of cities built out of old tin cans and boxes).
bouleversement [Fr] – literally 'overturning' (used in this context to describe a social revolution).
Centre National de la Recherche Scientifique (CNRS) – French National Research body.
Chaamba [Ar] – Arab tribe, formerly nomadising in much of Algeria's northern Sahara, and traditional enemies of the Tuareg: pronounced 'Shaambi'.
chech [Ar] – veil or head-cloth. There are many terms for the Tuareg veil and particular parts or features of it. The word *chech* is an Arabic term, known in Tamahak as *echchach* (see *tagelmoust*).
cheurfa (sing. *cherif*) [Ar] – Descendants of the Prophet.
Chinoui/Chnaoui (masc. sing. *chinoui*; masc. pl. *chnaoui*; fem. sing. *chinouia* or *chinouiette*; fem. pl. *chnaouia* or *chnaouiat*) [Tk] – a new Tuareg word meaning Chinese, used derogatorily to describe Algerians from the north.
commune [Fr] – small territorial division, roughly equivalent to an English parish.
Confédération des Touareg du Nord [Fr] – a French notion comprising the Kel Ahaggar and Kel Ajjer Tuareg.
Dag Rali [Tk] – vassal descent group of the Kel Ahaggar, traditionally attached to the drum group (*ettebel*) of the noble Kel Rela.
daira [Ar] – administrative division, smaller than a *wilaya* and roughly equivalent to a municipality (between commune and *wilaya*).
Djanet [Tk] – ancient desert town town in the extreme south-east of Algeria in the *wilaya* of Illizi. Recognized as a tourist centre because of its proximity to the rock paintings of the Tassili-n-Ajjer (pop. *c.*12,000).
djenoun [Ar] – evil spirits.
echchach [Tk] – see *chech*.
ehenen (sing. *ehen*) [Tk] – tent(s).
ehere-n-amadal [Tk] – a form of tributary land-rent (lit. 'the wealth of the land').

Glossary

Eid Es Rir [Ar] – Islamic religious festival.
ekerhei [Tk] – woman's headcloth.
El Molathemine [Ar] – wearers of the veil (see Ahl el litham).
elmengoudi [Tk] – an adolescent boy's first wearing of the veil. This is a family ceremonial occasion marking a boy's initiation or 'passage' from adolescence to adulthood.
ettama/tezama [Tk] – mystical power, a belief prominent in Aïr which is similar to the belief in *tehot* in Ahaggar (see *tehot*).
ettebel (pl. *ettebelen*) [Tk] – drum (lit.); also means drum group, a political unit of most Tuareg groups.
Fezzan [Ar] – region of south-west Libya.
FIS (*Front Islamique du Salut, Al-Jebha al-Islamiyya li 'l-Inqadh*) – gained the greatest number of votes in Algeria's national election of 1992, which was annulled by the military authorities.
foggara [Ar] – underground aqueduct.
Fondation Deserts du Monde – World Deserts Foundation, founded in 2002, head office is in Ghardaia (Algeria). President is Cherif Rahmani, Algeria's Minister for the Environment.
Front Islamique du Salut (FIS) – see FIS.
gandoura [Ar] – the Arab kaftan.
gens du nord, les [Fr] – French expression used by many Tuareg in Algeria's extreme south to describe Algerians from the north of the country (see *Chinoui/Chnaoui*).
Ghat – ancient desert town in south-west Libya.
GIA [Fr] – *Groupe(s) Islamique(s) Armé(s)*.
Grand Sud [Fr] – geographical term for Algeria's four southernmost *wilayat* of Illizi, Tamanrasset, Adrar and Tindouf. A slightly enigmatic term when used in a political context, sometimes associated with political regionalism extending into Tuareg areas of Niger and Mali. To be understood within its political-geographical context.
Groupe salafiste pour la prédication et le combat (GSPC) – militant Islamist group which broke away from the GIA in 1998. Led by Hassan Hattab.
guardiens du parc [Fr] – lit. 'the guardians of the Park', employed by the Ahaggar National Park. The French term is used by most Tuareg in preference to the official job description as *agents de conservation*.
guelta(s) [Ar] – natural rock water-hole. The Tamahak word is *agalmam*.
Hadj Bettus – Hadj Bettu was a local entrepreneur/'warlord' from Tamanrasset who acquired national notoriety and was gaoled in 1992 for ten years. The term Hadj Bettus is sometimes used by Algerians from the north as a derogatory term for Tuareg.
harratin (sing. *hartani*) [Ar] – caste of agriculturalists, known in Tamahak as *izeggaren*.
Hoggar [Ar] – Arabic for Ahaggar (mountainous region of southern Algeria).
Ibettenaten [Tk] – vassal descent group of the Kel Ahaggar, traditionally attached to the drum group (*ettebel*) of the noble Kel Rela.
ibubah (sing. *ababah*) [Tk] – male cross cousin.

Idjeradjeriouène [Tk] – vassal descent group of the Kel Ajjer. Their territory includes the *Oued* Djerat.
Iforas [Tk] – religious tribe, originating from Es Souk (ancient Tadmekka), Adrar n Iforas, Mali.
Ihaggaren (sing. Ahaggar) [Tk] – the nobility of Ahaggar.
ihwar [Tk] – to be red (see *izeggaren*).
Ikerremoien [Tk] – section of the Kel Rela, originating from Aïr.
iklan (sing. *akli*; fem. sing. *taklit*; fem. pl. *tiklatin*) [Tk] – slaves.
Iklan Taoussit [Tk] – vassal descent group of the Kel Ahaggar, traditionally attached to the drum group (*ettebel*) of the noble Kel Rela.
Illizi – town in south-east Algeria and capital of *wilaya* of Illizi. Formerly Fort Polignac (pop. *c.*20,000).
Imanrassaten [Tk] – noble *tawsit* of Kel Ajjer.
Imenan [Tk] – ancient noble tribe of Ghat/Ajjer region.
Imesseliten [Tk] – part of the Dag Rali *tawsit*, Kel Ahaggar.
imrad [Tk] – vassal; see Kel Ulli.
imuhagh [Tk] – term used by Kel Ahaggar to designate themselves.
imuhagh ouan aghrem [Tk] – translated literally, this means '*imuhagh* (Kel Ahaggar) of the gardens'; i.e. Tuareg who are sedentarised.
imzad [Tk] – violin, the traditional musical instrument of the Tuareg.
ineden (sing. *ined*) [Tk] – blacksmiths.
In Eker [Tk] – the former French atomic test base, 160km north of Tamanrasset.
ineslemen [Tk] – religious class.
In Salah [Ar] – town in southern Algeria, 658km north-north-west of Tamanrasset.
Institut de Recherches Sahariennes [Fr] – former French research body.
Irregenaten [Tk] – an Isekkemaren *tawsit* belonging to Kel Rela drum-group, living in both Ahaggar and Tamesna.
Isekkemaren [Tk] – a class of vassal amongst the Kel Ahaggar, thought to descend from unions between Arab men and Tuareg women at a time when the northern Tuareg made alliances with Arab tribes or tribes of mixed origin in exchange for certain land rights in Ahaggar.
Iwllemmeden [Tk] – large Tuareg federation in western Niger.
izeggaren (sing. *azeggar*) [Tk] – see *harratin* (from the word *ihwar*, to be red).
Kabyles – *Amazigh* (Berber) peoples of Northern Algeria, whose traditional home is the region of Kabylia.
Kaimakam [Ar] – Turkish title of governor.
karem [Ar] – the fast observed in the holy month of Ramadan.
kehal [Ar] – black material used for veils.
Kel [Tk] – 'people of', as in Kel Ahaggar, people of Ahaggar.
Kel Aghrem (*aṛrem*) [Tk] – lit. people of the gardens, i.e. sedentarists/cultivators.
Kel Ahaggar [Tk] – lit. people of Ahaggar, traditionally, the federation of Tuareg tribes and descent groups (*tawsatin*) who live in Ahaggar.
Kel Ahem Mellen [Tk] – early noble tribe in Ahaggar of uncertain origin, now with scarcely any living descendants.
Kel Ahnet [Tk] – vassal descent group of the Kel Ahaggar, traditionally attached to the drum group (*ettebel*) of the noble Taitok.

Glossary

Kel Aïr [Tk] – lit. people of Aïr, traditionally, the federation of Tuareg tribes and descent groups (*tawsatin*) who live in the Aïr Mountains of Niger.

Kel Ajjer [Tk] – lit. people of Ajjer, traditionally the federation of Tuareg tribes and descent groups (*tawsatin*) who live in and around the Tassili-n-Ajjer.

Kel Amadal [Tk] – people of the earth (see Kel Asouf).

Kel Arefsa [Tk] – section of Aguh-en-tehle.

Kel Asouf [Tk] – wicked spirits, sometimes known as Kel Had (people of the night), Kel Tenere (people of the empty places), Kel Amadal (people of the earth).

Kel Djanet [Tk] – lit. people of Djanet.

Kel Had [Tk] – people of the night (see Kel Asouf).

Kel Hirafok [Tk] – a section of the Dag Rali.

Kel Meddak [Tk] – a descent group (*tawsit*) of the Kel Ajjer, traditionally living on the plateau above Djanet.

Kel In Amguel [Tk] – lit. people of In Amguel.

Kel Rela [Tk] – noble descent group (*tawsit*) of the Kel Ahaggar.

Kel Tagelmoust [Tk] – lit. people of the *tagelmoust* (veil), a term used to describe the Tuareg (see *tagelmoust*).

Kel Tagmart [Tk] – lit. people of Tagmart (mostly Dag Rali).

Kel Tamanrasset [Tk] – a section of the Dag Rali.

Kel Tenere [Tk] – people of the empty places (see Kel Asouf).

Kel Terhenanet [Tk] – a section of the Dag Rali.

Kel Tinhart [Tk] – a section of the Dag Rali.

Kel Ulli [Tk] – lit. people of the goats, the term used to designate vassal descent groups (*tawsatin*) in preference to the term *imrad* (vassal), since it is deemed more in keeping with their predominant economic activity.

khamast [Ar] – traditional agricultural contract; from the Arab word *khamsa*, five (the Tuareg land-owner took four-fifths of the harvest and the *harratin* cultivator received one fifth).

khent [Ar] – type of veil.

marabout [Ar] – holy man.

mehariste [Fr] – camel rider, term used for French auxiliary camel corps.

Merabtine [Ar] – the Ahl Azzi (see Kel Rezzi), of religious descent, originating in Tuat – Tidikelt.

métayage [Fr] – system of cultivation in which the cultivator pays rent in kind (see *khamast*).

Metlilli – a town/village near Ghardaia (northern Algerian Sahara).

mihrab [Ar] – small mosque, usually marked out by stones.

mokadem [Ar] – holy man.

Mouadhi Chaamba [Ar] – a section of the Chaamba tribe (see Chaamba).

Mozabite – tribe originating from the Mzab.

Musée de L'Homme [Fr] – museum, Paris.

Oued [Tk] – river valley (Ar. *wadi*).

Oued Djerat [Tk] – a *oued* running north and issuing from the Tassili approximately 25km south-east of Illizi. It is famous for its prehistoric rock art.

oult ettebel [Tk] – a women through whom political succession is transmitted (see *agg ettebel*).

Qadiriya [Ar] – religious order.
Rehala [Ar] – Arabic tribe.
Relaydin [Tk] – section of the Aguh-en-tehle.
Sahara Français [Fr] – lit. French Sahara.
Sahraouis [Ar] – a term used somewhat derogatorily by northern Algerians to describe people of the desert, especially Tuareg.
Sanussi [Ar] – religious order.
Sanussiya [Ar] – see Sanussi.
Sonarem [Fr] – *Société Nationale de Recherches et d'Exploitations Minières*.
sufi [Ar] – mystic 'popular Church' of Islam.
tagelmoust [Tk] – the Tuareg veil (see also *chech*). Traditionally the *tagelmoust* is made from Sudanese indigo-dyed cloth.
Tahilahi [Tk] – a rock shelter (cave) in the Tassili near Ihrir, famous for its prehistoric rock art.
Taitok [Tk] – noble descent group (*tawsit*) of the Kel Ahaggar. Stripped of their authority by the French in 1918 for their continued resistance to colonial rule, they settled increasingly in Niger.
Taiwan – a derogatory term used by Tuareg for Algerian tourists from the north of the country, or Algerian emigrants living in France, who are called Taiwan because 'they are like the cheap spare parts made in Taiwan, compared to the expensive, original, quality spare parts – namely European tourists'.
taklit (pl. *tiklatin*) [Tk] – female slave (see *iklan*).
takouba [Tk] – the traditional Tuareg broad-sword.
taleb (pl. *tolba*) [Ar] – Quranic teacher.
Tamahak/Tamashek [Tk] – Tamahak is the language of the northern (Algerian) Tuareg. Tamashek (a close dialect) is spoken by southern Tuareg (Niger and Mali).
Tamanrasset [Tk] – the administrative capital of the *wilaya* of Tamanrasset, Algeria's extreme south (pop. *c*.100,000).
tamekchit [Tk] – exploitative social relationship whereby food is given as hospitality; deriving from *ekch*, to eat.
Tamesna [Tk] – plains in northern Niger.
Targuis [Ar] – incorrect and colloquial plural of Targui, deriving from Arab term Tuareg.
Tassili [Tk] – plateau (e.g. Tassili-n-Ajjer).
Tassili-n-Ajjer [Tk] – the plateau of the Ajjer region.
tawsit (pl. *tawsatin*) [Tk] – descent group.
tegehe [Tk] – federation.
Tegehe Mellet [Tk] – a noble tribe of Ahaggar, now very few in number.
Tegehe-n-Efis [Tk] – vassal descent group of the Kel Ahaggar, traditionally attached to the drum group (*ettebel*) of the noble Taitok.
tehot/tugarchet [Tk] – the evil eye.
tekerheit [Tk] – white woolen veil.
temazlayt [Tk] – contract of protection between nobles and vassals.
tesa [Tk] – stomach, mother's family.
tibubah (sing. *tababaht*) [Tk] – female cross-cousin.

Glossary

Tidikelt [Ar] – region to the north of Ahaggar.
Tidjaniya [Ar] – religious order.
tifinagh [Tk] – the Tuareg script.
Ti-n-Esa (Tit) [Tk] – small knoll close to Tit which was the site of the battle between the French and the Kel Ahaggar in 1902.
tirailleurs [Fr] – French auxiliary troops comprising local Arabs.
tiwse [Tk] – annual tributary payment.
tourisme sauvage [Fr] – 'unregulated' tourism.
Tuareg [Ar] – Arab word of uncertain origin, but possibly associated with the region of Targa and probably used by Arabs to refer to Berber (*Amazigh*) peoples of the Tripolitanian Sahara. Not used by Tuareg to designate themselves, except to non-Tuareg. Kel Ahaggar used the term to refer to the Fezzan region of southern Libya.
Tuat [Ar] – oasis region to the west-north-west of Tidikelt.
Ulad Ba Hammu [Ar] – Arab tribe of Tidikelt.
Ulad Dahane [Ar] – Arab tribe of Tidikelt.
Ulad Mokhtar [Ar] – Arab tribe of Tidikelt.
Ulad Yakhia [Ar] – Arab tribe of Tidikelt.
ult [Tk] – daughter of (see *ag*).
Union Nationale des Associations des Agences de Tourisme Alternatif (UNATA) – national association of tourism agencies in Algeria advocating more environmentally sustainable forms of tourism in the Sahara.
Uraren [Tk] – ancient noble tribe of Ghat/Ajjer region.
wali [Ar] – head of administration of the *wilaya*, appointed by the President and roughly equivalent to the former *Préfet*.
wilaya (pl. *wilayat*) [Ar] – *wilaya* is an administrative region, equivalent to a French *département*. During the War of Independence the FLN (*Front de Libération Nationale*) divided Algeria into six military regions, known as *wilaya*. The administrative head of a *wilaya*, appointed by the President, is the *wali*.
zawiyya [Ar] – religious lodge.
zeriba [Ar] – reed hut.
Zoua [Ar] – Arab tribe of Tidikelt.

Introduction:
Indigenous Rights and a Future Politic amongst Algeria's Tuareg after Forty Years of Independence

The seven other articles in this volume were originally planned as 'stand-alone' articles. One, 'The Lesser Gods of the Sahara', was in fact published elsewhere in 2002. While that article was in press, 'Ethnicity, Regionalism and Political Stability in Algeria's *Grand Sud*' was submitted for consideration to the editors of the *Journal of North African Studies* (JNAS). That resulted in the suggestion that I might edit a special issue of JNAS on the Algerian Tuareg. This was an opportune invitation, for which I am immensely grateful, for although the other articles were all at various stages of preparation, I had given no thought as to where they might be published. In bringing them together in one volume, I have retained their 'stand-alone' quality while taking advantage of the generosity of the editors of JNAS to indulge in more cross-referencing between the articles than would have been the case if they had been scattered through a multiplicity of journals.

A Minority Population

The Tuareg are part of the indigenous *Amazigh* people (generally known as 'Berbers') of North Africa. Their traditional lands range over some 1.5 million sq. kms of the Central Sahara and Sahel – an area roughly three times the size of France, their former colonising power. They now find themselves occupying large tracts of southern Algeria, northern Mali and Niger, with smaller pockets in Libya, Burkina Faso, northern Nigeria and Mauritania. Their precise numbers in any of these countries are not known: national censuses either ignore ethnic categories, as in Algeria, or are of dubious accuracy, as in Niger and Mali. Published figures range from 300,000 to 3 million, a difference which is largely accounted for by definitional confusion of 'who is a Tuareg': many former slaves and other formerly subordinate peoples, who still speak the Tuareg language (Tamahak in the north and Tamashek in the south), are often counted as Tuareg. According to government statistics, the southern Tuareg of Niger and Mali probably number around one million and 675,000 respectively. The northern Tuareg, who inhabit the mountainous regions of Ahaggar and the Tassili-n-Ajjer in southern Algeria, probably number between 25,000 and 30,000. This estimate is based on recent language surveys, which claim that there are some 25,000 Tamahak-speakers in Ahaggar and about 5,000 in the Tassili-n-Ajjer. These very approximate figures are further complicated by the facts that many Tuareg, especially in Niger and Mali, have been displaced from their former homelands following the pressures of drought and civil wars in the 1980s and 1990s, and that modern-day Tuareg, especially young men, are accustomed to travelling widely across the Sahara and surrounding regions in search of employment. Thus, for example, one now finds that most of the Tuareg donkey handlers working in Djanet and the surrounding Tassili are Kel Aïr.[1] Similarly, many Tuareg from Niger and Mali can be found working, or seeking work, in Tamanrasset.

On the basis of these figures, we can see that the Tuareg of Algeria comprise only about one per cent of the total population of Tuareg, while within Algeria they comprise only about 0.1 per cent of the national population. Indeed, they are now a minority in the region, comprising scarcely 10 per cent of the population of the *wilaya*[2] of Tamanrasset and only about 15 per cent of the region of Ahaggar.[3]

It might therefore be asked why this volume has been dedicated to such a numerically small population. There are several reasons. One is that the Tuareg, especially the northern Tuareg, have played a major role in both the history of the Sahara and French colonial expansion. Historically, they have punched far above their numerical weight. Related to this reason is the fact that their traditional territory, extending from around Ghadames in Libya in the north to the plains of Tamesna in northern Niger in the south,[4] is larger than the size of France and extends over some 20 per cent of Algerian national territory.

A further reason is that many of their cultural traits, notably their matrilineality and the veiling of their men (both of which are discussed in two of the articles in this volume[5]), have been the focus of interest since foreign travellers and ethnographers first came into contact with them. Indeed, the Tuareg not only became a household name in France after their massacre of the Flatters mission in 1881,[6] but they were also noted for their exotic customs, being referred to widely as the 'veiled men' or the 'blue-veiled warriors' of the Sahara, while several writers made much of their alleged matriarchy.

The decline in academic publications on the Tuareg in general, and the Algerian Tuareg specifically, since the 1960s is not a reflection of a decline in the interest of social and political scientists in the Tuareg. On the contrary, it

Introduction

is more a reflection of Franco-Algerian relations, the demise of scholarship in British (and perhaps continental European) universities, the poverty of research funding, and the fact that much of the Sahara, especially the Algerian Sahara, has been inaccessible to social scientists in recent years. The onset of Algeria's crisis, in which an estimated 100–150,000 people have been killed, following the army's annulment of the 1992 general election, which would have brought to power the world's first elected Islamist government, effectively closed the country to foreigners. Tuareg revolts in Niger and Mali in the first half of the 1990s, followed by the escalation of 'banditry' and insecurity in the northern parts of those countries, along with the Toubou revolt in north-east Niger, civil wars in Chad and the Sudan, the closure of Libya to most Westerners, along with the long-running dispute over the Western Sahara, has meant that very little research has been undertaken by social and political scientists in the Sahara for quite some time. Thus, when I returned to the Algerian Tuareg in 1999,[7] it was in a state of profound ignorance. I had not been able to find any reliable information on how they had fared over the preceding decade, during which they had experienced almost complete isolation from the outside world. Rumours and hearsay abounded, but facts were in short supply. In fact, it is probably not too far-fetched to suggest that our knowledge of the general well-being of the peoples of the Sahara at the end of the twentieth century was not much greater than it was at the beginning.

Thus, while social scientists still have an intrinsic interest in the same aspects of their socio-cultural organisation that interested them in earlier times, interest in and concern for the Tuareg has been enhanced as a result of the traumatic events that they have experienced in recent years. This concern has focused predominantly on the southern Tuareg of Niger and Mali, for whom the 1965–90 cycle of drought, with peak crises around 1973–74 and again in 1984–85, followed in the early 1990s by revolts against their respective governments, have been devastating. It is estimated that these events resulted in as many as 25 per cent of the Tuareg in Niger and Mali being displaced, most as refugees, from their former homes. Although the Algerian Tuareg have been fortunate in not having suffered the same traumas as their southern neighbours, the last decade, albeit for different reasons, has also been a disaster for them. Algeria's Tuareg have not, as many people might assume, been unaffected by Algeria's crisis.

The Tuareg as Part of Algeria and Algeria's 'Crisis'

One of the main reasons for bringing together this volume of articles is to rectify this imbalance. While quite a lot has been written on both the impact of drought on the peoples of the Sahel and the Tuareg revolts, nothing has been written on the impact of Algeria's 'crisis' on the Algerian Tuareg. Indeed, with the notable exception of Pandolfi's excellent study of the Dag Rali,[8] no extensive social anthropological research has been undertaken amongst the northern, that is Algerian, Tuareg since I worked amongst them in the 1960s and early 1970s, more than 30 years ago.[9] A key feature of that study is that it documented what happened to the Kel Ahaggar Tuareg during the traumatic years immediately following Algerian independence in 1962, when their society was more or less turned upside-down as a result of the new state's radical policies towards them. When talking to Algerian Tuareg today about those traumatic years, several French-speaking Tuareg have used the word *bouleversement* to describe what they experienced. But, since that time – the end of the 1960s – we are left with nothing but questions. How, for instance, did the Algerian Tuareg cope with and survive this *bouleversement* of their society? What has become of them in the intervening 30 or so years? And, more specifically, how have they been affected by Algeria's crisis of the 1990s? The articles in this volume are designed to answer these questions by providing an analysis of the social changes that have taken place amongst the Algerian Tuareg since the end of the 1960s. In that sense, they provide us with something of an 'ethnographic update'. But I am not sure whether they capture the extraordinarily complex and dynamic interface, what we might even call the dialectic, between the values and culture of traditional society, the key feature of which was its fundamental dynamic (see 'From Tit to Tahilahi'), and the profundity of the change and modernity that has overwhelmed this society, like so many others in the world, in recent years. As one colleague recently expounded, 'All peoples want to play in the World Cup'.

Or do they? In 1969 I tried, without success, to explain to Tuareg how men (Americans!) had recently visited and walked on the moon. Having already managed to drown a camel in Ahaggar, I was at a disadvantage and once again had to resign myself to being perceived as a little deranged. Some 35 years later, in the summer of 2003, I spent a week travelling through much of Central Europe by train (an exhilarating experience after the United Kingdom) to meet with a number of Tuareg who, as they like to say, 'now prefer to nomadise in Europe during the hot summer months!', to finalise the editing of this volume. In some respects, our conversations were more illuminating and interesting than what I have written here. They ranged through observations on the fashion and sexuality of passers-by on the station concourses, and the conclusion (fieldwork observation of body language!) that more than half were unhappy with their lot; the threat posed to world peace by the current US administration and whether George W. Bush or Tony Blair was the greater dissembler; the merits of the radio communication

Introduction

systems being used by the current hostage-takers (see 'Contested Terrain'); the technology of night vision and associated weapon systems being sought by the Algerian security forces; the cabals, divisions and intrigues within the Algerian government (see 'Contested Terrain'); whether there is any relationship between endogamy, genetic disorders and infant mortality amongst the Kel Ahaggar Tuareg, the need for genetic research (see 'The End of the Matriline?'), and the such-like. We also discussed at length how often and how far a certain nomadic cousin of one of the discussants had moved his herds out of Ahaggar during the last couple of years (see 'The Last Nomads'). As I flew out of Zurich, it dawned on me that these conversations were not much different from many I had held recently with Tuareg 'back home' in Ahaggar and the Tassili-n-Ajjer, and that one could now hold a more intelligent and better-informed conversation on global affairs with a Tuareg from the Central Sahara than with what I suspect is an increasing number of citizens in my own country.

As I have already intimated, the key question in regard to what has happened to the Algerian Tuareg in recent years is how they have been affected by the 'crisis' that followed the Algerian army's annulment of the 1992 general election. The answer, in a nutshell, and as several of the articles in this volume demonstrate, is profoundly. To the extent that most of these articles are concerned either directly or indirectly with the position of the Tuareg in Algeria and their relationship with the Algerian state, this volume is as much about Algeria as it is about the Tuareg. In fact, my reference to the Tuareg of Ahaggar and Ajjer (the Kel Ahaggar and Kel Ajjer) as 'Algerian Tuareg' rather than 'northern Tuareg', as would have been the case a generation or so ago, says much about their position in the world today.

Such a pointed reference to Algeria highlights two important issues. The first is the tendency of most analysts of Algeria and Algerians themselves to ignore the country's south. This is not in the least surprising when one considers that the vast bulk of the country's population (and most of its socio-political problems) lies within a 250–300km-deep corridor along its northern littoral. To most Algerians, the Sahara is a vast and predominantly alien space, known to many of them by little more than reference to the names of some of its predominant tribes and oasis-towns and as the source of the country's hydrocarbons. Some idea of the size of the Algerian Sahara can be grasped from the fact that the distance from Algiers to London is less than that from Algiers to the southern frontier at In Guezzam. It is consequently not surprising that throughout most of the country's 40 years of independence the central government's policy towards its Saharan territory has been limited largely to three overriding concerns: the hydrocarbons industry and its security, political relations with its neighbours (concerning the small matter of almost 6,000km of international frontiers), and international economic projects such as the trans-Saharan highway (still far from finished) and the proposed Nigerian–Algerian pipeline. Until the last year or two, little serious consideration had ever been given to either tourism or the value of the Sahara's rich cultural heritage. Algeria is now learning that it cannot ignore its extreme south. This region may contain only a minuscule proportion of the national population, but it covers roughly a fifth, or perhaps more, of national territory and, as at least two other articles[10] in this volume show, is becoming an area of increasing strategic and political importance.

The second issue concerns the relationship between the Tuareg and the Algerian state and centres on such diffuse and largely subjective concepts as 'Algerianisation', 'assimilation', 'incorporation', 'ethnicity' and the construction of political identities. The issue is encapsulated within a statement made by a group of Tuareg in Tamanrasset in response to my question of whether they saw themselves primarily as Tuareg or Algerians. I sensed that the question had never been put to them before, at least not quite so starkly. It was discussed with much deliberation for a long time. They had no trouble in agreeing that they were 'Algerian Tuareg'. But, although they recognised that they were Algerian citizens in a juridical and national sense, in as much as they carried Algerian passports and other such documents and, as such, had certain entitlements, they had little cultural sense of being 'Algerian'. 'I am first and foremost a Tuareg, an Algerian Tuareg. I do not know what it is to be an Algerian', said one of them, tapping his head, as if to make the point that being an 'Algerian', as distinct from being a 'Tuareg', was a cultural step that involved a lot of mental transformations that had not yet been made. These discussants were men in their forties and upwards. If the same question had been put to a group of young Tuareg men half their age, who had grown up in school with Arabic supplanting Tamahak as their first language, and who had experienced national military service, I suspect that there would have been less equivocalness.

Even if most Algerian Tuareg think of themselves primarily as 'Tuareg' rather than as 'Algerians', any such contemporary discussions about ethnic and national identities are a far cry from the years immediately following Algerian independence, when for most Tuareg the word 'Algerian' was almost synonymous with 'enemy' and usually mentioned in a sense of fear and tone of derision. Having lived amongst the northern Tuareg, the Algerian Tuareg, in the years immediately following Independence and again at frequent intervals over the last four years, it is evident that their relationship with, and their perception of, the Algerian state has changed enormously. Although it is much easier to draw on anecdotal evidence to describe this change in relationship and perception over this 40-year period, I have tried to provide a more detailed analysis of it in 'Ethnicity, Regionalism and Political Stability in Algeria's *Grand Sud*'. However, because both the Tuareg and the Algerian government are probably two of the most enigmatic parties in the world, even to each other, I will add a little more to it here, not only because it is the fundamental dynamic of this large and politically sensitive tract of the Sahara, but because it is one theme that runs in various ways through all these articles.

In the years immediately following Algerian independence, what little reference that was made to the Tuareg by both Algeria's media and government was usually couched within the conceptual framework of a supposed 'Tuareg problem'. I have tried to analyse this notion elsewhere in this volume ('Ethnicity, Regionalism and Political Stability in Algeria's *Grand Sud*'). However, as it is a predominantly political notion, it inevitably raises questions about my personal outlook towards the Tuareg, as well as the extent to which such politically sensitive research can be undertaken in a country in which it is virtually impossible to undertake serious empirical research on the ground. If I had requested permission from the Algerian government to undertake detailed empirical research into the construction of local political identities, Tuareg attitudes to the Algerian government and similar matters, I doubt very much that it would have been granted, although I am fairly sure that the findings would reveal a far better disposition towards the government and its institutions than its members might surmise. Much of what I have written on this question is therefore necessarily subjective. Nevertheless, this subjectivity is based on a fairly extensive social anthropological knowledge of the Tuareg, as well as a reasonable appreciation of the many difficulties faced by Algeria since Independence. However, in the inevitable absence of solid empirical research, the reader is entitled to know something of my personal outlook towards Algeria and its peoples and the extent to which my writing might be deemed as being unduly influenced by any strong sentiments either towards or against the Tuareg and the Algerian state.

I first visited Algeria as a young student in 1964, less than two years after Independence. The purpose of that visit was simply to see something of the countries of North Africa and the Middle East and their desert regions. My most vivid memories of Algeria were not so much the Sahara and the Tuareg, who at that time were reputedly in a state of revolt against the new Algerian government (see 'Ethnicity, Regionalism and Political Stability in Algeria's *Grand Sud*'), but the bars and cafés of Algiers in which I spent literally dozens of hours listening to the stories that young, middle-aged and occasionally old men told me of Algeria's War of Independence. I still retain the images of the lifting or parting of apparel to reveal the scars of cigarette burns and other physical tortures, along with poignant memories of being invited to the victims' homes, being introduced to their friends and relatives and being told the most horrific stories of one of the world's most appalling wars. In the next couple of years I read all I could about Algeria's Revolution and its early revolutionaries and martyrs and travelled extensively throughout almost every region of the country. There is scarcely a town in Algeria that I did not visit. I learnt more from the people of Algeria than I ever learnt from a university, and that is a debt that I hope I have been able to repay a little in the last few years. My affection for Algeria as a whole is consequently no less than that for the Tuareg, with whom I spent most of my time in Algeria between 1964 and 1971/72, during which time I wrote a PhD thesis on 'The Social Consequences of Algerian Development Policies for the Tuareg of Ahaggar'.

I like to think that I achieved objectivity in writing on Algeria and the Tuareg, which is derived from a balance of affection and understanding for both parties. That is not to imply that I see the Tuareg through rose-tinted spectacles or condone all the policies and practices of the Algerian government. On the contrary, there is much about Algeria, especially its archaic and intractable bureaucracy, the absence of adequate political institutions, its inadequate political representation, the crippling divisions within its government and its resistance to change, and the abuse of authority at almost all levels, of which I, along with most Algerians, can only be critical. There is also much that has taken place during the terrible drama of the last 15 years that can never be condoned. But these are all problems that Algerians will work out for themselves without the interference of external parties. For there is much about Algeria that gives its people an extraordinary resilience and which holds out great hope for their future.

The Tuareg's 'Indigenous Rights' in Algeria

My lack of partisan allegiance to the Tuareg is perhaps reflected in my decision to abandon the original sub-title of this volume, which was to have been *Social Change and Indigenous Rights*. My reason for dropping this reference to indigenous rights was because I felt that its inclusion in the title might be perceived as suggesting either that Algeria was denying such rights to the Tuareg, or that the situation of the Tuareg in Algeria with regard to their indigenous rights was worse than in neighbouring countries. I discussed this change of title at length with individual Tuareg. Their views embrace two arguments. One is that the term 'indigenous' is fraught with definitional problems. Even if we accept the UN's and IWGIA's (International Work Group on Indigenous Affairs) classification that the Tuareg are the indigenous population of this part of Africa, there is much ambiguity and ambivalence over who precisely is a Tuareg. This complex problem of ethnic identity and

Introduction

categorisation is analysed in 'Ethnicity, Regionalism and Political Stability in Algeria's *Grand Sud*'. As many Tuareg themselves agree, the term 'indigenous' soon becomes conflated with the idea of 'local peoples', not all of whom would be regarded as Tuareg in terms of their own internal social and historical categories. Discussions with Tuareg on the subject of ethnic identity usually tend to slip rather quickly from concepts of ethnicity to notions of regionalism and regional identity, with the result that the notion of who and what is 'indigenous' becomes rather confused and of questionable analytical use.

The second argument is much more important. It concerns the extent to which the Tuareg's indigenous rights, and indeed their human rights, have been suppressed or safeguarded by their respective governments. This question is becoming increasingly pertinent as we approach the end of the UN's nominated Decade of Indigenous Peoples in 2004. The Decade effectively came into being on 26 August 1994 with the submission of a Draft Resolution by the UN Commission on Human Rights' (CHR) Sub-Commission on Prevention of Discrimination and Protection of Minorities entitled Draft United Nations Declaration on the Rights of Indigenous Peoples. The following year the CHR established an open-ended inter-sessional working group to elaborate the Draft Declaration (CHR Resolution 1995/32). The working group is now (2003) in its ninth session. Whether the Declaration will be adopted within the framework of the Decade is still a little uncertain, as a number of substantive issues, notably those relating to 'collective rights', 'self-determination' and 'third party' issues, are still being discussed. However, even if there is a delay in the final adoption of the Declaration, there are already a number of existing international instruments that recognise the collective rights of indigenous peoples, such as the two international covenants (ICCPR and ICESCR), the International Convention on the Elimination of Racial Discrimination, the ILO Convention No.169 on Indigenous and Tribal Peoples (1989), the UNESCO Declaration on Race and Racial Prejudice (1978), the African Charter on Human and Peoples' Rights (1981), the Convention on Bio-Diversity, and the Universal Declaration on Cultural Diversity (UNESCO 2001), among others. The two most important of these instruments, which are likely to achieve increased prominence and importance for indigenous peoples such as the Tuareg in the next few years, as the question of 'indigenous rights' achieves an increasingly higher profile in the world, are the ILO Convention and the UN's Draft Declaration.

Algeria has received widespread admonishment in recent years from both internal and external sources for the abuse of both human and indigenous rights.[11] The latter have centred on the situation of the indigenous *Amazigh* peoples. However, many external commentators on Algeria and the Maghrib in general tend to oversimplify the situation by lumping together all the various *Amazigh* populations of North Africa, and especially those of Algeria, as part of what they refer to generally as the Berber 'problem' or 'situation'. Because the Tuareg are also Berbers, they are often assumed to be subject to the same levels of human rights abuse and denials of indigenous rights as the Kabyles and other *Amazigh* peoples of the north. For instance, the demonstrations that greeted President Bouteflika when he visited Djanet and Illizi in the summer of 2001 were assumed by many commentators to be part of the Berber unrest that had broken out in the north of the country a few months earlier. That was not the case at all. As I explain elsewhere in this volume (in both 'Ethnicity, Regionalism and Political Stability in Algeria's *Grand Sud*' and 'Contested Terrain'), the Tuareg demonstrations had little if anything to do with the Berber unrest in the north of the country, but were a specific protest against the quality of governance in their *wilaya* (Illizi) and their demand for the removal of the *wali*,[12] whom they regarded as both corrupt and incompetent.

The Tuareg have never had strong political links with Berber groups in the north of the country. Although they share certain cultural traits,[13] the Tuareg are politically peripheral to the '*Amazigh* movement' of the northern Maghrib. Not only is the situation of the Tuareg, in terms of their indigenous and human rights, quite dissimilar from that of the Berber populations of the north of the country, especially that of the Kabyles,[14] amongst whom there has been widespread unrest in the last few years,[15] but they recognise that their situation is very different.

In the same way as there are major differences between the situation of Algeria's Tuareg and Berber peoples in the north of the country, so there is a major difference between the situation of the Algerian Tuareg and that of their southern neighbours in Mali and Niger. The Tuareg in both Niger and Mali have taken up arms against their respective governments in recent years, with both rebellions breaking out almost simultaneously in May–June 1990.[16] The causes of the rebellions in both countries stemmed from a combination of deep-seated economic and political marginalisation. In both countries, the Tuareg had been effectively excluded from any form of political incorporation into the post-colonial state. Although peace was finally established in the two countries in 1996 (Mali) and 1998 (Niger), it is debatable whether the initial grievances and the fundamental causes of the revolts have been resolved. Both countries still have much to do if they are to meet the terms and conditions of the major international instruments that have and still are being developed to safeguard the rights of indigenous peoples such as the Tuareg.

The situation of Algeria's Tuareg is very different. If one considers the two main instruments that I have already mentioned, the Draft United Nations

Introduction

Declaration on the Rights of Indigenous Peoples and the ILO Convention No.169 on Indigenous and Tribal Peoples,[17] it soon becomes clear that Algeria has done considerably more than her southern neighbours to ensure the human rights and most of the indigenous rights of its Tuareg peoples. Earlier this year, I attempted, with the help of Kel Ahaggar who were conversant with Algeria's civil and family law, to calculate the extent to which Algeria might be deemed to be in compliance with these two instruments. The exercise is not a very fair test for a number of reasons. First, as far as I am aware, while the Algerian government is probably only vaguely aware of these instruments, members of the local/regional administration would almost certainly have no knowledge of them. Moreover, Algeria, along with all other African countries, has not ratified the ILO Convention, nor has it attended the IWGIA sessions (although there is a Berber representative on the Working Group). In other words, neither instrument is currently legally binding on the country. If they were, it is most likely that the compliancy levels would be higher. Second, and not surprisingly, there is considerable duplication between the articles contained within the two instruments. Third, some of the articles have little or no applicability to the Tuareg's specific situation or are concerned solely with implementation and are therefore irrelevant.

If we look first at the UN Draft Declaration, it contains 43 articles giving a total of some 69 clauses, of which it would seem that Algeria is more or less in compliance with 44. Of the remainder, 13 are inapplicable or to do with implementation and are therefore not relevant, or, in the case of one, was only relevant during the colonial period. That means that Algeria is compliant in the case of 79 per cent of the applicable clauses. This leaves 12 clauses (21 per cent) on which Algeria would appear not to be directly compliant, or in which either the wording or subject of the clause raises further questions that are either ambivalent or ambiguous in the current situation. There is no clause in which Algeria can be said to be categorically 'non-compliant'.

In the case of the ILO Convention, there are 44 articles giving a total of 101 clauses, of which it would seem that Algeria is in compliance with 57. Thirty-three are non applicable as they are irrelevant or to do with implementation. That means that Algeria is compliant in the case of 84 per cent of the applicable clauses. That leaves 11 clauses, on nine of which Algeria would appear not to be directly compliant, or in which either the wording or subject of the clause raises further questions that are either ambivalent or ambiguous in the current situation. In the case of only two clauses might Algeria be deemed to be 'non-compliant'.

I am sure that there are some Tuareg who would argue that this interpretation is overly generous to the Algerian government. For instance, in the case of 23 of the 170 clauses on which Algeria does not appear to be directly compliant and the two of apparent non-compliance, most Tuareg would probably argue that the government was non-compliant. The majority of these possible 'non-compliances' relate to 'culture', 'education' and 'language' issues, contained in such clauses as:

- 'Education programmes and services for the peoples concerned shall be developed and implemented in co-operation with them to address their special needs, and shall incorporate their histories, their knowledge and technologies, their value systems and their further social, economic and cultural aspirations' (ILO 27.1);
- 'Children belonging to the peoples concerned shall, wherever practicable, be taught to read and write in their own indigenous language or in the language most commonly used by the group to which they belong. When it is not practicable, the competent authorities shall undertake consultations with these peoples with a view to the adoption of measures to achieve this objective' (ILO 28.1);
- 'Measures shall be taken to preserve and promote the development and practice of the indigenous languages of the peoples concerned' (ILO 28.3);
- 'Indigenous people have the ... right not to be subjected to ... any form of assimilation or integration by other cultures or ways of life imposed on them by legislative, administrative or other measures' (UN Draft Dec. 7d); and so on.

While it is true that the Algerian government has made little or no effort to further the development and practice of indigenous language, and that 'Arabisation' has been the central plank of its educational and cultural policy in the region, the government would most likely argue that such measures might be taken if and when the instruments were ratified, but that in the meantime, they are impracticable. Tuareg might also argue that Algeria is in non-compliance with the clause not to 'recruit indigenous individuals against their will into the armed forces ...' (UN Draft Dec. 11a). The Algerian government, for its part, would no doubt argue that conscription applies to all citizens and that all Algeria's indigenous peoples are full citizens. It might even point to the few cases of young Tuareg men who have been exempted from conscription as a result, it would seem, of requests from their families that they are the only able-bodied son and are needed in the nomadic camps.

Further areas on which most Tuareg would probably argue that Algeria was not compliant relate to those articles and clauses covering the right of indigenous peoples to 'maintain and strengthen their distinct political, economic, social and cultural characteristics, as well as their legal systems',[18] and a number of similar clauses relating to the maintenance of and respect for their own 'institutions', and so on. If these clauses had to be implemented now, they would present a number of difficulties, as a result of Algeria's socialism in the 1960s and 1970s having subverted most tribal and kinship structures.[19] Amongst the Tuareg, this subversion of most of the traditional political and associated cultural institutions extended from the complete abolition of the traditional tribal political system to such things as the abolition of the traditional naming system, which I describe in 'The End of the Matriline?'. The immediate problem for any contemporary consideration of the reinstatement or recognition of indigenous rights is that these actions were undertaken more than a generation ago. Even if both the Tuareg and the Algerian government now wished to reinstate them, it would be extremely difficult, if not impossible to do so. Moreover, the Algerian government would no doubt argue, with justification, that some of the institutions that it abolished, such as 'slavery', certain land-holding arrangements and *métayage* systems, were both contrary to human rights and incompatible with a modern, 'socialist' state.[20] It would also no doubt argue that the new system of political representation that it introduced was not discriminatory, treating all peoples equally as 'Algerian citizens'. There is, however, one residual consequence of those changes that might conceivably present problems not only for the future implementation of any indigenous rights legislation, but also for the development of future political dispensations within the region. This is that although the Tuareg have equal rights of political representation in Algeria's new political system, they are nevertheless a demographic and hence a political minority in their own region. Beyond their formal but democratic representation in local and regional assemblies, in which they tend to be a minority, and the rather haphazard and informal links between certain individual Tuareg of questionable legitimacy and certain government channels, there are no obvious vehicles for the expression of Tuareg political grievances, other than the 'lining of the streets' and the sort of public demonstrations that greeted President Bouteflika when he visited the region in 2001. This potential political vacuum in a region as politically sensitive as Algeria's south, and in which indigenous rights might well become an issue in the future, could, as I have suggested in 'Ethnicity, Regionalism and Political Stability in Algeria's *Grand Sud*', spell danger.

Although a number of the Articles in the UN Draft Declaration, such as indigenous peoples' right of self-determination, might be anathema to the Algerian government, discussion on such sensitive articles is fairly far advanced. For instance it is now generally recognised that the right of self-determination is established in international law and that it does not necessarily either threaten territorial integrity and national unity or normally entail the right of secession from independent states. According to Norway,[21] for example, a country containing a significant indigenous population, self-determination exercised within states includes the right of indigenous peoples to participate at all levels of decision-making in legislative and administrative matters and in the maintenance and development of their political and economic systems. Within Algeria's current narrow and inadequate confines of political representation, the government would no doubt argue that Tuareg do already participate in these levels of decision-making. While that is debatable, the main point of what I am saying is that the human and indigenous rights of Algeria's Tuareg are more assured than those of other Tuareg groups and many of the world's other indigenous peoples. Indeed, if the UN's Draft Declaration were to be ratified tomorrow, Algeria would find itself further down the road to full compliance in the case of her Tuareg population than might be imagined.

By focusing in this way on the Algerian Tuareg's human and indigenous rights as if they were some sort of checklist, we are likely to miss three important points. The first is that the absence or inadequate provision of some of these rights, such as those pertaining to the provision of healthcare, certain educational resources and so on, is more often a symptom of the underdevelopment of the region than the outcome of discrimination against any one group within it. Second, and as most Tuareg would, I think, agree, one of the outstanding elements of Algeria's social, economic and political development of its extreme south since Independence has been the fairness with which policies, no matter how appropriate, have been implemented.

I have documented elsewhere a number of examples of this 'fairness' and how much it surprised and impressed the Tuareg in the years immediately following Algeria's independence.[22] Perhaps the greatest surprise for many Tuareg encountering the new Algerian government's agencies for the first time was to find themselves being treated, contrary to their widely held expectations of discrimination, as 'Algerian citizens'. On entering local government offices they were provided with identity cards that gave particulars of their name, place and date of birth, marital status, number of dependents, but no reference to their ethnicity or mode of existence. When they sought employment at the Labour Exchange, for example, they found that jobs were allocated on a 'points system' in such a way that labour opportunities, except in the case of specifically skilled labour, were allocated on the basis of equal distribution in relation to social needs. Priority was given to men with the greatest number of dependents, regardless of whether they were nomadic Tuareg or ex-slaves living in Tamanrasset. If, for example, 12 jobs were available, six would be given to married men with children, three or four to married men without children or bachelors, and a maximum of only

Introduction

25 per cent to workers resident in other regions. A nomadic Tuareg married with children thus had better prospects of being given unskilled employment than an unmarried ex-slave living in Tamanrasset.

The third point is that the Algerian government is currently beginning to address some of the more ambiguous cases of possible non-compliance with both the ILO Convention and the UN Draft Declaration. The key issues, as far as the Tuareg are concerned, relate to their right (as indigenous peoples) to determine and develop priorities and strategies for the sustainable development and use of their lands. This is a complex area, which focuses especially on the way in which tourism has and will be developed in Algeria's south. It is discussed in detail in the final article in this volume, 'Contested Terrain'. Tourism is regarded by the Tuareg as 'their industry', and the way in which it has developed in the last few years, along with the wider issue of environmental and heritage conservation, lies at the heart of what I have described elsewhere as the 'last significant battle of the Central Sahara'.[23] Algeria's more constructive approach to these critical problems has been manifest in two very recent and extraordinary developments. The first was a regional conference on 'Tourism in the Tassili and Ahaggar',[24] organised by the *wali* of Illizi under the auspices of the Ministry of Culture and Communication, at Djanet in March 2003. The background and significance of this conference are explained in 'Contested Terrain'. The second development was the launch in December 2002 of the World Deserts Foundation (*Fondation Déserts du Monde*). Although ostensibly a global institution, the Foundation is very much an Algerian initiative, being the brainchild of Algeria's Minister for the Environment, M. Cherif Rahmani, who is also the Foundation's President. A key aim of the Foundation is 'to promote the sustainable economic development of desert regions'. This involves 'decisions and actions being taken in partnership with local desert peoples; giving encouragement to local institutions; recognising the rights of the local people to natural resources and creating cultural platforms, communication links and the means of meeting together so as to give a voice to the peoples of these areas'. In the context of the Algerian Sahara, these are bold words. The first step in meeting them, as far as Algeria's Tuareg are concerned, lies in the Minister's support for the immediate commissioning of a scientific research report which will analyse the problems of tourism development in the *Grand Sud* and provide a base for the development of '*le Tourisme Alternatif et Responsable*'[25] in the region. In the light of the damage that has been inflicted on Saharan tourism, especially in Algeria, by the 'Hostage Crisis' (see 'Contested Terrain') that overwhelmed the region during the spring and summer of 2003, it is unlikely that the Algerian government will not adopt the main recommendations of this report. If that is done, then Algeria will be compliant with most, if not all, of the ILO's and UN Draft Declaration's clauses relating to such issues as economic development, land and natural resource development, environmental and cultural protection, and so on.

The Problems of Modernisation and the Invasion of *les gens du nord*

The majority of the problems facing the Tuareg today are what one might call, somewhat euphemistically, 'the problems of modernisation'. A conversation with any reasonably knowledgeable Tuareg about 'social change' soon comes down to the subject of 'modernisation', and that for all its virtues there are almost as many drawbacks. This is a subject on which I touch in some depth in 'The End of the Matriline?'. Tamanrasset is now a large town – it calls itself a city. When I began writing these articles, I put its population at around 100,000. Now (2003), less than two years later, local people are suggesting that it is probably approaching 150,000! According to the manager of Tamanrasset's main bank, the town contains 48 nationalities (he means ethnic groups). If one allows for a little geographical licence by regarding the south-west–north-east flow of traffic (people, contraband and so on) across the Sahara as the east–west axis, then Tamanrasset can now be regarded as one of the more sociologically and ethnographically interesting cross-roads of Africa. The dusty, isolated little oasis of some 4,000 souls that I first visited in 1964 is now a pulsating, and for some people a frightening, cosmopolitan African town, whose bounds can be scarcely walked in a day. And with this huge infusion of peoples has come a host of new social problems and diseases, mostly sexually transmitted (including AIDS), smugglers, bandits, illegal immigrants, refugees, desperation, poverty, racketeers, drug dealers and all the wretchedness of modern-day Africa that has turned this dusty and charming little Saharan town into a rapidly modernising African city with all the attendant social and health problems that are associated with rapid and largely unfettered urbanisation. The town's problems of public health, housing shortages, unemployment and educational resource pressures and the such like, are more to do with issues of international development and the shortcomings of international development agencies than the question of 'indigenous rights'. They are part of a global problem that goes beyond the confines of Algeria. Indeed, the way in which Algeria is coping with and attempting to manage such problems on a regional (one might soon start using the notion of 'pan-Sahara') basis reflects a certain 'coming of age' and recognition of its international duties and commitments as the most developed and powerful country in this vast region.

However, while Tamanrasset's explosive growth and consequent pressure on resources owes much to the difficulties being experienced in the Sahel and further south, the town's problems have been exacerbated by Algeria's own internal crisis, as thousands of people from the north have sought refuge for themselves and their families in the relative safety of Saharan oasis-towns such as Tamanrasset. I have the strong impression that local Tuareg are inclined to see Tamanrasset's problems as emanating more from the north than the south. This is partly because they have a greater understanding, sympathy for and identification with the peoples of Niger and Mali than the peoples of the north, who are seen as being associated with the root cause of the international isolation and consequent difficulties they have experienced over the last decade (see 'Contested Terrain'). However, as I have tried to explain in 'Ethnicity, Regionalism and Political Stability in Algeria's *Grand Sud*', this sense of being 'invaded', as local people describe it, by *les gens du nord*, with all the provocative and inflammatory notions of 'clash of cultures' and 'disrespect' that it entails, has the potential for becoming an increasing political problem in the region, and one which is already turning peoples' heads towards Niger and Mali.

Three issues are at stake here. One is the feeling amongst local people, especially Tuareg, that Algerians coming to the extreme south, whether as government 'functionaries' or to live on a more permanent basis, not only have no interest in or understanding of their culture, but also are disrespectful of it.[26] As I have explained in 'Ethnicity, Regionalism and Political Stability in Algeria's *Grand Sud*', this 'disrespect' is manifest in such things as referring to the local peoples, especially the Tuareg, derogatorily as Sahraouis or Hadj Bettus.[27] Such 'disrespect' may often be in a joking context, and as such is understood by local people. However, far more serious at a political level is the growing awareness amongst local people that much of the damage being done to the region's rich cultural and environmental heritage, notably its prehistoric rock art, especially in the form of graffiti and other types of despoliation, is being inflicted by *les gens du nord*.[28] On my return to Tamanrasset in 1999, a group of local Tuareg took me one afternoon to the local beauty spot of Imlaoulaouene, a series of *gueltas* (rock water pools) in a deep gorge some 16km north of the town. On arriving there, I was shocked to see that graffiti, mostly in Arabic, had been scrawled all over the rock walls. Bloated flies gorged on the entrails and other remains of three animals (goats and sheep) that had been killed and eaten there the night before. Dozens of empty cans, plastic bags and containers and other rubbish were scattered in and around the *gueltas*. The Tuareg, who had not previously seen this damage, were enraged by it and asked if I would write a letter of complaint, in my capacity as a tour company director, to the Director of the Hoggar (Ahaggar) National Park, who was responsible for the protection and conservation of the site, and the local Director of Tourism. On receiving the letter, they requested the army, which was deemed responsible for the damage, to clean up the gorge. I returned to Imlaoulaouene with the Tuareg a few months later and saw that there had been some semblance of a clean up and that all the graffiti on the canyon walls had been smeared with mud. A month or two later, heavy rains removed the mud and re-exposed the graffiti for all to see that the damage is permanent!

The Quality of Governance

This anecdote takes me to the second issue, which concerns the quality of Algeria's governance. Algeria's Tuareg no longer have the same misgivings about the Algerian government as they did in the years immediately following Independence. On the contrary, if detailed field research were undertaken today, it would probably reveal that most of them were broadly supportive of most government policies, at least in as much as they were aware of them. And they would certainly be found to be strongly supportive of the government's stance against Islamic fundamentalism. The Tuareg have not only remained indifferent to Algeria's Islamist movement,[29] but they have been quick to identify it as the cause of most of their current misfortunes. Their main criticism of the government relates not so much to its policies as to the quality of its governance. During the last couple of years especially, there have been a number of issues that have brought into question the calibre of government officials in the extreme south. Many of these issues, such as the looting of cultural artefacts, the poor quality of administration by key government agencies responsible for the management of the Ahaggar National Park, tourism and environment conservation and, since the spring of 2003, the kidnapping by alleged Algerian Islamists of 32 European tourists who were travelling in the region, are examined in detail in 'Contested Terrain'.

Finding good administrators to work in Algeria's Sahara has always been one of the government's biggest headaches. It is rare for 'high-flyers' to volunteer to work in this difficult part of the country, which many regard as a punishment posting, or one that is certainly not conducive for fast-track promotion. While this is something that has always been understood by the people of the region, it is something that they are no longer so ready to accept. Indeed, the gist of the message given to President Bouteflika from the crowds lining the streets in Djanet and Illizi when he visited the region in the summer of 2001 was: 'If you want us to remain part of Algeria, give us good governance'.

What, it might be asked, has led to this increased politicisation of the extreme south? This is a question which I have tried to analyse in 'Ethnicity, Regionalism and Political Stability in Algeria's *Grand Sud*'. However, as that article was written in early 2002 and before the dramatic events of 2003, I have the opportunity to expand on it here. Many commentators are inclined to explain such political manifestations in the south as an extension of the Berber disturbances that became so prominent in the north of the country in the spring and early summer of 2001. I do not hold with this view, as I have found very little awareness of these northern Berber issues amongst local peoples, beyond the general, one might even say nationwide, complaint about the inadequacy of political institutions and political representation in general. Rather, I think that there are two more regionally specific reasons. The first is an undercurrent that has been expressing itself on various occasions throughout much of the last decade.[30] It stems from the fact that the prosperity of Ahaggar and the Tassili-n-Ajjer depends almost entirely on tourism. For ten years, as a result of Algeria's Islamist crisis, this major source of income dried up. Although almost everyone in the region suffered from the cessation of tourism, it is the Tuareg who have suffered most. Thus, while most people in the region are generally supportive of the government's stance against the Islamist movement, they are very aware that Algeria's crisis, which is predominantly a product of the country's northern regions, has cost them dear. They have suffered for Algeria, and are therefore no longer prepared to tolerate what they regard as second-rate government. Many local people, especially Tuareg, are increasingly expressing the sentiment that poor governance is simply another manifestation of disrespect for their region and their culture. Bouteflika, politically sensitive to such feelings, immediately dismissed the Illizi *wali* and replaced him with a top-class administrator.[31] The citizens of Tamanrasset are still waiting for such a response, arguing, in the meantime, that Tamanrasset is the most 'international' city in the country after Algiers in terms of the number of foreign visitors and therefore warrants a higher quality of governance.

The Implications of the 'Hostage Crisis'

The second reason is related to the first but stems from a specific incident, namely the kidnapping of 32 European tourists by alleged Algerian Islamists in the Algerian Sahara in February–March 2003. The details of this event are outlined in 'Contested Terrain'. This crisis, which has enveloped most of the Algerian, Niger and Malian Sahara for almost six months,[32] has highlighted three facts which Tuareg in all three of these countries have been aware of for some time. The first is that the Central Sahara consists of vast spaces over which the three governments involved (Algeria, Mali and Niger) have little or no effective control. The second fact is that the hostage crisis, like Algeria's overall political crisis, is enormously damaging to Tuareg interests. In the same way that Algeria's Islamist crisis in the 1990s brought tourism in Algeria to a standstill and substantially reduced tourism in the adjoining desert regions of Niger and Mali,[33] so the current hostage crisis is having the same effect. Third, Tuareg are fully aware that the hostage-takers, like most of the more prominent contraband traffickers, have moved into their traditional lands from northern Algeria,[34] and that the insecurity they have generated in the region is now causing them more harm than good. Moreover, it is becoming widely apparent from the increasing amount of information being released to the media that elements of the Algerian security forces are complicit in the affair.[35] In other words, they see this damaging business as a further intrusion into their domain of Algeria's ongoing Islamist crisis.

These three facts appear to be leading the Tuareg in all three countries to the realisation that the governments of these three countries now need their help and co-operation more than the Tuareg have any need of their governments. This stark fact was more or less admitted in July 2003, when the Malian government suggested, on becoming the recipient of the hostages and their captors, that this sector of the Sahara was now effectively beyond the control of the states and that the three countries should consider the creation of some sort of joint security zone.[36]

Towards a New Saharan Politic and the Potential Development of Tuareg Regions

I am now of the opinion that the Central Sahara, or at least that part of it which traditionally belonged to the Tuareg, has reached an interesting and perhaps critical watershed. This is because the key issues underlying the current complex state of affairs, namely the loss of tourism resulting from Algeria's 'Islamist problem', the 'invasion' of the region by *les gens du nord*, the threats being posed to the region's cultural and environmental heritage, the poor quality of local governance, and the security weaknesses exposed by the hostage crisis, have coalesced in a way that will almost certainly herald the development of a new politic, not only in the Algerian Sahara but throughout all Tuareg regions.

It is not yet clear how this politic will develop, as much will depend on how the current hostage crisis is resolved and what revelations of complicity and skulduggery emerge in its aftermath. But I think two possible scenarios, which are not mutually exclusive and which present enormous opportunities for both the people and governments of the region, might emerge.

One scenario may develop through the intervention of Algeria's Minister of the Environment, Cherif Rahmani, and the activities of the World Deserts Foundation of which he is the President. As I have explained in 'Contested

Introduction

Terrain', the whole question of the Sahara's environmental conservation has reached almost iconographic status amongst not just Tuareg 'environmentalists', as I refer to them, but amongst a wide swathe of the local population. 'Environmentalism', seen especially as the protection and conservation of the region's rich natural and cultural heritage within a new framework of environmentally sustainable tourism development, has become a major issue. The 180 or so members of UNATA (*Union Nationale des Associations des Agences de Tourisme Alternatif*) have already requested Minister Rahmani to commission a scientific research report to provide a base for the development of '*le Tourisme Alternatif et Responsable*' in *Le Grand Sud*. If this report is commissioned, which seems likely, and the government adopts and implements its main recommendations, the 'last significant battle of the Central Sahara'[37] will have been won. If that happens, it will open up a whole new politic in the Algerian Sahara, which will not only enable the Algerian government to comply with all the clauses of the main 'indigenous rights' instruments, but also presage a significant step forward in Tuareg–Algerian relations.

The second scenario, which is likely to develop concurrently with the first, was hinted at by the Malian government during the course of the current 'hostage crisis' when it admitted that the states concerned were unable to assure the security of this large sector of the Sahara. Such security can never be attained without the full support and collaboration of the Tuareg populations. This is not to imply that the Tuareg favour the present state of insecurity or that they are opposed to their respective governments. It is, quite simply, that they regard these lands as their traditional domain and they blame their respective governments for the current state of insecurity that is threatening their livelihoods. In Algeria's case, the problem stems primarily from its ongoing Islamist crisis. In the case of Niger and Mali, it is that the fundamental causes of the Tuareg rebellions of the 1990s have been only partially addressed. Notwithstanding the many development projects scattered throughout Tuareg regions, notably the agricultural irrigation schemes in Aïr and the agro-pastoral initiatives in much of the Niger Bend country, tourism is recognised by nearly all Tuareg as being at the heart of any development strategy that will enable them to control and manage their own lands and resources and thus achieve their own rightful place in the global economy. But, while the current state of insecurity prevails, tourists will stay away from their lands.

Insecurity is not the only problem threatening Tuareg interests. The Tuareg in all Saharan countries – Libya, Algeria, Niger, Mali, and even Mauritania – are becoming increasingly conscious of the fact that many of their lands, notably Tassili-n-Ajjer, Ahaggar, Tassili-ouan-Ahaggar, Aïr, Ténéré and the

Adrar-n-Iforas, are being seen as comprising a unique tourism product, akin to ecosystems such Antarctica and the Amazon Rain Forests. The way in which this product has been developed (exploited) in recent years has been extremely damaging to both the natural and cultural environment and the long-term interests of the local peoples concerned. Tuareg in all these regions are becoming increasingly aware that many of the parties that have been hitherto involved in this development, including elements of their own governments, have been motivated by short-term, 'get-rich-quick' interests. Local peoples in all these countries have already seen what damage can be done to their environment and cultural heritage by both mass tourism and *tourisme sauvage*.[38] In Algeria, awareness of the damage done by mass tourism in Ahaggar and the Tassili-n-Ajjer in the 1980s led to the formation of UNATA and the 1989 Tamanrasset Conference on environmentally sustainable tourism.[39] The citizens of Libya's Acacus region saw 45,000 tourists disgorged onto the runway at Ghat's little airport between December 1999 and April 2000, and subsequently counted the cost in at least 40 permanently damaged rock art sites. In Niger, the Aïr Mountains and the adjoining Ténéré desert have been almost vacuumed clean of prehistoric artefacts. The scale of this looting of the Sahara's prehistoric artefacts, predominantly by European collectors and for commercial sale, is immense. With the arrival of the Internet in 2001, Tuareg have been able to scan one website after another displaying and advertising their looted heritage. There is now an upsurge of anger spreading across Tuareg regions as local people become increasingly aware of the scale and consequences of this catastrophe.[40]

The development of a new politic, which seems to be gathering pace across much of this vast region, is emerging from the fact that local people, notably the Tuareg, now realise that their governments have not only been inept in both safeguarding their regions' cultural and natural heritage and in developing an environmentally sustainable tourism industry, but also that they can no longer ensure the region's security.

The realisation and acceptance of these two facts by both governments and people alike may now not be so difficult. This is because the tragic events of the last year, notably the looting of the Sahara[41] and the kidnapping of 32 European tourists, have demonstrated to both the governments and the local peoples alike that they have a common interest in ensuring the sort of security which is so demonstrably lacking, and initiating new policies orientated primarily to the development of environmentally sustainable forms of tourism along the lines advocated in the resolutions of the Djanet Conference of March 2003[42] and by organisations such as UNATA.

What I am saying may sound reminiscent of the calls that have been made at various times since the independence of these countries, by certain

Introduction

Tuareg activists and outsiders such as Libya's Colonel Qadhafi and neo-colonial Tuareg romanticists (mostly French), that the Tuareg should unite and form some sort of unified political entity in the south-central Sahara. This idea has never received much support, partly because it threatens the territorial sovereignty of the countries concerned and partly because at no time in their history have the Tuareg ever been politically unified. I am not advocating such a development now. However, I do believe that the current groundswell for a new politic in this part of the Sahara, emanating from the growing realisation of the region's insecurity, the threat of environmental catastrophe and the urgent need for the development of an environmentally sustainable tourism industry along the lines of the principles already established by the Tamanrasset Conference, the Djanet Conference and UNATA, calls for the consideration of some sort of entity, perhaps along the lines of a vast 'trans-border' international park. Such a park, managed by a board representing both the governments and the indigenous peoples, and incorporating one of the world's most valuable and fragile cultural and environmental heritage systems, might stretch along a north-east–south-west axis from Ghadames, the Oubari sands and the Fezzan in Libya, through the Tassili and Ahaggar ranges to the Adrar-n-Iforas, and along the other directional axis from Tuat-Tidikelt to Kawar and the Bilma sands. The fact that most of this vast territory largely coincides with the limits of the Tuareg's traditional lands should not necessarily be seen as a way of reinvigorating the idea of a Tuareg political entity in the Sahara. Rather, by focusing on the Park's potential for generating environmentally sustainable development, the governments of the four countries directly involved (Libya, Algeria, Niger, Mali) would be able to take a lead in ensuring those indigenous rights to which I have already drawn attention and which are in any case going to be demanded of them within the next few years. Such a collaborative development is probably the only way to ensure the security of this vast region, which, in any case, is a precursor for any such development schemes. Countries of the Sahara talk much about pan-Saharan collaboration and development. Now is an opportune time to put fine words into practice.

Although Algeria has a smaller Tuareg population than its southern neighbours, it is the richest and most powerful state in the region. Moreover, it already has the considerable experience of having already established two major national Parks in the region.[43] It is also responsible for safeguarding the greatest 'heritage' of all these areas.[44] Without a major initiative from Algeria, any development along these lines will remain stillborn. However, it is just possible that the initiatives shown by Algeria's Ministry of Culture and Communication,[45] and the lead being given by the World Desert Foundation and its President, Cherif Rahmani, with its anticipated report on the future development in Algeria's Sahara of *Un Tourisme Alternatif et Responsable*, will be the catalyst that this new politic will need.

The Lesser Gods of the Sahara

NOTES

I would like to acknowledge the Economic and Social Research Council (ESRC), the British Academy and the Leverhulme Trust for their most generous support.

1. Kel (Tamahak), 'people of'. Aïr is the mountain range in Niger that runs from Agades in the south towards the Algerian border in the north, reaching just over 2,000m in various points.
2. *Wilaya* is an administrative region, equivalent to a French *département*. During the War of Independence the FLN (*Front de Libération Nationale*) divided Algeria into six military regions, known as *wilaya*.
3. The *wilaya* of Tamanrasset is larger than Ahaggar as it includes the region up to and including In Salah.
4. The plains of Tamesna are not in the physical region of Ahaggar. However, following the defeat of Muhammad Kaoucen in 1916, Tamesna was given to the Kel Ahaggar by the French as reward for Moussa ag Amastane's support. Similarly, it might be argued that the regions of Tuat and Tidikelt fell within the domain of the Tuareg in as much as they obtained much of their foodstuffs from these oases prior to French occupation. See J. Keenan, 'From Tit (1902) to Tahilahi (2002): A Reconsideration of the Impact of and Resistance to French Pacification and Colonial Rule by the Tuareg of Algeria (the Northern Tuareg)', in this volume, pp.27–66.
5. J. Keenan, 'Dressing for the Occasion: Changes in the Symbolic Meanings of the Tuareg Veil'; and J. Keenan, 'The End of the Matriline? The Changing Roles of Women and Descent amongst the Algerian Tuareg', both in this volume, pp.97–120 and 121–62 respectively.
6. There are many published accounts of the Flatters expedition. I have recently written a commentary on the expedition: 'How and Why the Tuareg Poisoned the French: Some reflections on *efelehleh* and the motives of the Tuareg in massacring the Flatters expedition of 1861', in Barnaby Rogerson (ed.), *North Africa Travel*, vol.1 (London: Sickle Moon Books 2001) pp.75–91.
7. J. Keenan, 'The Father's Friend: Returning to the Tuareg as an Elder', *Anthropology Today* 16/4, Royal Anthropological Institute, London (Aug. 2000) pp.7–11.
8. P. Pandolfi, *Les Touaregs de l'Ahaggar* (Paris: Karthala 1998).
9. J. Keenan, *The Tuareg: People of Ahaggar* (London: Allen Lane 1977).
10. J. Keenan, 'Ethnicity, Regionalism and Political Stability in Algeria's *Grand Sud*'; and J. Keenan, 'Contested Terrain: Tourism, Environment and Security in Algeria's Extreme South', both in this volume, pp.67–96 and 226–65 respectively.
11. Algeria is not the only Maghrib country to be accused of suppressing indigenous rights. Similar criticisms are levelled against Morocco, while Tunisia's benign dictatorship is also accused of human rights abuses.
12. The *wali* is the head of a *wilaya's* administration, equivalent to a French *préfet* in a *préfecture*. The *wali* is appointed by the President.
13. Although Kabyles and Tuareg speak a Berber language (Tamazaght and Tamahak/Tamashek respectively) and recognise its common roots, most Kabyles and Tuareg whom I have questioned have said that it takes six–nine months to learn each others' language.
14. The Kabyle region is known as Kabylia. It is centred on the Djurdjura Mts, about 100–120km west-south-west of Algiers. The capital of Kabylia is Tizi Ouzou.
15. The most extensive outbreak of unrest was in the spring of 2001.
16. For a summary account of the rebellions in Mali and Niger, see J. Keenan, 'The Situation of the Tuareg People in North and West Africa', in *The Indigenous World, 2001–2002* (Copenhagen: International Working Group for Indigenous Affairs 2002) pp.353–64.
17. The UN Declaration is only in Draft stage, while Algeria is not a signatory to the ILO Convention.
18. UN Draft Declaration, article 4.
19. See H. Roberts, *The Battlefield Algeria, 1988–2002* (London: Verso 2003) p.16.
20. These major changes have been described in Keenan (note 9). A summary account of them

Introduction

is given in Keenan, 'Ethnicity' (note 10).
21. 'Report on the 6th Session of the Commission on Human Rights Working Group on the Declaration on the Rights of Indigenous Peoples', in *The Indigenous World 2000–2001* (Copenhagen: International Working Group for Indigenous Affairs 2001) pp.414–54.
22. These are documented in 'The "Algerianization" of the Kel Ahaggar', Keenan (note 9) ch.15, pp.258–90.
23. J. Keenan, 'Thirty years of change and continuity in Ahaggar (1971–2002)', *The Tuareg: People of Ahaggar* (London: Sickle Moon Books 2002) new preface. See also J. Keenan, 'The Sahara's Indigenous People, the Tuareg, fear Environmental Catastrophe', *Indigenous Affairs* (Quarterly Journal of the International Working Group on Indigenous Affairs) 1 (2002) pp.50–57.
24. The Tassili-n-Ajjer and Ahaggar are the two main tourist regions of Algeria's extreme south. They coincide more or less with the *wilayat* of Illizi and Tamanrasset.
25. This is the aim of UNATA (*Union Nationale des Associations des Agences de Tourisme Alternatif*), which has requested M. Cherif Rahmani, in his capacity as Minister of the Environment and President of the World Deserts Foundation, to commission the report. UNATA's head office is in Tamanrasset. Its background, and the reasons behind this request to the Minister, are detailed in Keenan, 'Contested Terrain' (note 10).
26. A common complaint is that senior government officials do not have sufficient understanding of the south, its customs, regional issues and so forth. A pertinent example, frequently cited by the Tuareg, concerns how the last two *walis* of Tamanrasset delayed the subsidy payments due to camel owners as they did not understand why the Kel Ahaggar kept their camels in Tamesna in Niger. This lack of knowledge and understanding on the part of the region's senior administrator did much to fuel political tension in the region. For details, see J. Keenan, 'The Last Nomads: Nomadism amongst the Tuareg of Ahaggar (Algerian Sahara)', in this volume, pp.163–92.
27. See Keenan, 'Ethnicity' (note 10).
28. See J. Keenan, 'The Lesser Gods of the Sahara', in this volume, pp.193–225; and also J. Keenan, 'Tourism, development and conservation: A Saharan perspective', Proceedings of the Conference on Natural Resources and Cultural Heritage of the Libyan Desert, Tripoli, Libya, 14–21 Dec. 2002, *Libyan Studies* 34 (2003, in press).
29. An exceptionally good account of Algeria's Islamist movement is to be found in Roberts (note 19). See p.129 for comments on Tuareg.
30. Examples of these grievances are given in the Appendices to Keenan, 'Contested Terrain' (note 10).
31. This move was widely appreciated and probably the major contributory factor behind a highly successful conference held in the *wilaya* in March 2003. For details of this conference, see Keenan, 'Contested Terrain' (note 10).
32. At the time of writing, mid-August, the hostage crisis had still not been resolved.
33. Although it is true that Algeria's crisis had a 'knock-on' effect on tourism in Mali and Niger, the primary reason for the collapse of tourism in those two countries was the Tuareg rebellions.
34. The best known of these 'emirs', as they are now known, are Mokhtar ben Mokhtar and Abderazak Lamari (el Para), both of whom have several aliases. These two both originate from northern Algeria, although Mokhtar ben Mokhtar is a Metlilli Chaamba and can accordingly claim to be a 'man of the desert'. Since 11 September 2001 and the subsequent US invasion of Afghanistan, a considerable number of Pakistan and Afghan elements have spread into the region, especially northern Mali, in an attempt to 'Talibanise' it. Western and local intelligence services have recently made much ado about the alleged linkage of these elements to *al-Qaeda*.
35. This has generated a sense of 'betrayal' amongst Algeria's Tuareg.
36. This is in line with the US security strategy, which now sees this part of Africa becoming the base for major threats to US interests.
37. See Keenan, *The Tuareg* (note 23).
38. This is the term given to tourists who travel in the region in their own vehicles and without

using the services of local travel agencies or registered guides. Most of this type of tourism is illegal in the Algerian regions of Ahaggar and Tassili, as these regions are National Parks, which should not be entered in this way. Following the hostage crisis of 2003, Algeria is now enforcing strict visa controls to try and put an end to this sort of tourism, which has been largely associated with the looting of the Sahara's cultural artefacts.

39. See Keenan, 'Contested Terrain' (note 10) for details of the Tamanrasset Conference.
40. The Tuareg's struggle to avert this catastrophe, through what I have referred to as the 'last significant battle of the Central Sahara' is described in Keenan, 'Contested Terrain' (note 10).
41. The looting of the Sahara has not been confined to the last year. On the contrary, it has been going on for some time. However, it was only in 2002–03 that it was given significant prominence in the media and so drawn to the widespread attention of local peoples. For details, see Keenan, 'Contested Terrain' (note 10).
42. Ibid.
43. The Tassili-n-Ajjer Park, a UNESCO world heritage site, was established in 1984. The Ahaggar (Hoggar) National Park, the largest single park in the world, was established in 1987. For details, see Keenan, 'Contested Terrain' (note 10); and Keenan (note 26).
44. The Tassili-n-Ajjer, for example, just one of Algeria's prehistoric heritage sites, has been described as 'the site of the world's greatest collection of pre-historic art'. See Keenan, 'The Lesser Gods' (note 28).
45. This includes the possibility of major new conservation developments in the Tassili and Ahaggar National Parks, and elsewhere in the Sahara, and the Ministry's backing of a major film on Algeria's Saharan heritage and the associated problems of its conservation. The title of the film, *The Lesser Gods of the Sahara*, is taken from the article of the same title in this volume.

From Tit (1902) to Tahilahi (2002): A Reconsideration of the Impact of and Resistance to French Pacification and Colonial Rule by the Tuareg of Algeria (the Northern Tuareg)

The northern Tuareg have no written records of their history. This is because their script, *tifinagh*, has very limited usage, while Arabic, particularly in its written form, has been little known by them until recently. The main contemporary source material of the most critical period in their history, from the time when the French began to push south into the Sahara in the second half of the nineteenth century until about 1920 when they were deemed to be pacified, is of French origin. It consists mainly of French military archives,[1] reports written by French army officers who were involved in the conquest and exploration of the Sahara, the reports and records of administrators and a number of semi-official scientific and ethnological reports. Even the most valuable studies of that period, notably Duveyrier's *Les Touareg du Nord* (1864), Bissuel's *Les Touareg de l'Ouest* (1888) and Benhazera's *Six Mois chez les Touareg du Ahaggar* (1908), are written largely from a French perspective.[2]

When I first stayed amongst the northern Tuareg in the 1960s,[3] I found that their memories of this traumatic period were hazy and had been confused by the radical changes that had taken place under French colonial rule. Nevertheless, I was able to tap many of those memories for valuable insights into both the events that had occurred around the turn of the century, as well as the socio-political structures of the northern Tuareg at that time. The conclusion that I reached was that the 'French version' told only half the story. In particular, it made virtually no reference to the fact that northern Tuareg society at that time was in the midst of an extremely complex, dynamic and multifaceted revolution, nor that this revolution was being exacerbated by the varied perceptions and implications of France's encroachment into the Central Sahara. The many facets of Tuareg resistance and collaboration, which were articulated through the complex interplay of both class and political factional interests, could themselves only be understood within this revolutionary context.

Two things immediately struck me on my return to the northern Tuareg in the late 1990s. One was that much history had already been lost: the Tuareg had already forgotten the details of much that had taken place before and during the years of pacification. No more than a handful of the eldest Tuareg had even limited personal experiences of those times, while many knew little, or had only very confused knowledge, of some of the key events and personages of that era.[4] The second thing that struck me was the way in which many of the more significant determinants of those events, notably the different roles played by both social classes (nobles and vassals) and political factions within those classes in their resistance to or collaboration with the French, had been reinterpreted by Tuareg in ways which 'made sense' in the light of their subsequent knowledge and post-colonial experiences.

This article attempts to capture and analyse key elements of this crucial period in Tuareg history before they are swept away into a world of mythology in which an imperialist perspective, with all its cultural and racial arrogance, still dominates the literary terrain.

From Contact to Conquest and Pacification (A French Perspective)

The bare bones of the history of France's contact with and conquest of the northern Tuareg (seen largely from a French perspective) are as follows.

The French capture of Algiers in 1830 led eventually, after several bitter campaigns against Abdel Khader and other local 'resistance leaders', to Algeria being declared French in 1848. France's first contacts with the Tuareg,[5] at least in the Ajjer region, appear to have been reasonably amicable. The influential Sheikh Othman[6] of the religious Iforas tribe accepted an invitation from the governor general to visit Algiers, following on from which the French made an alliance with the Sheikh and the Kel Ajjer leader Ikhenoukhen.[7] In 1859 the young French geographer Henri Duveyrier travelled amongst the Kel Ajjer (as a guest of Sheikh Othman) for several months, and a commercial Treaty (of Ghadames) was signed in 1862. In spite of these seemingly amicable overtures, this initial period of exploration was followed by a series of troublesome events. The Dutch explorer Miss Tinné was murdered by Tuareg in 1869. A year later, two Frenchmen, Joubert and Dourneaux-Duprée, were also murdered by Tuareg. As a result contact between the French and the Tuareg remained extremely limited.[8] Indeed, by 1880 no European had yet entered Ahaggar.

That situation was to end in disastrous circumstances in 1881 when Colonel Flatters entered Ahaggar with a military column of some 90 men[9] to reconnoitre a route for a proposed trans-Saharan railway. In one of the most notorious incidents in French colonial history, the column was massacred by

From Tit to Tahilahi

Kel Ahaggar Tuareg, with only 11 'permitted' survivors managing to struggle back across almost 1,000km of desert to the safety of Ouargla.[10] The shocking outcome of the Flatters expedition put a stop to any further French penetration into the Central Sahara until the end of the 1890s. As M. Belin, the military commander of the *Cercle de Laghouat*, explained at the time,[11] military reprisal against the Tuareg would be a hazardous and uncertain business, which could become acutely embarrassing and difficult for France at the international level. With considerable foresight, Belin remarked that the desired results could be achieved just as surely by depriving the Tuareg of the vital food resources which they obtained from the oases of Tuat.

The Flatters massacre brought an effective halt to any further southwards sorties. It was not until 1899,[12] 18 years later, that the Flamand-Pein expedition pushed south to occupy In Salah.[13] This was followed shortly afterwards by the occupation of Tidikelt and the oases of Tuat and Guerara. The consequences of this occupation for the Tuareg, especially the Kel Ahaggar, were as Belin had predicted. The reaction of the Kel Ahaggar to this encroachment was to raid the camps of Arabs under French authority.[14] In March 1902, however, the people of Tidikelt had suffered enough from Tuareg raids.[15] They asked Captain Cauvet, the military commander at In Salah, to authorise a punitive expedition against the Kel Ahaggar. Lieutenant Cottenest, with some 130 voluntarily enlisted *meharistes*,[16] left In Salah on 23 March to make a reconnaissance of Ahaggar and inflict a punitive raid on the Kel Ahaggar.[17]

Cottenest's patrol travelled through the Mouydir (Immidir) and Tefedest ranges to Ideles and then on to Tazrouk, Tarhaouhaout and Tamanrasset without contact with the Tuareg. On 7 May 1902 the patrol left Tamanrasset on its return northwards. Forty kilometres north of Tamanrasset, near the little settlement of Tit, the patrol was attacked by a force of some 300 Kel Ahaggar. After two-and-a-half hours fighting and the reported expenditure of 14,000 bullets by Cottenest's men, the Tuareg retreated leaving 93 dead[18] on the ground. Cottenest lost 6 men.[19]

The battle of Tit[20] shocked Ahaggar. The Kel Ahaggar's notions of their invincibility and territorial sovereignty were shattered, and their submission to France can be dated as beginning from that day. In early 1903, Colonel (later General) Laperrine, the senior military commander of the Saharan oases, sent Lieutenant Guilho-Lohan on a follow-up tour through Ahaggar. He encountered no significant resistance.

Some Taitok, suffering from France's occupation of Tuat, sought peace in 1901. Others sought refuge in the Ajjer region from where they continued to resist. Accordingly, in 1903 Lieutenant Besset was sent on a police visit to the Ajjer region. Although Besset came under attack from Sidi ag Keradji, the old

Taitok chief, other Taitok under Aziouel ag Ser'ada did submit.[21] In the following year (1904), Moussa ag Amastane, who at that time was a significant leader amongst the Kel Ahaggar, rode to In Salah with many of his followers to negotiate peace. He was received with great ceremony and courtesy. In his negotiations with Captain Metois, the *Chef d'Annexe*, he guaranteed the cessation of hostilities by the Kel Ahaggar and the security of the trade routes on condition that France also assured peace in Ahaggar. Sidi ag Keradji eventually followed in the steps of Moussa ag Amastane and made his way to In Salah. During the police tour of Ahaggar in the summer of 1905 Captain Dinaux officially invested Moussa ag Amastane in the name of France as *Amenukal* (supreme chief) of Ahaggar,[22] and Sidi ag Keradji as the *Amenukal* of the Taitok and Kel Ahnet.

The submission of the Kel Ahaggar enabled France to link up with her Sudanese territories.[23] On 18 April 1904 Laperrine achieved the long-awaited liaison by meeting a Sudanese contingent under Captain Théveniault at the wells of Timaiouine, about 350 miles to the west-south-west of Tamanrasset. The meeting established the frontier between Algeria and French West Africa.[24] Another straight line, disregarding the social, economic and political interests of the local people, in this case the Tuareg, was drawn on the map of Africa.[25]

By this time, the French also saw Ajjer territory as relatively tranquil. Besset had reported in 1903 that the dissident Kel Ahaggar who had sought refuge in Ajjer, as well as the Kel Ajjer themselves, were in disarray. In the following year (1904) Captain Touchard received the submission of several Kel Ulli ('vassals') at Djanet. Indeed, Bernard and Lacroix, writing in 1906, went so far as to state that *'la question touareg est aujourd'hui résolue ... La question de la pénétration saharienne ne doit donc plus encombre notre politique'*.[26] Moussa ag Amastane remained loyal to his word and in 1907 was invested as a Commander of the *Légion d'Honneur* for his services to France.[27] By 1908 French garrisons had been built at Temassinine (Fort Flatters), Illizi (Fort Polignac) and Tarhaouhaout (Fort Motylinski).[28]

However, in spite of this considerable French presence and the apparent tranquillity of the Ajjer region, the Kel Ajjer were still not pacified. In 1913, some 300 of them, led by Inguedazzen (the *Amenukal*), Bubekir ag Allegoui and Sultan Ahmoud of Djanet, attacked a 45-strong French unit under the command of Lieutenant Gardel at Essayen, a few miles to the south-west of Ghat. As at Tit, the Tuareg were heavily defeated.[29] Nor was the Battle of Essayen the end of it. Within months of the outbreak of the First World War, the Sanussi revolt against the Italian and French 'infidels' spread like wildfire through the Sahara. By 1917 France's hold on her Saharan territories was precarious, with their retention owing much to the role of Moussa ag Amastane.

France's last military engagement against the northern Tuareg was on 27 July 1920. Moussa and a force of Kel Ahaggar joined the French in defeating the Kel Ajjer at the Col d'Assakao, 50km north of Djanet.[30]

A Reassessment of the French Perspective

This summary account of France's conquest and pacification of the northern Tuareg reflects a predominantly imperialistic perspective. Although not factually incorrect, it is very misleading, verging on the mythological, in a number of crucially important respects. Not only has it contributed to a very distorted notion of the social structure and dynamics of Tuareg society at the time of the French arrival, and what is meant by 'traditional' society, but, because of the Tuareg's own lack of written records, it has also contributed to their own increasingly misconstrued notions of their history.

French Colonial Policy

Before trying to 'set the record straight', as it were, we need to have a clearer understanding of France's colonial policy in the Sahara, and the Algerian Sahara in particular. There is a danger, especially amongst those more familiar with British colonial policy, in assuming that France shared the same level of interest in her colonies as did the British. Compared to Britain, whose empire became of central political and economic importance, France's colonies were of peripheral importance to the affairs of the metropolis. Indeed, even when France did create an independent ministry for the colonies in 1894,[31] France's Saharan regions still fell under the responsibility of four separate ministries![32]

France did not set out to occupy the Sahara. At no time did she have plans to garrison or colonise it.[33] The remoteness of the Sahara in government thinking was demonstrated by the fact that no governor general visited Ahaggar until 1932. Throughout the nineteenth century, French policy towards the Sahara lurched from one objective to another.[34] Her limited sorties into the desert were circumscribed by little more than fear of upsetting the Turks to the east and the Sultan of Morocco to the west.[35]

France's attitude and policy towards the Sahara were epitomised in the conquest of the Tuat in 1899–1900.[36] If there was a policy for the Sahara at that time, it was a restriction on further expansion or the creation of new posts and the retention of what was already in French possession. Tuat was therefore strictly 'off limits', especially as its claim by the Sultan of Morocco was recognised and guaranteed by Britain. However, for those few Frenchmen pre-occupied with the conquest of the Sahara, as well as those still transfixed by the idea of a trans-Saharan railway, the Tuat was a military target of major importance.[37] Not only was it on the direct route to Timbuktu, now seen as the most likely terminus of a trans-Saharan railway, but, as Belin had advised almost two decades earlier, it was the Tuareg's Achilles heel.

The occupation of the Tuat by French forces in 1899–1900, under the guise of a geological expedition (the Flamand-Pein expedition), was an ingenious exercise in subterfuge and duplicity. The plan was instigated primarily by Captain Théodore Pein, with the connivance of his friend, Captain Ferdinand Levé, the military secretary to the governor general of Algeria. Standing orders at that time required all officers to consult Algiers before ordering an operation in the Sahara. However, it was the willingness of independent-minded military officers to bend, or simply ignore, orders from superiors that enabled France ultimately to conquer the Sahara.[38] The strategy of Pein and Levé, like a number of other military officers, was to take unscheduled initiatives, provoke fights ('incidents') and thus oblige Algiers to despatch punitive expeditions. They played a game of brinkmanship in which they placed the French government in embarrassing positions, knowing that such embarrassment was less than the embarrassment of withdrawal.

The invasion of Tuat caused the French government considerable military and diplomatic problems.[39] But, as the 'colonialists' had foreseen, their action was ultimately given grudging sanction by the French government.[40] The announcement of the war minister in November 1901 that the Saharan oases would be provided with no more than the minimum number of troops to police the Tuat was an effective admission and acceptance of France's permanency in the region.[41] But the announcement was also an attempt to rein in these headstrong military officers. In particular, the minister sought to deter them from attempting to conquer Ahaggar. Unwisely he left it to military officers on the spot, the senior of which at this time was Henri Laperrine, to interpret this policy.

Cottenest's punitive raid into Ahaggar in 1902 saw military opportunism and dissemblement being developed to a fine art. At the time of the raid, Laperrine was commander of the oases, Pein was the commandant at Ouargla and Cauvet was the commander at In Salah. Cauvet authorised Cottenest's raid without reference to the higher authority of Laperrine. Thus, although Cauvet did not seek authorisation from Laperrine for fear that Laperrine might have orders forbidding such expeditions, he clearly felt confident that Laperrine would not disapprove such action. 'I had no orders', Cauvet later confessed.

> There were none at In Salah. I even avoided asking Laperrine who might have received some or who would have felt obliged to ask for some. Therefore I did not overstep my orders. The distinction is perhaps a trifle subtle, for I know exactly what the reply would have been if I had proposed to send my people on a tour of the Hoggar. But it exists nevertheless.[42]

It is almost inconceivable that Cauvet would have authorised Cottenest's raid without knowing that he had Laperrine's support. Indeed, the fact that Laperrine and Pein both sent out raids at the same time in order, it must be presumed, to distract the Tuareg from Cottenest's raid, suggests a fairly well-planned strategy on the part of French military officers in the Sahara.

In July 1902, following Cottenest's unauthorised raid into Ahaggar, the minister repeated his call, saying that the commander of the Saharan oases must adopt a purely passive role of local defence. In a futile attempt to strengthen the control of government over military adventurers, the French parliament passed a law making the southern territories of Algeria the direct responsibility of the governor general in Algiers rather than the commander of the 19th military division.[43] Officers such as Laperrine, Pein[44] and Cauvet operated independently by simply ignoring or circumventing such orders.

Following the conquest of Tuat, the interpretation of French policy in the region was left largely to Laperrine. His policy towards the Tuareg was basically twofold. The primary policy was to impose a trade embargo against those who did not submit to French authority. Although this policy was not new, having been initiated after Flatters's disastrous expedition, it moved into top gear with the invasion of the Tuat. By controlling the Tuareg's main market of Tuat, Laperrine hoped to starve dissidents into submission.[45] Laperrine's second policy was to use the Tuareg's existing socio-political structures to administer French control. However, as I shall show later, the 'traditional' socio-political structures which France claimed to have preserved had already been turned completely upside down in the course of pacification. What replaced them was a façade.

Misconceptions Inherent in the French Perspectives of Tuareg History

French perspectives on the conquest and pacification of the Tuareg contain a number of fundamental misconceptions of Tuareg society. Two in particular permeate most of the colonial literature on the subject.

La Conféderation des Touareg du Nord

The first of these misconceptions was what the French frequently referred to as *La Conféderation des Touareg du Nord*.

The Tuareg comprised eight groups. Six were to be found in what is now Niger and Mali; the two most northerly, the Kel Ahaggar and Kel Ajjer, inhabited respectively the mountains of Ahaggar and Tassili-n-Ajjer in what is now southern Algeria.

We have little knowledge of the tribal groupings and socio-political structures of the northern Tuareg before the middle of the seventeenth century. Before that time, the Tuareg of Ajjer, Ahaggar, the Adrar-n-Iforas and northern Aïr fell under the rule of the Imenan, who lived at Ghat and Djanet and whose chiefs held the title of sultan.[46] From what little we know of those times, it seems that the Tuareg under their rule grew tired of their tyranny and exactions. With the assistance of some of the Tuareg tribes of Niger, notably the Uraren, they overthrew them. The Tuareg of Ajjer and Ahaggar may have been to some extent unified in the era up to the mid-seventeenth century, albeit in subjugation to the power of the Imenan. It is important to appreciate, though, that since that time they have formed two separate and independent groups which at no time could be considered as forming a single social or political entity.[47] Indeed, and in spite of occasional intermarriages between them, the relationship between them has more often been one of enmity, as epitomised in the three-year war which raged between them from 1875 to 1878.

The idea that the Kel Ajjer and Kel Ahaggar formed some sort of social or political confederation was a colonial invention, and the cause of frequent misinterpretation of political realities in the Central Sahara. In fact, there were very significant differences between the two groups.

Once such difference was in their economic bases. Although both groups were essentially nomadic pastoralists, the Kel Ajjer had greater agricultural and commercial resources and were consequently much less dependent on pastoralism than the Kel Ahaggar. Both Ghat and Djanet were fertile oases. Djanet, in particular, which in 1914 supported a population of 1,200,[48] enabled the Kel Ajjer to develop a significant agricultural economy. In Ahaggar, by contrast, there were no significant settlements and little agricultural development until after French pacification.[49] Djanet was also an important commercial centre, being on three trans-Saharan trade routes.[50] This important commercial traffic enabled Djanet to earn revenue from the supply of camels and other related services and to exchange dates, salt and medicinal plants for millet, livestock and manufactured goods. The caravan trade passing through Ahaggar and under the control of the Kel Ahaggar[51] bore little comparison to that which passed through Djanet and the control of the Kel Ajjer. The Kel Ahaggar envied the Kel Ajjer and hankered after the rights to organise the protection of the great trans-Saharan caravans.[52] Indeed, the importance of this trade to the Kel Ajjer was such that one of the demands of their chief, Brahim ag Abakada, on finally submitting to the French in 1919, was that all supply caravans in the Tassili-n-Ajjer should be reserved for them.[53]

Although there appears to have been little significant numerical difference between the Kel Ahaggar and Kel Ajjer in pre-colonial times,[54] it seems that

Djanet's position on the caravan routes made the Kel Ajjer the more important of the two groups at that time. However, the internecine wars of 1875–78, in which the Kel Ahaggar were ultimately victorious, so weakened the Kel Ajjer that the Kel Ahaggar had probably become the dominant group by the end of the nineteenth century.

Another key difference between the Kel Ahaggar and Kel Ajjer was the latter's more prolonged resistance to the French. There were three reasons. The first was that the comparative sanctuary offered to the Kel Ajjer in Turkish-held Fezzan protected them from French reprisal raids.[55] The second reason was the relatively weaker position of the nobles in Ahaggar, caused by factional interests amongst the nobility and the increasing independence of many vassal groups. The third reason was the key role of the *Amenukal* of the Kel Ahaggar, Moussa ag Amastane, in assisting the French in their subjugation of the Kel Ajjer, an act which has served to further the longstanding hostility between the two groups.

I shall elaborate on all three of these factors later. But first, let me focus for a moment on the last-mentioned act, namely the role played by Moussa ag Amastane in the final defeat of the Kel Ajjer. It goes some way to explaining the French misconception of *La Confédération des Touareg du Nord*.

In spite of the apparent tranquillity of the Tassili-n-Ajjer region following the submission of various Kel Ulli (vassal) groups to Captain Touchard in 1904, Captain Niéger's mission to Djanet in 1909 and Captain Charlet's establishment of a French garrison[56] at Djanet in 1911, the Kel Ajjer were by no means pacified. In 1913 some 300 of them attacked a French column at Essayen. Although heavily defeated, resistance against the French simmered on in the Fezzan and flared up again within months of the outbreak of the First World War.

The fan behind this resistance was the *sufi* brotherhood of the Sanussi,[57] who by 1900 had established remarkable control over Cyrenaica and, to a lesser extent, over parts of Tripolitania and Fezzan. The basis of their power lay in their control of the important Tripoli–Bornu/Wadai trade routes. It was principally for fear of losing this economic wealth to the colonial powers[58] that they adopted such a strong anti-colonial stance. They had hindered the Foureau-Lamy[59] expedition's acquisition of provisions in 1900,[60] and in 1901 had received at their headquarters in Kufra a delegation of Uraren who were alarmed by the French advance. But it was not until after the outbreak of the First World War that they really became active among the Tuareg.

Pushed by the Turks, the Sanussi launched their *jihad* against the Italian and French infidels.[61] On 23 December 1914 the Italians abandoned Ghat to Sidi Mohammed el-Abed[62] and the Kel Ajjer chiefs Sultan Ahmoud, Bubekir ag Allegoui and Inguedazzen. The influence of El-Abed, the Sanussi representative for the Fezzan, was now substantially enhanced and his position of unchallenged authority provided a rallying point for the leaders of Tuareg resistance, both amongst the Kel Ajjer and in Niger, where Kaoucen ag Ouantigidda,[63] a Tuareg from Damergou, led a Sanussi-backed offensive against the French.

The roles of the Kel Ahaggar and more especially that of Moussa ag Amastane in the Sanussi revolt are particularly interesting. Some Kel Ahaggar nobles, notably the Taitok, joined Kaoucen in his resistance to the French. Many Kel Ahaggar, Kel Ulli and Isekkemaren also joined the Sanussi cause. However, the position of Moussa was more ambivalent. The French had doubts about his loyalty to them during the height of the Tuareg resistance. However, we do know that he declined the overtures of El-Abed, who wrote to him in May 1916, calling on him to join the *jihad* – as well as those of Kaoucen who wrote to him in January 1917, exhorting him '*n'accepter ni l'humiliation, ni la honte, ni la soumission à ceux qui adorent les idoles. Comment pourrait-on vivre avec les vipères et les scorpions?*'[64]

On 26 February 1916, a force of 1,000 men under the command of Sultan Ahmoud and Abdessalem, the *Kaimakam* of Ghat,[65] armed with artillery and machine-guns and backed by Sanussi and Turkish troops, left Ghat to take Djanet. After an 18-day siege the Djanet garrison of 45 men (two of whom were French) surrendered, a day before French reinforcements arrived from Fort Polignac. Lieutenant Colonel Octave Meynier recaptured Djanet on 16 May and immediately advanced on Ghat. However, with Ghat surrounded and at his mercy, he received an order from Paris to cease the campaign and withdraw.[66] With the French withdrawal, the Sanussi revolt spread like wildfire across the Sahara. After coming under a series of attacks in the Tassili-n-Ajjer, the French were forced to evacuate Djanet on 21 July leaving Ajjer territory almost completely under Sanussi control.[67] By early 1917, France's position in the Sahara was tenuous. The entire Ajjer territory was in a state of insurrection. Kaoucen had succeeded in inciting most of the Aïr Tuareg to revolt. The situation in Ahaggar, where the French priest Charles de Foucauld had been murdered at Tamanrasset in December 1916, was no better.[68] Faced with such widespread resistance, Laperrine, now a general, was recalled from the Somme to take command of all French Saharan territory. He returned on 2 February 1917 to find the small number[69] of troops disorganised, ill-equipped and in very low morale.[70] For most of the first half of 1917, French troops and convoys continued to be attacked with impunity.[71] By July, however, the tide began to turn. A band of Kel Ajjer was repulsed at Tadjemout (2 July); dissident Kel Ajjer began to withdraw from Ahaggar as hunger ravaged the region; and two of the most prominent Kel Ahaggar rebels[72] asked for pardon. This sudden change in attitude was reinforced by re-

From Tit to Tahilahi

equipped French forces showing for the first time that they were prepared to go on the offensive.[73]

The role of Moussa ag Amastane in this offensive was critical. By August 1917[74] there was a movement towards submission in Ahaggar. In September he led a delegation of Kel Ahaggar nobles to In Salah to plead the case of the Kel Ahaggar dissidents and negotiate their terms of pardon.[75] In the beginning of 1918, he undertook a number of raids against Kaoucen, notably at Talarak in February and Agangan in March. While these actions were decisive for the French,[76] they also paid big dividends for the Kel Ahaggar as the French handed over to Moussa and his 'tribe' (*tawsit*), the Kel Rela, thousands of camels captured from the Kel Aïr. This huge increase in the size of the Kel Ahaggar's camel herds presented them with a major problem. They did not have sufficient carrying capacity in Ahaggar, and their traditional camel-grazing areas around Tin Zaouaten and the Adrar-n-Iforas were no longer accessible in view of the new frontier restrictions and the independence of the Iforas. With Laperrine's approval, the Kel Ahaggar effectively annexed the region of Tamesna in northern Niger. Such a 'buffer' zone between the 'northern' and 'southern' Tuareg was clearly of strategic value to the French.[77] Since that time the Kel Ahaggar have kept the bulk of their camels in Tamesna. It is interesting to note that most of the important wells in the region were dug by the Kel Ahaggar – the wells of In-Abangerit being the work of the Irregenaten.[78]

Having dealt with Kaoucen, Moussa turned his attention to helping the French forces attack the camps of dissident Kel Ajjer. In October and November he raided Kel Ajjer camps between Djanet and Admer and in the Anahaf massif in the east of Ahaggar.[79] He continued raiding the Kel Ajjer throughout 1919. Fort Polignac was reoccupied in February 1920, with Djanet finally being reoccupied with a permanent French garrison in July. The French installed Moussa as the ruler of Djanet, granting him the sovereign rights formerly held by the Sultan Ahmoud, along with the ownership of all the gardens that were owned by Bubekir ag Allegoui. On 27 July Moussa led the Kel Ahaggar alongside French troops to crush most of the remaining Ajjer dissidents at the Col d'Assakao.

At the time of Moussa's death,[80] precisely five months after the battle of Assakao, his authority, supported by the French, was unprecedented since the time of the fall of Imenan Sultans around 1660. Ahaggar was united under his command; he was the ruler of Djanet, and he controlled much of northern Niger.

I believe that the explanation for the misconception of a *Confédération des Touareg du Nord* derives from this unprecedented concentration of power in the personage of Moussa ag Amastane. Such a concentration of authority, as ruler of both Ahaggar and Djanet, was immensely convenient for Laperrine, whose policy was to use the Tuareg's existing socio-political structures to administer French control. In this case, however, we are looking at a colonial construct which had nothing to do with traditional society, in as much as the Kel Ajjer had never fallen under the rule of the Kel Ahaggar. However, we must be careful not to insinuate that such 'colonial structures' were entirely without local support. Indeed, Moussa himself had long striven for such an outcome. As early as 1905, when he learnt that the Iforas were to fall under the administration of French West Africa and not Ahaggar, he had asked the French authorities to compensate him by naming him as 'chief' of the Kel Ajjer.[81] Laperrine had even written to the governor general, asking that Moussa's request be granted, confirming that it would merely be the implementation of the implicit promise that Captain Cauvet had made to him.[82] Although the imposition of Moussa as ruler of Djanet exacerbated the cleavage between the Kel Ajjer and Kel Ahaggar, especially when the French decreed on Moussa's death that the rights over the gardens of Djanet would devolve to his successor (as *Amenukal* of Ahaggar), Akhemouk ag Ihemma,[83] it was readily abetted by Moussa ag Amastane and no doubt most of the Kel Ahaggar.

With Ahaggar and Ajjer being placed under a single ruler, it is easy to see how the idea of a confederation of Kel Ajjer and Kel Ahaggar could have gained credibility amongst the French.

The Dynamics of 'Traditional' (Pre-Colonial)[84] *Society*

The second and perhaps greatest misconception inherent in most colonial literature on the Tuareg has been its failure to recognise the dynamic nature of their 'traditional' society.[85] The society which the French encountered when they finally penetrated Ahaggar was not just 'dynamic'; it was, I believe, on the brink, if not in the midst, of a major social, political and economic revolution. In short, the conventional picture of 'traditional' society and its prevailing socio-political structures through which the French sought to administer their control over the region is far removed from social, political and economic reality.

The dynamics of traditional Tuareg society need to be understood on two interrelated levels. The first is in terms of the dynamics inherent in the fundamental cleavages of traditional or pre-colonial society. The second is in terms of the way in which external forces have worked on and been mediated by these cleavages.

Pre-colonial society was characterised by four main cleavages:

1. that between the Kel Ajjer and Kel Ahaggar;
2. that between the two main classes of Ihaggaren ('nobles') and Kel Ulli ('vassals');

3. that between the 'noble' descent groups (*tawsatin*, sing. *tawsit*) themselves, notably, in the case of the Kel Ahaggar, the Kel Rela and Taitok, and finally;
4. cleavages between political factions within the nobility themselves.

The Kel Ajjer/Kel Ahaggar cleavage has been described above. I will therefore deal in turn with the remaining three before focusing on the way they have been affected by external factors.

Ihaggaren ('Nobles') versus Kel Ulli ('Vassals')

The noble–vassal division was the fundamental cleavage within all Tuareg groups. However, as a result of the ongoing conflicts between drum-groups (*ettebelen*, sing. *ettebel*), individual nobles and the two main classes themselves, the nature of noble–vassal relations was rarely static or changeless. It is consequently difficult to present a precise picture or analysis of noble–vassal relations, since at any one moment they seem to have been in the process of or on the brink of change. Any description of the relationship can therefore be little more than an abstraction.

The origin of this division probably arises from the Ihaggaren's control of the use of physical force in the form of their exclusive ownership of camels and weapons, notably the *takouba* (sword). We know that the Kel Ulli were, as the French themselves commented, 'warriors in their own right' at the time of the French conquest. However, it is not at all clear when they acquired rights to camels and weapons. For example, Duveyrier, writing in the middle of the nineteenth century, is quite emphatic that the Kel Ulli carried the same weapons as the Ihaggaren and were equally capable warriors.[86] Heinrich Barth, on the other hand, who visited the Kel Ajjer at about the same time as Duveyrier, recorded that the vassals had no rights to possess iron spears and swords.[87] The same contradiction is found amongst more recent writers. Lhote, for instance, states that it was only recently, and with reluctance, that the Ihaggaren yielded the right to carry the *takouba* to the Kel Ulli.[88] Nicolaisen, for his part, regards Barth's observations as spurious, and states that all Tuareg confirmed to him that in the past noble and vassal Tuareg did not differ in regard to weapons.[89]

I can do little more than throw some rather speculative light on what is meant by 'recent' and 'in the past'. We know very little about the political groupings in either Ahaggar or Ajjer in the immediate wake of the overthrow of the Imenan. We do know that the Kunta[90] to the west and south-west of Ahaggar were defeated resoundingly by the Kel Ahaggar around 1755, indicative that the Kel Ahaggar were a significant fighting force at that time.

It was around that time or shortly afterwards that the Kel Ahaggar reorganised[91] themselves into the territorial and political groupings which remained in place until the French conquest. This reorganisation resulted in the creation of three drum-groups (the Kel Rela, the Taitok and the Tegehe Mellet), each comprising a single noble *tawsit* to which was attached a number of subordinate or 'vassal' *tawsatin*. It is conjectural whether the nobility held exclusive rights over specialised weapons prior to this division. What we do know is that the division was unequal, resulting in an imbalance of power between the three drum-groups. It is logical for us to surmise that this imbalance of power between the three groups and their need to control and protect their respective territories and resources, not only from each other but also from foreigners, created a situation in which the nobility would have wanted to make their vassals a more effective auxiliary fighting force. Indeed, that was almost certainly the case, for we know that the nineteenth century was characterised by more or less continuous conflict between the Kel Rela, Taitok and Tegehe Mellet in their struggle for overall domination of Ahaggar. If vassals did not have rights to the *takouba* before, it was certainly in the interests of the nobility to yield the right to them around this time. The terms 'recent' and 'in the past' may thus refer to the second half of the eighteenth century, which would also accord with Duveyrier's observations.

However, the Kel Ulli's acquisition of specialised weapons is only part of the answer. In this vast, sparsely populated region warfare usually took the form of raids, with success often dependent on speed and cunning rather than numbers. Raiding parties usually only numbered a few dozen (or less) specialised, well-armed, mounted men, and booty consisted mostly of livestock, particularly camels, which could be driven off quickly. In this form of warfare, the camel was paramount. It was the Ihaggaren's exclusive possession of camels, as much as arms, that made them a specialised warrior class. According to Foucauld,[92] the Kel Ulli possessed no camels at all before the latter part of the eighteenth century, while throughout the nineteenth century they possessed only a few of their own. Gradually, however, the Kel Ulli acquired possession of their own camels. We can only speculate on the process whereby this happened. Wittingly or unwittingly the Ihaggaren were partly, if not wholly, responsible, for as it was in their interests for their Kel Ulli to be wealthy (for reasons explained below), the Ihaggaren encouraged them to join them in raids or to use the nobles' camels left in their care to undertake raids on their own account.[93] In this way, and through such large-scale operations as the Ajjer–Ahaggar war (1875–78), the Kel Ulli were able to acquire possession of their own camels. This process of acquisition almost certainly accelerated during the second half of the nineteenth century as a result of the general escalation of warfare and raiding associated with the prolonged Ajjer–Ahaggar war, attacks against encroaching French patrols, and the almost constant feuding between the drum-groups themselves. In short, there is ample evidence to show that by the beginning of the twentieth century (the time of the French arrival), and probably even earlier, the Ihaggaren no longer held exclusive control over the means of physical force. By that time the Kel Ulli were camel owners in their own right and equally capable warriors. Indeed, given the numerical superiority of the Kel Ulli, it can be argued that at the time of the French arrival it was the vassals, not the Ihaggaren, who comprised the largest fighting force in Ahaggar, and probably also in Ajjer.

This shift in the balance of physical power between the two main classes had critical implications for the fundamental relationship between them. The Kel Ulli, as their name tells us, were 'goat-breeders' and, as such, comprised the subsistence base of traditional society. The Ihaggaren, in contrast, comprised a warrior aristocracy. The traditional relationship between them was expressed formally within the relations of the drum-group (*ettebel*) and informally within the relationships known as *temazlayt* and *tamekchit*.[94]

Within the *ettebel*, the political subordination of the Kel Ulli and Isekkemaren *tawsatin* was expressed in an annual tributary payment of allegiance (known as *tiwse*) and the annual payment of a 'land-rent' known as *ehere-n-amadal* (lit. 'wealth of the land'). *Tiwse* payments were normally paid by whole *tawsatin*, or sections of *tawsatin*, to the drum-chief (*amrar*), although there were several instances of *tiwse* being paid to other prominent noble families.[95] *Tiwse* payments comprised subsistence goods such as goats, millet, butter and dates.

No one could enjoy rights to the land without the explicit or implicit authorisation of the drum-chief, in return for which he paid an annual *ehere-n-amadal*. For cultivators and other 'foreigners' who came into Ahaggar increasingly after the middle of the nineteenth century, this land-rent constituted a real levy. For Kel Ahaggar *tawsatin* (Kel Ulli and Isekkemaren) it was largely symbolic and minimal in amount, usually comprising products associated with a particular region, such as donkeys, occasionally mouflon and the ubiquitous goat. What was significant about this payment, in contrast to *tiwse* payments, is that it was paid only to the drum-chief and not to any other nobles.[96]

Unlike the *tiwse* and *ehere-n-amadal* payments, which were formal, institutionalised arrangements, the *temazlayt* relationship was more informal, more socially complex and, in view of its disintegration around the time of pacification, more difficult for us to describe and analyse.[97] Marceau Gast described *temazlayt* as a 'contract of protection'.[98] In early times, the Kel Ulli, as their name tells us, were the main producers. Their goat herds provided both themselves and the Ihaggaren not only with numerous food products (milk, cheese, butter, meat), but the materials used in the manufacture of many essential artefacts. As such they had to suffer the exactions of the Ihaggaren and other groups within the *tegehe*,[99] as well as foreign raiders. In the latter instance it was the responsibility of the *Amenukal* to ensure the defence of the *tegehe*, but it seems that he was often powerless to prevent raids that went on within Ahaggar. Consequently, the Kel Ulli, without camels and specialised arms, were obliged to turn to the Ihaggaren for their protection. It was for this reason, as Gast says, that the Kel Ulli would choose a warrior from among their nobility to protect them personally, in return for which they gave him a special tribute in kind – the *temazlayt*. Each group of Kel Ulli, or productive unit, thus had a protector at the local level, while in the event of large foreign raids all the warriors of the drum-group or *tegehe* would join together on the command of the *Amenukal* in what could be regarded as the 'national' defence.

The *temazlayt* relationship was the primary means whereby the Ihaggaren were able to appropriate sufficient surplus labour from their vassals to meet their subsistence needs. In this respect the relationship was the fundamental means whereby the diverse economic activities of the two classes were integrated within an overall 'pastoral-cum-raiding' economy. The form of this appropriation, or rather the 'unequal' exchange basis of the relationship, was expressed in the various rights and obligations of the two parties. Unlike the drum-chief, the *temazlayt* leader had no judicial authority over his Kel Ulli, nor could he summon them to war or raid unless they were interested. Furthermore, if the Kel Ulli did undertake raids, either on their own or under the leadership of their *temazlayt* leader, half the booty was given as tribute (*aballag*) to the drum-chief. The rights of the *temazlayt* leader were essentially economic. *Temazlayt* payments provided the nobility with valuable goat-breeding products. The associated but more generalised institution of *tamekchit*, whereby Ihaggaren could claim food from the Kel Ulli, enabled them to obtain more or less anything they needed for their subsistence. Ihaggaren would consequently camp close to their Kel Ulli, who were obliged to feed and provision them. The Kel Ulli, however, received certain compensation, not least of which was the assurance of protection. Moreover, as Ihaggaren were frequently away raiding, they would leave most of their livestock, notably camels, in the care of their Kel Ulli, who then had certain usufruct rights over them. The more important of these rights was that they could use the Ihaggaren's camels for their own caravan or raiding expeditions.

Although the rights of the Ihaggaren appear to have been extensive, it was clearly in their interests to ensure that their Kel Ulli were rich and well-protected, for they were dependent on them to a very large extent for much of their subsistence. In the case of persistent or excessive demands, it appears that the Kel Ulli always had the right to refuse their requests. More important, and perhaps the ultimate sanction against over-exploitation, the Kel Ulli could turn to another noble for protection.[100]

This description of *temazlayt* is an idealised abstraction drawn from a range of historical sources. In practice we know that the balance of power between the Ihaggaren and Kel Ulli, in terms of access to camels and weapons and hence their fighting ability, had been undergoing a more or less continuous process of change. The result was that the Kel Ulli were almost certainly the most powerful element in Ahaggar, in terms of their numbers and fighting ability, throughout much of the latter part of the nineteenth century (and possibly earlier). Under such circumstances, the traditional basis of the *temazlayt* relationship no longer found justification in the prevailing social reality. While the origins of the relationship may have been predominantly symbiotic, it almost certainly became the site for more or less continuous conflict between the two classes. Indeed, we have considerable evidence from the early French reports and travelogues on the region, as well as the oral accounts given by Tuareg themselves during the course of the last century, to suggest that Kel Ulli, during the late nineteenth and early twentieth centuries were becoming increasingly confident in rejecting the demands of the Ihaggaren. They were acting increasingly on their own initiative in both the political and economic domains.

Ahaggar, at the time of the French arrival, was on the brink or in the midst of a class revolution.

'Noble' versus 'Noble'

The precise circumstances under which the division of the Kel Ahaggar into three drum-groups took place in the middle of the eighteenth century are not clear.[101] The outcome was three drum-groups, each headed by a noble *tawsit* (Kel Rela, Taitok and Tegehe Mellet) with the Kel Ulli and Isekkemaren *tawsatin* distributed between them. The Kel Rela got the lion's share of the division and it was not long before both the Taitok and Tegehe Mellet began to feel that they had been treated unfairly. Both the Taitok and Tegehe Mellet attempted to overcome the dominance of the Kel Rela but both were convincingly defeated. Although the Tegehe Mellet never again became sufficiently strong to challenge the Kel Rela, the Taitok remained a threat to the pre-eminence of the Kel Rela throughout most of the nineteenth century. Many of the raids within and around Ahaggar during this period can only be understood within the context of this long-standing conflict between the Kel Rela and Taitok. For example, it seems that Taitok raids on Arabs under

French authority in the Tidikelt in 1900, following the French occupation of the Tuat in 1899, may have been designed to embarrass the Kel Rela and implicate them in French retaliatory action. Similarly, the Taitok's alliance with Kaoucen and their seemingly greater resistance to the French in the period of the Sanussi revolt may have been driven as much by their desire to redress their position in Ahaggar as any belief in a *jihad* or resistance to colonialism.[102]

It is significant that the 'Taitok problem' was not resolved within the framework of 'traditional' society, but by the forces of French colonialism. During the Sanussi revolt they had joined Kaoucen and sought refuge in Aïr. When they returned to Ahaggar in 1918 they did not receive a pardon, as was the case with all other dissidents except those responsible for Foucauld's murder. Rather, they were stripped by the French of their political authority and rights to all land in Ahaggar and placed under the overall command of Moussa ag Amastane. This measure was not simply to punish them for their dissidence. On the one hand it was part of the reward 'package' to Moussa ag Amastane for his loyalty (along with his installation as ruler of Djanet and effective annexation of Tamesna). On the wider plan, however, it was part of France's strategy to increase the authority of the *Amenukal* and the Kel Rela in Ahaggar (the so-called 'traditional structures') so that they could be more easily used to administer French control.[103] In effect, the French exiled the Taitok from Ahaggar. Stripped of their *ettebel*, they moved progressively towards the south-west. Animosity towards the Kel Rela continued, and in 1935–36, when a few Taitok tents were pitched close to a Kel Rela encampment at the wells of Aloua, a fight broke out which resulted in their chief, Mohammed ag Mohammed, being gaoled in Tamanrasset. Once again the Taitok felt they had been treated unjustly and moved more and more towards Niger. By 1938 there were only about 30 Taitok in Ahaggar, and in 1945 they became formally attached to the Niger administration with their Kel Ulli remaining attached to the Algerian administration.[104]

There was similar rivalry amongst the Kel Ajjer between the noble Uraren and Imanrassaten. Their rivalry was expressed in the complex interplay of external alliances.[105] Erwin de Bary,[106] for instance, who stayed with the Kel Ajjer in 1876, noted that German and English travellers were deemed to be under the protection of the Imanrassaten, while the French were considered as clients of the Uraren.

Political Factions within the Nobility

The dynamism and political complexity of Ahaggar and Ajjer at the time of the French encroachment and conquest was further compounded by the emergence of major political factions amongst the northern Tuareg, especially the Kel Ahaggar.

Although the massacre of the Flatters expedition (1881) drew attention to these factions,[107] we can trace their emergence to the death of the *Amenukal* El Hadj Akhmed in 1877, and perhaps even earlier. El Hadj Akhmed's reign as *Amenukal* of Ahaggar (1830–77) was extraordinary for a number of reasons, not the least of which was that he effectively succeeded as *Amenukal* before the death of his predecessor, Ag Mama. The reason for this unprecedented event was because Ag Mama had evidently reached a very old age. His longevity was the cause of considerable consternation, not only in Ahaggar, but also throughout much of the Sahara. He was not only blind, but also seemingly quite incapable of governing. The need for a stronger authority was felt as far afield as In Salah and Timbuktu, where there was concern for the security of the trade routes, as well as among neighbouring Tuareg who were anxious to maintain the state of good relations that seems to have existed for most of the previous generation.[108]

The difficulty in resolving the many legitimate claims of possible successors was overcome by finding the three important conditions for succession in the person of El Hadj Akhmed, the brother of the influential Sheikh Othman and a member of the Iforas tribe of the Kel Ajjer confederation, but who belonged to the Kel Ahaggar and the Kel Rela through his mother. As a marabout (holy man) he was respected; as a stranger, or outsider, his succession destroyed local rivalries; and, as the son of one of Ag Mama's sisters, his succession conformed to the traditional rules of matrilineal descent.[109] El Hadj Akhmed was not only a warrior of repute, but also much respected throughout the region for his maraboutic status, intelligence and wisdom. It is perhaps a little far-fetched to call him a statesman, but his diplomacy and farsightedness certainly brought relative peace and stability to Ahaggar in as much as his reign seems to have been something of a golden era in Ahaggar.[110] At his death many of his qualities and much of his wisdom lived on in the person of his stepson, Khyar ag Heguir.

Khyar was the son of Lella Tiguent, a matrilineal granddaughter of Sidi ag Mohammed el Khir (and consequently *oult ettebel*).[111] After the death of Heguir, Khyar's father, Lella Tiguent married El Hadj Akhmed. He took an exceptionally close interest in his stepson, so much so that Khyar grew up under the guiding eye of the *Amenukal* and was closely associated with all matters of government. Although Khyar was the protégé of his stepfather and also *agg ettebel* (through his mother), he was not directly in line to succeed to the position of *Amenukal*, which passed to El Hadj Akhmed's mother's sister's son, Aitarel.

We know that Khyar was frustrated in his ambition to become *Amenukal*,[112] and in this respect was constantly opposed to Aitarel. But the opposition between them seems to have been more deep-rooted, stemming from a fundamental difference in policy. Khyar condemned the Flatters massacre and even went so far as to communicate his views to the French. We do not know how far Khyar was prepared to go in his more conciliatory policy towards the French, but there are indications that he was prepared to enter into negotiations with the French after the Ajjer war if he had been in command of Ahaggar. Neither do we know the extent to which Khyar's more conciliatory stance towards the French was influenced by his antagonism to Aitarel, nor the extent to which Aitarel's decision to attack Flatters's expedition may have been influenced by Khyar's opposition. We can surmise, however, that an overwhelming victory over such a large and well-armed force of 'invading infidels', particularly if the number of casualties was relatively low, would have enhanced his position. He would not only have gained prestige as a great strategist and 'defender' of Ahaggar, but would also have reduced the attraction and credibility of Khyar's more collaborationist policy towards the French.

Aitarel's position regarding the Flatters massacre and his policy towards the French is more ambiguous than I have perhaps implied. While his antagonism to Khyar may have pushed him more towards resistance than collaboration with the French, there is reason to believe that he could not prevent his two nephews, Attici and Anaba ag Amellal, from attacking Flatters. This stemmed from the fact that, although his two nephews were Kel Rela by their mother, their father was a Tegehe Mellet, and they played on whichever parentage suited them best.[113] The Flatters massacre took place in Tegehe Mellet territory (on the eastern side of Ahaggar), which lay beyond Aitarel's jurisdiction. Attici certainly used the attack on Flatters as a means of building up his own following in Ahaggar.[114]

Although the Flatters massacre put an effective stop to any further French penetration into the Sahara for nearly 20 years, it is wrong to assume that there was no contact between France and the northern Tuareg during those years. On the contrary, there was considerable communication between the parties, including a delegation of Tuareg to Algiers in 1892,[115] with the consequence that France was well aware of the emergence of factions within Ahaggar that were more or less well disposed towards them. Aitarel had somehow managed to maintain a degree of centralised authority over Ahaggar in spite of both the Taitok's increased autonomy and the faction centred around Khyar ag Heguir. With his death in 1900, the forces of internal dissent were once again let loose. The rightful successor was Mohammed ag Ourzig, the son of Aitarel's eldest sister. Mohammed, however, was old and lacking the necessary qualities of leadership. Most of the nobles and all of the Kel Ulli preferred Attici, the elder son of Aitarel's younger sister. Although both were opposed to a settlement with France, Attici had already acquired a reputation for courage and energy. His vehement opposition to any peaceful settlement with France was also firmly established.

The situation was resolved (one might say inflamed), by the fanatical marabout Abidine al-Kunti of the Kunta proclaiming 'two Sultans with the same title'. The appointment of two *Amenukals* merely accentuated the state of anarchy that was developing within Ahaggar. In addition to the rivalry between the two *Amenukals*, a third faction, which had developed around Khyar ag Heguir, was gaining greater adherence. It was not through Khyar, who was now an old man in his eighties, but through his nephew, Moussa ag Amastane. Moussa, like El Hadj Akhmed, was a 'foreigner'. His mother, who was *oult ettebel*, had married an Ikerremoien, who, although assimilated into the Kel Rela, were originally from the southern Tuareg. Moussa had already acquired a great reputation as a warrior for his raids against the Iwllemmeden Tuareg and considerable influence amongst neighbouring groups, especially the Iforas of the Adrar among whom he spent much of his youth. Moussa also had the reputation of being a good and just man, an advocate of peace in the mould of El Hadj Akhmed and his old uncle Khyar. His emergence as an alternative force in Ahaggar arose largely from his growing influence among the Kel Ulli, who were becoming increasingly weary of the tiresome conditions resulting from the embargo on Tidikelt and the dispute between Attici and Mohammed ag Ourzig, both of whom were claiming *tiwse* from them.

The emergence of political factions was not limited to the Kel Rela. Around the turn of the century, splinter groups were also emerging amongst the Taitok, the majority of whom under the old Taitok chief, Sidi ag Keradji, were resolute in their defiance of the French. In 1901, however, certain Taitok and a number of their Kel Ulli, suffering as a result of the French occupation of the Tuat, abandoned their resistance and asked the French for pardon. This defection left the remainder of the Taitok weakened and isolated in their resistance under the leadership of Aziouel ag Ser'ada and Sidi ag Keradji. Aziouel submitted to Laperrine two years later, and in view of Sidi's continued defiance, was invested by the French with the title of Chief of the Taitok. It was not until some months after Moussa ag Amastane's submission to the French in 1904 that Sidi ag Keradji followed in his footsteps. In 1905 the French invested him with the title of *Amenukal* of the Taitok and Kel Ahnet.

The Role of External Factors

We can thus see how the inherent dynamic generated by the structural cleavages of pre-colonial society had brought the northern Tuareg, especially the Kel Ahaggar, to a state of almost anarchic disunity. As I have already suggested, 'traditional' society was on the brink, if not already in the midst, of a social and political revolution, or what the French might more appropriately term *un bouleversement*, at the time of their arrival. The big question, however, is the extent to which this state of affairs was caused or merely exacerbated by external factors.

Two points can be made. The first is that the origins of three of the four main cleavages, namely those between the two confederations, between noble *tawsatin* and between the two main classes, all predate the arrival of the French. Perhaps only the emergence of the political factions within the nobility, notably amongst the Kel Rela, can be attributed entirely to external forces in the form of France's encroachment into the Sahara. However, even here there is some evidence to suggest that the emergence of the resistance and collaborationist factions amongst the Kel Rela may have stemmed as much from the personal antagonism between Khyar ag Heguir and Aitarel as from policy differences.

The second point is that colonial pressure played a part in exacerbating all four cleavages. Let me look briefly at each in turn. At first glance, it might be argued that the cause of the Ahaggar–Ajjer war (1875–78) was a purely internal matter. That may have been so. However, it would certainly not have dragged on for so long, or at least not involved such an intensity of fighting, if the Turks, who saw an opportunity to establish themselves at Ghat, had not answered the Kel Ajjer's call for assistance.[116]

Similarly, although the Kel Rela–Taitok cleavage goes back to the eighteenth century, there is little doubt that it was exacerbated by the French encroachment. The reason for this is that the authority of the *Amenukal* in Ahaggar was increasingly being challenged during the last two decades of the nineteenth century as a result of the emergence and increasing polarisation of political factions amongst the Kel Rela, which, with the death of Aitarel in 1900, threw the region into a state of complete disunity. This enabled and encouraged the Taitok to operate with increasing autonomy, to the extent that by the time of the French occupation of Tuat and Tidikelt they could be regarded effectively as an almost entirely separate force within Ahaggar.[117] An indication of how great this cleavage had become is that the French (in 1905) invested Sidi ag Keradji with the title of *Amenukal* of the Taitok and Kel Ahnet.

The transformation of noble–vassal relations was also accelerated considerably by the French encroachment and subsequent pacification of Ahaggar. On the political front the Kel Ulli's seizure of the political initiative, in which they gave their support to Moussa ag Amastane, was a consequence of the emergence of political factions among the Kel Rela and the state of near-anarchy that erupted on Aitarel's death in 1900. But it was also a direct consequence of the occupation of Tuat and Tidikelt. As Belin had foreseen, the eventual occupation of these oases deprived the Kel Ahaggar of access to vital markets. It also posed a serious impediment to their raiding exploits outside Ahaggar, which enabled them to overcome, or at least reduce, the consequences of drought and famine. Even by 1896 it seems that the need to establish new markets outside Ahaggar was being felt. In that year members of the Dag Rali and Aguh-en-tehle (Kel Ulli of the Kel Rela) undertook for the first time, on their own initiative and independently of the Ihaggaren, a caravan to Damergou in Niger to exchange salt they had mined in Amadror for millet. Why these Kel Ulli suddenly decided to take this initiative is not altogether clear. There had been severe drought and famine in Ahaggar and Ahnet in 1882,[118] but the period 1886–1900 seems to have been one of relatively good pasture, except for an attack of locusts in 1893 and drought in 1897 and 1900. It must be supposed, therefore, that the need to establish new markets was created more by the anticipated deprivations resulting from French encroachment than by pastoral conditions within Ahaggar. Further evidence of this need to establish new markets was seen in 1903 when Kel Ahaggar (mostly Isekkemaren) sought dates as far afield as the Fezzan.[119]

Under such political and economic conditions, the exactions of the Ihaggaren became intolerable and we can see how and why the Kel Ulli began to take the political and economic initiative. By the time of French pacification, the Kel Ulli were operating almost entirely on their own account. They owned their own herds of goats and camels, were well-armed (and with guns) and were proven warriors. They were developing new markets, establishing their own gardens (with the labour of their slaves and *harratin*), refusing to pay *tiwse* and rejecting the demands of their *temazlayt* masters.

A Façade of Traditional Society

I think we can conclude that external factors, especially in the form of the colonial presence, more than exacerbated the cleavages of traditional society; they changed it fundamentally. Faced with such a social and political revolution, it was impossible for the French to use the traditional socio-political structures to administer their control of the region, for those structures were in the process of being literally overthrown.

The picture of Tuareg society that France presented to the world after the final pacification of Ahaggar and Ajjer in 1920 was a semblance – almost a caricature – of traditional society. If France wanted to administer her control through traditional socio-political structures, she had to modify those structures to her own designs. In Ajjer, where all the nobles remained adamantly opposed to the French, this meant reducing their power and authority over their vassals. This was done by splitting up the tribes and making them submit to France one by one. A chief (*amrar*), responsible to the military commander of the area, was appointed for each tribe, with special seals of office being designed to represent each of these novel divisions.[120]

In Ahaggar, it meant reversing the socio-political revolution that was in place by increasing the power and authority of the nobility, notably the Kel Rela, and centralising that authority in the office of the *Amenukal*. If the two confederations could be brought together to form one single political and administrative entity, so much the better.

In Ahaggar the first step was to find a suitable and reliable leader. Such a person was Moussa ag Amastane, whom the French invested with the title of *Amenukal*.[121] The second step was to ensure the wealth and dignity of his own people, the Kel Rela. This was done by giving Moussa's followers the booty (camels) they amassed in assisting the French in their suppression of dissidents such as Kaoucen and the Kel Ajjer and by stripping their rivals, the Taitok, of their power and authority in Ahaggar. There is a certain irony in the fact that France's policy of administering their control through 'traditional structures' involved removing one of its key elements – the Taitok! Under the French, and in the personage of Moussa ag Amastane, the office of the *Amenukal* was strengthened enormously, investing it with a political authority which had been absent before.[122] Although the concept of the individual authority of an *Amenukal* did not exist before Moussa, it became imprinted in much French colonial literature. At the time of Moussa's death in 1920, he was the ruler of Ahaggar, Djanet and much of northern Niger. But his power was held at the behest of the colonial authority. The reality was that neither he nor his successors, nor the other chiefs, had any real political autonomy. Nevertheless, the French maintained the appearance of traditional authority by sanctioning their titles and trappings of political office, and preserving – and at times even reinforcing – what could best be described as many of the 'feudal' elements of pre-colonial society. But it was a façade, constructed by the colonial authorities, beneath which the Tuareg no longer had any real political autonomy. The political role of the *Amenukal* and other chiefs was as intermediaries and effectively limited to negotiating, when the occasion arose, the form and details of decisions made elsewhere.

Some Final Considerations

The Role of Drought in Weakening Tuareg Resistance

The Tuareg's resistance to the French encroachment and eventual conquest was severely weakened by a number of factors. One was the protracted war (1875–78) between the Kel Ajjer and Kel Ahaggar, which severely dissipated the strength and resources of both federations. Moreover, the recuperation of these losses, both demographically and in terms of livestock, would have been retarded by the severe drought and famine of 1882.[123] Indeed, drought and famine played a critical role in undermining Tuareg resistance. 1911 saw the start of a prolonged period of drought,[124] which left the Tuareg, especially those of the Tassili-n-Ajjer and Fezzan, in great economic hardship. In 1914 there was further disaster in that locusts were so abundant that the Tuareg agriculturalists had to replant their crops three times.[125] Laperrine's ability to move onto the offensive in 1917 was certainly aided by the fact that the Kel Ahaggar were being tormented by hunger and that the Kel Ajjer, faced by such hardship, withdrew from the region. Captain Perdriaux reported that by 1917, *'la misère régne partout, des gens meurant de faim, dans la montagne les indigènes se pillent entre eux pour pouvoir subsister'*.[126] The Uraren called 1917 the 'Year of Famine' and 1918 the 'Year of Fever'.[127] The grimmest picture of all was that painted by *Maréchal de Logis* Lapierre, the commanding officer at Djanet when it was captured by the Sanussi in 1916. He was taken prisoner and held by El-Abed, along with five other Frenchmen and two Italians, at the small oasis of Ouaou el-Kebir deep in the Libyan desert. On 16 August 1917 he wrote that Fezzan was completely ravaged by drought and locusts, and in his report from Kufra, dated 21 June 1919, he stated that from the end of January 1918 until August, Ouaou el-Kebir suffered a near total lack of provisions. Only one small convoy reached them in that time, and their provisions for six months consisted of just tea, sugar, coffee and a few dates. By August when he was taken to Kufra, between five and ten people were dying daily, and the only survivors were himself, one Italian, three Sanussi Moqaddems and a gardener.[128] As Graham commented, 'The extreme hardship caused by these conditions must have been a significant factor in the collapse of resistance to the French, the demise of the Fezzan into more or less anarchy, and the ease with which the French finally subjugated the remaining Tuareg'.[129]

The Role of Moussa ag Amastane

Many of the questions that surround this crucial period in Tuareg history will remain unanswered. The role of Moussa ag Amastane, for instance, the most crucial personage of this period, is likely to remain enigmatic. However, in view of Algeria's (and the Tuareg's) more revisionist interpretation of these events, we can perhaps throw a little more light on the context of his 'collaboration'.

There are several points that need to be made. The first, and perhaps the most important, is that Moussa's 'submission' to the French at In Salah in 1904 is shrouded in ambiguity.[130] The key document (reproduced in the Appendix) can be interpreted quite clearly as recognising Moussa's political autonomy, albeit within some sort of unspecified dependency on the colonial authorities. At the same time, it painstakingly makes no reference to any form of tributary tax or levy with regard to possible French occupancy of Ahaggar and/or Tuareg submission to the French. Indeed, the document's primary emphasis could easily be interpreted as its concern for the safe movement of commercial goods and traffic throughout the region. The development of commercial relations was clearly high on the minds of both parties, with Moussa actually requesting that the French establish a settlement at Tadjemout (near Arak) as a commercial centre (see Appendix). But, above all, the document agreed to between Moussa and the French authorities at In Salah makes absolutely no mention of any submission on the part of the Kel Ahaggar.

The French were fully aware of these ambiguities. Moussa, for his part, almost certainly saw his 'submission' as little more than an agreement of protection – more in the context of a peace treaty – that would bring a number of benefits, especially in the realm of commerce, while recognising his political autonomy within Ahaggar.

The second point to be made is that we must look at Moussa's actions from his perspective and from within the context of the prevailing internal dynamics of Kel Ahaggar society. Moussa and the French arrived on the political scene in Ahaggar at about the same time. And that scene was one of near anarchy in which both he and the Kel Rela risked being overwhelmed by what was, to all intents and purposes, a concurrent palace and class revolution. The French presence merely intensified the structural changes and internal dissensions among the northern Tuareg. Under such circumstances, I doubt whether Moussa saw his liaison with the French in terms of 'collaborating' or 'selling out' to a 'colonial oppressor'. It is more likely that he saw the liaison as providing him with the support he needed to manipulate what were essentially internal changes in the dynamics of Tuareg society. His personal position in Ahaggar at that time was tenuous: although he was *agg ettebel*, there were at least three other potential successors to Aitarel who were as well if not better placed genealogically than he.[131] Moreover, his following in Ahaggar, although growing amongst the Kel Ulli, was marginal. He clearly anticipated that the delivery of the benefits that he saw as emanating from liaison with the French (economic gain, control over trade routes, peace and so on) would help eliminate internal opposition by enhancing his personal position in Ahaggar as well as that of his own *tawsit* – the Kel Rela.

'Collaboration' and 'resistance' are difficult terms for us to use, as they present us with contradictory categories which carry the danger of being loaded with the political connotations of modern, Western political structures and ideologies.[132] In the case of the Tuareg, as with many other such societies, actions associated with 'collaboration' and 'resistance' can only be fully understood within the context of all the other concurrent conflicts. If it were now possible to ask Moussa ag Amastane if he saw his actions as those of a 'collaborator', he in turn might well ask whether the 'resistance' of Attici, Mohammed ag Ourzig, Inguedazzen, Sultan Ahmoud and their followers, as well as the Taitok, was really driven by different motives. The point that needs to be stressed is that their initial reactions to the French encroachment and presence all stemmed from predominantly internal considerations. Attici's and Mohammed ag Ourzig's 'resistance' to France was almost certainly driven as much by their struggle for supremacy in Ahaggar as for ideological reasons, while the initial concerns of Kel Ajjer nobles were to retain control over their Kel Ulli. Indeed, it has been suggested that the only genuine resistance to French colonialism, at least after about 1903, was during the period of Sanussi-backed action (1916–18).[133]

The Role of Islam and the Brotherhoods

This reference to the Sanussi revolt raises the final consideration, namely that of the contradictory influence and roles played by the Islamic Tidjaniya, Qadiriya and Sanussiya brotherhoods in this period. The most influential of these brotherhoods in the Algerian Sahara in the late nineteenth century was the Tidjaniya, whose policy was to collaborate with the colonial authorities. Si Ahmed, the fabulously wealthy head of the Tidjaniya, had married a young French girl – Aurélie Picard. Moreover, the Tidjaniya saw their support for the French as a means of getting the upper hand in their inter-brotherly conflict with the Sanussiya and thus recovering some of the ground that they had lost to them in this part of the Sahara. Indeed, the Tidjani order played a significant role in assisting France's push into the Sahara. They supported the Flatters expedition,[134] developed and maintained contacts between the Tuareg and the French in the years following its massacre,[135] and played a key role in the establishment of the 'pro-French' faction in Ahaggar. In their inter-brotherly conflict, the Sanussi directed their activities more towards those whom they knew to be opposed to French advances, such as the Ajjer Tuareg around Ghat and Ghadames, while the Tidjani saw their opportunity in supporting those who might be prepared to support the French. Both Sheikh

Othman and El Hadj Akhmed, for example, had kinship links with prominent members of the Tidjani order, while by the end of the century at least a dozen Kel Ahaggar notables, including it seems Aitarel, were affiliated to them or at least in close contact with them.[136] Indeed, throughout the pre-conquest years the Tidjani provided the main network through which the French were able to maintain a modicum of communicative contact with the Tuareg of both Ajjer and Ahaggar.

The role played by the Tidjani order in supporting the French advance into the Sahara cannot be overemphasised. Neither can that of the Kunta Muslim legal scholar, Bay al-Kunti (1865–1929).[137] Bay was the bridging point between the Tuareg *ineslemen* and the Moorish *zawiyya*, notably those of the Qadiriya brotherhood. He lived at Teleya in the Adrar, near Kidal, but his influence extended throughout the Sahara. Norris describes him as 'arguably the most important religious teacher of the twentieth century in the Sahel. Many were his pupils, of profound significance his ideas'.[138] Bay considered that opposition to the French was futile, and in keeping with the collaborationist policy of both the Tidjaniya and Qadiriya, he extolled pacifism towards the French penetration – a doctrine which went some way to facilitating the French conquest of the southern Sahara. Bay had a profound influence on Moussa ag Amastane, who grew up in the Adrar and was one of Bay's pupils.

Many of the French who came into contact with Moussa commented on his religiosity, something which set him apart from most other Tuareg. Foucauld described him as 'a fervent Muslim, pious, brave, intelligent, a friend of wealth and peace, a man of his word'.[139] Benhazera, who spent six months with the Kel Ahaggar shortly after the French arrival confirmed his religious fervour. He described how 'he passed his nights in prayer, constantly telling his beads, being first affiliated to the Tidjaniya and then later to the Qadiriya, of whom he had become a *mokadem* (holy man)'.[140] The genuineness of his religiosity is debatable. Many, such as Bourgeot, believe his becoming a *mokadem* was simply '*s'auréoler d'un titre maraboutique*'.[141] Although maraboutism would certainly have enhanced his political status, there are indications that Moussa's life did undergo a considerable change when he was about 30 (that is, c.1897) in the form of an enhanced religiosity, which can be attributed to the spiritual mentorship of Bay al-Kunti.[142] Along with his strong pacifism, Bay would also surely have pointed out to Moussa the prosperity of those Kunta who had co-operated with the French.

We can therefore see that the predominant religious influences on the northern Tuareg, and especially on Moussa ag Amastane, came from the Tidjaniya and Bay al-Kunti, both of whom strongly advocated co-operating with the French. The only religious call for resistance to the colonial presence came from the Sanussiya and Abidine al-Kunti, the fanatical nephew of Bay whose views were diametrically opposed to those of his uncle.[143]

We can see the battle for influence between these two ideologies being played out in the attempts of El-Abid and Kaoucen to persuade Moussa to join the *jihad* against the infidel. There has been much surmise about Moussa's actions during the critical year of 1916–17. Moussa's loyalty was widely doubted amongst the French on the grounds that he did not support them at the height of the Sanussi revolt and because many Ahaggar Kel Ulli and Isekkemaren went over to the Sanussi cause. The reality of the situation was probably a little more complex. Moussa's precise movements during this period have never been entirely clear, although most records indicate that he spent much of this time in the Adrar-n-Iforas where he would almost certainly have discussed his position with his spiritual mentor. It is fairly safe to assume that Bay would have encouraged Moussa to try to persuade Kaoucen to abandon his resistance to the French. We do not know what passed between Kaoucen and Moussa, other than that Kaoucen held Moussa under some form of house arrest, from which he escaped to rejoin the French in March 1917 and take the lead in a number of decisive raids against Kaoucen. By the end of 1917 the Sanussi revolt had all but collapsed; Fezzan had fallen into a state of anarchy and El-Abid was without influence. Although most Tuareg formed a nominal attachment to the Sanussiya during this period, there seems to have been little penetration of Islamic values. The prevailing view amongst most Tuareg seems to have been that the French had been defeated (they had, after all, withdrawn from Ghat and Djanet) and were abandoning their position in the Sahara.[144] Under such circumstances their attachment to the Sanussi cause must be seen as little more than a politically expedient means of achieving their own ends.

Revising History: On the Road from Tit to Tahilahi

In the spring of 2002, I travelled with a small group of Kel Ahaggar from Tamanrasset to a rock shelter in the Tassili-n-Ajjer called Tahilahi, a journey of several days. We stopped on the way at Ti-n-Esa (Tit), to pay respects on the centenary of the Kel Ahaggar's great defeat. Our subsequent conversation inevitably took us back to Moussa ag Amastane, the role of the French in Ahaggar and many other aspects of twentieth-century Tuareg history. Several things struck me most forcibly about our conversations (until we reached Tahilahi!).

The first was how little the present generation of Tuareg knew of their past. Names such as Kaoucen, Bay al-Kunti, Abidine, the order of succession, and even the names of some of the *Amenukals*, were lost to them.

A second thing that struck me was how much of this 'forgotten' history was being reinterpreted in the context of more recent events. One such example concerned the Taitok. In the 1960s, my enquiries about the Taitok, compared to those about the Kel Rela, were invariably met with disinterest. They seemed to have been regarded rather in the context of the 'second' rank of nobility, and as having 'lost out' to the Kel Rela. Now, some 40 years later, they were being spoken of in quite different terms, the gist of which was that the Taitok (not the Kel Rela) were the greatest of warriors and the true 'heroes' of those distant times. Whereas the Kel Rela had collaborated with the colonialists, the Taitok had continued to fight and resist them, so much so that France's only recourse was to expel them from the region. This interpretation of history was stretching a point, but it reflected the revisionist spirit of the new, post-colonial Algeria and, in the case of the Kel Ahaggar, the 'Algerianisation' of the Tuareg.[145] The word 'Taitok' now carries a sense of respect, and those Taitok who have returned to Algeria in recent years are being treated, so it seems to me, as if they are returning war heroes, albeit three or more generations later. On several occasions my travelling companions referred to them jocularly, as *'anciens combattants'* or, in the context of modern-day Algeria, as *'anciens moujadhins'*. It was notable that in this reinterpretation of history, my companions knew few of the names of the prominent Taitok or the details of the raids and battles of those times.[146]

Moussa ag Amastane has also been subjected to such revisionism. I recall that in the 1960s his name was always mentioned with veneration, being spoken of as a man of great, almost superhuman, qualities: a great warrior and leader, a marabout, farsighted, wise beyond his years and so forth. (Why else would he have been invested as a Commander of the *Légion d'Honneur*?!). Now, on several occasions, I was asked rhetorically (in the contextual categories of resistance and collaboration) if Moussa was not a collaborator – a 'sell-out'. I was also aware of my travelling companions discussing him in tones which carried a suggestion of disrespect as they poked fun, albeit jokingly, at his reputed obesity and ugliness; reasons they suggested for his rejection in marriage by Dassine ult Ihemma[147] and his taking two slave-girls as wives instead.

To reach Tahilahi, which involved a climb and walk of several hours onto the plateau of the Tassili-n-Ajjer, we were obliged to take on a local guide. Before we had even set out there were massive disagreements between the guide, a Kel Ajjer, and my four Kel Ahaggar travelling companions about almost every conceivable aspect of the trip. By the end of the first day, the language was 'blue', bordering on fisticuffs, as vitriolic insults were traded. They began with barbed digs about such minor things as the state of the donkeys, the direction we were following, where we would camp for the night

From Tit to Tahilahi

and so on, but became music to my ears as insults and accusations began to dig deep into the Kel Ahaggar–Kel Ajjer war of 1875–78 (they had forgotten the dates – it might have been yesterday!), their respective treachery and vindictiveness (which quite clearly had not changed!), how they had no sense of humour, and how it was a mistake (as proven) even to travel in their country, and so forth! We left Tahilahi a day earlier than planned, but my faith in history had been restored.

APPENDIX

The following is the text of the agreement between capitaine Métois and Moussa ag Amastane at the time of their meeting in In Salah in January 1904. The text was prepared by Métois and presented to Moussa, who added additional points. This is a particularly important document for the Kel Ahaggar as the French colonial authorities considered it as the basis of their submission. J. Métois, *La soumission des Touaregs du Nord* (Paris: Challamel 1906) p.33, described the occasion as follows:

> *nos négociations furent faciles. Je rédigeai sous la forme d'instructions à l'amenokal des Touareg, titre que je reconnaissais à Moussa, les exigences du gouvernement français. Moussa les accepta entièrement et me demanda que deux modifications qui, toutes deux constituaient une aggravation du document, au point de vue targui.*

Moussa added the last sentence of clause 1 and clause 10.

Texte:

1. Moussa ag Amastan exercera le commandement de tout le territoire de l'Ahaggar et de ses dépendances. Il y assurera la liberté et la sécurité des voyageurs et des commerçants venus de la France ou des pays qui lui sont soumis. Un esclave portant de l'or sur la tête pourra traverser le Ahaggar en toute sécurité.
2. Moussa ag Amastan recevra un burnous d'investiture et un cachet, comme les caïds des régions soumises, mais il conservera son titre d'aménokal et exercera le commandement, avec le concours de la djemna, suivant les usages de son pays.
3. Le chef d'annexe d'In-Salah sera son intermédiaire, tant pour lui transmettre les ordres du Gouvernement Français que pour transmettre à celui-ci les demandes formulées par Moussa ag Amastan, soit en son nom propre, soit au nom de ses gens.
4. Moussa ag Amastan remettra au chef d'annexe d'In-Salah, la liste complète des tribus, fractions ou sous fractions placées sous son commandement, et des campements qu'elles occupent habituellement. Dans tout le territoire ainsi déterminé, et pour toutes les fractions ainsi dénommées, les troupes de Gouvernement Français ne feront pas acte d'hostilité. Les habitants pourront en conséquence s'approcher des camps militaires, où ils seront reçus amicalement et vendre aux soldats les produits dont ils disposent.
5. Toute infraction aux stipulations de l'article précédent sera signalée par Moussa ag Amastan au chef d'annexe si elle a été commise par un militaire, et par le chef d'annexe a Moussa ag Amastan si elle a été commise par Moussa. Le coupable sera puni.
6. Dans le cas où un homme des Imouhar méconnaîtrait l'autorité de Moussa ag Amastan, celui-ci le signalerait au chef d'annexe qui pourrait alors le châtier.
7. D'une manière générale, Moussa ag Amastan exercera lui-même, et avec le concours de ses gens, la police de son territoire. Dans le cas où il aurait affaire à un ennemi qui lui serait supérieur en nombre, il en informerait le chef d'annexe qui le seconderait au moyen des troupes dont il dispose.
8. Afin de bien affirmer aux yeux de tous la collaboration étroite qui existe entre le Chef de l'annexe d'In-Salah et Moussa ag Amastan pour la protection du commerce et le maintien de

la paix, les gens qui serviront Moussa ag Amastan exécuteront ses ordres de police et lui serviront d'intermédiaires avec le Chef d'annexe, recevront de Gouvernement français une indemnité mensuelle de 15 francs. Leur nombre sera fixé en raison des crédits accordés par le Gouvernement français, et le Chef d'annex pourra, pour récompenser ceux d'entre eux qui se seront plus particulièrement fait remarquer par leur zèle, leur confier un fusil de l'Etat, avec les munitions qu'il comporte.

9. Dans les territoires voisins du Ahaggar et actuellement soumis à la France, les Imouhar seront recus amicalement, et devront s'abstenir de tout acte d'hostilité.

Le chef d'annexe fera connaître à Moussa ag Amastan les modifications qui pourraient être apportées à la situation politique du pays; de même qu'il fera connaître à ses collègues de Tombouctou, de Gogo, de Tahoua et de Zinder que le Ahaggar est maintenant en paix avec la France, et que ses habitants doivent être reçus partout en conséquence.

10. Afin de faciliter les relations entre le Ahaggar et le Tidikelt, le Chef d'annex d'In-Salah s'occupera de la création d'un village à Tadjemout où des Harratin du Ahaggar pourront cultiver et où des travaux seront exécutés pour l'aménagement des cultures.

NOTES

I would like to acknowledge the Leverhulme Trust for its most generous support.

1. The *Archives Historiques de la Guerre* (AHG) are housed by the *Service Historique de l'Armée de Terre* in the Château de Vincennes.
2. There are also few contemporary Arabic records of France's conquest and pacification of the northern Tuareg.
3. I was able to draw on Johannes Nicolaisen's recently published *Ecology and Culture of the Pastoral Tuareg* (Copenhagen: University of Copenhagen 1963), probably the first unbiased assessment of the northern Tuareg.
4. Paul Pandolfi, *Les Touaregs de l'Ahaggar* (Paris: Karthala 1998) p.108.
5. The first European to traverse Tuareg country was the Frenchman René Caillé in 1828, crossing the Tanezrouft to the west of Ahaggar from Timbuktu to Morocco. Gordon Laing of the Yorkshire Light Infantry journeyed from Tripoli to Timbuktu in 1824–26, but was murdered at In Arouane, about 200 miles north of Timbuktu. His journey is particularly interesting in that he made contact with Sheikh Othman.
6. Sheikh Othman was also the brother of El Hadj Akhmed, the *Amenukal* (supreme chief) of the Kel Ahaggar from 1830 to 1877. El Hadj Akhmed's father had married a noble Kel Rela of the Kel Ahaggar. Because group membership was determined by matrilineal descent, El Hadj Akhmed was deemed a Kel Rela.
7. Ikhenoukhen is sometimes spelt Akhenoukhen. Nicolaisen (note 3) describes him as neither *Amenukal* nor *Amrar*, but as the 'practical' leader of the Tuareg of the Tassili-n-Ajjer, having 'supreme political and judicial authority'. H. Duveyrier, *Les Touaregs du Nord* (Paris: Challamel 1864) called him *Emir*.
8. Duveyrier had tried unsuccessfully to persuade the French government to appoint a consul to Ghadames.
9. The precise number of men is not clear as the way in which Chaamba guides and cameleers were counted varies according to different reports. The column consisted of 11 Frenchmen, 47 Arab *tirailleurs* and 30-odd Chaamba cameleers and guides.
10. There are many accounts of the Flatters expedition. In English, see J. Keenan, 'How and Why the Tuareg Poisoned the French: Some Reflections on *efelehleh* and the Motives of the Tuareg in Massacring the Flatters Expedition of 1881', in Barnaby Rogerson (ed.), *North Africa Travel*, no.1 (London: Sickle Moon Books 2001); see also J. Keenan, *The Tuareg: People of Ahaggar* (London: Allen Lane 1977) p.72f.
11. June 1881.
12. French interest in the Tuareg during the intervening years was regenerated in 1887 when Taitok raided a group of French auxiliaries (the Mouadhi Chaamba) at Hassi Inifel. Many

From Tit to Tahilahi

Taitok were captured and moved by the French to Algiers before being set free. This led to Bissuel's (1888) study of the western Tuareg. Two of the Taitok prisoners were taken to Paris in 1889; for details, see Keenan, *The Tuareg* (note 10) pp.80–1.
13. During the 18 years between the Flatters massacre and the occupation of Tidikelt there were several 'contacts' between the French and the Kel Ahaggar and Kel Ajjer. Details of these delegations, and the role played by the religious brotherhoods in facilitating them, notably the Tidjani (Tijaniya) order, have been documented by Pandolfi (note 4) p.411–26.
14. Tuareg raids on Tuat and Tidikelt were not without causalities. In summer 1900, the Taitok had been taught a bloody lesson by Caid Baba following a raid on the Kel Ahem Mellen of the Mouydir (Immidir) and In R'ar region, while a short time later the same Caid heavily counter-raided a group of Ibettenaten and Iforas from the Adrar at the water-hole of Ouallen, about 200km south of Tidikelt, as they were returning southwards after pillaging the oases of Aoulef and Akabil.
15. While it is true that some residents of Tidikelt were suffering the exactions of the Tuareg, the impact of the French seizure and occupation of the Tuat was an economic disaster for both the region, its peoples and much of the wider Sahara.
16. Cottenest was the sole Frenchman. The *meharistes* comprised members of the Ulad Ba Hammu, Ulad Mokhtar, Zoua, Ulad Yakhia and Ulad Dahane tribes of Tidikelt. See M. Gast, *Alimentation des populations de l'Ahaggar* (Paris: Mémoires du CRAPE VIII 1968) p.21.
17. There were also fears for the safety of Ahl Azzi caravans passing through Ahaggar at the time.
18. The number of Tuareg dead has never been established precisely as many died subsequently from their wounds. Most accounts put the number between 100 and 150. See Pandolfi (note 4) p.91.
19. AHG 1H1036, 1 June 1902.
20. The battle is generally known in most literature as the Battle of Tit. Kel Ahaggar, however, know it better as the battle of Ti-n-Esa, after the name of the rocky hillock near the village of Tit, at whose base the battle ensued.
21. In view of Sidi ag Keradji's stance, Aziouel was invested by the French with the title of 'Chief' of the Taitok.
22. The French authorities had invested Moussa with the title of *Amenukal* when he negotiated peace with them at In Salah in 1904, although he did not assert this title until the Kel Ahaggar themselves proclaimed him as *Amenukal* in his own right.
23. This essay focuses on France's conquest and colonisation of the northern Tuareg. It should, however, be noted that France's Sudanese territories benefited even less from France's 'civilising mission' than the Algerian Sahara. The conquest of the Tuat can hardly be compared to the atrocities committed by Voulet and Chanoine's barbaric Central African Mission of 1898–99 that left a trail of wanton slaughter and butchery from the Niger bend, across what is now central and southern Niger, north-western Nigeria and eastwards towards Chad. For an account of the Central African Mission, see M. Mathieu, 'La Mission Afrique Centrale', thèse du 3ème cycle, University of Toulouse-Mirail, 1975.
24. *L'Afrique Occidentale Française* (AOF).
25. This frontier was established officially by the Ministry of the Interior and the Colonial Ministry on 7 February 1905. There is no record of the Kel Ahaggar ever having been consulted over the location of this frontier, which deprived them of one of their most valuable pasture areas, the Adrar-n-Iforas, as well as a number of 'tribes' in that area who wanted to remain allied to the Kel Ahaggar rather than the Iwllemmeden Tuareg. See A. Richer, *Les Touaregs du Niger (Région de Tombouctou-Gao): Les Oulliminden* (Paris: Larose 1924) pp.186–8.
26. A. Bernard and N. Lacroix, *La pénétration saharienne (1830–1906)* (Alger: Imprimerie algérienne 1906) p.174.
27. This followed his organisation of a raid against certain Kel Ajjer to avenge the killing of a French *mehariste* and raids on Kel Ahaggar camps.
28. About 40 miles south-east of Tamanrasset.

29. The Tuareg suffered some 70 dead compared with two of the French unit, AHG 1H1070; see also V. Gardel, *Les Touareg Ajjer* (Alger: Baconnier 1961); and *Le Journal Officiel de la République Française*, 10 Nov. 1913.
30. The Kel Ajjer aptly named 1921 as 'the year of peace'; J. Dubief, 'Les Oûraghen des Kel-Ajjer: Chronologie et nomadism', *Travaux de l'Institut de recherches sahariennes* XIV (1956) pp.85–137.
31. Until 1894, the colonial department was an adjunct to either the Ministry of the Marine or the Ministry of Commerce, directed by a civil servant.
32. The new ministry was only responsible for some of the colonies. While most of Algeria fell under the Ministry of the Interior, the Saharan territories came under the responsibility of the Ministry of War. Morocco and Tunisia, on the other hand, came under the Foreign Ministry.
33. Britain was more than happy to leave the Sahara (excepting Egypt and the Nile) to France. The Anglo-French convention of 1890 allocated to France the territory running south from her Mediterranean possessions, namely Algeria and Tunisia, to a line running from Say on the lower Niger to Barruwa on Lake Chad. British minister Lord Salisbury, who was responsible, said, 'It is what a farmer would call "very light land". We have given the Gallic cockerel an enormous amount of sand. Let him scratch it as he pleases'. D. Porch, *The Conquest of the Sahara* (London: Cape 1985) p.127.
34. It is not only questionable whether France ever had a clear policy towards her Saharan territories, but it could be argued that it was not until the 1950s, when the Algerian Revolution was well under way, that France first saw an economic use for the Sahara, and then as a nuclear testing ground and a source of oil.
35. Paris's disinterest in the region was reflected in the loose determination of both borders. Turkish interests were recognised as lying to the east of the 6th meridian, while the Sultan of Morocco's claim to the Tuat (including Tidikelt and Guerrara) was recognised by several European countries, including Britain.
36. Tuat is the name generally given to a complex of three oases that curl around the Plateau of Tademait. Together they are shaped like a U opening to the east. The Gourara makes up the northern arm, Tidikelt the southern, with the Tuat being an extension of the Saoura Valley to the west. The main town of Gourara is Timimoun and of Tidikelt, In Salah.
37. During the 1890s any further conquest of the desert was stalled by the diplomatic issue of the Tuat. Several European nations, including Britain, supported the Sultan of Morocco's claim over Tuat. Paris feared that the seizure of the oases would spark a diplomatic incident. However, in 1899, with the British army bogged down in a war with the Boer republics, French colonialists saw their opportunity to occupy Tuat.
38. Porch (note 33) p.210, described Pein as having achieved the status of master craftsman in the useful art of blurring that fine line between initiative and insubordination.
39. The conquest of Tuat had proven so costly that, for the first time in the history of French colonial conquest, there was a serious possibility that the government might order the French army to withdraw from a conquered piece of Africa. The French had requisitioned 35,000 camels in Algeria to feed the Tuat expeditions of 1900 and 1901. Of these 25,000 had perished from thirst or inexpert handling by novice French cameleers.
40. At the time, the government of Prime Minister Waldeck-Rousseau was in difficulty. The Dreyfus Affair had reached its climax and there were talks of a possible coup. Waldeck-Rousseau therefore fell back on a tactic frequently adopted by governments in the Third Republic: he offered Eugène Etienne's Colonial Party, with its 102 seats, a free hand in Africa in return for support on the domestic front. This partly explains the spasmodic nature of French colonial expansion and why there was so little rationale behind it. Porch (note 33) p.223.
41. The inhabitants of the Tuat were soon in revolt against the French invaders, forcing France to allocate far greater military resources to the region than intended. Porch (note 33) p.224, raised the question of why there were so many revolts against French occupation. He suggested two reasons. First, because the French army was stationed in France, with its primary aim to defend the north-east border, it had no reservoir of knowledge or experience

of colonisation. Second, because the initial invasions were prepared by stealth. Because French colonial officers knew that conquests would meet political opposition, they conspired with colonialists in Paris to find a pretext for new advances … The territory would be seized, provoking the inevitable political storm. The colonial soldiers would then be forced to lie low while the politicians and propagandists in Paris praised the benefits and minimised the costs of the new conquest. As territory once seized could never be relinquished without a loss of diplomatic face, the opposition, after initial protests aimed at embarrassing the government in the short term rather than at rolling back colonialism, would then forget the matter.

42. Ibid. p.261. Algiers did attempt to recall Cottenest when they heard about his raid, but by then he was beyond reach.
43. Porch (note 33) p.240.
44. Pein had no intention of following such orders. On being warned, before Cottenest's raid into Ahaggar, to 'to calm things down', he wrote to Cauvet at In Salah, 'In my four years in Ouargla, I have received nothing but criticism, which has never stopped me from doing what I thought was my duty', Porch (note 33) p.249.
45. Gardel, AHG 1H1070, refers to a French threat to close the Tunisian market of Ben Gardane to Fezzan Arabs should they be involved in any anti-French activity with the Kel Ajjer. See A. Bourgeot, 'Les échanges transsahariens, la Senoussiya et les révoltes twareg de 1916–1917', *Cahiers d'Etudes Africaines* 18 (1978) p.164; A. Bourgeot, 'Les mouvements de résistance et de collaboration (Algérie) de 1880 à 1920', paper delivered at the Symposium on 'Resistance in Nomadic Societies: The Colonization of the Sahara: 1880–1940', at the 82nd Annual Meeting of the American Anthroplogical Association, Chicago, 16–20 Nov. 1983, p.11, published in *Annuaire de l'Afrique du Nord* (1984). Laperrine also hoped to redirect trans-Saharan trade, through their control also of Timbuktu, away from both English and Turkish hands.
46. The Imenan were *cheurfa*, descendants of the Prophet. Even today, although completely fallen from power and no more than a handful in number, they are still recognised by Tuareg for their religious status.
47. The division of the Kel Ahaggar into the three drum-groups of the Kel Rela, Taitok and Tegehe Mellet dates from around the middle of the eighteenth century, Keenan, *The Tuareg* (note 10) p.25f.
48. M. Museur and R. Pirson, 'Une problématique de passage chez les populations du Hoggar-Tassili: du nomadisme à la sedentarité', *Civilisations* 26/1–2 (1976) p.67.
49. The Tuareg had attempted some diffident gardening, using their slaves, in the vicinity of Ideles around 1840, but they proved unsatisfactory and it was not until 1861 that renewed efforts were made at both Ideles and Tazrouk.
50. Kanem–Bornu–Damergou–Aïr–Tripoli; Iferouane–Ghat; and Kano–Zinder–Agades–Tripoli. Museur and Pirson (note 48) p.68.
51. The most important market in Ahaggar was at Abalessa, where merchants came from Tidikelt each spring to sell leather goods, riding camels and above all slaves. Abalessa was also a staging post for caravans journeying from the Sudan to Tidikelt. See C. de Foucauld, 'Chez les Touaregs: Taitoq, Iforas, Hoggar – Journal de voyage de Père Charles de Foucauld, mars–septembre 1904', *Bulletin de Liaison Saharienne* 3 (1951) pp.20–30; *Bulletin de Liaison Saharienne* 4 (1951) pp.19–32.
52. M. Benhazera, *Six Mois chez les Touareg du Ahaggar* (Alger: Jourdan 1908) p.69.
53. Maurice Vacher, 'L'Amghar des Ajjers: Brahim ag Abakada', *Le Saharien* 80 (1982) pp.4–5.
54. Duveyrier (note 7).
55. The French government refused to grant its troops a right of hot pursuit east of the 6th meridian for fear of offending Turkish or Italian sensibilities.
56. Charlet established his garrison in the Sanussi *zawiyya*. His initial hesitancy to use a religious building for his garrison was overcome on learning that the *zawiyya* had only been

built in 1903–04 and, in the words of the Tidjani Caid Andennebi Ben Ali, who was accompanying Charlet's column, that it was more a fort than a mosque with its defensive position making it inaccessible to the weak, sick, old and lame. See AHG 1H1068; and C. Charlet, 'L'Oasis de Djanet', *Bulletin de la Société de Géographie d'Alger et de l'Afrique du Nord* 17 (1912) p.132f.

57. The Sanussi order was founded in Mecca in 1837 by an Algerian holy man, Sidi Muhammad b. 'Ali al-Sanussi (1787–1857). On his return to Algeria in 1841 he learnt of the progress of the French occupation of his home country and settled instead in Benghazi. On al-Sanussi's death the headship of the order went to his son Sayyid al-Mahdi, under whom the order became a force in the Sahara. Al-Mahdi moved the headquarters to Kufra in 1895 and in 1899 to Qiru between Borku and Tibesti. M. Abun-Nasr Jamil, *History of the Maghreb*, 2nd edn. (Cambridge: Cambridge University Press 1971) pp.305–6.
58. Before the Italian invasion of Libya in 1911, the Sanussi were particularly worried about French encroachments into the Sahara. In 1900, the Sanussi were the dominant power in the Fezzan and the Central Sahara and had slowly increased their influence in southern Tripolitania and advanced it towards the west.
59. This was the first French expedition actually to cross the Sahara. The expedition left Ouargla in October 1898 travelling to the east of Ahaggar to the Tenere and Aïr (Iferouane) before reaching Agades in July 1899 and Lake Chad in January 1900.
60. L. Lehuraux, *Les Français au Sahara* (Alger: Editions les territoires du Sud 1936) p.83.
61. Libya had been invaded by the Italians in 1911.
62. Sidi Mohammed el-Abed ben Cherif Mohammed ben Ali es Sanussi was the brother of Sidi Ahmed al-Sharif, head of the Sanussi order.
63. Kaoucen, a member of the Ikaskasen *tawsit* (descent group), was born near Agades around 1882, but left his country with the arrival of the French around 1904–05 and participated in the battle of Ain Galakka in the Tibesti. He was a notable anti-French agitator, renowned throughout much of the Sahara for his courage and audacity. He affiliated to the Sanussi order in 1909 and became a close confidante of Sidi Mohammed el-Abed and was appointed governor of Fezzan in 1915. He had been in Ghat in the summer of 1916, but returned to Aïr in the autumn, where he offered immunity to all Tuareg who joined him in revolt against the French. He continued his resistance until killed by Turkish partisans at Murzuk in January 1919. See A. Bourgeot, 'Les échanges transsahariens' (note 45) p.171.
64. AHG 7N2129.
65. Appointed by El-Abed.
66. Much colonial literature sees Paris's decision to withdraw as a grave error. Seen in the wider context of the First World War, Paris's decision to maintain only existing posts and not to open up a new theatre of war is more intelligible.
67. The French suffered further losses at *Oued* Ihan (16 Sept.), *Oued* Tabelbalet (28 Nov.) and *Oued* Amastane (3 Dec.). Fort Polignac was evacuated on 23 December, following the Sanussi capture of a supply train between Fort Flatters and Fort Polignac in late October.
68. For political reasons, many French reports state that the group which attached Foucauld was comprised solely of Sanussi and that Kel Ahaggar were not involved. In fact, some 14 Ait Lowayan Tuareg were involved.
69. On 1 October 1916, the Oasis Command of Southern Algeria comprised only 37 French officers, 66 other French ranks, 1,254 regular indigenous troops and 366 irregulars; AHG 1H1072.
70. For example, poor food had resulted in a bout of scurvy breaking out in Fort Polignac; AHG 1H1072, Report of Dr Gavart, dated 1 Nov. 1916.
71. In the Tassili-n-Ajjer there were attacks during February at Ain el Hadhadj, Tahebert and Temassint. In Tamesna (Niger) there was an attack on In Abangarit on 12 March. In April the Dag Rali saw their opportunity to avenge the battle of Tit by routing a French column in the *Oued* Ilaman. This was followed by an attack on a French patrol at In Eker (15 June). On 8 May Sultan Ahmoud attacked Fort Flatters and a convoy at Hassi Tanezrouft four days later. Colonel J. Ferry, 'Le Sahara dans la Guerre, 1914–1918', *Revue Historique de l'Armée* 23/4 (1967) pp.85–96.

72. Notably the two Kel Rela (noble) leaders, Anaba and Souri ag Chikat.
73. The first such offensive was by Lieutenant Lehuraux at Tehi-n-Akli (25 July). Although of little military significance, the attack had great effect on the morale of the Tuareg as it showed that the French were prepared to take the offensive.
74. By this time the Kel Ajjer had retreated from Ahaggar towards the Fezzan.
75. Pardon was granted by the governor of Algeria to all but Foucauld's assassins.
76. J.-L. Triaud, 'Un mauvais départ: 1920, l'Aïr en ruines', in E. Bernus *et al.* (eds.), *Nomades et commandants: Administration et sociétés nomads dans l'ancienne A.O.F* (1993) pp.93–100:

> Les efforts des Français allaient tendre dès lors à reprendre le contrôle du Massif de l'Aïr. Ils allaient être aidés de façon décisive par Mûsa ag-Amastan ... L'aide de Mûsa fut d'abord militaire ...: il amenait avec lui plus de 300 combattants montés à chameau et entraînés à la guerre du désert. Ainsi, le 1 mars 1918, joua-t-il un rôle important au combat d'Akarao (sur la bordure orientale de l' Aïr), qui rejeta définitivement Kawsan et les restes de son armée hors du Massif. Mais c'est au plan politique que son action devait être déterminante. Tous les Touaregs qui désiraient abandoner la lutte mais redoutaient les répresailles françaises vinrent se mettre sous sa protection et firent leur soumission par son entremise. L'arrivée de l'Amenokal en Aïr (février 1918) relança donc les ralliements sur une grande échelle. Sans son concours, la reprise en mains du Massif aurait coûté beaucoup plus de temps et d'efforts aux Français.

77. Gast (note 16) p.37n, records that Laperrine left the Kel Ahaggar with a number of rifles to prevent any reprisal action by the Kel Aïr.
78. Laarmech, their chief who was responsible for this work, died in 1954.
79. On 28 October, Moussa, along with contingents of the French Saharan Company from Tidikelt, even entered Djanet, but without installing themselves permanently.
80. 27 Dec. 1920.
81. AOM 22H67.
82. In a letter to the Governor-General, dated 25 Sept. 1905, Laperinne wrote:

> J'ai l'honneur de solliciter de votre haute bienveillance de rattacher les Azdjer à l'annexe du Tidikelt et de décéder que les tribus dont l'amenokal Moussa agg Amastân amenènerait la soumission à la France seraient placées sous son commandement. C'est d'ailleurs ce que le commandant Cauvet lui avait promis implicitement et ce sera pour lui une compensation de la perte des ifoghas de l'Adrar.

Pandolfi (note 4) p.104n.

83. The French soon realised the error of their ways and in 1933, in an attempt to ingratiate themselves with the Kel Ajjer, agreed to return the gardens to the Kel Ajjer through the personage of Sultan Ahmoud's son. However, Akhemouk took the move as a sleight to his honour and obliged the French to abandon it.
84. The term 'traditional society' is best understood as being synonymous with pre-colonial society, i.e., Tuareg society before the arrival of the French in Ahaggar (prior to *c*.1902). However, it is essential to appreciate that pre-colonial society was itself inherently dynamic and subject to almost continuous change.
85. This is, of course, a generalisation to which there are a few notable exceptions such as Marceau Gast, André Bourgeot, Paul Pandolfi, and Edmond and Suzanne Bernus.
86. Duveyrier (note 7) p.334.
87. H. Barth, *Reisen und Entdeckungen in Nord- und Central Afrika in den Jahren 1849 bis 1855*, 4 vols. (Gotha: 1857–58) p.257 (French trans. Paris: Didot 1863).
88. H. Lhote, *Les Touaregs du Hoggar* (Paris: Payot 1944, 1955) pp.373–4.
89. Nicolaisen (note 3) p.437.
90. The Kuntas claim descent from the North African conqueror Uqba ibn Nafi, although they are probably of Berber origin. The name 'Kunta' comes from the maternal father of Sidi Muhammed al-Kunti. Sidi Muhammed's mother is said to have been a daughter of

The Lesser Gods of the Sahara

Muhammed Alim b. Kunta b. Zazam, the chief of the Idawkil Sanhaja; quoted in I. Hamet, 'Les Kounta', *Revue de Monde Musulman* XV (Sept. 1911) p.307. Through their intermarriage with such prestigious western Sahara tribes as the Tajakanat, they succeeded in elevating their social status to a point where their Arab ancestry is accepted; quoted in C.C. Steward, with E.K. Stewart, *Islam and Social Order in Mauritania* (Oxford: Clarendon 1973) p.36f.

91. This was probably more of a reactive process. Prior to the 'reorganisation', it seems that all vassals may have fallen under the control of the dominant 'nobility', the Tegehe-n-ou-Sidi, whose chief, the *Amenukal* Sidi ah Mohammed el Khir, came under increasing pressure from other noble groups who demanded that they too should have their own vassals. For details, see Keenan, *The Tuareg* (note 10) p.25f.
92. C. de Foucauld, *Dictionnaire Touareg–Française, dialecte de l'Ahaggar*, 4 vols. (Paris: Imprimerie nationale de France 1951–52) p.534.
93. Although a proportion of the booty captured by Kel Ulli was given to the *Amenukal* and their *temazlayt* masters, the remainder became their possession.
94. The *temazlayt* relationship is explained in detail in J. Keenan, 'The Last Nomads: Nomadism amongst the Tuareg of Ahaggar (Algerian Sahara)', in this volume, pp.163–92.
95. *Tiwse* was officially abolished by the administration in 1960. For details of *tiwse* and *eheren-amadal* paid by certain *tawsatin*, see Keenan, *The Tuareg* (note 10) pp.36–41.
96. Any caravans passing through the territory of the drum-group paid dues to the drum-chief and not to the tenants of the sub-areas through which they passed.
97. For a fuller analysis of the *temazlayt* relationship, see Keenan, *The Tuareg* (note 10) pp.44–52; and J. Keenan, 1976, 'Some theoretical considerations on the *temazlayt* relationship', *Revue de l'Occident Musulman et de la Méditerranée* 21/1 (1976) pp.33–46.
98. Temazlait (Contrat de protection chez les Kel Ahaggar), *Encyclopédie Berbère*, Edition Provisoire, Cahier No.7, 10 Nov. 1972, UNESCO, Université de Provence.
99. The term *tegehe* is probably best translated as 'federation'. The Kel Ahaggar, for example, were a *tegehe* comprising the three drum-groups (*ettebelen*) of the Kel Rela, Taitok and Tegehe Mellet.
100. Although it was said that Kel Ulli could 'choose' a protector, there was considerable evidence to suggest that *temazlayt* partners were to some extent inherited; Keenan, *The Tuareg* (note 10) p.44f.
101. Ibid. p.25f.
102. For details of the struggle between the Kel Rela and Taitok, see ibid. pp.63–92.
103. The French also took it upon themselves to 'modify' traditional structures by stripping the Taitok chief, Amr'i ag Mohammed of his authority and replacing him by Mohammed ag Mohammed.
104. The few that remained in Ahaggar were descendants of the old chief Amr'i ag Mohammed. They lived in the vicinity of Abalessa and according to the 1949 census comprised 9 men, 10 women, 14 children and 10 slaves.
105. Duveyrier (note 7) p.355.
106. Erwin de Bary, *Le dernier rapport d'un européen sur Ghât et les Touareg de l'Aïr (traduit et annoté par H. Schirmer)* (Paris: Libraire Fischbacher 1898) p.33.
107. Of the three Kel Ahaggar drum-groups, only the Kel Rela and Tegehe Mellet were involved in the Flatters massacre. The Taitok were preoccupied elsewhere with raids of their own at that time.
108. The key reason for this was because the former *Amenukal*, Sidi ag Mohammed El Khir, had married his two sons, Younes and Ag Mama, to daughters of the Taitok.
109. Succession is matrilineally adelphic, a complex system which allows considerable flexibility in the emergence of 'strong men'. For details, see Keenan, *The Tuareg* (note 10); and J. Keenan, 'Power and Wealth are Cousins: Descent, Class and Marital Strategies among the Kel Ahaggar (Tuareg – Sahara)', *Africa* 47/3 (1977) pp.242–52, and 47/4 (1977) pp.333–42.
110. Even at the outbreak of the Ajjer war (in which he was killed), it seems that he was

reluctant to commit the Kel Ahaggar to battle and only yielded to the pressure of the *tegehe* as a whole.
111. Details of the Kel Ahaggar's matrilineality and descent system are explained in more detail in J. Keenan, 'The End of the Matriline? The Changing Roles of Women and Descent amongst the Algerian Tuareg', in this volume, pp.121–62; and Keenan, *The Tuareg* (note 10) p.107f.
112. We know this from, amongst other things, the letter of M. Feraud to the minister of foreign affairs on 13 May 1881, quoted by Benhazera (note 52).
113. M. Gast, 'Compléments à la rubrique Attici ag Amellal', *Encyclopédie Berbère*, Cahier 25, 1980.
114. Attici was known as 'Léopard, fils de la panthère' by the French; Foucauld (note 51) part 2, p.32.
115. See, for example, P. Pandolfi, 'Tijaniyya et Touaregs du Sahara central à la fin du XIXème siècle: l'exemple de la délégation de 1892', *Islam et sociétés au sud du Sahara* 10 (1996) p.25–41; and Pandolfi (note 4) pp.411–26.
116. After their first major defeat at the hands of the Kel Ahaggar, the Kel Ajjer chief Ikhenoukhen asked the Turkish Bey of Murzuk for support. The Bey consented, and supplied the Kel Ajjer with 400 Arab soldiers recruited and armed by the Bey, on the condition that if the campaign against the Kel Ahaggar was successful, the Turks would have the right to build a garrison at Ghat. With the Bey's support, the Kel Ajjer inflicted a massive defeat on the Kel Ahaggar (eventually to be redressed). The Turks held the Kel Ajjer to their agreement and established themselves in Ghat.
117. In 1887 the Taitok, on their own initiative, raided the Mouadhi Chaamba, who were French auxiliaries, at Hassi Inifel. Many of the Taitok were taken prisoner and moved to Algiers, where they were detained before being set free. Their capture caused considerable interest and led Bissuel to undertake a study of the western Tuareg (Taitok and Kel Ahnet), published in 1888. See Keenan, *The Tuareg* (note 4) pp.81–2.
118. C. de Foucauld, *Poésies touaregues*, 2 vols. (Paris: Leroux 1930) pp.59–60.
119. This may have been a consequence of the influence of the fanatical marabout Abidine, who forbade the eating of dates from Tuat and Tidikelt on religious grounds. This venture was not repeated, possibly as a result of hostilities with the Kel Ajjer. Further attempts to establish new markets were made in 1908 when Kel Ahaggar sought rice from Gao and in 1912 when they sought millet from Anderamboukane.
120. AHG 1H1066, dated 1 Sept. 1909; AHG 1H1085, dated Aug. 1911; cited by T. Graham, 'Resistance and Collaboration among the Northern Tuareg, 1900–1920', unpublished MA thesis, SOAS, University of London, 1985, p.27.
121. Moussa did not actually assert this title until the Kel Ahaggar themselves, tired of anarchy, proclaimed him *Amenukal* in his own right.
122. Elections of *Amenukals* subsequent to 1920 reflected the new 'power' of the Kel Ulli. The first evidence we have of the Kel Ulli exerting their greater power and hence influence on this succession was in their support for Attici in 1900. See Keenan, *The Tuareg* (note 10) p.82.
123. Foucauld provides a vivid picture of the horror of this drought: There was a shortage of milk due to the depletion of the herds, and little wheat as a result of locust attacks. About eight Taitok and Kel Ahnet, accompanied by a few Kel Rela, set off on a raiding expedition in the hope of alleviating the situation and did not return for eight months. During their absence the Taitok and Kel Ahnet women were without milk, meat, grain and men to go on caravans in search of supplies. Many died of hunger and lack of clothing. Foucauld (note 118) pp.59–60.
124. Rainfall in 1913–14 was apparently the lowest ever recorded; F.A. Fugelstad, *History of Niger 1850–1960* (Cambridge: Cambridge University Press 1983) p.90.
125. Lhote (note 88) p.362.
126. AHG 1H1074, report dated 8 Dec. 1917; quoted by Graham (note 120) p.32.
127. Dubief (note 30) p.115.
128. R. Couret, 'L'embuscade de Hassi-Tanezrouft et la mort du Brigadier Paul Bechet au

Fezzan (1916–1918)', *Revue Historique de l'Armée* 23/4 (1967) pp.97–109; and *Maréchal de Logis* Lapierre (commanding officer at Djanet in 1916), report dated 1920 quoted by Graham (note 120) pp.32–3.
129. Graham (note 120) p.33.
130. Pandolfi (note 4) p.98, annex 3, and passim.
131. According to Foucauld, there were four candidates: Attici, Mohammed ag Ourzig, Sidi Mohammed ag Rotman and Moussa ag Amastane; C. de Foucauld, 'Chez les Touaregs (Taitoq, Iforas, Hoggar) mars–septembre 1904', *Bulletin trimestriel des amitiés Charles de Foucauld* 117 (1994–95) p.23.
132. Graham (note 120) p.34.
133. Ibid. p.35. Graham also suggests that it is more appropriate to classify the Tuareg's stance after 1903 as one of refusal to co-operate with the French rather than as resistance.
134. Flatters led two expeditions to Tuareg country, one in 1880 and a second in 1881 which was massacred. Both were supported by the Tidjani order.
135. The Tidjani also gave their support to the Foureau-Lamy expedition which crossed the Sahara (via Ahaggar) in 1899.
136. Foureau, at the time of his expedition (1899), reckoned that there were at least 15 notables in Ahaggar who were affiliated to the Tidjani order; F. Foureau, *D'Alger au Congo par le Tchad* (Paris: Masson 1902) p.34; Pandolfi (note 4) p.419; while Lhote, writing in 1944, stated that the Tidjani was the brotherhood with the highest number of affiliates in Ahaggar. These were notably amongst the Kel Ulli and Isekkemaren *tawsatin* of the Dag Rali, Iheyawen-Hada, Kel In R'ar and Kel Tazulet; Lhote (note 88) pp.190, 199–201.
137. His full name was Sidi Mohammed b. Sidi 'Umar b. Sidi al-Muktar. His grandfather Sidi al-Mukhtar was without parallel among religious leaders in the southern Sahara at the beginning of the nineteenth century.
138. H.T. Norris, *The Tuaregs: Their Islamic Legacy and its Diffusion in the Sahel* (Warminster, Wilts: Aris and Phillips 1975) p.169.
139. Foucauld (note 51) part 1, p.26. Similarly, in a letter to Commandant Lacroix, dated 26 November 1907, quoted in Captain Lecointre, 'Les Touareg Hoggar: Petite Société Berbère en face de l'Islam et du monde arabe', *Contre d'études sur l'Afrique et l'Asie modernes* 2152 (1953) p.8.
140. Benhazera (note 52) p.135.
141. Bourgeot, 'Les mouvements de resistance et de collaboration' (note 44) p.21.
142. Pandolfi (note 4) pp.93–4.
143. Abidine was renowned throughout the Sahara for his opposition to the French. After the French capture of Timbuktu he sought refuge in Ahaggar, where he took a wife from amongst the Kel Ahnet. His qualities as a marabout and a warrior enabled him to exert considerable influence on the affairs of Ahaggar. He urged Kel Ahaggar to attack all French or allied convoys and to break off all ties with Tidikelt, declaring that their dates were *haram* (forbidden by religion).
144. According to Captain Depommier, Moussa stated that: '*Tous les Touaregs de toutes classes du Hoggar sans exception étaient convaincus d'après les bruits lancés du Fezzan et de Ghat et habilement répandus dans toutes les tribus, que les Français étaient à bout et allaient, comme les Italiens, évacuer complètement la region. Les évènements semblainet corroborer ces dires*', AHG 7N2129, dated Feb. 1917.
145. See J. Keenan, 'Ethnicity, Regionalism and Political Stability in Algeria's *Grand Sud*', in this volume, pp.67–96.
146. Sadly, none of them remembered my near namesake, Kenan ag Tissi ag Rali, who had raided the French auxiliaries at Hassi Inifel in 1887 and was taken prisoner to Algiers and then to Paris by M. Masqueray, the Director of the *Faculté des Lettres* at Algiers.
147. Dassine, a Kel Rela, was renowned for both her beauty and intelligence and courted by many prominent nobles. Her first marriage was to Bouhen ag Khebbi ag Adebir, whom she left to marry Aflan. She was a friend of Charles de Foucauld and influential in the affairs of the country. See Keenan, *The Tuareg* (note 10) p.99.

Ethnicity, Regionalism and Political Stability in Algeria's *Grand Sud*

Introduction

Most political analyses of Algeria are limited to the country's northern regions. This is not at all surprising, considering that the vast bulk of the country's population, some 95 per cent, is located to the north of a line running roughly from around El Oued in the east to around Bechar in the west. Nevertheless, even though the country's extreme south is of little demographic significance, it should not be ignored for it is likely to play an increasingly important strategic and political role in the country's future.

The term 'south' in contemporary Algeria is fraught with ambiguity. Anyone familiar with the country's news media will know that places to the south of the Ouarsenis, Hodna and Aures massifs are usually referred to as being in the 'south' of the country, with the word 'south' being a euphemism for the country's vast Saharan territory. In this article I focus on Algeria's 'extreme south', a region, roughly the size of France, which comprises the massif of Ahaggar and the surrounding Tassili ranges,[1] the most significant of which is the Tassili-n-Ajjer to the north-east of Ahaggar. These two regions – Ahaggar and the Tassili-n-Ajjer – are the traditional home of the Kel[2] Ahaggar and Kel Ajjer Tuareg respectively. Both regions now fall within Algeria's two *wilayat* of Tamanrasset and Illizi.[3]

Political analyses of Algeria's extreme south, such as they are, have tended to focus on what has generally been referred to as the 'Tuareg problem'. This was, and still is, a dynamic concept, elusively difficult to define, which has taken on new perceptions and meanings, both symbolic and real, over the 40 or so years since Algeria's independence. In the years immediately following Independence (1962), it reflected the Tuareg's lack of incorporation into the Algerian state at the time of Independence and the Algerian government's fear that their resentment of the new order might lead to political unrest or even armed revolt.

The aim of this article is not merely to highlight and explain the political significance of Algeria's extreme south, but also to show how the effective resolution of the 'Tuareg problem', in terms of the Tuareg's incorporation into Algeria, has given rise to new political and social dynamics that are transcending and blurring many of the region's old cultural and social categories. In short, the 'Tuareg problem' of today is not only a conceptually different social construct to the 'Tuareg problem' that existed in the first years after Independence, but its continued use as an analytical tool is of highly questionable value. Indeed, any current analysis of the country's extreme south in terms of a 'Tuareg problem' is likely to lead to two dangerously misleading consequences. First, it is likely to mask both the emergence of new social and political forces as well as the increasing political and strategic importance of the region within the national entity. Second, it carries the danger of both failing to identify the current causes of potential political unrest in the region and failing to recognise the greater inherent potential for political unrest that these causes may ignite.

The Tuareg and the 'Tuareg Problem'

The Tuareg are Berber, predominately nomadic, pastoralists whose traditional homes are the central and southern Saharan massifs of Ahaggar and Tassili-n-Ajjer in Algeria, Aïr in Niger and the Adrar-n-Iforas in Mali, and the extensive plains surrounding these massifs.

Today the Tuareg are reckoned to number a little under two million. About a million of them live in Niger and about 675,000 in Mali, where they comprise a fraction over 10 per cent and 7 per cent of the total populations respectively. Current population censuses in Algeria make no reference to ethnic categories. We therefore do not know the precise number of Tuareg in the country. However, according to recent language surveys there are only some 30,000 Tamahak speakers (the language of the Tuareg) in the regions of Ahaggar and Ajjer: 25,000 in Ahaggar and 5,000 in Ajjer.[4] Such a number constitutes less than 0.1 per cent of the national population. Indeed, even in their own traditional regions of Ahaggar and Tassili, the Tuareg (excluding their slaves) have been a numerical minority since about the 1940s.[5] At Independence, Tuareg nomads in Ahaggar numbered a little over 5,000[6] in a total population of 13,000.[7] Today the Tuareg comprise scarcely 10 per cent of the population of the *wilaya* of Tamanrasset, and only about 15 per cent of the region of Ahaggar.[8]

The notion of a 'Tuareg problem' stems from the earliest days of French colonial penetration into the Sahara, when it was associated with the Tuareg's long and determined military resistance to colonial rule and pacification.[9] More recently, the notion has referred to the possibility that they might oppose and even revolt against the independent, post-colonial governments of Niger, Mali and Algeria, as has indeed been the case in both Niger and Mali.[10] In Algeria, however, given that the Tuareg comprise such a small minority, it is debatable whether there has ever really been a serious 'Tuareg problem'.

Political Stability in Algeria's Grand Sud

Notwithstanding these qualifications, the notion of a 'Tuareg problem' is not entirely without relevance to the understanding of Algeria's extreme south, not least because the Algerian government has never totally discounted the possibility of a Tuareg uprising. There are three reasons for this. One is that although the Tuareg comprise such a small minority, their traditional lands cover more than 20 per cent of the national territory. Another is that there has always been a concern that the Tuareg of Niger, Mali and Algeria could unite and form some sort of united political entity in the south-central Sahara. The recent Tuareg revolts in Niger and Mali, along with the provocative encouragement of Libya's Colonel Qadhafi, have given some credence to such a possibility. Finally, there is still a residual anxiety stemming from the experiences of the new Algerian administration in the years immediately following Independence.

Three issues in particular coloured the new Algerian administration's perception of the Tuareg in those early years. The first was the north's inherent view and understanding of the Tuareg, which had been bolstered by France's veneration for the Tuareg and its attempt to preserve, as far as possible, the social and political structure and institutions of their traditional society.[11] The Tuareg are Berbers, not Arabs, and their social organisation and culture were very different from that with which most Algerians of the north, even Kabyles, were familiar. Moreover, the Tuareg saw the Arabs to their north (notably the Chaamba) as their traditional enemies; a categorisation which – along with the Tuareg's rapacious reputation as the once-great warlords of the Central Sahara – was preserved by the French.

Second, and related to the first issue, was the fact that the initial Algerian administration that took over in Tamanrasset after Independence was not in firm control of the region. The Algerians, mostly young men, who took over the administration of the extreme south, saw the region as a 'foreign' country, far from home[12] and populated by a largely alien culture – that of the predominantly nomadic Tuareg. For them, the region was potentially hostile and inhospitable. Such feelings were reciprocated by most Tuareg, who were inclined to see the new administration as inherently antagonistic and intent on destroying what was left of their traditional way of life. It is consequently not surprising that it took the newly independent state some half-dozen or more years to get its act together in the Sahara.[13] Indeed, as far as the extreme south is concerned, I will argue later that it was not until after 1992 that the national government in Algiers took a firm grip on the region.

The third issue was a bizarre, almost comical incident in 1963–64. It occurred when five Tuareg, on returning from a six-month caravan to Niger, were led to believe that the new administration had rescinded its decree on the abolition of slavery. The five rode on the small settlement of Otoul[14] to reclaim their former slaves. Two slaves were killed and two wounded[15] in the affray. The five Tuareg were arrested and imprisoned in Ouargla.[16] Not surprisingly, the incident cast a long shadow. It provoked widespread rumours of a Tuareg revolt, which gave further credence to the notion of a 'Tuareg problem' and heightened the political tension that hung over the region during those early years of Independence.

The Resolution of the 'Tuareg Problem'

If we are to understand the specific nature of the political currents and forces at play in southern Algeria today, we need to return for a moment to the decade immediately following Independence, for the way in which the 'Tuareg problem' was resolved at that time has gone a long way to shaping the region's current social and political terrain.

The Algerian state would no doubt like us to believe that the resolution of the 'Tuareg problem' in the years immediately following Independence was the natural outcome of its policies. Tempting though such an interpretation might be, it is incorrect for at least two reasons. First, it must be recognised that circumstances quite beyond the control of the state played important roles. Second, it is very doubtful whether the government at that time had any clear policy as to how it was going to incorporate or assimilate the Tuareg into the new Algerian state.

To understand how the Tuareg were incorporated into the Algerian state and how that process has contributed to the sculpting of the present political landscape, we first of all need to analyse the social and political structure and subsistence base of Ahaggar society at the time of Independence, and the radical changes that they underwent during the 1960s.

The Social and Political Structure of Ahaggar at Independence

Although major political, economic and social changes had taken place in Tuareg society both prior to and during the French colonial period,[17] France's policy of using traditional socio-political institutions to administer their control meant that many of the social and political structures of traditional society were preserved. Consequently, at the time of Algerian independence, the semi-feudal, rigidly hierarchical socio-political categories of traditional Tuareg society, together with many of their associated rights and privileges, provided the fundamental social and political constructs of Algeria's extreme south.

When the French finally pacified the Tuareg, they classified the various social groups and classes as either 'white Tuareg' or 'black Tuareg', in accordance with the highly dubious criterion of skin colour and the predominantly racist ideology of the time. By about 1950 'white' and 'black' Tuareg found themselves being reclassified by ethnologists and other external agents as 'Tuareg' and 'non-Tuareg'. The Tuareg themselves (as distinct from 'black Tuareg' or 'non-Tuareg') comprised two main social classes: nobles and vassals. Nobles (Ihaggaren; sing. Ahaggar) were traditionally camel breeders who formed a warrior aristocracy based on their exclusive control over camels and certain arms, which enabled them to wage war, raid and control trans-Saharan caravan routes.[18] The vassals, as their name Kel Ulli (people of the goats) implies, were traditionally goat pastoralists. From around the middle of the nineteenth century onwards, Kel Ulli began to fight alongside their 'noble' overlords and to undertake raids on their own behalf.[19] As a result, they were able to acquire camels and specialised weapons, and by the end of the nineteenth century were warriors and camel-owners in their own right.[20]

A third category of Tuareg are the Isekkemaren, who are recognised as descending from unions between Arab men and Tuareg women at a time when the northern Tuareg made occasional alliances with Arab tribes, or tribes of mixed origin, in exchange for certain land rights in Ahaggar. Isekkemaren, who outnumbered the nobles by about four to one, held a slightly ambiguous status, being regarded as a slightly superior form of 'vassal' in terms of the nature of their political subordination and their various economic rights and obligations within the drum-group (see below).

The main social grouping amongst nobles, vassals and Isekkemaren was the *tawsit* (descent group; plur. *tawsatin*), membership of which was determined matrilineally.[21] Around the middle of the eighteenth century there were three territorially compact and more or less politically autonomous drum-groups (*ettebelen*, sing. *ettebel*) in Ahaggar. Each comprised one noble descent group, from which the drum-group took its name, and a varying number of subordinate Kel Ulli and Isekkemaren descent groups, who paid tributary dues to the chief of the drum-group. In addition, individual nobles held feudal-type relations with individual vassals' families within their drum-group.[22] By the end of French pacification, two of the noble *tawsatin* had become so numerically and politically weak that Ahaggar was effectively dominated by one noble descent group, the Kel Rela, whose chief held the title of *Amenukal* (supreme chief).

Other groups categorised as 'Tuareg' included the Ibettenaten, who were once considered as 'noble' but reduced to vassal status; the Irregenaten, who are considered as descending from Arab men from the south and women of the Ibettenaten and who were assimilated into the Kel Rela drum-group at about the same time as the Isekkemaren; the Ahl Azzi (known as Kel Rezzi), who were Arab nomads of marabout status from the In Salah region who married into and settled among the Tuareg of Ahaggar; and certain religious groups, known as *ineslemen*.[23]

The 'black' or 'non-Tuareg' consisted of slaves (*iklan*, sing. *akli*), cultivators (*izeggaren*, sing. *azeggar*; Arab. *harratin*) and blacksmiths (*ineden*).

The etymological meaning of *iklan* probably derives from a *k-l* root meaning 'to be black', and refers to their skin colour. They were originally brought to Ahaggar and Ajjer by raiding expeditions in the Sudanese regions and raids on the trans-Saharan slave caravans. By the late 1940s they numbered around 1,700 compared with a Tuareg population of about 4,300.[24] This ratio was not reflected uniformly among the various *tawsatin*, as in Ahaggar nearly half of all *iklan* were owned by two *tawsatin*: the noble Kel Rela and the vassal Dag Rali, who were both outnumbered by their slaves.[25]

The word *izeggaren*, which derives from the verb *ihwar* (to be red), refers to the dark colour of their skin, and is used to designate the dark-skinned *harratin* cultivators (many of ancient Negro origin), who came into the region from the oases of Tuat and Tidikelt in increasing numbers after 1861,[26] when the *Amenukal* invited them to cultivate the land on behalf of the Tuareg. Although technically free men, their position as dependent clients of the Tuareg, working the land on a contract basis (the *khamast*) that entitled them to only one-fifth of the harvest, meant that their living conditions could be described in degrees of poverty. From a few hundred at the end of the nineteenth century, they numbered about 3,000 in Ahaggar by the end of the 1940s, compared with a Tuareg population of some 4,300.[27]

Ineden (blacksmiths) formed an endogamous caste that was found amongst all Tuareg groups, although they were few in number in Ahaggar and Ajjer compared to southern Tuareg groups in Niger and Mali.[28]

Prior to the middle of the nineteenth century, Ahaggar (and Ajjer) society consisted solely of the Tuareg (Ihaggaren, Kel Ulli and Isekkemaren) and their slaves, along with a few *ineslemen* and *ineden* families. Since then, and especially since French pacification in the early part of the twentieth century, the pluralist nature of Ahaggar and Ajjer society has been augmented by the steady immigration into the region of other smaller non-Tamahak-speaking groups: first the steady inflow of *harratin*; then Arabic Chaamba who arrived as French auxiliaries and later acquired certain land rights; marabout (*cheurfa*) religious families who followed the French 'push' south and attached themselves in increasing numbers to various Tuareg groups; and Mozabite and Metlilli merchants, who came into the region after Tamanrasset and then Djanet were established as administrative and commercial centres.[29]

By the time of Algerian independence, the population of Ahaggar had grown to 13,000, almost equally divided between 'nomads' and 'sedentarists'. The 6,500 or so nomads consisted almost entirely of Tuareg and their slaves. The sedentarists consisted primarily of *harratin*, who by 1962 could be estimated as numbering around 4,000, townspeople belonging to the families of merchants, along with an increasing number of people attached to the French civil and military administrations, as well as an increasing number of formerly nomadic Tuareg and Arabs who were beginning to settle in the main villages and commercial centres, notably Tamanrasset and Djanet.[30]

These social categorisations were predominantly 'external' constructs, based fundamentally on ethnic-racial criteria. The indigenous categorisations of Tuareg society were more meaningful in that they better reflected its social, political and economic dynamics. A key word in the indigenous categorisation of Ahaggar society is *imuhagh*.[31] Linguists[32] who have studied the various Tuareg languages consider that *imuhagh* may be the noun derived from the verb *aheg*, meaning 'to raid' or 'plunder'. Although we have minimal information on the usage and meaning of the term before the time of Duveyrier (1864), it may have been used in a restrictive sense to designate the 'raiders', that is the Ihaggaren, who until about the mid-nineteenth century retained exclusive control over camels and certain weapons: the means of warfare and raiding. By the beginning of the twentieth century, the term seems to have been extended to designate everyone whose language was Tamahak. By then, that group comprised the Ihaggaren, the Kel Ulli and Isekkemaren, who were now warriors in their own right, as well as their slaves and a few *ineslemen* and *ineden*. In other words, the term *imuhagh* seems to have been extended to designate the inner 'we' of traditional society. The 'they' comprised the later in-migrating groups of *izeggaren/harratin* (cultivators) and the other predominantly Arabic-speaking minorities. This rather heterogeneous 'they' was characterised by two features: Tamahak was not their mother tongue, and they settled for the most part in the growing cultivation centres. They came to be referred to collectively as Kel Aghrem (*aṛrem*), meaning literally 'the people of the cultivation centres' (that is, small villages, hamlets), or in other words sedentarists as opposed to nomads.

It would seem that the extension of *imuhagh* to include the Kel Ulli, the Isekkemaren and their slaves was more than just the recognition of the distinction between the traditional 'pastoral-cum-raiding' economic formation and agriculture. It was the ideological expression of an opposition between lifestyles, between nomadism and sedentarism. This was most clearly seen in the case of freed slaves and the absorption of foreign nomads: freed slaves who settled in the cultivation centres were no longer classified as *imuhagh* but as Kel Aghrem, while those few who managed to establish themselves in a nomadic-pastoral way of life were still referred to generally as *imuhagh*. Similarly, a few immigrant Arab nomads, such as the Ahl Azzi (Kel Rezzi), who married into, and settled with, certain Kel Ahaggar groups, also came to be referred to as *imuhagh*.

Thus, while the French system of administration effectively retained the rigid social and political hierarchy of traditional society, and injected it with political, social and economic meaning, Tuareg themselves were perhaps beginning to see and classify their society more in terms of a distinction between lifestyles. This distinction became more pertinent in the years immediately following Algerian independence when it came to take on a political dimension.

The Subsistence Base of the Kel Ahaggar at Independence

At the time of Independence, the Kel Ahaggar's subsistence economy was supported by five main pillars: animal husbandry (goat and camel pastoralism); salt caravans trading locally mined salt for millet from the Damergou region of southern Niger; *harratin*-cultivated gardens; wage labour; and the institution of slavery. By the mid-1960s most Kel Ahaggar spoke of all these activities as if they had all been part of their traditional way of life, even though both cultivation and the salt caravans did not become significant components of their subsistence economy until the early part of the twentieth century, and wage labour not until the 1950s.[33] In the years immediately after Independence, the notion of 'traditional' applied to almost anything that existed prior to Independence. Especially anomalous was their reference to wage labour as being 'traditional', when manual labour in all its forms had always been regarded with disdain. The opportunity for wage labour at that time was provided mostly by the French atomic test site at In Eker.[34] Comparatively few Tuareg worked at In Eker before Independence, although several sent their slaves to work there on their behalf. However, with the abolition of slavery after Independence, Tuareg themselves took to working at In Eker in increasing numbers. Although this extraordinary transformation in their attitude to manual labour was triggered predominantly by the pressure of survival, it was also partly explained by the fact that In Eker was controlled by France and not Algeria.[35] The new Algerian administration was perceived by most Tuareg as being hostile towards them. In Eker, by contrast, was something that they 'knew' and had experienced. Many Kel Ahaggar felt that their employment by the French at In Eker provided them with a certain immunity and independence from the Algerian administration.

The immediate impact of Algerian independence on the Kel Ahaggar economy was not as great as might be supposed. Although the abolition of slavery meant that there was less labour available for mining salt and for tending the caravans and the herds, the departure of the slaves brought some relief by reducing the number of mouths to be fed. Furthermore, although all systems of *métayage* labour were abolished, not all *harratin* were in a position to exercise their new-found freedom. Many Tuareg, still regarding themselves as the landowners, continued to exact dues from them. Similarly, although the terms of trade for the purchase of millet in Niger deteriorated significantly between 1962 and 1965–66,[36] the caravans continued to run and at least provide the Kel Ahaggar with a supply of millet.

Thus, although the first three or four years of Algerian independence saw the loss of their slaves and a demise in the amount of foodstuffs accruing from the caravans and their gardens, the nomadic economy was able to survive as pasture for both goats and camels remained adequate and more cash income came into the camps from working at In Eker.[37]

The 'Collapse' of the Nomadic Economy

If by 1965 the Kel Ahaggar thought they had weathered the introduction of Algerian 'socialism', they were grievously mistaken. Following Boumediènne's coup in 1965, a new, hard-line *sous-préfet*, M. Aktouf, arrived in Tamanrasset. He immediately set about eradicating all traces of slavery and *métayage* labour, and developed small agricultural co-operatives to help overcome the problem posed by 'liberated' slaves congregating in *bidonvilles* around Tamanrasset.[38] Aktouf's actions coincided with the onset of drought, thus making the nomadic camps increasingly dependent on the salt caravans and wage labour. But, in 1966, the government blocked the importation of millet and the French withdrew from In Eker. By the end of 1966, four pillars of the Kel Ahaggar economy had been effectively destroyed, while the fifth, pastoralism, was being undermined by drought.

Aktouf offered the nomads no compromise. In his view the Tuareg had played no part in the creation of Algeria; they had given nothing, had nothing to offer, and were politically unimportant. He saw nomadism as backward and an obstacle to modernisation. They either accepted his policies or left Algeria!

Under these conditions, the distinction between sedentarist and nomad – Kel Aghrem and *imuhagh* – took on an overtly political dimension. *Imuhagh* increasingly saw Tamanrasset, the outlying villages and cultivation centres, with their rapidly expanding population of former slaves and *harratin*, as the domain of the Algerian state, which they berated as the main cause of their increasing poverty and hardship.

The determination of the majority of *imuhagh* to maintain their nomadic existence said as much about their aversion to a sedentary life and their fear of the Algerian administration (especially in Tamanrasset), as it did for their resilience and ingenuity. Their survival during this period was dependent on a precarious and often incidental assortment of incomes. Scattered rains, although not breaking the drought, gave hope of an improvement in pastoralism; a few clandestine caravans returned from Niger with small but invaluable amounts of millet; a few ex-slaves and *harratin* who had chosen to remain with their former masters produced a modicum of garden produce in a number of small, isolated cultivation centres; public works gangs (repairing the *pistes*) provided wage income to a handful of nomads; intermittent distributions of Foreign Aid grain found its way into some of the camps, while a trickle of tourists contributed marginally to cash income.

The question remains as to whether the Tuareg ever considered taking up arms against the government at this time.[39] Although the Algerian government was spoken of in hostile terms, I do not think that any serious thought was given to rebelling. There were many reasons for this. One was that the fate of those Tuareg who had rebelled against the Malian government in 1961 was still fresh in their minds. Not only had President Keita of Mali crushed the rebellion, with disastrous consequences for the Tuareg, many of whom fled to Ahaggar to seek refuge among the Kel Ahaggar, but he had been helped by the Algerian *Armée de Libération Nationale* (ALN),[40] a fact that had not gone unnoticed in Ahaggar. In addition, and quite apart from their realisation of their own inadequate numerical and military strength, an important factor mitigating against an uprising was the lack of leadership among the Kel Ahaggar. The *Amenukal*'s recruitment into the Algerian political hierarchy as a vice-president and salaried Deputy of the National Assembly compromised his position, which for many Kel Ahaggar became one of ambiguity.[41] Moreover, the Kel Rela, who might have provided some leadership, were not affected by this predicament as most of them had already abandoned a nomadic lifestyle and settled in Tamanrasset.[42]

Most Kel Ulli and Isekkemaren, however, had little choice but to brave it out in their nomadic camps in a state of increasing hardship and poverty, or settle in the cultivation centres. Although a small number of *imuhagh* did begin to develop economic links with villages and even began to settle 'temporarily' in them while developing and working their own gardens, the majority remained in the camps, clinging to the hope that the following year would bring an amelioration in pastoral conditions, the removal of the caravan embargo and the reopening of In Eker.

This rather dismal account of nomadic subsistence in 1968 was, as it perhaps sounds, the last gasp of 'traditional' nomadic society. If that sounds overly dramatic it is because the end of 1968 marked the turning point, or what we might regard as the end of the *imuhagh*'s resistance to 'modernisation', at least in as much as their resentment and fear of the Algerian administration and their avoidance of Tamanrasset underwent an almost total *volte-face* within a matter of a few months. While the calamitous state of the nomadic economy was the overriding pressure on the *imuhagh*, it does not explain the amazing speed of their transformation and incorporation into the new order, which can be dated – quite precisely – to a few weeks between December 1968 and spring 1969, a period during which a most extraordinary series of events unfolded in Tamanrasset.

The catalyst of these events was the government's decision in 1965 to extend primary education to nomads by constructing boarding annexes alongside the main village schools. The Kel Ahaggar, who had hitherto experienced very little schooling, were opposed to this development on two grounds. First, children were an important source of labour in the nomadic milieu. Second, they feared that the government was trying to take their children away and draft them into the army. In both 1966 and 1967 most nomads managed to avoid the poorly co-ordinated net that was thrown over them by the administration. However, Aktouf was determined to break the back of their resistance and in 1968 ordered military vehicles to scour the nomadic camps. While this succeeded in raising school attendance, his coercive measures merely hardened the nomads' resistance towards both schooling and the administration in Tamanrasset.

Fortunately for all concerned, Aktouf's drive through the camps coincided with the appointment of a new local Director of Education, an ex-patriot (M. Laporte) with much experience of both nomads and education in Algeria. Realising the potential damage of Aktouf's actions, Laporte immediately set out to subvert the stringent guidelines imposed from Algiers. His first initiative was to persuade the townspeople of Tamanrasset, in the name of charity, to invite the nomad children into their homes for the religious festival of *Eid Es Rir*. This social experiment was a great success. With the exception of a few of the elder nomadic children, who remained aloof in their attitude to the townspeople, most of the younger children made many friendships and established fictive familial bonds with their 'adopted' families. *Eid Es Rir* was followed a short time later by a five-day holiday over Christmas. This was too short a break to justify the closure of the boarding house. Laporte, however, realising that nomads would never accept schooling until it was made voluntary, sent the children home to their camps for the short holiday break. The *sous-préfet*, who was neither consulted nor informed of this decision, had grave misgivings that any would return. To his amazement, every child returned to school on time, with many being accompanied by their parents!

The nomads realised that they had misjudged Aktouf in that he had kept his word and was a man who could be trusted: their children had been returned to them sooner than expected, and unharmed. What was more, the children told their parents and elders of the conditions in the school: new clothing, good quality food, caretakers who knew the nomadic environment and befriended them, and townspeople who had taken them into their homes!

The transformation of the attitude of the nomadic community towards Tamanrasset, its townspeople and the Algerian government was immediate and extraordinary. The boarding house was seen more as an 'hotel' than a school, where their children would be fed and well-cared for while the drought-induced hardship in the camps continued. And, more pertinently, nomads began coming into Tamanrasset almost immediately, claiming that in having given their children to the government they had paid a tax[43] and were now demanding rights in return! In particular, they demanded wage labour. In this, they were also to be surprised, for in 1969 Sonarem, the national mineral exploration company, began recruiting labour for the establishment of a big base in the region. The nomads were even more taken aback to find that labour was allocated on a 'points system' geared to social needs that cut across ethnic and other such cleavages. With the exception of specifically skilled jobs, labour was allocated according to points in such a way that priority was given to locally married men with dependent children, regardless of whether they were nomadic Kel Ahaggar or ex-slaves living in Tamanrasset. Moreover, in addition to finding that they were afforded the same rights as other Algerian citizens, they also found little or no prejudice towards them on the part of the townspeople.[44]

The Initial 'Algerianisation' of the Tuareg

The incorporation of the Tuareg into the Algerian state has involved three closely inter-related processes that are contextually distinct, yet closely linked conceptually: Algerianisation, Arabisation and Islamisation. I shall say more about the later two in a moment, as they have become more pronounced in the last decade than in the 1960s and 1970s. As a cognitive process, this first stage of incorporation, which followed the remarkable events of 1969, was marked by the Tuareg's notion of being part of a redistributive tax system: having 'given' their children, they now had the right to make demands on the government! So quick was this change in attitude that by 1970 Tuareg were actually referring to themselves as 'Algerian Tuareg' and a few even as 'Algerians', largely to make the point that they too had rights to the labour market, the boarding school and other such institutions and amenities of the newly socialist state.

At a more demonstrable level, the process of Algerianisation, especially during this early phase, was associated with the Tuareg's increasing immersion into a sedentary environment. As the impediments to the nomads' traditional ways mounted, especially the deterioration of pastoral conditions, so sedentarisation became the only viable course of action open to them. In almost all nomadic societies, however, sedentarisation is neither an instantaneous nor an 'all-or-nothing' process, but tends to be characterised by various stages of 'semi-sedentarisation' – stages which are not necessarily defined etymologically in geographical, residential or economic terms, but primarily in terms of changing cognitions. This was very apparent in Ahaggar following Aktouf's emphasis on the primacy of agriculture and his denigration of nomadism as being archaic and contrary to modernisation. Under these circumstances, the indigenous classification of Ahaggar society in terms of *imuhagh* and Kel Aghrem – nomads and sedentarists – came to reflect more than a difference between lifestyles: it took on a political meaning, reflecting the distinction between the ancient, traditional or 'pre-Algerian' order and that of the new Algerian state, with its emphasis on agriculture, the development of agricultural co-operatives and a social order constructed on the values of the new national socialism. Sedentarisation at this time (the late 1960s and early 1970s) consequently involved more than just a change of lifestyles; it involved immersion into and acceptance of the new Algerian order.

For the Tuareg to re-evaluate and to take on new perspectives towards the Algerian state was one thing; for them to replace their traditional value system with that of the new Algerian order in a matter of a few years, was quite another. For sedentarisation to be complete or final, the legitimation of the nomad's actions must be confirmed and validated in terms of the ideas and assumptions held by the sedentary society's definition of social reality. In Ahaggar and the Tassili-n-Ajjer at that time, this reality was that of the new Algerian state. Thus, for a nomad to become a sedentarist he must accept and maintain the new Algerian order. Within this cognitive framework sedentarisation could therefore not be conceived as anything but a partial and reversible process, for otherwise it would merely have resulted in a total disconfirmation of the Kel Ahaggar's existing ideas and definitions of social reality. Although many nomads began to sedentarise during this period, they could therefore not be regarded as 'sedentarists'; for their settlement, although often taking on an air of permanency, did not imply a complete acceptance of the Algerian order. Rather, it was seen as an act of expediency, legitimised in terms of the ideas and assumptions of the traditional order and expressed in such statements as 'until the rains come'.[45] Thus, although an increasing number of nomads became sedentarised in a residential sense, and in so doing demonstrated an increasing acceptance of the new Algerian order,[46] it is debatable whether many of them became wholly 'sedentarist' at a cognitive level. Indeed, it is significant that while ex-slaves who moved from the nomadic to the sedentary milieu became reclassified as Kel Aghrem (as distinct from *imuhagh*), Tuareg did not reclassify themselves in this way, but spoke of themselves as *imuhagh ouan aghrem* (*imuhagh*, or Tuareg, of the villages).

The Second Stage of Incorporating the Tuareg (Kel Ahaggar)

The radical changes that virtually turned Ahaggar society upside town in the late 1960s and early 1970s were not only very quick, but also traumatic for all concerned, none more so than the Kel Ahaggar who experienced a great 'shock', which is possibly why their incorporation and assimilation into the new Algerian state was more successful than might have been imagined only a few years earlier.

In spite of the success of these 'shocks', the Kel Ahaggar could not be regarded as fully 'Algerianised' until nomadic pastoralism was recognised and accepted as part of the social reality of the new order. There is no precise date when this happened. Unlike the 'shock' treatment of the late 1960s, the second and more pervasive stage of the Kel Ahaggar's incorporation was a more gradual and ongoing process throughout the remainder of the 1970s and the 1980s.

Two policies in particular marked this second phase of incorporation. One was the government's progressive dismantling of several of the Tuareg's remaining political and cultural practices and institutions. By the mid-1970s virtually all the vestigial symbols of the Kel Ahaggar's former political rights and institutions had been removed. The most notable amongst these was the transfer of the drum (*ettebel*) – the symbol of the *Amenukal*'s supreme political authority – from the *Amenukal*'s camp to the *mairie* of Tamanrasset. This highly symbolic gesture was followed by no *Amenukal* being appointed on the incumbent's death in 1975.[47] This meant that the Kel Ahaggar no longer had any official political representation other than as local residents of the *commune* and the *wilaya* and as citizens of Algeria.[48]

A more subtle act of 'deculturation', and one which will have far-reaching, long-term implications, was the abolition of the traditional system of naming. The traditional system consisted simply of a single first or 'given' name being prefaced to the father's name, such as Mohammed ag (son of) Ahmadu ag ... and so on, or, in the case of women, Fatma ult (daughter of) Mohammed. The key feature of this system of naming was that it enabled Tuareg to reckon their descent relatively unambiguously over several generations, sometimes as many as seven or eight. This was of crucial importance in a society in which the basic principle of social organisation was descent, and especially in a society in which political power and almost all other rights were located within lineages and transmitted according to complex rules and principles of group membership and descent. However, in the 1970s, the Tuareg were told to drop the 'ag' or 'ult' and take a 'proper' family name. The reason given them by the government was to facilitate the computerisation of documents. Perhaps surprisingly, there was no resistance to this move, which effectively removed their fundamental identity – their names – at a stroke. On the contrary, most Tuareg seem to have taken it in a spirit of good humour, with many seizing the opportunity to rearrange their kinship ties or simply distance themselves from bothersome kinsmen! In practice, the abolition of the 'ag/ult' system is already contributing to genealogical amnesia and accelerating the decline of the relevance of descent and kinship as the fundamental social organisational principles of Tuareg society.[49]

The second significant policy of this period was the government's gradual recognition of the social and economic importance of nomadic pastoralism. While this partly reflected the government's failure to match its rhetoric towards the agricultural sector with investment and reform, it also signalled a more pragmatic recognition of the importance to the region's economy of tourism and the development in 1984 and 1987 respectively of the Tassili[50] and Hoggar (Ahaggar) National Parks, both of which are integrally associated with the nomadic milieu. Tourism contributed an important source of income to the nomadic community during the 1960s. With drought conditions persisting for much of the 1970s, the increasing number of tourists visiting both Ahaggar and Ajjer provided an increasingly important economic prop to what was left of the nomadic way of life.[51] This was reinforced by the employment opportunities created by the two National Parks.[52]

The 'High-Point' of the Extreme South's Development

It could be argued that the end of the 1980s marked something of a high-point in terms of both the economic and political development of Algeria's extreme south and the incorporation and assimilation of the Tuareg.

Although the majority of Tuareg were now settled, the 1987 census showed that there were still 4,471 nomads in the *wilaya* of Tamanrasset.[53] Of particular significance was the fact that the government was now recognising nomadism as part of the region's cultural heritage. Both Parks were providing nomads with employment; some 15,000 tourists a year were visiting the region (Ahaggar and Ajjer); Djanet was a thriving town of some 10,000 inhabitants, while Tamanrasset, a *wilaya* capital since 1974, had grown to some 40,000. Surely, the notion of a 'Tuareg problem' now belonged to history.

And yet, by the end of the 1990s, the character of the region had changed almost unrecognisably, both physically through a more than doubling of the population, but also socially and politically through the emergence of a raft of issues and associated grievances that have the potential to spill over into wider political unrest.

The Impact of Algeria's 'Crisis' on its Extreme South

Although the violence that engulfed Algeria following the army's annulment of the 1992 general election[54] was restricted largely to the north of the country, this 'crisis' had profound effects on the extreme south. However, these effects can only be fully appreciated in the context of a number of local issues, two of which in particular have had a major bearing on developments in the region.

The 'War-Lord' Syndrome

The first of these relates to the emergence in the region of a certain Hadj Bettu as a local 'war-lord'.[55] By the beginning of the 1990s he was in effective control of most of the region's business, both legal and clandestine,[56] including widespread gunrunning and the provision of a 'private' army in Niger.[57] The emergence of Hadj Bettu's 'fiefdom' in the south is an indication of both how far the south had drifted away from the direct control of Algiers and how widespread corruption throughout the country facilitated the emergence of such a phenomenon. There is an irony in the fact that Bettu's activities seem to have been brought to the attention of certain elements in the army command following the assassination of President Mohammed Boudiaf in June 1992. Shortly before his assassination, Boudiaf had made a major speech promising to stamp out corruption throughout the country, in local and central government as well as in the army. Did the President have Bettu in his sights? The official line is that Boudiaf was assassinated by an Islamic fundamentalist. But amongst the many rumours and theories that still abound, many of which incriminate the army, the army's attention was drawn to Hadj Bettu and the anarchic state of affairs that reigned in Ahaggar.

The army immediately set about reining in the country's extreme south. Tamanrasset was turned into the country's sixth military region, under the command of a general directly responsible to Algiers. Bettu was gaoled[58] and Algiers took a much closer interest in the reorganisation of the region's administration. Indeed, as I have already suggested, it was not until this time that the national government in Algiers took a firm grip on the country's extreme south. Over the next decade, the population of Tamanrasset more than doubled as military and government officials poured into the region.

Refugees from Mali

The second local issue which has had a major bearing on developments within the region was the influx of an estimated 40,000 or so Tuareg refugees into Ahaggar from Mali. The last of these refugees returned to Mali in 1998–99, but their presence in Ahaggar for much of the decade did much to strengthen ties between the Algerian and Malian Tuareg (see below).

The 'Invasion' of les gens du nord

Algeria's 'crisis' has had two major consequences on the extreme south. One is that it led many people to move to Tamanrasset with their families so that they would be safe from the troubles of the north. Following the influx of military and government personnel after 1992, local people now speak of having been 'invaded' by *les gens du nord*. The 1998 census revealed that the town's population had risen to 82,000 from around 40,000[59] in the late 1980s.[60] The population of the *wilaya* also more than doubled, growing from 95,822 in 1987 to some 210,000 in 1998.

Isolation and the Collapse of Tourism

The second major consequence of Algeria's 'troubles' in the north was that tourism in the region fell from an average of 15,000 per year to almost zero.

With the region becoming increasingly isolated and almost literally cut off from the outside world as a result of political instability along Algeria's southern frontiers (the Tuareg revolts in Niger and Mali) and the escalation of violence in the north of the country, it was difficult to ascertain how Algeria's Tuareg, especially the few remaining nomads, were being affected by and responding to this sudden cessation of tourism and the wave of political instability washing over much of the Central Sahara. Rumour and hearsay fell into two broad categories. One was that Tuareg, suffering the loss of income from tourism, had reverted to traditional ways, with many of them allegedly roaming the mountains of Ahaggar, armed with Kalashnikovs, and raiding what little trans-Saharan traffic dared to venture into these parts. The other was that the remaining nomads had been forced to abandon their tents and settle in the villages.

The Response of the Tuareg

I consequently returned to Ahaggar and the Tassili-n-Ajjer during this time to find out what lay behind these seemingly contradictory stories. Although there were widespread manifestations of cultural revivalism in Niger and Mali, which is not surprising in the light of the recent Tuareg uprisings in those countries, I found few apparent signs of this phenomenon in either Ahaggar or Ajjer. Stories of Kalashnikov-wielding Tuareg holding sway in Ahaggar seemed to have been a legacy from Hadj Bettu's earlier gun-running operations, while attacks on traffic were associated almost entirely with the troubles in Niger and Mali and trans-Saharan smuggling and banditry (see below), all of which had little to do with the Tuareg of Algeria. Neither had the Kel Ahaggar fully sedentarised. Although the number of nomadic Kel Ahaggar appeared to have declined from some 4,000 at the end of the 1980s to perhaps no more than 3,000 by the end of the 1990s, these few were nevertheless still surviving in their nomadic milieu, in spite of the collapse of tourism.[61]

In practice, I found that a far more complex and intricate situation had been developing, the key to the understanding of which is to be found in the way the Algerian government, by the late 1990s, had wittingly or unwittingly largely 'incorporated' the Algerian Tuareg into the Algerian state. The most striking manifestations of this assimilation are the noticeably greater Islamisation and Arabisation of the Kel Ahaggar since the early 1970s. The increased Islamisation of the region is a reflection of the more fundamentalist doctrines that have permeated the country over the last decade or so and which are now apparent in such things as the almost total observance, even amongst the nomads, of *karem* – the fast during the holy month of Ramadan.[62] The increased Islamisation of the Kel Ahaggar has been paralleled by their far greater usage of Arabic, especially among the younger generation, whose preference for Arabic over Tamahak is not simply the outcome of their having been taught in Arabic for a generation, but because they see 'Arabism' – to use their own words – as *chic*, *à la mode* and the essence of modernity.[63]

However, the key element of the government's incorporative strategy towards the Kel Ahaggar during these difficult times has been the economic and ideological support that it has given to the nomads through its 'Parks' policy. Decreed in 1987 as an act of environmental conservation, and with half an eye on the development of the tourism industry,[64] the Ahaggar National Park has provided the government with the means through which it has compensated the nomads for their loss of income from tourism. By September 2000 the Park was employing 550 people, mostly Kel Ahaggar, as *agents de conservation* or, to use their own term, *guardiens du parc*. This 'employment', regarded by most Kel Ahaggar as a euphemism for 'social security', involves a negligible amount of 'work'.[65] But, as a 'social security' policy, it has almost certainly saved the remaining nomadic Kel Ahaggar from severe poverty: an outcome that could have had significant political repercussions.[66]

The Emergence of New 'Issues' and Grievances in the South

Why, if the Tuareg have been so thoroughly incorporated and assimilated into Algeria, have the last two or three years seen the emergence of a combination of 'new' issues and grievances in the region that have the potential for fuelling widespread political unrest? Before itemising the specific issues, it should be made clear that the answer is not to be found within the traditional context of the 'Tuareg problem', but within the new sense of regionalism that is taking hold of the extreme south and which is in large part being galvanised by these issues.

These issues themselves can be categorised into those over which the Algerian government has direct influence, which I refer to as 'internal', and those which are largely beyond its control, which I refer to as 'external'.

The main external factor impinging on Algeria's extreme south is trans-Saharan 'smuggling', especially of cigarettes.[67] Much of this contraband trade is in the hands of 'bandits', some of whom are thought to be protected by elements in Algeria's own military establishment, while others are believed to be associated with armed Islamic 'terrorist' groups in northern Algeria. For example, Mokhtar ben Mokhtar, generally regarded as the largest such *contrabandier*, and who has been responsible for several attacks on Algerian facilities throughout much of the Sahara, especially in 1998, is believed to have linked up with Hassan Hattab's Armed Islamic Group (GIA),[68] with the result that cigarette smuggling is intimately associated with the establishment of armed Islamist training camps south of the Algerian border and the movement of both arms and men between these camps and the north. While much of this activity skirts the regions of Ahaggar and Ajjer, it has contributed to security problems in Algeria's Saharan territories and the destabilisation of the southern frontier.[69] Such activities pose two political dangers. One is that they provide an attractive alternative to burgeoning unemployment. The other is that the professed ideologies of some of these bandits, which are discussed below, have inflammatory connotations both within and beyond the region.

A second 'external' factor, the implications of which are discussed further on, is the Commission on Human Rights Working Group's (CHRWG) 'Draft Declaration on the Rights of Indigenous Peoples'. The Tuareg are designated as one of the world's indigenous peoples. Should the Declaration be adopted by the UN General Assembly in its present form, the implications for all 'Tuareg' countries will be considerable.

Three 'internal' issues (see Postscript, below) can be identified: the lack of both government strategic planning and consultation with local people in regard to long-term regional economic development, especially the region's tourism industry; the imposition of government policies and administrators without consultation with the local people; and the sense that 'local people', especially in Tamanrasset, are being 'swamped' by the 'invasion' of *les gens du nord*.

The future of the tourism industry, because of its scale and complexity, cannot be dealt with in this paper,[70] other than to point out that many local people, especially those Tuareg (Kel Ahaggar and Kel Ajjer) who are involved in it, believe that the government's short-term approach, which is seen as encouraging forms of 'mass tourism' and 'quick bucks' at the expense of environmental and patrimonial conservation, is taking the region to the brink of an environmental catastrophe which will have dire consequences for the long-term economic future of the region and its peoples.[71] All three of these issues, however, and others that could be mentioned, may be regarded as expressing the same broad level of grievance, namely that 'local people' feel that they have little or no say in matters that concern them.

Towards a New Regionalism – *Le Grand Sud*?

While this complaint is commonplace in most corners of the country, its significance in Algeria's extreme south is that it is not coming from any one social or 'ethnic' (that is, Tuareg) group, but rather from within a much broader regional context, which is best understood in its 'we'/'they' context. The 'they' are the increasing number of people from the north of the country who have 'invaded' (to use local parlance) the region in the last few years. The locals' perception of themselves as a specific 'we' group is being fuelled by the sense that they are being overwhelmed by *les gens du nord*.[72]

The descriptive nomenclature used by the two groups towards each other is revealing in that it says much about the nature of this division and the regional identities that it is helping to foster.

I have come across only one new term in the local language for these new social categories. This is the word *Chinoui/Chnaoui*, from the French *chinois* – Chinese.[73] It is the collective name given, somewhat derisorily, by both Kel Ahaggar and other people of the region, to the people from the north of the country (that is, *les gens du nord*). The explanation for why northerners are called 'Chinese' is because 'they are white and behave like foreigners'. In similar vein, Algerian tourists from the north of the country, or Algerian emigrants living in France, are called Taiwan because 'they are like the cheap spare parts made in Taiwan, compared to the expensive, original, quality spare parts – namely European tourists'.

A *Chinoui* would most likely refer to the people of the region as 'southerners', using the term Sahraouis, or if they were wearing a *chech* (veil) and *gandoura* he would probably call them Targuis or Hadj Bettus. Although the use of such terms by *Chnaoui* is often considered by locals to be conveying a sense of derision, their usage probably tends more to reflect the northerners' lack of knowledge of the region and its social categories.

In the case of local people, the terms they would use to describe themselves would depend on the context and to whom they were speaking. A Tuareg talking to a *Chinoui* would not refer to himself as either *imuhagh* or Kel Ahaggar, as the *Chinoui* would not know what he was talking about. He would be more likely to describe himself as 'a Tuareg from Ahaggar', or the 'Hoggar'. Similarly, a *hartani* would not refer to himself as a *harratin* or an *izeggar*, but would probably describe himself with reference to his ancestral origin, saying that he was from In Salah or the Tuat. Likewise, an ex-slave would be unlikely to make reference to his slave origins and almost certainly not use the term *akli*, but would refer to himself as a Dag Rali or Aguh-en-tehle, that being the name of the Tuareg *tawsit* to which he or his forbears had been attached. He might also just refer to himself as a Tuareg from Ahaggar.[74]

There is, as far as I know, no single term amongst the people of the region to express their notion of 'we'.[75] However, in contradistinction to the 'they', the 'we' tend to think of themselves increasingly in a regional context, as the people of the region, defining this context, albeit rather loosely, as being born in the region, or, more especially, having parent(s) or other ancestors who originated or were born in the region. Within this 'we' group, depending on the context, people still use the old terms that describe their ancestry and origins, such as: *imuhagh*, Kel Aghrem, Ihaggaren, Kel Ulli, Isekkemaren, *kel ..., iklan, ineden, ineslemen, hartani* and so on.[76]

Thus, while the old social categories still exist and have meaning in an historical context, their current lack of political content reflects the success of Algeria's incorporation policy. However, it can also be argued that it has been the very success of this policy that has given rise to the emergence of regionalism as a potentially destabilising political force. The abolition of all traditional political institutions and offices, with little to replace them, except for the informal role played by Hadj Moussa, the half-brother of the former *Amenukal*,[77] on behalf of the Kel Ahaggar, has had the effect of limiting the ways in which any dissatisfaction, especially amongst the Tuareg, might be expressed, thus increasing the likelihood that it will find expression through new and more unconventional channels.

Precisely what these channels may be is not easy to see at the moment. Following the Berber unrest in early summer 2001, it was reported in some of the national media that this unrest affected all Berber areas, including the Tuareg south. This was not correct. The Tuareg have never had strong political links with Berber groups in the north of the country and there was no such Berber-oriented unrest in either the Tamanrasset or Illizi *wilayat*.[78] However, in late mid-summer President Bouteflika, concerned that the Tuareg might ally themselves with the Berber unrest in the north, visited Tamanrasset, Djanet and Illizi. At Djanet he was presented with a letter, signed by 157 of the most prominent residents of the town, complaining about the *wali*, Mohammed Ouba.[79] He was greeted in the main street with a mixture of respect and ribald chanting, the message of which was quite clear: 'If he [the North] didn't want the South to be part of Algeria, he was just to let them know!'

Although many might like to interpret this taunting challenge to the government within the context of the prevailing Berber unrest in the north, the nature of the demonstration and the message that it gave to the government was not linked to the events in the north. In Illizi, the message was even more direct. People lined the streets, chanting and clapping and demanding that the President get rid of the *wali*. Bouteflika took note, and on returning to Algiers he ordered the dismissal of Mohammed Ouba. The removal of the *wali* was seen by the people of both *wilayat* as a great victory for the south. A short time later the national press reported Ouba as being one of the twelve *walis* dismissed by the President for their responsibility for the Berber unrest in the north of the country! Although people in the north were probably none the wiser, those in the south knew why Ouba had been dismissed. It was also soon common knowledge throughout the south that Ouba had been investigated by the procurator fiscal for embezzling funds.[80] In the *wilaya* of Tamanrasset the *wali* returned home on an extensive period of 'sick leave'. On his return, the 'locals' remarked on how well he was now performing! (see Postscript, below)

The demonstrations that greeted the President were particularly significant in that they were a concrete expression of the new sense of regionalism that has swept both *wilayat* in the last two or three years. The chant to the President also conveyed what must have been a worrying message for him, in that the people made it quite clear that they did not need to be part of Algeria and saw a beckoning home further south. The challenge was stated firmly and clearly: if the north wants the south to remain part of Algeria, then it must listen to its demands.

Attractions across the Southern Borders

The most worrying aspect of this new regionalism for the government is not that it is an expression of the division between the country's north and south, but that the people of the south may begin to look southwards – across the borders – for their political and economic future.

Four factors lie behind this southwards reorientation:

1. Increased ties with the peoples of Mali and Niger, especially amongst the Tuareg, following revolts in both Niger and Mali in the 1980s and early 1990s. Although most Malian refugees have since returned home, their

presence in Ahaggar strengthened the bonds between Algerian and Malian Tuareg enormously. Malian Tuareg now say that as their 'brothers' in Ahaggar helped them in their time of need, so too will Kel Ahaggar find a welcome in Mali.[81]

2. The peoples of Ahaggar, especially the Tuareg, perceive *les gens du nord* as being disrespectful of the peoples of Ahaggar and Ajjer, and their cultures. This disrespect is reflected in their general designation of all 'southerners' as Sahraouis or more disparagingly as Hadj Bettus. Northerners are perceived as being uninterested in learning about the region and its peoples; as viewing the local economy opportunistically, especially its tourism industry; and as having no concern for either the region's sustainable development or environmental conservation. At a political level this disrespect is perceived as being manifested in the lack of consultation in local/regional policy- and decision-making, and in the appointment of unsuitable administrators from the north. While this perception is widely articulated in Tamanrasset, it is no longer found so extensively in the *wilaya* of Illizi. Since the dismissal of Ouba, a new *wali* of the highest calibre has replaced him. The new *wali* soon earned the respect and support of local people. The fear is now being expressed that he will be moved to a more important posting elsewhere.

3. The perception amongst local people that the north is afraid that the economic development of the south will lead to the south developing a sense of independence from the north. For example, people of the south believe that the north is jealous of their ability to develop a tourism industry (when there is no possibility of such development in the north), and of the fact that some of the latest oil and gas developments are in the *wilayat* of Tamanrasset and Illizi.[82]

4. The north's fear that the south's increased sense of economic development and economic autonomy will be fuelled by the current bandying of the politically charged concept of *Le Grand Sud*. Technically, the term *Grand Sud* refers to Algeria's four *wilayat* of Tamanrasset, Illizi, Adrar and Tindouf. Politically, however, the term carries far more dangerous connotations, being associated with the idea of some sort of independent political entity in the Sahara. Whether this entity is limited to southern Algeria or is more pan-Saharan, embracing adjoining territories of neighbouring states, remains part of its phantasmal quality.

The notion of *Le Grand Sud* has been given more relevance in the last few years by Mokhtar ben Mokhtar's avowed claim to be fighting for its 'Liberation'. He states that his 'war' is against the Algerian state, not its peoples, and that as a 'man of the Sahara' himself,[83] his professed ideology, written boldly across the windscreen of his main 'command' vehicle, and fast entering into local folklore, is: *LA LIBERATION DU GRAND SUD*. Given his operational bases in Niger and Mali, and his affinal relations in Mauritania, the notion of *Le Grand Sud* is beginning to take on a connotation similar to the idea of a single Tuareg political entity being carved out of the three or four Saharan countries in which the Tuareg live. Given the new southwards perspective of the people of Ahaggar and Ajjer, and their closer ties with the people (mostly Tuareg) of Niger and Mali, the ideology of *Le Grand Sud* could easily take on a popular and, for the Algerian government, dangerous appeal.

Another factor which should not be discounted entirely is the contribution of Libya's Mohammed Qadhafi to the potential destabilisation of Algeria's southern border regions.[84] Only a few thousand Tuareg actually live in Libya (in the extreme south-west of the country), but Qadhafi has long promoted the idea of some sort of Tuareg political entity or Libyan satellite state encompassing the traditional Tuareg regions of Libya, Algeria, Niger and Mali. It has recently been reported that he has once again been sending 'humanitarian' aid to Tuareg groups in Niger and Mali.

These factors have all contributed to the emergence of a broadly regional identity in Algeria's extreme south, the political relevancy of which has superseded the more traditional and historically oriented ethnic identities and the old Tuareg–Arab/Algerian cleavage. In this political reorientation, the notion of 'the south' and 'people of the desert' could well find expression in the inflammatory notion of *Le Grand Sud*.

Conclusion: The Question of 'Indigenous Rights'[85]

Algeria cannot take the continued political stability of its extreme south for granted. Any one of a number of issues, not all of which are directly within the government's control, could lead to its political destabilisation. The most likely of these, however, is one that I have mentioned only cursorily. It is the UN's 'Draft Declaration on the Rights of Indigenous Peoples', which is due for ratification before the end of 2004. The Algerian government would therefore be wise to take immediate action on issues over which it does have direct control, before people in the south become aware of the human and environmental rights that will be conferred on them by the Declaration. In particular, it would be wise to implement a long-term plan for the sustainable economic development of the region, in which primacy is given to the redevelopment of the tourism industry within the framework of a much more rigorous environmental conservation policy. It would also be prudent to ensure greater representation of local people in matters relating to policy development and administrative appointments in the region, especially within the fields of tourism, the administration of the Parks and the incorporation of environmental concerns within the development and implementation of far-reaching sustainable development policies. As for the question of the UN's Draft Declaration on Indigenous Rights, Algeria's more socialist policies, compared to Niger and Mali, already meet many of the main requirements of the Declaration. However, if the issues touched on in this essay are left to fester for much longer, the Declaration might well prove to be the catalyst for political unrest throughout the potentially inflammable area of *Le Grand Sud*.[86]

Postscript

This article was written at the beginning of 2002. Since then a number of crucial developments have taken place in regard to the 'internal' issues identified in this article, notably: (1) the lack of both government strategic planning and consultation with local people in regard to long-term regional economic development, especially the region's tourism industry; and (2) the imposition of government policies and administrators without consultation with the local people. Between September 2002 and July–August 2003 a number of crucial events, including the disappearance (taken 'hostage') of 32 European tourists, occurred within these two broad areas that are likely to have a significant impact on the immediate political and economic development of Algeria's extreme south. These events are described and analysed in a further article in this volume, 'Contested Terrain: Tourism, Environment and Security in Algeria's Extreme South'.[87]

NOTES

I would like to acknowledge the Economic and Social Research Council (ESRC) and the Leverhulme Trust for their most generous support.

1. In the Tuareg language of Tamahak the word *tassili* means plateau. The Tassili ranges form an encirclement of uplifted sandstone scarps and plateaux around the crystalline massif of Ahaggar.
2. *Kel* means 'people of' in Tamahak.
3. Although the northern borders of both *wilayat* extend a little further north than the geographical limits of Ahaggar and Tassili-n-Ajjer, their more northern parts, notably In Salah, fell within the Tuareg's pre-colonial spheres of influence. The Tuareg were conquered by the French in 1902.
4. The source of this language survey is not clear, being posted on the Internet. However, it is close to my own estimate, which puts their number at a likely maximum of 30,000.
5. J. Keenan, *The Tuareg: People of Ahaggar* (London: Allen Lane 1977) p.355.
6. At Algerian independence, the Kel Ahaggar numbered about 5,000 and the Kel Ajjer somewhat less, ibid.
7. In addition to the nomadic Tuareg a few more, no more than a few hundred, would have been

counted as sedentarists. The Algerian census of 1966 put the population of the *arondissement* of Tamanrasset (Ahaggar) at 16,124, ibid. pp.355–61.
8. These figures must be regarded as approximate. The 1998 census of the *wilaya* of Tamanrasset gave a total population of about 210,000. However, the census was undertaken in August when many people are on holiday in the north. It also excludes military personnel. The Tamanrasset *wilaya* includes In Salah, whose population of about 50,000 should be subtracted to give an approximate population for the region of Ahaggar.
9. See J. Keenan, 'From Tit (1902) to Tahilahi (2002): A Reconsideration of the Impact of and Resistance to French Pacification and Colonial Rule by the Tuareg of Algeria (the Northern Tuareg)', in this volume, pp.27–66.
10. Political unrest and open revolt by the Tuareg has been a feature of both Niger and Mali during much of the 1980s and 1990s.
11. I have argued elsewhere (note 9), that France's attempts to 'preserve' Tuareg society and govern through the Tuareg led to a quite anachronistic situation. Elements of Tuareg society that might otherwise have evolved in their own way were cut short and preserved like a 'museum society' in aspic, while others were changed significantly.
12. One of Algeria's more surprising statistics is that the nation's capital is nearer to London than it is to its southernmost border.
13. The difficulty was compounded by the fact that France retained an element of control for a few more years over parts of Algeria's Saharan territory as a result of her oil interests and her continued presence at their atomic test bases at In Eker and Reganne.
14. Twenty kilometres north of Tamanrasset.
15. The only injury to the Tuareg seems to have been to a sixth, who refused to join the affray and was shot accidentally in the foot!
16. This incident, its background and consequences are discussed in detail elsewhere, Keenan (note 5) p.206f.
17. French colonial rule is deemed to have run for 60 years, from the defeat of the Tuareg at the battle of Tit (40km north of Tamanrasset) in 1902 until Independence in 1962.
18. The historical origin of the 'noble–vassal' division is dealt with elsewhere, Keenan (note 5) pp.13, 52; and idem (note 9).
19. Kel Ulli outnumbered Ihaggaren by about 8 to 1.
20. There is substantial evidence to suggest that, by the time of the French military conquest and pacification at the beginning of the twentieth century, vassals were beginning to reject many of the burdensome demands nobles made on them, and that Ahaggar may have been on the verge of a social revolution. See Keenan (note 9).
21. The Kel Ahaggar's system of descent is discussed in detail in J. Keenan, 'The End of the Matriline? The Changing Roles of Women and Descent amongst the Algerian Tuareg', in this volume, pp.121–62.
22. This complex and involved relationship, known as *temazlayt*, is discussed in depth in J. Keenan, 'Some theoretical considerations on the *temazlayt* relationship', *Revue de l'Occident Musulman et de la Méditerranée* 21/1 (1976) pp.33–46; and Keenan (note 5).
23. Some *ineslemen* were of vassal status while others were considered more noble.
24. For a detailed account of the position and condition of slaves in Ahaggar, see Keenan (note 5) pp.95–100.
25. Some *tawsatin* owned very few slaves.
26. There had been no cultivation in Ahaggar before that date, although some diffident cultivation had been attempted near Ideles about 20 years earlier.
27. Keenan (note 5) p.355.
28. Claude Blanguernon, *Le Hoggar* (Paris: Arthaud 1955) p.59, writing in the 1950s, stated that in Ahaggar they numbered only 17 men, 20 women and 40 children, with about ten slaves. Their origin, like that of most groups in Tuareg society is obscure, but according to most traditions they are of Jewish origin.
29. The first shops were established at Tarhaouhaout (Fort Motylinski) in 1916–17. By 1929 six had been established at Tamanrasset, Keenan (note 5) p.341.

Political Stability in Algeria's Grand Sud

30. By this time, the Kel Ahaggar, numbering around 5–5,500, had become a minority in their own region.
31. It should be noted that terms such as *amacheg* and *amajeg*, which are used by certain southern Tuareg and which are regarded as being homologous to *imuhagh*, have slightly different restricted and broader meanings, Keenan (note 5) p.104f.
32. Notably H. Duveyrier, *Les Touaregs du Nord* (Paris: Challamel 1864); C. de Foucauld, *Dictionnaire Touareg–Française, dialecte de l'Ahaggar*, 4 vols. (Paris: Imprimerie nationale de France 1951–52); M. Benhazera, *Six Mois chez les Touareg du Ahaggar* (Alger: Jourdan 1908); and K.G. Prasse, 'L'Origine du mot Amazig', *Acta Orientalia* XXIII/3–4 (1959) pp.197–200. However, Prasse, *Manuel de grammaire touarègue (tahaggart)*, 3 vols. (Copenhagen: Editions de l'Université de Copenhague/Akademisk Forlag 1972–74) later rejected this meaning.
33. Cultivation did not become a significant component of the Kel Ahaggar's economy until after French pacification, while the first salt caravan was not until 1896, and then only in response to the pressure of French encroachment to the north of Ahaggar. Salt caravans to Niger did not become a regular annual event until the 1920s.
34. In Eker is 100 miles north of Tamanrasset. Construction of the atomic test site began in 1956–57.
35. A condition of the Evian agreements was that France would retain rights over In Eker for a number of years after Independence.
36. For details, see Keenan (note 5) pp.230–1.
37. In 1964 there was an average of 1,100 workers on the base at any one time. As most were employed on a monthly shift basis, this represented a workforce of 2–3,000. The total wage bill was approximately £15,000 per month, with most labourers receiving about £20–£25 a month. The labour exchange in Tamanrasset estimated that Kel Ahaggar comprised 80 per cent of the In Eker labour force. This figure is almost certainly too high as it probably refers to the percentage of the labour force that did not come from Tamanrasset and includes sedentarists (Kel Aghrem) from the many outlying villages and cultivation centres.
38. Twenty such co-operatives were established in Ahaggar between 1966 and 1969.
39. At the time, I was aware of the presence in Tamanrasset of *agents provocateurs*, but am inclined to think that their actions were directed more towards ex-patriots and visiting foreigners such as myself, rather than the Tuareg population.
40. After independence the ALN was renamed the *Armée Nationale Populaire* (ANP).
41. Many Kel Ahaggar began to look for political leadership towards the *Amenukal*'s half brother, Hadj Moussa. But his position was equally ambiguous and compromised.
42. Many Kel Rela had already settled in Tamanrasset before Algerian independence, having latched themselves on to the French administration as a means of preserving their more elevated status.
43. They used the word *tiwse*, the Tamahak word for tribute, and the French word *impôt*!
44. A further bonus was that the government lifted the embargo on caravans in 1969, although by then the traditional salt–millet trade had almost entirely been replaced by mechanised, commercial enterprises.
45. This was manifested in their attempts to reaffirm and validate their socio-cultural values and traditionally orientated definition of social reality by their regrouping and encapsulating themselves as a 'sub-society' within the wider sedentary community. In some instances, such as the settlements of Tagmart and Terhenanet, whole descent groups settled in homogenous communities. More often, the nomads tended to form their own little residential and social nuclei or 'quarters' within villages, with their social and economic ties ranging outwards to the surrounding camps of their descent group sections rather than inwards to the village community itself. In many centres, where cultivable land formed little basins and terraces along several miles of an *oued*, a chain of tiny settlement clusters became interspersed over several kilometres of the *oued*. This is typical of many villages, such as Hirafok (Dag Rali), Mertoutek (Ait Lowayan), Tahifet, In Dalag and Tarhaouhaout (Aguh-en-tehle) and many others. The quality of the gardens can be a good indication of whether such clusters are occupied by Tuareg or ex-slaves and *harratin*!

46. The process of sedentarisation varied enormously between descent groups, depending on such factors as local pastoral conditions, access to alternative resources, the nature of relations with former nobility now living in Tamanrasset, and above all the nature of social relations with ex-slaves and *harratin* in agricultural centres in their region. Where the emancipation of slaves and the abolition of the *métayage* system had given risen to conflict, as for example around Abalessa and at Otoul, Tuareg tended to keep away from such areas. Where such relations were better, a whole range of economic co-operation began to develop between the nomadic and sedentary communities and families. For example, there were many instances of nomadic Tuareg and former *harratin* co-operating in running clandestine caravans, no longer trading salt for millet but *harratin*-grown wheat for sheep and goats from nomads in Niger and using the Tuareg's camels. At a local level, Tuareg nomads might look after or more usually exchange livestock in exchange for garden products. Occasionally, former slaves and *harratin* might work with a Tuareg in developing and maintaining a garden. Almost every conceivable form of economic co-operation began to develop between the nomadic and sedentary milieus.
47. This was Bay ag Akhemouk, who had been appointed *Amenukal* in 1950.
48. In practice, Bay's younger half-brother, Hadj Moussa, became the effective political representative of the Kel Ahaggar, not because of his relationship to the former *Amenukal*, but through his position as an elected Deputy of the *wilaya* of Tamanrasset, which was created in 1974. Hadj Moussa was not *agg ettebel*, meaning that he did not belong to the descent line that would have permitted him to accede to the title of *Amenukal*.
49. The impact of this change in nomenclature is discussed in more detail in Keenan (note 21).
50. The Tassili-n-Ajjer National Park was designated by UNESCO as a World Heritage Site in 1984.
51. Kel Ahaggar were employed as guides, cameleers, drivers, cooks and so on.
52. Some 80 'guardians' were employed officially by the Tassili Park, while many more were employed within the tourism industry. In September 2000, the Ahaggar National Park employed 550 people, mostly Kel Ahaggar.
53. This included the region of Tidikelt.
54. The elections were won by the FIS and would have brought to power the world's first elected Islamist government. The army's annulment of the elections led to the outbreak of militant and terrorist activity by certain Islamist groups. The spiral of violence that took hold of the country in the ensuing years has seen an estimated 100,000 people killed.
55. Hadj Bettu is apparently of local origin and of mixed descent.
56. The expression 'doing a Bettu' entered the colloquial language at this time. It means suddenly coming across or making a large amount of money by 'uncertain' means!
57. This led to protests from the Niger government.
58. He was released from gaol in 2002.
59. The population had already increased tenfold, from around 4,000, in the preceding 20 years.
60. As the 1998 census was taken in August, when many people are away on holiday, and also excludes the military, the real population of Tamanrasset can now almost certainly be estimated as being in excess of 100,000.
61. For a detailed discussion of the state of nomadism in Ahaggar and Ajjer at this time, see J. Keenan, 'The Last Nomads: Nomadism amongst the Tuareg of Ahaggar (Algerian Sahara)', in this volume, pp.163–92.
62. During the month of Ramadan in 1999, I visited many remote and predominantly Tuareg communities, both nomadic and settled, amongst whom the observance of the fast was almost total, whereas only three years ago, so my informants told me, it was largely disregarded. For social implications of Islamisation, see Keenan (note 21).
63. This is not to suggest that Islamic fundamentalism has found fertile ground in the region. On the contrary, most Kel Ahaggar blame Islamic fundamentalists for the collapse of 'their' tourist market and have been supportive of the government and army in their fight against 'terrorists'. It is also interesting to note that several amongst the more educated and 'wordly-wise' Kel Ahaggar now refer to the increasing strands of 'Islamo-fascism' in government.

64. Although the government has at various times paid lip-service to the development of a tourism industry, it has never made more than the most half-hearted efforts to encourage such development, and has frequently obstructed initiatives in that direction.
65. For example, the *chef de poste* at Mertoutek, which is typical of the Park as a whole, recorded not a single tourist between the end of 1993 and December 1999! A few Kel Ahaggar have refused to accept such 'employment' on the grounds that it is demeaning.
66. The average monthly wage, according to my estimates, is around DA 7,000 (*c*.£70). Further government assistance to nomads has taken the form of issuing all nomadic families with a large tent, while the local administration has on occasion given small amounts of assistance, such as when some 250 camels were killed by falling on ice in the high mountains of Atakor. See Keenan (note 61).
67. The main international brand is Philip Morris, whose products, notably Marlboro cigarettes, are trans-shipped through Niger and Mali, then into Algeria and the North African market, with many being 'smuggled' on into Europe.
68. Hassan Hattab who, along with Mokhtar ben Mokhtar, claims to deplore gratuitous violence (their actions are directed against the 'state', not the 'people') has subsequently broken from the GIA to form the *Groupe salafiste pour la prédication et le combat* (GSPC). Among its many attacks on the 'state', Hassan Hattab's GSPC was held responsible for the attack on a military convoy at Teniet El-Abed, in the Aures mountains south of Batna on 4 January 2003, which killed 43 and wounded 19 soldiers. According to official Algiers sources, the GSPC is affiliated to *al-Qaeda*.
69. This problem is explored in more depth elsewhere in J. Keenan, 'Contested Terrain: Tourism, Environment and Security in Algeria's Extreme South', and 'Introduction: Indigenous Rights and a Future Politic amongst Algeria's Tuareg after Forty Years of Independence', both in this volume, pp.226–65 and 1–26 respectively.
70. The many questions surrounding tourism development in the region are examined in Keenan, 'Contested Terrain' (note 69). For further details of the problems associated with tourism development in the Central Sahara, see J. Keenan, 'Tourism, development and conservation: A Saharan perspective', Proceedings of the Conference on Natural Resources and Cultural Heritage of the Libyan Desert, Tripoli, Libya, 14–21 Dec. 2002, *Libyan Studies* 34 (2003, in press); J. Keenan, 'The Development or Re-development of Tourism in Algeria', in Mohamed Saad (ed.), *Transition and Development: The Algerian Experience* (2002). For a more descriptive account of tourism in the region and associated environmental damage, see J. Keenan, *Sahara Man: Travelling with the Tuareg* (London: John Murray 2001).
71. See J. Keenan, 'The Sahara's Indigenous People, the Tuareg, Fear Environmental Catastrophe', *Indigenous Affairs* 1 (2002) pp.50–57.
72. This phenomenon is much more characteristic of Tamanrasset than Djanet which, with its population of some 12–13,000 (estimated), is not only much smaller but has a far smaller percentage of *gens du nord* in its population.
73. Masc. sing. *chinoui*; masc. pl. *chnaoui*; fem. sing. *chinouia* or *chinouiette*; fem. pl. *chnaouia* or *chnaouiat (ettes)*.
74. It is for this reason that foreign visitors to the region find themselves meeting so many Tuareg!
75. The terms Kel Ahaggar and *imuhagh* are both too exclusive in that they refer to Tuareg of Ahaggar and Tamahak speakers respectively.
76. With people from the outside they would adapt their denomination in order to make themselves understood – i.e. they would use terms that describe their regional identity.
77. This does not mean that Tuareg are not represented in the Algerian political order. On the contrary, it could be argued that they are probably 'over-represented' in terms of the number of both deputies and senators and members of the local *wilaya* assemblies who are of Tuareg origin. However, this representation is as elected/appointed representatives of political parties and not specifically as representatives of the Tuareg 'ethnic community'. Amongst the Kel Ahaggar, Hadj Moussa, a former Deputy and the half-brother of the former *Amenukal*, Bay ag Akhemouk, who is himself without *ettebel* (traditional right of political

succession), has for a long time been regarded by both the Tuareg and the government as the effective 'spokesman' and 'representative' of the local Tuareg. Indeed, most Tuareg believe that the government will not readily contravene Hadj Moussa. However, Hadj Moussa is currently 85 years old and Tuareg do not know who, if anyone, will take up his role on his death. Hitherto, he has played a major role in resolving conflicts between Tuareg and the government, at both 'group' and individual levels. His death could conceivably leave a dangerous vacuum in local politics.

78. I was in the region twice during the summer of 2001 and neither saw nor heard of any unrest that was associated with the Berber unrest in other parts of the country.
79. The President had been sent a similar letter the previous year in the name of the citizens of Tamanrasset, complaining about the actions of the new *wali* and saying that they could not be held responsible for might happen in the region if the government continued to foist dissatisfactory administrators upon them. Extracts of the letter were printed at regular intervals in the national press.
80. One local mayor had actually refused to hand over funds to the *wali* because he was aware of the embezzlement.
81. Several Kel Ahaggar have indeed gone to Mali to find work, mostly in the tourism industry, following the effective collapse of tourism in Ahaggar as a result of Algeria's security situation.
82. These are the two new BP projects at In Salah and In Amenas. Although In Amenas is not in the Illizi *wilaya*, BP's office is in Illizi.
83. Mokhtar ben Mokhtar is a Metlilli Chaamba.
84. Qadhafi's relationship with or support for Mokhtar ben Mokhtar and other bandits operating in the region is not clear, although it is widely believed that Libya has been and perhaps still is involved in the arms traffic.
85. The question of the Tuareg's indigenous rights is discussed in detail in Keenan, 'Introduction' (note 69).
86. The Declaration will give indigenous peoples collective rights, territorial rights and, above all, rights of self determination. Many countries, including France and most other EU members, the United States, Brazil and Australia are not keen that indigenous peoples acquire rights of self-determination. They are therefore obstructing the ratification process. As France has no indigenous peoples, one can only suppose that her obstruction of the Declaration is on behalf of her former colonies. In the case of the Tuareg, these are Algeria, Niger and Mali. For more details, see Keenan, 'Introduction' (note 69).
87. These issues are also discussed in the concluding remarks of Keenan, 'Introduction' (note 69).

Dressing for the Occasion: Changes in the Symbolic Meanings of the Tuareg Veil

An analysis of the substantial body of literature that has been written on the Tuareg, including that by Arabic writers in pre-colonial times, would probably reveal that the most commented upon custom of the Tuareg is the veiling (*anagad*) of their men.[1] Reference to the wearing of the veil by Tuareg men can be traced back to the writings of several early Arabic authors such as El Bekri (1028–94)[2] and Ibn Batutah,[3] whose journeys in the fourteenth century certainly took him into Tuareg country. If that turned out to be the case, it would not be surprising, as the veiling of Tuareg men is not only an ancient custom but has probably always been the most dominant symbol of 'Tuaregness'.

Until recently, the veil was worn by all Tuareg men from puberty throughout their adult lives. An adolescent boy's (*elmengoudi*) first wearing of the veil was a family ceremonial occasion marking his initiation or 'passage' from adolescence to adulthood. Throughout his adult life a man would rarely be unveiled, either when travelling alone, when asleep, when eating or with other people. Women, by contrast, do not wear a veil, but a headcloth (*ekerhei*) which is also taken at puberty, but which is quite different to the man's veil. It is black, much shorter, and is not wrapped around the head, but partially draped over it without concealing the face.

Not surprisingly, the French commented extensively on veiling amongst the Tuareg, writing much on the possible functions and meanings of the veil and why its use was restricted to men, for it was this practice, perhaps more than their many other distinctive characteristics, notably their alleged 'matrilineality',[4] which set the Tuareg so distinctly apart from surrounding Arab peoples.

When I first visited the Kel Ahaggar in 1964, less than two years after the end of colonial rule, the veil was worn almost universally by Tuareg men, who could easily be distinguished from other men, even at a distance, by the mere fact that they were veiled. During the years that I lived and worked amongst them, between 1964 and 1972, it was not often that I saw a Tuareg man unveiled. However, those were turbulent years for the Tuareg of Algeria. Confronted by the demands of a newly independent Algerian state, their society experienced severe shocks and underwent significant changes. A complex array of political, economic, ecological and social forces threatened their predominantly nomadic pastoralist lifestyle, obliging increasing numbers of them to turn towards a more sedentary way of life, with several of them even settling in the main administrative town of Tamanrasset. At the end of that period, around 1971, I wrote a paper on the Tuareg veil, in which I concluded, with reference to these changes, that 'the acceleration of this process, and the consequent de-pluralisation of Ahaggar society may lead to further considerable changes in both the traditional belief systems and social structure of Tuareg society, *with the possible disappearance of the veil in its traditional form and meaning*' (emphasis added).[5]

On returning to Ahaggar in 1999 for the first time since 1972, more than a generation later, the first things that struck me on arriving in Tamanrasset (apart from the growth of the town from some 4,000 to 100,000 inhabitants) was that I could not immediately see any Tuareg. That was not because they had disappeared. Rather, it was because I had been accustomed to looking for veiled faces, and the veil is now worn comparatively infrequently by Algerian Tuareg (Kel Ahaggar and Kel Ajjer)! As I had foreseen, the veil had indeed disappeared amongst the Algerian Tuareg in much of its traditional form and, as I shall explain, in most of its traditional meaning. Nevertheless, it soon became apparent that although the veil is now worn much less frequently by Algerian Tuareg, it is still a dominant symbol of 'Tuaregness'. As in the past, the Tuareg still sometimes refer to themselves as Kel Tagelmoust (people of the veil). This distinctiveness is also still widely recognised by Arabs, amongst whom the Arabic counterpart, El Molathemine or Ahl el Litham (wearers of the veil), may occasionally be heard in common parlance,[6] although most Algerians, especially those who have moved into the Sahara from the north of the country in recent years, are today more likely to refer to Tuareg, especially if they are wearing a *chech* (veil) and *gandoura*, as Targuis or Hadj Bettus.[7] Both terms refer implicitly to the Tuareg custom of veiling, although both, especially the latter, are considered by Tuareg to convey a sense of derision.[8]

Since returning to the Tuareg in 1999, I have had the opportunity to travel widely amongst them, both in Algeria, Libya and the countries of the Sahel. Across this extensive geographical area, one finds Tuareg communities, families and individuals ranged across the whole spectrum of modernity–traditionalism. Within the same extended kin network one can converse with commercial pilots, government ministers,[9] businessmen who 'summer' in European capital cities, and nomadic pastoralists still moving their herds in search of pasture. Such is the complexity of modern-day Tuareg society. But, like a sensitive weather-vein, there is no greater tell-tale indicator of 'modernity' and 'traditionalism', and the values and beliefs that they entail, than individuals' general deportment of the veil.

In this article, I consider the range of symbolic meanings that have been attached to the veil over this critical period of time, that is from traditional pre-colonial times, through the colonial period, to the present – a period of almost exactly one hundred years, or much longer if we include the entire pre-colonial era. I focus on the veil's multivocality in various systems of ideas and beliefs, and the levels of meaning in each of those systems which have invested it at various times with both affective and cognitive functions. It is only through an appreciation of the changes that have taken place in these various levels of meaning, especially over the last generation, that we can make sense of the considerable range of deportment of the veil that is now found across various Tuareg groups, ranging from its near disappearance from the streets of Tamanrasset to what might seem its almost exaggerated usage amongst many Tuareg communities in Niger and Mali.

However, before embarking on this analysis, it is useful to provide both a summary description of the veil and its physical properties, as well as a brief account of the many interpretations that have been ascribed to its functional properties and symbolic meanings by both European and Arabic writers, as well as the Tuareg themselves, over the last century or so.

The Physical Properties of the Veil

The traditional veil (*tagelmoust* or *alechcho*) is a piece of Sudanese indigo-dyed cotton, 1.50–4.0m long and 0.25–0.50m wide and made of individual strips of cotton sewn together.[10] The cloth is wrapped around the head to form a low turban (*amaoual-oua-n-afella*), with one fold being brought across the face to form the veil (*amaoual-oua-n-aris*), so that the top of the veil usually rests on the bridge of the nose, and the bottom (*agedellehouf*) falls across the face to the upper part of the chest. The turban covers the forehead so that when the veil is at its highest there is only a narrow slit around the eyes. At its lowest the veil may fall below the mouth, thus exposing the entire face. The position of the veil varies between these two extremes.

The term *tagelmoust* or *alechcho* is reserved for this Sudanese indigo-dyed cloth made of individual strips, and is not used for the industrially manufactured fabrics, notably muslin, which have been promoted increasingly by the presence and activity of Arab merchants since about 1920, with the consequent introduction into the vocabulary of Arabic terms such as *echchach* and *khent* alongside such Berber words as *alechcho*, *tekerheit* and so on, which relate to the traditional artisan level of production. The ascendancy of Arabic influence in the vocabulary thus reflects the transition to another level of technology.[11] A further type of veil is that known as *khent*, which is a manufactured indigo-coloured cloth, intermediate in both cost and quality between the *alechcho* and the *echchach*. Today, the *tagelmoust* is rarely seen. It is worn almost exclusively on ceremonial and festive occasions, and then predominantly by the 'noble' class. More frequently worn, even at ceremonial and festive occasions, is the *khent*. Although the *khent* may be worn for everyday use, such usage is now uncommon in Algeria. The most common type of veil now worn by all Algerian Tuareg (Kel Ahaggar and Kel Ajjer), particularly for general day-to-day use is the *echchach*. When I lived amongst the Kel Ahaggar in the 1960s and 1970s, the *echchach* was almost exclusively white, black or dark blue (not indigo) in colour. It is made of manufactured muslin, is much cheaper and readily available in many of the shops of Tamanrasset and elsewhere. Today, the *echchach* – made of material imported almost exclusively from China – may be of an almost infinite variety of colours, with pastel ranges (lilac, yellow,[12] olive green, pink and so on) being currently especially common. Bright, bold colours, such as 'fire-engine' red, are also not uncommon, especially among young men.

Although veiling is an ancient custom, there is an element of uncertainty in the literature with regard to both the colours and the material of the veil prior to the earlier part of the twentieth century. Marceau Gast states that the famous indigo veil only became widespread among the Kel Ahaggar quite recently; until 1920, most of them still wore the *tekerheit*, a white woollen veil with coloured bands that came from Tripoli.[13] Foucauld, writing during the second decade of the twentieth century, states: *'les étoffes employées pour cet usage (le voilement) sont toujours très minces, habituellement de coleur indigo, quelquefois blanches, et très rarement noirs'*.[14] Benhazera, writing a decade earlier, is not particularly illuminating on this matter, stating that the veil consists of a single strip of deep blue or black cotton fabric.[15] He does mention, however, that black material (*kehal*) used for veils was brought from Damergou and Aïr, and that both blue and white cotton material, and the white muslin *chech* were brought from Tidikelt and Tuat.[16] Sudanese indigo cotton has been known in Aïr since ancient times,[17] and it is not easy to understand why it does not seem to have become widespread in Ahaggar, as Gast suggests, until fairly recently. It may be that the caravan trade between Ahaggar and Damergou, which only became a regular annual event from the 1920s onwards, opened up and maintained a more regular trade between Ahaggar and the south.[18] As for the Kel Ajjer, we know from the writing of Henri Duveyrier, who travelled amongst the Kel Ajjer in the mid-nineteenth century, that black and white cotton veils seem to have been prevalent amongst them at that time, for he made a distinction between the use of the black and white veils and skin colour, saying that the true Tuareg (nobles in particular) preferred the black cotton veil, while men of 'inferior race' (with Negroid blood) usually wore the white cotton veil.[19] If that was true in Duveyrier's time it certainly was not so a century later when veils of both colours were worn by all classes alike. It is also interesting to note that Francis Rodd, writing in 1926 with reference to certain districts in Aïr, made the same distinction between the wearing of dark indigo or black veils by the nobles and white veils by servile tribes.[20] We can therefore conclude, a little cautiously, that there may have been some sort of distinction in veil colour between the classes in earlier times, and also that the indigo veil was probably worn predominantly by the noble class.

Interpretations and Explanations of the Veil

In spite of numerous hypotheses, several of which have a romantic appeal, the origin of the Tuareg veil remains obscure and conjectural. So, too, did the function of the veil long perplex those who had contact with the Tuareg. Over the years, many unsatisfactory arguments and explanations were put forward as to the origin and function of the Tuareg veil, with little attention being given to its functional interpretation as a dominant symbol until Robert Murphy's seminal analysis of social interaction among the (southern) Tuareg in 1964.[21]

Duveyrier (1864), the first to write comprehensively about the Tuareg, saw the veil in terms of its hygienic functions; it protected the eyes from the sun and sand, and the mouth, nostrils and ears from dehydration.[22] Most other writers have rejected such an explanation, as it does not explain why Tuareg men remained veiled in their camps or when asleep, and why women are unveiled.

Among the more romantic explanations is the suggestion, made especially by Arabs, that the veil functioned to mask Tuareg raiders from their enemies. This explanation is equally unsatisfactory as recognition is afforded by numerous other features apart from the face. In this vein, one might mention the malevolent remarks made by certain Arabs that Tuareg veil their faces to hide their ugliness![23]

Most explanations, however, have touched upon the mouth in one way or another. Foucauld stated that it was shameful to be unveiled and thus expose the mouth,[24] while Gautier, in observing that evil spirits were believed to enter the body through the mouth, recognised some sort of taboo surrounding the mouth and considered that there was consequently a good psychological necessity for covering it.[25] This opinion was shared not only by Abdel Djalil,[26] but also by Henri Lhote, who considered that there was undoubtedly some sort of taboo surrounding the mouth that was associated with the veil. While emphasising that it was shameful to expose the mouth before women, he also pointed out that these associations were accentuated among the nobility, who, being conscious of their elevated status, regarded the taboo concerning the mouth to such a degree that they never discarded the veil before women, parents or other respected persons. Lhote thus saw the taboo as pertaining not only to women but also to all other respected persons such as father, mother, maternal aunts and uncles, older cousins and brothers, chiefs, marabouts and so on. Although he had little doubt that the veil and its origin were related to this taboo concerning the mouth, he admitted that the inapplicability of veiling amongst women could not be explained.[27]

Bourgeot's conclusions expressed the same dilemma. He saw the veil as having a utilitarian function in protecting the head from the sun and preventing dehydration of the nasal passages and throat. He also mentioned the Tuareg's proneness to headaches and their response to these afflictions by raising the veil to its highest, thus giving them the impression of relieving the complaint by stopping its penetration. In this behaviour he saw an association with Gautier's remarks, but added that such functional explanations, even if correct, still did not explain why women and children went unveiled.[28]

Johannes Nicolaisen, who worked amongst the Tuareg in the 1950s and early 1960s, considered that both hygienic and magico-religious explanations, namely the belief that the veil gave protection against persons having an 'evil-eye' or 'evil-mouth' (*tehot* – Ahaggar; *tugarchet* – Aïr), were insufficient. Instead, he argued that the main function of the veil was social. He saw this as being manifested in the covering of the mouth, nose and brow when in the presence of foreigners (especially women) and parents-in-law (especially mothers-in-law).[29]

In spite of this prompt towards the 'social', explanations for variations in the style in which an individual might wear his veil still tended to be seen by many authors in terms of tribal variations.[30] Others, notably Lhote, considered that these variations, especially in regard to the changes that an individual might make to the position of his veil and therefore how much of his face was exposed, could be interpreted in terms of dominant traits (either permanent or temporary) within the individual's character. Lhote therefore saw the position of the veil more in terms of individual psychological characteristics rather than in terms of the social situation, as suggested by Nicolaisen. For example, he considered that a veil that was always worn in the same way and always in the correct position indicated a steady and serious character, while the full exposure of the forehead, through the turban being at its highest, was a general indication of a jovial character, and so on.[31]

Dressing for the Occasion

Social Interaction and the Veil

This sort of psychological explanation, associating the manner of deportment of the veil with individual character traits, has little or no validity. On the contrary, these variations in the style, position and arrangement of the veil are to be understood, as Robert Murphy[32] recognised, in terms of the symbolic significance of the veil with relation to communication in the social interaction process, and its association with certain magico-religious beliefs. Murphy saw the position and style of an individual's veil as being more a reflection or communication of his expected role-behaviour in a particular social situation. In other words, the 'self', 'character' or 'personality', or whatever Lhote means precisely by *'un trait dominant du caractère de l'individu'*,[33] is to some extent concealed, for, as Murphy recognised, the wearing of the veil by the Tuareg symbolically introduces a form of distance between their selves and their social others: 'the veil', as Murphy recognised, 'provides neither isolation nor anonymity, but bestows facelessness and the idiom of privacy upon the wearer, and allows him to stand somewhat aloof from the perils of social interaction, while remaining a part of it'.[34]

Among the Tuareg, men will frequently make slight readjustments, or merely the gesture of readjustment, to the position of their veils. These may occur while participating in conversation, as a person enters or leaves the group, at the approach of a particular person (perhaps unknown), or even as the subject or tone of the conversation changes. This dynamic aspect of the veil can only be understood, as Murphy recognised, through the concept of 'social distance' and an understanding of Tuareg kinship behaviour.

The display of social distance, as Radcliffe-Brown pointed out, may be pronounced in ambivalent or ambiguous relationships.[35] In such situations, when the outcome of the interaction is uncertain or unpredictable, because of some indeterminacy or involvement of contrary interests, the expression of distance or reserve in one form or another promotes a degree of autonomy and flexibility of action.[36]

A key feature of 'traditional' Tuareg society, and one that was still predominant in the 1960s, was the predominance of endogamy, both within social classes and within descent groups themselves.[37] The result of this practice was that members of a social group, especially the domestic camp, might be able to trace their relationships in multifarious and often contradictory ways: bonds of incorporation and solidarity within the social group were charged also with the antithesis of affinality and alliance.[38] Relationships within the social group may therefore be charged with ambivalence and ambiguity, with the result that social interaction may be a precarious affair. While this ambivalence was partially mediated by the restrictive use of classificatory kin terms and well-defined kinship behaviour, the necessary clear demarcation or segregation of roles was seen in the ritual behaviour attached to the veil.

In 1971–72, I wrote:

> The position of the veil signifies the degree of respect or deference that is expected of a particular social position. Between two actors, the one to whom respect is owed will usually wear his veil lower, so that generally speaking, the lower the veil, the greater the role status. The veil will, therefore, be worn relatively higher in the company of such persons as parents-in-law, senior kinsmen, and persons addressed as *Amrar* (such as section or tribal chiefs, old men, etc.), whether or not they are relatives. The veil thus symbolises the relative status and degree of respect that is expected of an individual in various role performances. Under certain circumstances, however, this pattern may be inverted, so that the highest status is symbolised by the veil at its highest, and vice versa. Situations in which this may arise are: when a person of high status, such as the *Amenukal* (supreme chief) or an important chief, wishes to underline or emphasise his role performance or, for example, when an Ihaggaren (noble) wishes to stress his higher class status before members of the Imrad or Isekkemaren.[39]

The veil is thus a symbolic manifestation of role status. However, in practice the situation is complicated, particularly at the level of kinship roles, by the ambivalence of so many relationships. Although marriage necessitates a definite reorganisation of the ties of relationship, adjustment to the new condition is by no means automatic or merely a matter of simple reclassification.[40] The opportunity of change in status allows selective adjustment on the basis of personal preference and degree of social significance. Amongst the Kel Ahaggar, the selection of new roles for more distant kin is relatively straightforward, but in the case of close kin, as for example the change from mother's brother to father-in-law, many circumstances have to be considered. It is in such ambivalent situations, when a degree of social distance is essential, that the veil functions symbolically to remove a portion of Ego's identity from the interaction situation and allows him to act in the presence of such conflicting interests and uncertainty.

Murphy distinguished two aspects of distance. First, the external dialogue maintaining the interaction situation, and second the internal dialogue of Ego maintaining Ego.[41] The first aspect, by cutting down the range of stimuli and creating a diffuseness of his behavioural stance, enables Ego to 'play it cool', while the second aspect, by symbolically removing part of his own identity from the interaction situation, is protecting the vulnerability of the self against penetration. Three interrelated functions of the veil are thus discernible: first,

Dressing for the Occasion

it signifies the relative status and degree of respect between role players; second, it acts as a mask by reducing the range of stimuli; and third, it affords protection to the self image by symbolic withdrawal of part of the actor's identity. The second and third functions are different categories of distance: the external dialogue is a manifestation of 'reserve', while the internal dialogue is a manifestation of 'privacy'. These two aspects of social distance, although analytically distinct, are fused in the interaction process.

'That the Tuareg withholds himself while communicating, and communicates through removal, is not a contradiction in terms, but a quality of interaction'.[42] What do the situational attitudes of the veil communicate? First, there is the possibility of role conflict; during the process of interaction the actor may take on a different role to which a different degree of respect and behaviour is expected. This may be signified unambiguously by a readjustment of the position of the veil *vis-à-vis* his social others. Second, the veil, apart from partially concealing the behavioural stance of an actor, is itself communicating the intent and disposition of the actor. The veil reduces the range of facial stimuli, but does not conceal the identity of the individual. By revealing only the immediate area around the eyes, all labial expression is concealed. Labial gestures, in contrast to ocular gestures, contain a greater element of unconscious or uncontrolled expression. Thus the veil not only protects the self-image by concealing most 'unconscious' gestures, but allows a universally perceptible form of communication which, by expressing or communicating such information as social position, status, respect, familiarity and so on, communicates in what way and through what channels certain information, such as feelings and emotions, may be expressed. In other words, Ego is taking his cues, not from the other's facial gestures, but primarily from his veil, and vice versa. The veil thus becomes an object of orientational significance in the interaction process. It symbolises social values, not only by expressing what type of behaviour is expected between actors, but also by symbolising what behavioural stance an actor is likely to adopt in a situation. As the interaction progresses, so each actor's behavioural stance will change, and be manifested in the changing attitudes of the veil (and/or other expressive gestures). Ego can thus largely evaluate the response to his own strategy by reference to the veils of others, which give him a measure by which he can formulate his expectations and evaluations of further alternative course of action.[43]

Other Uses and Beliefs Associated with the Veil

The social values that are symbolised by the veil in the interaction process are only part of the 'spectrum' of referents attached to the veil. They do not explain why the veil is worn by men only, or why – at least until recently – it was worn when alone, or when sleeping. It is necessary, therefore, to look at other uses and beliefs associated with the veil.

It is not so much the actual movement or change in position of the veil that symbolises social values, but rather its movement in relation to the mouth. Thus, if we can understand the implications of meaning and beliefs that surround the mouth, then we may be able to perceive the whole range of meanings that are invested in the veil.

Most writers on the Tuareg have commented on the fact that Tuareg say that it is shameful to expose the mouth. That was certainly true in the 1960s, although today, as I shall explain presently, such a view is no longer so widely held. Even so, Tuareg today are still familiar with their traditional saying that 'the veil and trousers are brothers'. The relationship between the two garments is that both cover external orifices: the trousers the genital region and anus, and the veil the mouth. These orifices were (and to some extent still are) considered as zones of pollution, and it was therefore deemed extremely disrespectful and shameful to expose them before others. Nevertheless, even in traditional times, the mouth was exposed occasionally, as, for instance, in the case of persons of very high status who might allow the veil to fall below the mouth, and also in the case of persons of lowest status. Only in the case of a Hadj could the veil be divested entirely, although in his case it was not his secular status, but his sacredness, that exempted him from shame. What were the beliefs that invested the veil with its sacred meaning?

By the end of the colonial period in 1962, many Tuareg, possibly the majority, still believed that many internal illnesses were caused by the Kel Asouf (*djenoun* – wicked spirits) and that the veil protected against their entry into the body. A similar notion related to the belief in *tehot*, the 'evil eye' or 'evil mouth'. *Tehot* is the fear of laudatory words that express desire or envy. This belief still makes a strong impression on the daily lives of Kel Ahaggar (and other Tuareg groups), so much so that great prudence is shown in praises that are addressed to the animals, family or possessions of others. One is also equally inclined to be modest in speaking of one's own actions, for the force of *tehot* is still believed by many Tuareg to harm men and even kill animals. While the main protection against *tehot* (and *ettama* or *tezama* – a related belief prominent in Aïr) is afforded by the wearing of Islamic amulets, some Tuareg suggested to me when I was with them in the 1960s that the veil also protects against *tehot*. Some supporting evidence for this might be found in Westermarck's writings on ritual and belief in Morocco.[44] However, the impression given to me by the Kel Ahaggar in the 1960s was that although many of them felt that the veil might afford protection against Kel Asouf entering the body, they were more reluctant to commit themselves regarding the significance of the veil in respect of *tehot*, leading me to conclude that this belief was probably more widely held among less esoteric or 'enlightened' members of Tuareg society.

This association between the veil and the Kel Asouf helps to explain why men remained veiled when alone in deserted places, for it is there that the Kel Tenere (people of the empty places) are to be found, and when asleep, for it is then that the Kel Had (people of the night) are active.

The reason why women are unveiled may be partially explained by their impurity and status in Islam, but more so, I would suggest, because the veil is attached more to the ritual of social relations than to the belief in the Kel Asouf. In traditional society, a woman was not a public figure in the same way as a man, and took no roles in the political arena. Similarly, it is surely because a boy has little or no social or political status that he does not wear the veil, rather than because the position of adulthood entails a greater susceptibility to attack from the Kel Asouf: on the contrary, it is recognised that babies and young children are most susceptible to the effects of the Kel Asouf.

Although the veil is associated with the beliefs in the Kel Asouf, it is not this association which invested the veil with its sacredness, for it is the intrinsic properties of the veil that were, and in some quarters still are, alleged to afford protection against these spirits rather than any sacred symbolism. In short, the veil's parts are not equal to the whole. The sacredness of the veil, as Murphy also pointed out,[45] is found in the ritual of social relations, and in the sentiments of shame and pollution that are associated with the mouth. In 1970–71 I wrote that:

> even the most powerful chiefs wear the veil, while the Hadj may divest himself of it, since it is his dignity and esteem that endues him with status that relieves him from all sense of shame and respect before others. The status of the chief is secular, while that of the Hadj is sacred, and the symbolism of the veil in social relations belongs to the sacred.[46]

Apart from changes in tense from present to past, there is little in this analysis that differs from what I wrote some 30 years ago. For instance, I wrote then of 'the most powerful chiefs wearing the veil'. Today, in Algeria at least, one cannot talk of chiefs in any meaningful political sense as they no longer have a place in the political structure of the country. The point of this article, however, is not whether we can still talk of 'chiefs' in the traditional political sense, but whether those same individuals – recognised as chiefs or otherwise – might still wear the veil. The question thus becomes: why is the veil no longer worn so widely amongst Algerian Tuareg and, on the occasions that it is worn, what symbolic values and beliefs are attached to it?

As already mentioned, Tuareg society in Algeria, especially in Ahaggar,[47] underwent a veritable social revolution in the decade following Algerian independence. A complex array of political, economic, ecological and social forces resulted in the traditional political system being dismantled and subordinated to the political institutions of the new state. Much of the traditional class structure was consciously and coercively abolished; the land was freed for those that worked it; the traditional salt caravans to Niger were blocked; several years of drought brought the pastoral economy to its knees; and education was made compulsory for nomadic children.[48] Kel Ahaggar society experienced dramatic changes in those few years. One such change, perhaps a little less traumatic than many of the others, and which I was able to observe with fascination, was the way in which certain Tuareg tended, on occasion, to discard the veil. In those years the occasion was very specific: it was when they were outside the Tuareg social milieu. These Tuareg, at that time still relatively few in number, were mostly those who had entered new roles in the developing and modernising outside world of Tamanrasset and its environs, in such positions as secretaries, mechanics, works foremen, labourers and so on. Similarly, several of the nomadic children who had been in the boarding school for a few years would go completely bareheaded, in spite of having reached puberty.

What I was observing at that time was a twofold process.

1. Tuareg were beginning to leave their social milieu more readily, to work in Tamanrasset, at the mines of Laouni, the Sonarem base at In Eker and so on. This process was tending to lessen the significance of ethnic cleavages within Ahaggar society and to alter the basis of social integration, as social positions in these new situations tended to be determined more by occupational ability than by criteria of ethnicity, kinship, class or other such characteristics.
2. Certain traditional beliefs, such as those in the Kel Asouf, were being dissipated, primarily as a result of the increased Islamisation and Arabisation that accompanied the new 'Algerianisation' of the region, but also with the associated increase of schooling and other modernising processes.

During the first few years of this process (that is, up to about the end of the 1960s), it was difficult to conclude that these changes signified a breakdown in the beliefs surrounding the veil and the ritualisation of Tuareg social relations, for these Tuareg would revert immediately to their traditional dress, especially the veil, on returning to their camps. On returning to the camp the Tuareg was once again involved in the ambiguous and ambivalent kinship relationships that characterised Tuareg society. In those conditions, no matter what his degree of emancipation or integration into the external society of Tamanrasset or elsewhere, the veil afforded him a degree of protection from the conflicting interests of essentially ambivalent roles.

By the end of that decade (1962–72), when I left Ahaggar, this situation was becoming more complex. During the mid-1960s, the number of Kel Ahaggar (apart from Kel Rela) spending any length of time in Tamanrasset was very few. By the early 1970s, as a result of rapidly improving economic, ecological and social conditions, and especially a marked decrease in the state of antagonism between Tuareg and other ethnic groups, such as former *harratin*, ex-slaves and the Algerian authorities themselves, many Kel Ahaggar, notably some of the more traditionally minded Kel Ulli descent groups,[49] were beginning to spend much more time in Tamanrasset, and even to settle there. Within the short space of a few years, I was able to witness the stage on which social interaction took place being enlarged considerably from the camp to the town. This was an extremely complex social development, characterised above all else by the widening of social networks, not only between different groups of Tuareg but also between Tuareg groups and the plurality of other rapidly growing social and ethnic groups in the region.[50] That was the situation in 1971 when I left Ahaggar and which I concluded might lead to further considerable changes in both the traditional belief systems and social structure of Tuareg society, *with the possible disappearance of the veil in its traditional form and meaning.*

There have indeed been further considerable changes in the belief systems and social structure of Tuareg society in the 30 or so intervening years, and although the veil has by no means disappeared, both the manner of its wearing and the symbolic meanings attached to it have changed – perhaps, as we might expect, in almost equal measure to the far-reaching changes in other facets of their society.

Of the many changes that have taken place in Tuareg society in the last 30 or so years, two broad 'constellations' of change can be singled out as having had major consequences for the wearing of the veil. These are what I would call the 'Islamo-Arabisation' and the 'social externalisation' of Tuareg society. Let me examine these two rather broad concepts in turn.

First, the Islamo-Arabisation of (Algerian) Tuareg society.[51] The greater Arabisation of the region, as reflected in the educational system in which all schooling is in Arabic, has been a major strand of state policy throughout the post-Independence era. Islamisation, however, has been a more muted strand of state policy, but one which has become more closely associated with Arabisation in recent years, partly, it would seem, in response to the more pronounced fundamentalist doctrines that have permeated the country since the early 1990s and which have been manifest, for example, in the Tuareg's much stricter observance, even amongst the nomads, of *karem* – the fast during the holy month of Ramadan.[52] Arabism, however, and perhaps even 'Islamo-Arabism', are today almost euphemisms for 'modernity'. For the young men of Algeria's south, both Tuareg and non-Tuareg, the modern world, especially as it is portrayed to them through the new media channels, is both 'Arab' and 'Islamic'. To paraphrase many of the young Tuareg men of Ahaggar: Arabism is *chic*, *à la mode* and the essence of modernity.

The belief systems of a more modern and more orthodox Islamic world have gone a long way to replacing those of the Tuareg's more animist form of maraboutic Islam. For example, belief in the Kel Asouf, Kel Had, Kel Tenere, Kel Amadal and so on, has been relegated amongst all but some of the eldest Tuareg to a bygone folklore. Whereas 30 years ago I was able to have serious discussions, especially with elder Tuareg, about the prevalence of Kel Asouf and the protection afforded against them by the veil, any such discussion today is likely to be met by laughter and denial of their existence, let alone their association with veiling. Similarly, while *tehot* still makes a strong impression on the daily lives of most Kel Ahaggar, any question as to whether the veil can afford protection against it is now likely to be met with an almost complete denial, or with comments such as 'perhaps there might be some old people who believe it'.[53]

Second, let me now explain what I mean by the 'social externalisation' of Tuareg society. Traditional Kel Ahaggar society was characterised by a high level of endogamy at a number of levels. First, in spite of a number of earlier marital alliances with external Arab tribes, such as the Chaamba, Rehala and Ahl Azzi (Kel Rezzi), most Tuareg marriages were within the *tegehe* ('federation', that is, Kel Ahaggar, Kel Ajjer and so on). Second, there was a high level of endogamy within classes. Marriages between Ihaggaren (nobles) and Kel Ulli (lit. 'people of the goats' – 'vassals') were almost unheard of.[54] Third, there was a high level of endogamy within the *tawsatin* (descent groups; sing. *tawsit*) themselves, and that within the *tawsit* the most common marriages were with cousins of one sort or another.[55] It is sufficient for the purposes of this article merely to point out that a survey undertaken amongst the Kel Ahaggar in the 1960s revealed a level of endogamy amongst some *tawsatin* approaching 95 per cent.[56] With the average *tawsit* numbering only a few hundred people, one can thus see how kinsmen might be related to each other in multifarious ways, and how such relationships could therefore be fraught with ambivalence and uncertainty.

This feature of Tuareg (Kel Ahaggar) society, in which its basic social structural arrangements tended to look inwards, has changed dramatically since the 1960s. This is now manifested at a number of levels, of which the most fundamental is that of marriage. Marriage patterns amongst the Kel Ahaggar and the changes that have occurred in them during the course of the last century, and especially the last generation, are analysed elsewhere in this volume.[57] That analysis reveals that marriage patterns over the last generation, and it would seem especially during the last decade or so, have become, and are continuing to become, less endogamous at all levels. For instance: amongst the Dag Rali, a Kel Ulli *tawsit*, there has been a decline in *tawsit* endogamy from 93–95 per cent in the 1960s to 78 per cent today (2003). In the case of second marriages, *tawsit* endogamy is now below 70 per cent. And within the *tawsit* itself, marriages are being contracted increasingly with more distant kinsmen, the percentage of marriages with first cousins having fallen from 25 per cent to 12 per cent. Amongst the 'noble' Kel Rela, the decline in *tawsit* endogamy is even more marked, from 70.5 per cent in the 1960s to 41.5 per cent today. And, within the *tawsit*, the percentage of marriages with the actual or classificatory matrilateral parallel cousin, the preferred marriage, has fallen from 32 per cent to 11 per cent. The many reasons for this trend are discussed in detail in the above-mentioned analysis, the main points of which are that:

1. Many of the political, economic and social forces that encouraged *tawsit* endogamy in the past have either dissipated considerably or withered away altogether.
2. The fundamental relations between the various Kel Ahaggar classes, and between Tuareg and non-Tuareg, notably ex-slaves and *harratin*, have been completely transformed since Algerian independence. Although there are still comparatively few marriages between the noble Kel Rela and previously subordinate classes,[58] there has been a marked increase in recent years in the number of marriages between Kel Ulli *tawsatin*, Kel Rezzi and Isekkemaren *tawsatin*. The declining significance of the traditional class structure of Kel Ahaggar society is nowhere better seen than in the workplace, whether that workplace be in 'state' employment or in the rapidly developing entrepreneurial business sector, such as tourism. Employment in both sectors is based almost entirely on merit and ability, and there are several incidences of Tuareg of noble descent working for or in partnership with Tuareg of traditionally lower status. With group membership still determined matrilineally, the last of the traditional barriers or cleavages within Kel Ahaggar society was probably the effective social prohibition on Tuareg women marrying non-Tuareg of traditionally inferior status, notably ex-slaves and *harratin*. Until the 1990s, such marriages were virtually 'unheard of' in Ahaggar. However, with thousands of Malian Tuareg seeking refuge in Ahaggar in the 1990s,

following the drought and the Tuareg uprising against the government, several dozen, perhaps even hundreds, of Malian Tuareg women married local *harratin* men and the descendants of former Kel Ahaggar slaves as a means of acquiring Algerian rights! Although most Kel Ahaggar with whom I have discussed this behaviour described it as 'shocking',[59] they nevertheless rationalised it as being a response to 'exceptional circumstances', leaving the door open, it would seem, for the acceptance of further possible 'exceptional circumstances'!

This increased openness and 'externalisation' of Tuareg society is reflected in the emergence in the last few years of a new sense of 'regionalism' and a corresponding 'regional' identity in the south of the country, especially amongst the peoples of Ahaggar and Ajjer.[60] This is not to imply that the old social categories and ethnic identities of traditional Tuareg society are no longer relevant. That is not the case, for they still have meaning in an historical and social context. It is simply that they lack political content and political relevancy in the new Algerian order.

3. There has been a marked decline, over the last generation or so, in the importance of both descent and kinship as the main social organisational principles of Kel Ahaggar and Kel Ajjer society. This is demonstrated most clearly when comparing various aspects of current social life with how they were in the 1960s. Perhaps the best examples of this are the decreased importance of the matriline, changes in marital strategies and marriage patterns and the changed naming system, all of which are examined in a further article.[61] One of the main results of these and other such changes in social organisation is that the current kinship system has become more 'elective' than 'prescriptive'. Elsewhere, I have documented a particularly amusing, but nevertheless highly significant, outcome of the new naming system, introduced in the 1970s, which afforded Tuareg the opportunity of dissociating themselves from bothersome kinsmen by the simple mechanism of taking another name![62]

4. Alongside a diminution in the proportion of Tuareg in both the total population of the region and in most residential areas, Tuareg residency patterns have become more geographically dispersed and elective. The population of Ahaggar[63] at the time of Algerian independence was 13,000 (excluding In Salah), of which the Kel Ahaggar comprised almost 50 per cent. According to the 1998 census (which under-counted the population), the population of Ahaggar (the *wilaya* of Tamanrasset, which now includes In Salah) numbered some 210,000, of which the proportion of Kel Ahaggar is estimated at some 10 per cent (or perhaps 15 per cent if In Salah is excluded). In Tamanrasset itself (est. 100,000) the number of Kel Ahaggar is estimated at a few thousand and probably no more than 10 per

cent of the town's population. The two main reasons for this diminution in the proportion of Tuareg are the much faster rates of population growth amongst the *harratin* and ex-slave populations and the massive migration into the area, especially from the north of Algeria, but also from countries to the south.[64]

During this period (1962–2002), the residential pattern of Kel Ahaggar has changed considerably. First, the proportion of Kel Ahaggar living a nomadic or semi-nomadic lifestyle has fallen from around 90 per cent in 1962 to around 15 per cent today.[65] Some 85 per cent of Algerian Tuareg now live in large towns such as Tamanrasset, Djanet or Illizi; large villages such as Ideles, Tazrouk, In Amguel, Abalessa, Amsel and so on; or small hamlets and cultivation centres such as Mertoutek, Tit, Otoul, Tamdjert, Terhenanet, Tagmart and many others, most of which are becoming established villages in their own right. With the exception of a small number of villages, such as Terhenanet, Tagmart and Ifrak (amongst the Dag Rali), Tamdjert (Kel In Tunin), and so on, in which whole descent group sections have tended to settle together in a fairly socially homogenous manner, Tuareg now find themselves living increasingly cheek by jowl with individuals and families from other social classes and ethnic groups, or in the case of the main towns, perhaps people from outside the region altogether. Second, the bulk of the Tuareg population still living in the nomadic milieu comprises mostly old people, women and children; most men of working age are away from the camp working or looking for work elsewhere.[66] Many of these men may be working far away outside the region, perhaps at In Salah, Illizi or further north, or across the border in Mali, Niger or Libya, and return home as infrequently as once a year.

Compared with traditional times, we are looking at a much greater geographical dispersion and range of movement of Kel Ahaggar, in which such factors as occupational opportunity now outweigh traditional, predominantly kinship-based prescriptions of residency. Even amongst the remaining nomadic elements, the abolition of traditional tribal (*tawsit*) land rights means individual families and groups are freer to move their herds over greater distances into lands where access might have been prohibited by traditional customary arrangements.[67]

5. Occupational-business links and alliances are now of far greater economic and socio-political importance to most Kel Ahaggar than traditional kinship-oriented ties. Such external links and alliances tend to extend far beyond the geographical confines of traditional economic activity, such as the former caravan trade. For instance, many Tuareg, not merely in Algeria but also in Niger and Mali, are occupied within the tourism-

transport business sector (including clandestine activities), which involves them in links that extend not only across these countries, but through both marriage and business alliances (and the use of the Internet) into European and world markets. Most Tuareg are conscious of these expanding linkages and networks, with some even referring to them as part of the 'Tuareg diaspora'. While the notion of a Tuareg diaspora is appropriate for the response of many Niger and Mali Tuareg to the droughts of the 1970s and 1980s and the subsequent rebellions against their governments, it is not really applicable to Algeria's Tuareg, who have suffered neither such extreme drought conditions nor such marginalisation and repression from their government. Nevertheless, Algerian Tuareg have become increasingly worldly-wise. Many of them travel extensively in the Sahara and Sahel, especially in the tourism-transport business,[68] while as many as a dozen or more Kel Ahaggar and Kel Ajjer will regularly pass the hot summer months in Europe, where they will not only 'holiday', but work on drumming up business for their tourism agencies. This international network is becoming increasingly important in their business, social and political lives, particularly in creating and establishing their place in the modern world as the Sahara's travel and tourism operators.[69]

The New Meanings of the Veil

It is evident, from what I have said so far, that many of the traditional symbolic values and meanings attached to the veil have fallen away, become less significant or been transformed altogether. The association between the veil and certain magico-religious beliefs would now seem to be held by increasingly few Tuareg, and then more commonly within the context of significant *rites de passage* and other ritual occasions. The majority of Tuareg, especially the younger generations, no longer believe that it is shameful to expose the mouth, although most would seem to be aware of the traditional beliefs and the customs surrounding them and would be inclined to respect them in the traditional milieu, which might be the camp, the company of elders, close kinsmen and so forth. Furthermore, as kinship relations become increasing less prescriptive, ambiguous and ambivalent, so the role of the veil as a symbolic referent in the communication process has diminished. This is not to say that the veil no longer plays such a role. Indeed, one can still see the veil as a communicative symbol in the traditional camp environment, in some of the villages, such as Terhenanet or Tagmart, where kinsmen of the same section still live cheek by jowl, amongst older Tuareg, as a mark of deference towards parents-in-law and other persons to whom respect should be shown, and sometimes between persons of markedly different social status.

Dressing for the Occasion

In such situations, one can still interpret the interaction process from the position, movement or gestures of movement of the veil. But these occasions now tend to be cameos, and the observer has to watch out for them!

So, who wears the veil now, and when? Few Tuareg, if any, have divested themselves entirely of the veil. It will be worn, for instance, by nearly all Tuareg on the sorts of occasions outlined above, but in the case of younger generations often more as a matter of social etiquette and respect, than in terms of its many traditional values and meanings. It will also be worn decorously by almost all Tuareg on festive and ceremonial occasions. In most such instances, however, we are witnessing the expression of only the vestigial elements of a once complex and multifaceted symbol, whose traditional values and meanings are, by and large, understood and adhered to only by the older men, and especially those still living in the nomadic and more traditional milieu. For instance, one such nomad, who works occasionally as a guide for a Tuareg tourism agency in Tamanrasset, travelled into town to enquire about any forthcoming work. As he would have anticipated, he was invited to stay in the agency's house before returning to his camp. While there, the other three Tuareg present construed a ruse to see if they could divest him of his veil. With the connivance of the cook, they prepared a spaghetti dish without cutting up the spaghetti. Straight faces were kept for a minute or two as the old man struggled without success to raise just one strand of spaghetti to his mouth by passing it under his veil. As his spaghetti slipped and slithered in every wrong direction, the group broke into uproarious laughter. No one laughed more than the old man himself, who appreciated the joke, but who nevertheless refused to lower his veil and insisted that the cook cut the spaghetti into small pieces and then bring him a spoon! While waiting for the food to be brought back, he jocularly berated the younger men for their shameful and disrespectful eating habits.

At the other end of the age scale, young Tuareg men now tend to sport the veil as a fashion accessory, often buying the most outlandish colours that Tamanrasset's merchants can obtain. I was recently visiting a partially sedentarised encampment, containing about 20 individuals, alongside the Tefedest range in northern Ahaggar, when a most debonair young man, the 21-year-old elder son of the headman, returned to the camp after a few weeks employment at Illizi. He was dressed in a blue *gandoura*, over which he wore a black leather jacket, wrap-around sun glasses and a fire-engine red *chech* with *tagelmoust* (veil) which shrouded his entire head except for his spectacles. He was a stunning sight, and I wondered how his kinsmen would react to this invasion of fashion. His return was clearly welcomed and I did not hear any overt ragging or note of admonishment with regard to his dress, although I sensed from his body language a slight unease and wondered if his bold statement of modernity, perhaps even defiance, would last into a second day. In Tamanrasset, he would have been the toast of café society (although with his veil lowered!). Here, back in the camp some 200 miles from town, he was uncomfortably out of place, and on the morrow I noticed that he was dressed in a suitably drab *gandoura*, plain white *chech* with veil casually low.

In spite of both the many changes in the ideas and beliefs surrounding the veil and the dramatic changes in the overall situation of the Algerian Tuareg during the course of the last generation or two, there is one feature of the veil which has remained more or less constant. Indeed, in some regions, especially Mali and Niger, I would suggest that it might even have become more pronounced. That is the veil's symbolisation of 'Tuaregness'. Ask a Tuareg why he wears a veil and the most likely answer is: 'because I am a Tuareg'. This notion, or sentiment, of ethnic identity imbues the veil with a combination of political and affective qualities.

In Niger and Mali, where 'modernisation' is perhaps as much as a generation behind Algeria and where the traditional forms of social organisation and their values are far more widespread than in Algeria, the veil still retains many of the levels of meaning that I have described in this article, but which have been substantially transformed in Algeria. However, the Tuareg of Niger and Mali, unlike their counterparts in Algeria, both rebelled against their governments in the early 1990s in two rather bloody civil wars. Both uprisings were associated with a wave of cultural revivalism amongst the Tuareg in which the veil became the most overt and dominant symbol of Tuareg identity.

Although Algeria has not experienced a Tuareg uprising, and there has consequently been no such similar cultural revivalism in Algeria as in Niger and Mali, the veil is still a powerful symbol of ethnic identity and political expression amongst Algerian Tuareg, the manifestation of which can be seen on numerous, almost daily, occasions. In the 1960s, when there was considerable tension between elements of the Kel Ahaggar and the new Algerian administration, Tuareg would deliberately raise their veils when entering any government office or talking with a government official, knowing that this 'masking of their facial identity', to which they were not accustomed, served to irritate them! Of particular amusement to an external observer was to watch Tuareg walking down the main street of Tamanrasset. As they approached the offices of the *sous-préfet*, police and military (which were then in the town centre), they would raise their veils to their highest in a gesture of ethnic and political defiance, analogous perhaps to a one or two fingered gesture in modern Anglo-Saxon culture! Relations between the Algerian Tuareg and the government are now much better. Indeed, one might even postulate that the position and gestures associated with the veil symbolises the nature of that relationship. In 1999, a new *wali* was appointed to Tamanrasset, who, within no time at all, had managed to incur the anger and disrespect of many of the local people, not least the Kel Ahaggar. One of his first and more stupid decrees was that the town's taxi drivers, some of whom were Tuareg, were not to wear the veil while driving their taxis. The immediate response was for all drivers, whether Tuareg or not, to wear a veil! Moreover, most Tuareg, when entering the *wali*'s or the *wilaya*'s offices, will wear the veil not as a symbol of respect but in a manner and with a meaning that is reminiscent of the 1960s.[70] Similarly, when participating in the formal political domain, especially at local assembly meetings and other such arenas of local and regional government, Tuareg delegates will usually wear their finest robes and veil, not simply as a display of finery, but as a symbol of Tuareg identity, as if their very words, spoken from under the veils, thereby contained a greater degree of knowledge, respect and political authority.

NOTES

I would like to acknowledge the Leverhulme Trust for its most generous support.

1. The second most commented upon custom probably relates to their matrilineal traits. See J. Keenan, 'The End of the Matriline? The Changing Roles of Women and Descent amongst the Algerian Tuareg', in this volume, pp.121–62.
2. El Bekri, *Description de l'Afrique Septentrionale*, trans. MacGuckin de Slane (Paris: 1859).
3. Ibn Batutah, *Voyages d'Ibn Batoutah*, I–IV, trans. Detrémy and Sanguinetti (Paris: 1853–58).
4. The question of matrilineality amongst the Tuareg, and the Kel Ahaggar specifically, is examined in Keenan (note 1).
5. J. Keenan, 'The Tuareg Veil', *Revue de l'Occident Musulman et de la Méditerranée* 17/1 (1974) pp.107–18.
6. The term *litham* (Ar., veil), although commonly used by Oriental Arabs, is not widely known among Tuareg groups and little used among the Maghrib populations as a whole, whilst the term *echchach* (Ar., *chach*) has been in common usage amongst all Tuareg for some time and reflects the increasing Arabic influence. See A. Bourgeot, 'Le Costume Masculin des Kel Ahaggar', *Libyca* XVII/1 (1969) pp.355–76.
7. Hadj Bettu was something of a local 'entrepreneur-cum-warlord', running much of Ahaggar as if it was his personal fiefdom. He came to the attention of the Algerian government following the assassination of President Mohammed Boudiaf in June 1992 and was gaoled in 1992 for ten years. He was released in 2002 and now lives in Tamanrasset. For details, see J. Keenan, 'Ethnicity, Regionalism and Political Stability in Algeria's *Grand Sud*', in this volume, pp.67–96.
8. Use of these terms also tends to reflect northerners' lack of knowledge of the Tuareg region and its social categories.
9. I think there is actually only one Tuareg government minister in Niger. In Mali, the current prime minister is a Tuareg.
10. See C. de Foucauld, *Dictionnaire Touareg–Française, dialecte de l'Ahaggar*, 4 vols. (Paris: Imprimerie nationale de France 1951–52) vol.1, p.439 (fig.); and Bourgeot (note 6). Bourgeot, p.358, mentions finding an *alechcho* belonging to a noble (Kel Rela) measuring 10m in length, about 60cm wide and valued at 500 DA (c.£45). Because of its rarity, it would now be difficult to place a monetary value on this *alechcho*. Today, traditional indigo-dyed

The Lesser Gods of the Sahara

cotton is not usually found in the shops of Tamanrasset, although it can still be bought in shops in Agades (Niger) and other such towns further south. In 2002 I was in Agades with a Tuareg from Ahaggar who bought an *alechcho* of 4.5m after negotiating a price at between £6 and £8 per metre. The cloth was rolled into a 'stick' about the size of small baguette and sold in sealed, modern baking foil to prevent the indigo dye from dripping out.

11. Bourgeot (note 6) p.358.
12. See front cover picture of J. Keenan, *Sahara Man: Travelling with the Tuareg* (London: John Murray 2001).
13. M. Gast, 1965, 'Premier résultats d'une mission éthnographique en Ahaggar', *Libyca* XIII (1965) pp.325–32.
14. Foucauld (note 10) vol.3, p.1326.
15. M. Benhazera, *Six Mois chez les Touareg du Ahaggar* (Alger: Jourdan 1908) p.36.
16. Ibid. pp.67–8.
17. J. Nicolaisen, *Ecology and Culture of the Pastoral Tuareg* (Copenhagen: University of Copenhagen 1963) p.287.
18. The first salt caravan from Amadror (Ahaggar) to Damergou in Niger took place in 1896. This was organised by the Dag Rali and Aguh-en-tehle. It did not become a regular event for another generation.
19. H. Duveyrier, *Les Touaregs du Nord* (Paris: Challamel 1864) p.392.
20. F. Rodd, 'The origin of the Tuareg', *Geographical Journal* 67 (1926) pp.27–52.
21. R.F. Murphy, 'Social Distance and the Veil', *American Anthropologist* 66 (1964) pp.1257–74.
22. Duveyrier (note 19).
23. Bourgeot (note 6) p.360.
24. Foucauld (note 10) vol.3, p.1329.
25. Bourgeot (note 6) p.360.
26. R.P. Abdel Djalil, 'Aspects intérieurs de l'Islam', *Bulletin de Liaison Saharienne* V/16 (Mars 1964) p.29.
27. H. Lhote, 'Au sujet du Port du Voile chez les Touareg et les Teda', *Notes Africaines* 52 (octobre 1951) pp.108–10.
28. Bourgeot (note 6) p.361.
29. Nicolaisen (note 17) p.14; and J. Nicolaisen, 'Essai sur la réligion et la magie touaregues', *Folk* 3 (1961) p.114. Nicolaisen also considered, incorrectly, that the man's veil and the woman's headcloth were similar in form and shape, and served the same social functions – a fact which he saw proven in their adoption of the veil and headcloth respectively at initiation in Ahaggar, or at marriage in Aïr.
30. See, for example, J. Nicolas, 'Le voilement des Twareg: Contributions à l'étude de l'Air', *Mémoires de l'IFAN* 10 (1950) pp.497–503.
31. Lhote (note 27) p.110.
32. Murphy (note 21).
33. Lhote (note 27) p.110.
34. Murphy (note 21). Murphy is adopting much of the 'interactionist' approach of Goffman, who states that the individual's sense of worth and significance is threatened by his vulnerability and penetrability, E. Goffman, 'The Nature of Deference and Demeanour', *American Anthropologist* 58 (1956) pp.473–502.
35. A.R. Radcliffe-Brown, *Structure and Function in Primitive Society* (Glencoe, IL: Free Press 1952).
36. R.K. Merton, *Social Theory and Social Structure* (Glencoe, IL: Free Press 1957).
37. See J. Keenan, 'Power and Wealth are Cousins: Descent, Class and Marital Strategies among the Kel Ahaggar (Tuareg – Sahara)', *Africa* 47/3 (1977) pp 242–52, and 47/4 (1977) pp.333–42; and Keenan (note 1).
38. R.F. Murphy, 'Tuareg Kinship', *American Anthropologist* 69 (1967) pp.163–70.
39. Keenan (note 5).
40. R. Firth, 'Marriage and the classificatory system relationship', *Journal of the Royal Anthropological Institute* 60 (1930) pp.235–68.

Dressing for the Occasion

41. Murphy (note 21).
42. Ibid. p.1271.
43. E. Goffman, *The Presentation of Self in Everyday Life* (London: Penguin 1969) p.220.
44. E. Westermarck, *Ritual and Belief in Morocco*, 2 vols. (London: 1926) p.422.
45. Murphy (note 21).
46. Keenan (note 5).
47. This 'revolution' was probably more intense and traumatic amongst the Kel Ahaggar than the Kel Ajjer, as the former had probably retained more of their traditional social structures during the colonial era and were less sedentarised at the time of Algerian independence than the Kel Ajjer.
48. This applied to boys, not girls, for whom schooling, although encouraged, is still not compulsory.
49. In particular, the Dag Rali, and perhaps also the Aguh-en-tehle, both of whom are referred to in more detail elsewhere in this volume in Keenan (note 1).
50. The Tuareg were already a significant minority in the region by this time.
51. This is conceptually distinct from the 'Algerianisation' of Tuareg society, a concept which is discussed in more depth elsewhere in this volume in Keenan (note 7).
52. During the month of Ramadan in 1999, I visited many remote and predominantly Tuareg communities, both nomadic and settled, amongst whom the observance of the fast was almost total, whereas earlier, so my informants told me, it was largely disregarded.
53. In many societies, individuals are deemed to be most vulnerable to the dangers of spirits such as the Tuaregs' Kel Asouf during periods of transition and passage from one social state to another. In this context, it is interesting to note Pandolfi's description of the symbolic actions taken during Tuareg wedding ceremonies to protect the young couple from the dangers of the Kel Asouf. P. Pandolfi, *Les Touaregs de l'Ahaggar* (Paris: Karthala 1998) pp.332–4.
54. This 'class endogamy' was not practiced by the Taitok and Tegehe Mellet, the two other noble *tawsatin* in Ahaggar (nor, it seems, the Tegehe-n-ou-Sidi before them). The French noted several marriages between Taitok women and Kel Ahnet (Kel Ulli) on their arrival in the region at the beginning of the twentieth century. Indeed, Bissuel, writing in 1888 on the Taitok and Kel Ahnet specifically, remarked on the 'lessening of the gap' between noble (Ihaggaren) and vassal (Imrad) as families of the two 'castes' became tied together through marriage. H. Bissuel, *Les Touaregs de l'ouest* (Alger: Jourdan 1888). Amongst the Kel Rela, who have been the sole, effective 'nobility' in Ahaggar since the time of French pacification, there have been a few marriages between Kel Rela men and women from subordinate *tawsatin*. Such marriages do not threaten the Kel Rela's dominant position, as group membership is transmitted matrilineally. However, to this day, there has still been no marriage between a Kel Rela women and a Kel Ulli man. For details of such marriage patterns, see Keenan (note 1).
55. The nature of Kel Ahaggar marriage patterns is discussed in detail in Keenan (note 1).
56. Ibid.
57. Ibid.
58. There have always been occasional marriages between Kel Rela men and Kel Ulli women, but there are still no marriages between Kel Rela women and Kel Ulli men. For details, see ibid.
59. It was deemed most 'shocking' amongst the Kel Rela rather than other *tawsatin*. See my comments at the end of ibid.
60. This is discussed in more depth elsewhere in this volume in Keenan (note 7).
61. Changes in the importance of the matriline and marriage patterns are discussed in Keenan (note 1). Changes in the naming system are explained in Keenan (note 7).
62. Keenan (note 12) pp.110–11.
63. A more detailed analysis of Ahaggar's demography, along with reasons for its change, will be found in Keenan (note 7); and J. Keenan, 'Thirty years of change and continuity in Ahaggar (1971–2001)', in idem, *The Tuareg: People of Ahaggar* (London: Sickle Moon Books 2002).

64. The bank manager in Tamanrasset calculated that 48 nationalities (he meant ethnic groups) could now be found living in Tamanrasset! Keenan (note 12) p.18.
65. See J. Keenan, 'The Last Nomads: Nomadism amongst the Tuareg of Ahaggar (Algerian Sahara)', in this volume, pp.163–92.
66. Ibid.
67. Ibid.
68. For example, during the five winter months of 2002–03, one Tamanrasset resident, who owned his own vehicles, had worked in the tourism business in Algeria, Libya, Niger, Mali, Mauritania and Burkina Faso.
69. In terms of the number of foreign visitors, it is conceivable that Tamanrasset is Algeria's most 'international' town after Algiers.
70. For a more detailed analysis of Tuareg–government relations, see Keenan (note 7); and idem, 'Contested Terrain: Tourism, Environment and Security in Algeria's Extreme South', in this volume, pp.226–65.

The End of the Matriline? The Changing Roles of Women and Descent amongst the Algerian Tuareg

Most Europeans who encountered the Tuareg in traditional times, and by 'traditional' I here include the period of colonial rule up to the time of Algerian independence in 1962, were impressed by the position of women in their society. European writers, moreover, were clearly taken by their beauty and elegance. Rene Gardi, for instance, the celebrated Swiss journalist who travelled amongst the Kel Ahaggar in the early 1950s, commented repeatedly on how 'agreeable they were to the eye'. Such writers were also impressed by the prominent roles Tuareg women played in social life. Unlike the Arab societies to the north, Tuareg women, as Gardi remarked, 'had a lot to say in the affairs of the tribe'. They took part in the discussions of men and, unlike their Arab counterparts, were neither veiled nor secluded.[1] They owned slaves and livestock in their own right; the camp was their domain, and they were responsible for most of its affairs – the management of the goat herds, the preparation of food, the education of children, and many other aspects of its organisation; while even beyond the confines of the domestic environment they were the foci of much of social life. And in matters of love and marriage, Tuareg women had a freedom unknown amongst their Arab neighbours – a matter which greatly impressed Europeans who wrote about such customs extensively, but not always correctly. Women were also the 'poets' and musicians of society. Battles, raids, the valour of their men folk, other significant deeds and love stories were composed and recorded in verse and then recited in song to the accompaniment of their *imzads*.[2] The news of an *ahal*, as these recitals were called, would attract men from far afield, particularly when performed by an accomplished woman. For a young man, an *ahal* was an occasion of great social significance where he could court the girl of his fancy and pronounce his worth as a potential husband, while for a woman it was an opportunity to print her reputation indelibly on society. As the evening progressed, the intensity and tempo of the *ahal* increased until well into the night and early hours of the morning, with casual flirtations often giving way to the intimacies of mild love-making.

While such romantic features of Tuareg life enabled Europeans to identify more closely and readily with the Tuareg than the Arab societies to the north, they also tended to emphasise and focus attention on the fundamental significance of women in Tuareg society, which was that group membership and rights to succession of political office were transmitted through the matriline. Much of the traditional literature on the Tuareg consequently described them, without qualification, as a matrilineal society, while several writers, such as Murdock,[3] went so far as to describe their society as a 'matriarchy'.[4]

To talk of the Tuareg, or any other society for that matter, as patrilineal, matrilineal or bilineal is not very helpful, as we are rarely dealing with one single principle of descent, but rather a whole complex of rights and their respective rules of transmission. If we look at the various components of this whole complex of rights in traditional Tuareg society, namely group membership, succession to office, inheritance and residency, and the way in which they were transmitted, we are confronted with a more complex system, but one which enables us not only to make more sense of the Tuareg's 'matrilineality', but also to understand how the whole concept of 'descent', as well as the significance of the matriline, have in a sense been 'downgraded' over the last generation or so.

My concern in this article is to explain this phenomenon, namely how and why both descent and the matriline have been 'downgraded' in recent years. I also show how changes in the meaning and relevancy of descent, alongside such radical changes as sedentarisation and various other processes and elements of the 'modern world', notably the intrusion in recent years of certain Islamo-Arabic influences, have resulted in a considerable degradation of the position and roles of women in social life, while posing serious threats to their health and general well-being.

Modes of Descent (The Rules)

In 'traditional' Tuareg (Kel Ahaggar) society, the 'rules' of descent determined the way in which a considerable number of rights – notably group membership, succession to political office, access to land rights, the inheritance of property and residency – were transmitted. For instance, group membership, and especially *tawsit* (descent group) membership, among both the main classes – nobles (Ihaggaren) and 'vassals' (Kel Ulli – people of the goats) – was determined by matrilineal descent. 'It is the stomach', as Kel Ahaggar say, 'which colours the child'.[5] Succession to political office, in both classes, was also transmitted matrilineally, the right to succeed being transmitted adelphically through the line of brothers, thereafter the line of mother's sisters' sons (in order of genealogical seniority), and, finally, through the line of sisters' sons.

In the case of property rights, it is necessary to make the distinction between land rights (immovable wealth) and those over livestock (movable wealth). The rules of inheritance, which are discussed below, determined that livestock among both classes were transmitted for the most part through the patriline. Land rights, however, were held corporately by each *tawsit*. The nobility held sovereign rights over the entire territory of their drum-group (*ettebel*), while in the case of the subordinate Kel Ulli, tenant rights were transmitted in conjunction with political office, being vested in the chief as the representative of his *tawsit*.[6]

This apparent matrilineal bias is modified when we turn to the rules of residency[7] and inheritance. Residency in 'traditional' society was based fundamentally on a patrilineal axis. After a marriage, the wife remained in her parents' camp where she was visited by her husband. The length and frequency of visits and the duration of this arrangement depended on many factors, but was usually at least a year and might, in extreme cases, be as many as five, or even more, during which time the wife might give birth to one or more children. A camp (*ariwan*) usually comprised about 4–5 tents (*ehenen*, sing. *ehen*),[8] and was basically an agnatic unit, usually of about three generations in depth and centring around a structural core of male agnates (typically father, sons and children, but often brothers or male paternal parallel cousins). The move of the wife (and children) to the husband's *ariwan*, known as *azalay* (from the verb *azli*, meaning to separate), was an occasion of great ritual festivity which effectively marked the constitution of the new domestic unit. This move established a period of virilocal residence, which might last for the rest of the wife's life, although she might move back to her own people, especially if divorced or widowed when comparatively young and with young children.

If we now turn to the inheritance of 'wealth' (that is, movable wealth), which in 'traditional' society consisted mostly of individually held livestock, we see that it was determined among all classes (as it is today) according to the principles of Quranic law, which, while recognising the right of women to inherit, were orientated towards males and patrilineal kinsmen, so that a daughter inherited one share to a son's two, without regard to primogeniture. Such 'diverging devolution' is, as Goody noted, 'in a certain sense agnatic'.[9] Thus, while land rights were transmitted laterally in conjunction with succession to political office, and were held corporately by the matrilineal descent group, livestock were transmitted within the family, and predominantly within the *ariwan*, which, as we have seen, was a patrilocal unit.

Those were the 'rules' as they pertained to 'traditional' society, and which, as I have emphasised, were broadly operative when I stayed with the Kel Ahaggar during the 1960s and early 1970s. Before turning to the changes that have taken place since then, it is necessary to say something about the special relationship between a man and his mother's brother, because if, as the foregoing suggests, the transmission of wealth – the means of production – in the form of livestock, through the patriline contributed to the unity of the *ariwan*, then the special relationship between a man and his mother's brother (*anet ma*), who was unlikely to be resident in the same *ariwan*, would appear to present something of a contradiction in that this relationship allowed for a fairly substantial amount of livestock to pass from the patriline to the uterine nephew.

The nature of this 'transaction' was that the nephew had an institutionalised right to take anything that he might need from his mother's brother (*anet ma*) and, through the classificatory extension of this relationship, all other senior male kinsmen in his matriline.[10] This right seems to have been rarely abused, being controlled by a fairly strict moral code. In such a miserly environment, in which natural hazards such as drought and disease, in addition to the threat of pillagers, presented all groups with the habitual risk of losing a substantial proportion of their productive resources, the special relationship between a sister's son and his mother's brother – and by extension his matrilineal kin – provided a vital redistributive or insurance mechanism. If necessary, a man could replenish or maintain his own productive resources through the activation of his matriline, which, as a result of the patrilocal axis, tended to be dispersed through other *ariwan*. In short, we can see how the matriline, in the person of the *anet ma*, cut across the patriline to provide a more equitable distribution of wealth (productive resources) between the *ariwan* and the patrilocal *tawsit* sections to which they belonged, according to their varying needs.

We thus see that, while the 'power' of a *tawsit*, in terms of its land rights and political rights over subordinate groups, was transmitted through the matriline, the wealth accumulated through the exercise of those rights was not transmitted with them, but was redistributed through, and transmitted within, the patrilocal 'sections'.[11]

From what I have said so far, we can see that the various principles of descent amongst the Kel Ahaggar, at least at the ideational level, that is in terms of the rules governing the transmission of this complex of rights, tended towards bilineality.[12] However, when we focus on the fundamental class structure of the Kel Ahaggar and Kel Ajjer, the division between Ihaggaren (nobles) and Kel Ulli ('vassals'), and the extent to which each class manipulated these rules of descent, largely through the adoption of different marital strategies, we see that the nobility were predominantly matrilineal while the Kel Ulli veered towards patrilineality.

The End of the Matriline?

Marriage Systems amongst the Kel Ahaggar in 'Traditional' Times

Before looking at these strategies, their ensuing marriage patterns and the changes that they have manifested in recent years, let me first recapitulate[13] the salient features of Kel Ahaggar marriage in early times, namely the strong adherence to monogamy, the comparatively advanced ages of spouses at marriage, the arrangement of marriages and the frequency of divorce.

Monogamy was the rule amongst the Kel Ahaggar.[14] According to Pandolfi, the first known case of bigamy in Ahaggar was that of a Kel Rela (noble) in the middle of the twentieth century who became the butt of general disapproval for his action, especially amongst women. 'Women-power' certainly seems to have played the decisive role in the preservation of monogamy. What happened to a notable Aguh-en-tehle after he took a second wife has long remained fresh in peoples' memories: the women of Ahaggar sent him to Coventry until he got rid of one of his wives![15] The few cases of bigamy amongst the Kel Ahaggar since then[16] have been associated with situations where the man was away from home for long periods of time. Instances of such 'double residency' became associated with Tamesna, the rich camel pastures of northern Niger which were acquired by the Kel Ahaggar after the defeat of Kaoucen in 1917.[17] After that date, the Kel Ahaggar kept the bulk of their camels in Tamesna and spent much of their time there. It was consequently not unheard of for a man to take another wife and establish a second camp with her in Tamesna. For example, Dua ag Agg-Iklan, chief of the Dag Rali from 1902 to 1911,[18] first married a Dag Rali wife, Tekadeyt ult Ebekki, who lived in Ahaggar. Then, without divorcing Tekadeyt, Dua took a second wife from amongst the Irregenaten *tawsit* in Tamesna. The key feature of such 'bigamous' unions was that there was no communal residency: Tekadeyt's camp remained in Ahaggar while that of the second wife remained in Tamesna.[19] In fact, the key to understanding such marriages amongst the Dag Rali was 'residency': if a Dag Rali man married exogamously with a woman from another *tawsit*, she could not come to live with him amongst the Dag Rali. He must either go and live with her, amongst her people, or move with her, as has now become commonplace, and set up house in Tamanrasset. Indeed, Tamanrasset, which is only a short distance away from most Dag Rali encampments/villages, now plays a similar role as Tamesna in the case of both bigamous and exogamous marriages: it is seen as belonging to the 'outside world'. What takes place there is therefore seen as being 'an exception' to or 'outside' the traditional rules and customs of society. A few Dag Rali who had married second wives in Tamesna, like Dua ag Agg-Iklan, did in fact bring them back to Ahaggar. However, in each of these handful of cases, the 'external' wife,[20] whether the sole or secondary wife, was prohibited by the Dag Rali from living amongst them. Instead, the husband was obliged to live with her in Tamanrasset.[21]

In earlier times, according to ethnographies published in the early part of the twentieth century, Kel Ahaggar did not marry until comparatively old: around 30–35 years old in the case of men and 20–25 years old in the case of women. When I stayed with them some 30–40 years ago, the average marrying age seemed a little lower, with girls generally being in their late teens or early twenties when they married, and men a little older.

One of the features of the traditional marriage system was that although a man's first wife was usually chosen by his parents, or was at least subject to their (and other relatives') consent – with the mother playing the key role – a girl was not only free to refuse such a choice, but frequently did so. Indeed, Tuareg history and poems are studded with accounts of such refusals, the best known being associated with Dassine ult Ihemma, the recognised 'beauty' of Ahaggar around the turn of the twentieth century. Dassine was courted by many prominent nobles. The first to ask her parents and be given their permission to marry her was Admer ag Ammou. Dassine kept her counsel while Admer went ahead with the marriage arrangements. A few hours before the actual marriage, as the festivities were in progress, Dassine sent word to Admer, saying: 'Dassine greets you, but tells you to find a wife elsewhere'. Admer was livid, demanding that she be compelled to marry him, but Dassine's mother refused to step in.[22] Dassine continued to be courted the length and breadth of Ahaggar by such nobles as Bouhen ag Khebbi, Aflan ag Doua and Moussa ag Amastane, the *Amenukal* (supreme chief). Although Bouhen was the first to marry her, both Aflan and Moussa continued to court her and she soon left Bouhen, without bearing him any children, to marry Aflan. Moussa, anguished by this rejection, refused to touch another Tuareg woman and took two slave-girls as wives. Bouhen also took two slave-girls as concubines after Dassine left him. With such dramas, it is not surprising that many early writers on the Tuareg were confused, with some emphasising that marriages were arranged and others highlighting what they saw as the freedom of women to choose and reject spouses.

The frequency of divorce in traditional society is not easy to ascertain. This is because many, perhaps even the majority, of marriages that ended in divorce, did so either before the birth of children or before the *azalay*. If both, then there is little if anything by which to remember the marriage! These ephemeral unions are simply, and probably rather quickly, expunged from the genealogical record. Even so, divorce was neither uncommon nor frowned upon, with many divorces being explained by the fact that first marriages (unlike subsequent ones) were largely arranged, usually between close cousins (see below), and that the spouses were consequently good friends, and – as Tuareg themselves say – 'knew each other too well', like 'brother and sister', rather than 'in love'. For reasons that I shall explain presently, the frequency of divorce in recent years has clearly risen.[23]

Cultural Norms and Social Reality: The Intervention of Social Classes

I have already said that marriages were often arranged between close cousins. Nearly all literary references to marriage amongst the Kel Ahaggar state that the preferential marriage was with a cross-cousin, preferably the mother's brother's daughter, and that marriages tended to be endogamous within the *tawsit*. This was confirmed to me by the Kel Ahaggar when I stayed with them in the 1960s–1970s, although they were quick to point out that marriages took place with all sorts of cousin. In fact, if we construct their genealogies and then look at the actual marriages contracted, we see that not only were marriages with cousins other than the matrilateral cross-cousin more common amongst both classes (Ihaggaren and Kel Ulli), but that each class[24] seems to have had a distinct preference for different types of cousin marriage.

An analysis of marriage statistics collected amongst both classes in the 1960s revealed contrastingly different marriage patterns.[25] However, two features common to both classes were their high rate of *tawsit* endogamy (between 93 and 95 per cent amongst the Dag Rali and between 67 and 74 per cent amongst the Kel Rela) and the high propensity for marriage with cousins of one sort or another.[26] The second feature really stems from the first, in that with such high levels of endogamy over so many generations, and in *tawsatin* whose members number between, say, only 300 and 600, it is virtually impossible to marry anyone within the *tawsit* who is not a cousin of sorts! Nor does the system of nomenclature help us: all collaterals in a man's generation, with the exception of his true and half brothers, sisters and parallel cousins, are merged together as *ibubah* ('male', sing. *ababah*) or *tibubah* ('female', sing. *tababaht*), the term given to cross-cousins, whether matrilateral or patrilateral. But, with ongoing endogamy, most members of a *tawsit* may be related through matrilateral and patrilineal consanguineous and affinal ties, with the result that almost every member of the *tawsit* of a man's own generation may be categorised as a 'cross-cousin'. Thus, when Kel Ahaggar say that preferential marriage is with the *tababaht*, the term is not necessarily being used for the explicit designation of the mother's brother's daughter, but often classificatorily and implicitly to mean a 'cousin of sorts'; by a further extension of meaning, this may be almost synonymous with saying that preferential marriage is with a member of the *tawsit*!

If this sounds confusing for us, it is little less so for the Kel Ahaggar themselves![27] Therefore, let me turn first to the marital strategies of the Kel

Rela (nobles) amongst whom endogamy is slightly less and the categorisation of cousin marriages a little more clear-cut than amongst the Dag Rali.

Ihaggaren (Kel Rela) Marital Strategies

The Kel Rela were preoccupied in earlier times by three overarching political concerns, which were achieved in large measure by means of their marital strategies. These were: to reproduce the class structure and their dominant position within it; to overcome or reduce the threat posed to their pre-eminent position in Ahaggar by the Taitok and Tegehe Mellet;[28] and, at the more individual level, to secure access to political rights and status for their descendants within the Kel Rela *tawsit* itself.

Their position in the class structure was maintained by the practice of 'class endogamy'. Although there were a few marriages between Kel Rela men and women from Kel Ulli *tawsatin*,[29] there has never been an instance of a Kel Rela woman marrying a man from a subordinate *tawsit*.[30]

As I have described elsewhere,[31] the Kel Rela's supremacy in Ahaggar was not secured until the French conquest at the beginning of the twentieth century. Prior to that time, their supremacy was being threatened almost continuously by the Taitok and Tegehe Mellet. Many of the Kel Rela's exogamous marriages were with these two groups, especially the Taitok, with many of them being specifically designed acts of reconciliation or appeasement after periods of hostility between them.

Amongst the Kel Rela themselves, internal rivalries centred almost exclusively on access to political rights, especially those over the Kel Ulli. Although some Kel Rela families held specific rights over certain Kel Ulli sections and families, most of this political power, in the form of rights to dues of political allegiance (*tiwse*) and land-rents (*ehere-n-amadal*)[32] from the subordinate classes, was centralised in the position of the *Amenukal*. Within the Kel Rela, however, the right to succeed to the position of *Amenukal* was restricted to certain matrilineal 'sections' (matrilineages), which were referred to as being *agg ettebel* (lit. 'of the drum'). The Kel Rela originally comprised nine such matrilineal sections, although four were not *agg ettebel*, because either they had lost their rights to the *ettebel* in earlier times through marital misalliance or they had been incorporated into the Kel Rela without being granted access to the *ettebel*. Of the remainder, two dwindled in significance, leaving only three politically dominant *agg ettebel* matrilineages. Amongst these three, rivalry reached critical dimensions on several occasions.

For these nobles, descent was an issue of primary concern, for the ability of Kel Rela families to reckon and manipulate their genealogical descent in this inherent struggle and competition for power, especially in a matrilineally adelphic system of succession, was a major factor in determining their fortunes. To be *agg ettebel* was consequently of crucial importance. Thus, while Kel Rela might well have paid lip service to the preferred marriage being with the mother's brother's daughter, marrying directly into the matriline, through marriage with the matrilateral parallel cousin, was the specific strategy for retaining and limiting access to this power, and for securing these matrilineal sections as minimal corporate lineages in which the various political rights over subordinate groups and the economic benefits emanating through the exercise of those rights could be retained. Indeed, my analysis of Kel Rela marriages up to the 1960s revealed that 32 per cent of marriages with kinsmen and 78 per cent of all 'cousin marriages' were with the actual or classificatory matrilateral parallel cousin.[33]

We can thus see how and why bilineality amongst the Kel Rela was not underscored, for the importance and significance of descent lay with the matriline, through which political rights, power and status were transmitted, rather than with the patriline, which hardly necessitated the reckoning of genealogical descent, since inheritance effectively involved little more than 'being one's father son'. In fact, the question of inheritance rules amongst the nobility (and other Tuareg) in earlier times is not entirely clear. Although Islamic influences reached the Sahara around the eleventh century, the Kel Ahaggar have always been notoriously lax Moslems.[34] There are several literary references suggesting that a man may have inherited from his mother's brother.[35] Few of these references mention class differences, while most of them are ambiguous in that they do not make clear whether they are referring to inheritance of property or succession to political office. Thus, while we know that a man transmitted the 'symbols of his power' to his sister's son, such as his specialised weapons, it is not clear whether this may also have included his camels. If that was in fact the case at some time in the past, then we can see that the patriline amongst the nobility, even at the level of inheritance, was relatively unimportant.

Kel Ulli (Dag Rali) Marital Strategies

In the case of the Dag Rali, and other Kel Ulli *tawsatin*, the imbalance between the significance of the matriline and patriline was reduced, along with the relevance of descent as an organisational principle, as a result of their different political rights and means of acquisition of wealth, in comparison with those of the Kel Rela.

The political subordination of the Kel Ulli, expressed through their various tributary payments, provided the Ihaggaren with most of their subsistence products. The Ihaggaren's need to gain access to these rights and secure the transmission of their benefits was not paralleled amongst the Kel Ulli, who held no such rights over subordinate groups. On the contrary, the political rights of the Kel Ulli headmen ('chiefs' – *amraren*) offered few economic benefits, and were to a large extent the inverse of those of the *Amenukal* and other drum-chiefs, in that the chiefs of Kel Ulli *tawsatin* were primarily responsible for the collection and payment of the various dues owed to the *Amenukal* and other drum-chiefs.[36]

Thus, while most of the nobles' subsistence products were derived directly from their political rights, those of the Kel Ulli were derived predominantly from their internal resources and activities of goat breeding and, since the end of the nineteenth century, caravan trading. While the primary consideration of nobles was the maximisation of their political rights and power through the acquisition of access to the *agg ettebel* matrilineages, that of the Kel Ulli was the maximisation of their pastoral resources – goats and, in more recent times, camels.

The extent to which these economic interests may have been reflected in the Kel Ulli's marital strategies presents us with a major difficulty. This is because their economic resources and interests changed dramatically during the course of the two generations spanning the end of the nineteenth and beginning of the twentieth century. I have discussed this major change in the Kel Ulli's economic orientation in some detail elsewhere.[37] The salient point is that the development of the salt caravans to Niger, on such a huge scale, quite apart from their activities as 'warriors in their own right', must have required certain changes in their social organisation. In their 'traditional' role of goat-herders, the *ariwan* could function as a more or less independent and viable economic unit. The introduction of the camel and the development of large-scale caravan trading required a greater amount of economic co-operation, in terms of labour resources, than could be mustered within the *ariwan*.

This co-operation is seen in the relations between the *ariwan* and the *tawsit* section. In the Dag Rali, for example, there were four sections – the Kel Terhenanet, Kel Tamanrasset, Kel Tinhart and Kel Hirafok – each of which held corporate land rights over its own sub-areas within the overall territory of the *tawsit*. In earlier times, it may well have been that the structural organisation of these sections was similar to that of the Kel Rela sections in which membership was based on matrilineal descent. However, in the 1960s, and I suspect for some years before then, it was difficult to define these sections in anything except a territorial sense as patrilineally organised local groups. In the 1960s, as today, Dag Rali equate section membership with residency, which is predominantly patrilocal. Thus, although the section may be defined ideationally, like all Kel Ahaggar groups, in terms of matrilineal membership, in reality it was effectively nothing more than the higher-level structural equivalent of the *ariwan*: a larger, patrilineally organised, territorial group co-operating in camel breeding and caravan trading. In practice, one might even substitute bilineal for patrilineal, for with about 50 per cent of all Dag Rali marriages being endogamous within the section, most members were related through both lines, with confusion and ambiguity in kin relationship being paramount. In the 1960s, when I raised with them the matter of the matriline and patriline, especially in the context of the determination of group membership, the answer I received was invariably along the lines of: *tesa* (the stomach), which symbolises the mother's family, and *arouri* (the back), which symbolises the father's family, 'are the same thing'!

Whether this helps us to make much sense of the Dag Rali's marriage pattern is open to question. Unlike the Kel Rela, amongst whom we saw a strong statistical preference for marriage into the matriline – ideally with the mother's sister's daughter, the mother's sister's daughter's daughter, or a classificatory matrilateral parallel cousin – the actual marriages contracted amongst the Dag Rali are with cousins of all types, with little or no obvious statistical preference. In the 1960s, the matrilateral side outweighed the patrilateral side amongst first cousin marriages (parallel and cross) by two percentage points – a figure which is not statistically significant. This statistical bias was reversed (to one percentage point – also not significant) when the first descending generation (that is, once removed) was included. When classificatory cousins were included there was a nine percentage point bias favouring parallel cousins over cross-cousins, with patrilateral parallel cousins being strongly favoured (by 15 percentage points) over the maternal side. However, with the majority of kin marriages (44 per cent) being with distant kin (beyond second cousin) which could not be traced accurately, it is doubtful whether too much should be read into this apparent statistical preference, nor the fact that the most common marriage (22.5 per cent of kin marriages and 44 per cent of 'cousin marriages') was with patrilateral parallel cousins (actual and classificatory).

When I wrote on this subject in the 1960s, I explained the Dag Rali's marriage pattern, favouring as it appeared to do the patrilateral parallel cousin, and their tendency to equate section membership with patrilocality, on the basis of two related levels. One was the suggestion that the economic requirements and conditions of pastoralism, particularly those generated by the possession of camels and the development of caravan trading, outweighed purely political interests in the form of access to the *agg ettebel* matrilineages and chieftaincy. The other was the suggestion that it was a misconception, in spite of the structural significance of the patriline amongst the Kel Ulli, to assume a corresponding diminution in the relevance of the matriline. Rather,

The Lesser Gods of the Sahara

I suggested that the possible increase in the structural significance of the patriline may have been permitted, and even facilitated, by the greater ideational and ideological strength and relevance of the matriline.

In reviewing these suggestions some 40 years on, they still seem to 'make sense', but are still based on the same level of conjecture as they were then! This conjecture centres around the Kel Ulli's acquisition of camels and their consequent shift in the emphasis of their economic activity, from goat breeding to camel pastoralism – and all the activities that it permitted, notably warfare and caravan trading. We can thus envisage the Kel Ulli's acquisition of camels as bringing about a major change in their social and economic organisation, and not least in their gender roles: goats belong strictly to the domain of women, while camels belong strictly to the realm of men.[38]

We do not know when the Kel Ulli came to possess their own camels, except that it was probably towards the later part of the nineteenth century.[39] Unfortunately, neither do we know much about their descent, marriage and residency systems before that time. We therefore have no concrete knowledge on which to base the presumption that this revolutionary change in their material state generated changes in their social organisation. However, we do know that when goats were the Kel Ulli's main resource, the *ariwan* could operate as an economically viable and independent unit. This would not have been the case after the introduction of the camel, and especially the commencement of large-scale caravan trading, for these activities demanded greater labour resources, and consequently a wider field of economic co-operation, than could be mustered within the *ariwan* itself. This wider field was the section, which we might refer to as the 'camel unit' as distinct from the 'goat unit' of the *ariwan*. I can only hypothesise that with the acquisition of the camel, both patrilocality (if uxorilocality was in fact more pronounced in earlier times) and marriage with the patrilateral parallel cousin (actual and classificatory) became favoured as means of restricting the circulation of camels, and encysting the section as a more-or-less corporate unit. With a section endogamy rate of around 50 per cent, it does not take long before marriage to the cross cousin, who is now also likely to be resident in the section territory, achieves the same end. We can perhaps see a similar logic applying to *tawsit* endogamy: Kel Ulli *tawsatin*, notably the Dag Rali and Aguh-en-tehle, were the most favoured in terms of pastoral resources and almost certainly the wealthiest Kel Ulli in Ahaggar in terms of livestock holdings. In purely ecological and economic terms, exchange marriages with other *tawsatin* would therefore have procured them few benefits, but would have provided the other *tawsatin* with access to their resources.

The above hypothesis merely highlights the contradiction between their cultural and social systems. There is, as I suggested in the 1960s, more to be

The End of the Matriline?

explained than 'cultural lag', albeit possibly over a short period of time. Indeed, by ignoring what the people were saying, we are in danger of not seeing how their social systems really worked. My argument at that time was as follows.

Because of the residency pattern, a man found his maternal kin, especially his mother's brothers, dispersed further afield. Exchange marriages between sections, which made up just under half of all Dag Rali marriages, were thus predominantly with maternal kin. Exchange marriage took place between all four sections and it is interesting to note that the Kel Tamanrasset and Kel Terhenanet sections (who together form the Dag Rali proper) still speak of the Kel Tinhart and Kel Hirafok sections[40] as 'children of our mother's brother'. With the people themselves stating that the preferred marriage was with the mother's brother's daughter, we must ask what was so significant about that type of marriage, and section exchange marriages in general, in relation to section endogamy and marriage with the statistically predominant patrilateral parallel cousin (actual and classificatory).

Amongst the Kel Ulli, a clue to the significance of marriage to matrilateral cousins (both cross and parallel) may be found, I believe, in Maurice Bloch's comments on the morality of kinship and the notion of 'long-term' and 'short-term' security.[41] The Kel Ahaggar's cultural system was permeated by its strong matrilineal emphasis, as reflected in the traditional 'rules' of group membership, political succession, land rights and so on, and as seen in a man's general relationship with his matriline, especially through the classificatory extension of the term *anet ma* (mother's brother), who, they say, 'can always be counted on to render assistance'.

A man did not speak of his agnatic kin with the same sense of ideological and moral commitment, as he did of his matrilineal kin. On the other hand, it was a man's male agnatic kin amongst whom he resided and with whom he had to co-operate, particularly in camel breeding and caravan trading activities. This 'co-operation' was, in Bloch's sense, essentially 'short-term' and was not based on any strong ideological commitment. The fact that the structure of the section tended to centre on a group of male agnates was merely an expression of the necessary co-operation between them. Indeed, as I suggested, it may be that the relatively high frequency of marriages with the patrilateral parallel cousin (actual and classificatory) reflected the necessity of having continually to reactivate relationships that were characterised by a relatively low moral content in contrast to those of the matriline.

The activation of these kin ties, which were the most necessary in terms of economic co-operation but which had the least moral commitment, was essentially a short-term strategy, providing no long-term security. In fact, this strategy, by encysting these ties within the section, and so limiting their outward extension, was at the expense of the section's long-term security against such risks as drought, disease, pillaging and so on.

The long-term security was provided, as we have seen, by the matriline, in the form of a man's mother's brothers, who were usually found living further afield, certainly in other *ariwan*, but also in other sections. These relationships had a stronger moral content and could always be depended upon for meeting future and unknown needs.

This line of argument does not necessarily explain why the stated preferred marriage was with the mother's brother's daughter, as this marriage is with a cross-cousin and therefore not necessarily within the matriline. However, I believe that with the ambiguity and 'bilineality' of so many kin relationships, as a consequence of such tight section and *tawsit* endogamy amongst the Kel Ulli, it is becoming increasingly difficult, and makes little sense, to try and unravel the specific kinship content of many 'cousin marriages'. It may well be, to stick with Bloch's 'morality of kinship' argument, that we should not be interpreting this reference to the mother's brother's daughter literally, but rather as a reference to the importance of the mother's brother, and hence the matriline, which provided both *ariwan* and sections with their long-term security.

The '*bouleversement*' of Kel Ahaggar Society: Forty Years Later

The above analysis applies to what I have referred to as 'traditional' society, or, more specifically, Kel Ahaggar society up to the time of Algerian independence in 1962. More than 40 years – almost two generations – have passed since then. What has happened to Kel Ahaggar society in these intervening years cannot be described adequately in a matter of one or two words. 'Upheaval' is too mundane; 'revolution' implies force of arms; 'social revolution' suggests that internal forces may have played determining roles. The French term *bouleversement* perhaps comes closest to capturing the essence of what has happened, and it is a word that French-speaking Tuareg themselves find appropriate for describing what they have experienced over the last 40 years.

The new Algerian state had considerable difficulty in establishing itself in the Saharan regions,[42] and certainly did not get its act together in the extreme south of the country for at least half a dozen years.[43] That does not mean that it did not take decisive action. On the contrary, through a few hastily issued decrees, radical changes were wrought. Slavery was abolished; the land was made free to those who worked it;[44] the southern border was closed to caravan trade and the French withdrew from the atomic base at In Eker, effectively closing the one local centre employing manual labour. Within the short space

The End of the Matriline?

of a few years, four of the five pillars of the Kel Ahaggar's economy had been destroyed, while the fifth, and their most important, pastoralism, was being decimated by the coincidental onset of drought.[45]

These changes were not so serious for the noble Kel Rela, many of whom were already living in Tamanrasset, as they were for the nomadic Kel Ahaggar. For the nomads, each year brought new hope that good rains would regenerate pasture and that the caravans would be allowed to travel to Niger. But, by the end of the 1960s, and as I have described elsewhere, most nomadic Kel Ahaggar had few options but to sedentarise.[46] The sedentarisation of nomads is not a simple, straightforward geographical-cum-residential process. It is as much a cognitive process, whose social, psychological and other effects cannot be immediately ascertained. Amongst some *tawsatin*, notably the Dag Rali and Aguh-en-tehle, some sections were able to sedentarise within their own traditional territories around water points where they were able to establish their own ethnically homogenous, small village communities. At that time, the use of the word 'village' was not altogether appropriate, for what we saw was a few families and even whole *ariwan* move their camps, and then build reed and even a few stone huts alongside them, as if the settlement was little more than a number of *ariwan* coming together on a slightly more permanent basis. Several of the villages that are now well-established in the Atakor region, such as the Kel Terhenanet and Kel Tamanrasset centres of Terhenanet and Tagmart, and the Aguh-en-tehle centres of Taramut and In Dalag, witnessed this process during the 1960s, as they grew from tiny cultivation centres with a few transient gardens and the occasional reed hut and stone enclosure into small, vibrant villages of up to a hundred or so residents. In villages such as these, where sedentarisation was more ethnically homogenous and undertaken at their own pace, the transition from 'nomadism' to 'sedentarism' was less of a 'shock', less psychologically profound and less of a rupture of traditional social organisational patterns. Indeed, during those years, many of these 'villagers' still thought and spoke of themselves as 'nomads',[47] seeing their position as merely transient until the rains improved and the Algerian authorities relented on such matters as caravan passage to Niger.[48] By the time these things did improve in the 1970s, places such as Terhenanet and Tagmart had become more or less permanently settled communities.

It was not only the Kel Ahaggar's economic system which experienced radical shocks in the wake of Algerian independence; their political system, much of which had been preserved during the years of colonial rule,[49] albeit to facilitate France's administration of the region, was also effectively abolished. The Kel Ahaggar's political system had no standing within the new state. Within the new Algerian state, the Kel Ahaggar's political representation was reduced, quite simply, to that of 'Algerian citizens' and as members of their local *commune* and *sous-prefecture* and, after 1984, the *wilaya* of Tamanrasset in the case of the Kel Ahaggar and the *wilaya* of Illizi in the case of the Kel Ajjer. Traditional political rights of subordination, such as *tiwse*, and land right payments, such as *ehere-n-amadel*, were officially abolished with all other such rights, notably pastoral-grazing rights and rights over various natural resources, being subsumed within the regulations and administrations of the *commune, daira* and *wilaya*. The main political office of the Kel Ahaggar was that of *Amenukal*. The incumbent at the time of Independence was Bay ag Akhemouk. He was immediately appointed as a nominal vice-president of the country, but with most of the day-to-day negotiations involving the Tuareg and the new government being handled by his half-brother, Hadj Moussa, who was not officially *agg ettebel*. Amongst the 'subordinate' *tawsatin*, the position of chief was reduced to little more than a socio-historical category, with no effective political power being attached to it. The new state moved as fast as possible to remove all vestigial and symbolic elements of the Kel Ahaggar's former political system, with even Tamanrasset's main hotel having its name changed very symbolically from Hotel Amenukal to Hotel Tin Hinan! On the eventual death of Bay ag Akhemouk in 1975, the post of *Amenukal* was effectively abolished.

The new state, having effectively abolished the traditional political system, then abolished the traditional system of naming.[50] Tuareg were told to drop the 'ag' (son of) or 'ult' (daughter of) and take a 'proper' family name. The reason given them by the government was to facilitate the computerisation of documents. The key feature of the traditional system of nomenclature was that it enabled Tuareg to reckon their descent relatively unambiguously over several generations, sometimes as many as seven or eight. This was of crucial importance in a society in which kinship and descent were its basic social organisational principles.[51]

These socio-political changes have had two profound consequences. The first is that changing the system of nomenclature has already led to considerable genealogical amnesia. The traditional system enabled a man literally to 'read out' his ascent: for example, Mohammed ag (son of) Ahmadu ag Elwafil ag Heguir, and so on. By choosing a new family name from one of his ancestors, such as Heguir, Mohammed's new name is simply Mohammed Heguir. In this case, Ahmadu and Elwafil have been squeezed out of the reckoning. With Mohammed's brother perhaps choosing a different surname, even the genealogical link between siblings can become lost.[52] I have recently been updating the genealogical records I made in the 1960s. While it has not been difficult to catch up on the last 40 years, one consequence of the induced

The End of the Matriline?

'genealogical amnesia' is that only a few of the eldest men and women have been able to help me check my records of earlier generations.

The second major consequence of these changes, particularly those to the political system, is that descent has lost most of its relevance as a social organisational principle. In 'traditional' times, descent determined a whole bundle of rights and obligations, many of which were critical to one's social and material existence. Today, that is no longer the case. With no political offices or rights to be transmitted, nor any land or other such rights being restricted to members of particular *tawsatin* or lineages, and with no such corollary obligations stemming from group membership, the matriline has become increasingly irrelevant. Group membership was determined traditionally by matrilineal descent. Although most Kel Ahaggar, when specifically questioned, will still confirm that it is 'the stomach which colours the child', the tendency, especially amongst younger people, is now to associate group membership (such as Kel Tamanrasset, Kel Terhenanet) with the village in which they live. People now tend to describe themselves as Kel Tagmart (people of the village Tagmart) and so on. These villages were, and still are, patrilocally organised residency groups, more or less coinciding with the original *tawsit* sections, such as Kel Tamanrasset in the case of Tagmart. However, because of the high rate of section (that is, village) endogamy, and to the extent that descent still has any relevance, these groups (that is, villages) are effectively 'bilineal' residency groups. In fact, many residents of the village of Tagmart, who regard themselves as Kel Tamanrasset and who now even refer to themselves as Kel Tagmart, are in fact members of the Usenden section of the Aguh-en-tehle in terms of their maternal descent. While there is still considerable intermarriage between the Usenden section of the Aguh-en-tehle and the Kel Tamanrasset section of the Dag Rali, the individuals concerned are now more inclined to regard themselves as members of their father's residency group (their patriline) than their mother's lineage, and regard these marriages more as 'cousin' marriages than exchange marriages between two matrilineally defined groups. In similar vein, although traditional residency 'rules' still have some bearing in the few remaining encampments and 'sectionalised' villages such as Terhenanet, Tagmart, Ifrak and so on, they too have become increasingly inchoate, with residency being based now on little more than the general acceptance that a wife lives with her husband, who in turn lives where he works!

This diminution of the importance and relevance of the matriline has been aided and accelerated by the change in the naming system. Even in the traditional system, names for both males and females were those of one's father, which meant that it was easier to recall one's patriline than matriline. Now, with family names being taken from an ancestor chosen more or less at random, even the patriline has become conflated. The example of Bouhen ag Khebbi, whom I have already mentioned in the context of his marriage to two slave-girls, well illustrates the problem. In the 1960s I had traced almost 100 of his descendants over three and occasionally four generations. Now, 40 years later, they span at least five generations. When I spent two days earlier this year with an old Kel Rela man, who is recognised as knowing the Kel Rela genealogies, trying to trace out the fourth and fifth generations, we soon ran into an insurmountable difficulty: some of them bore Bouhen's name while others had chosen the name of some other ancestor for their family name. At the end of it, we were both totally confused and even beginning to wonder if there had not been two Bouhens!

Perhaps surprisingly, most Kel Ahaggar men with whom I have discussed this change in nomenclature, and the 'genealogical amnesia' which it induces, expressed no resistance or anger at a move which effectively removed their fundamental identity – their names – at a stroke. On the contrary, most Tuareg seem to have taken it in a spirit of good humour, with many of them seizing the opportunity to rearrange their kinship ties or simply distance themselves from bothersome kinsmen!

Women's 'Double Whammy'

The consequences of all these many and complex changes have not been 'gender-neutral'. On the contrary, I think we can argue that women – in colloquial parlance – have suffered something of a 'double whammy'. First, the decline in the relevancy of descent, especially the significance of the matriline, as a social organisational principle has, in a sense, undermined the pre-eminent position that women once held in society. Access to the matriline, which few Kel Ahaggar can now recall beyond a couple of generations, is no longer of any political importance and of little additional social importance. Second, for reasons that I will explain below, sedentarisation has had a far more profound effect on the roles of women than those of men.

In the traditional, nomadic milieu, most able-bodied men were away from their camps for much of the year. From the 1920s up until the 1960s, when the salt caravans to Niger were the focal point of the annual cycle of economic activity, men might be away for at least six months of the year. If these same men also went on caravan to Tuat and Tidikelt, or accompanied their slaves to the salt mines at Tisemt in Amadror, they might be away from their camps for as many as eight or nine months of the year. In earlier times, before the development of the caravan trade, men might also be away for equally long periods on raiding expeditions. Women were therefore left in charge of the camps for most of the year. They were in command of the day-to-day organisation of the tent and food preparation. They were also responsible for the management and care of the goat herds and the never-ending search for pasture and water, and it was women who decided on the location and movement of camps. They were also responsible for all that was involved in the care and education of the children. In contrast, men's work in the camp was limited to looking after camels, the bulk of which were kept in Tamesna (northern Niger) or in the care of slaves, certain aspects of the preparation and cooking of meat and the occasional hunting or similar exploit. For men, their time in the encampment was a period of festivity, rest and relaxation between the gruelling 'work'[53] of warfare, raiding or caravans. In short, women were in control of the domestic domain in the widest sense.

With sedentarisation, women's roles changed enormously. Although many of their daily responsibilities – such as looking after the tent, hut or stone house, caring for the livestock (goats and sheep), being responsible for the general preparation of food and caring for children – remained the same, these tasks tended to become more burdensome and irksome upon sedentarisation. There were two reasons for this. One was that Kel Ahaggar women no longer had slaves to help them in these tasks. Amongst some Kel Ulli *tawsatin*, notably the Dag Rali, slaves outnumbered Tuareg. Female slaves (*tiklatin*) especially undertook much of the women's work in the camp, notably tending the goats, preparing food, taking care of children and so forth, to the extent that the role of the Tuareg woman in the nomadic milieu was more that of 'camp manager'. In the village, the management aspect of many of these tasks fell away, with women becoming reduced more to the status of 'domestic workers', effectively doing much of the work that had been previously undertaken by their *tiklatin*. The second reason was that much of this work was now 'indoors', rather than in the open, as was the way in the encampments. The mere aspect of working behind a reed, mud brick or stone wall, as distinct from the hearth of an open tent, tended to set women physically more apart than was the case in the encampment, and thus added to the air of seclusion that was in keeping with the increased Arabisation and Islamisation that have accompanied the overall process of Algerianisation. Moreover, with the growth of village schools, and the increasing school attendance of 'sedentarised nomads', even the women's responsibility for the education of children was removed from their domain.

The temporal framework in which these changes took place is less clear. The reason for this is simply that I was not in the region between 1972 and 1999 and, with one notable exception, no studies were undertaken of these processes during this intervening period. Thus, with the exception of that one study, namely Pandolfi's work in the late 1980s and early 1990s amongst the Dag Rali in the village of Terhenanet, where I had also worked in the 1960s, we do not have a very clear picture of what happened during these intervening years.

By the time of Pandolfi's study, virtually all the Kel Terhenanet were settled in the village of Terhenanet. However, I believe that we should regard Terhenanet, along with other villages such as Tagmart, Ifrak and so on, where nomads settled in their own territories on an ethnically homogenous basis and more or less in their own time and under their own volition, as slightly special cases. I witnessed the first few years of sedentarisation in these centres. It was far less of a 'shock' to the nomads than in the cases of bigger villages or ones in which nomads had to settle alongside their former *harratin* garden-workers or ex-slaves. At places like Terhenanet, Tagmart and Ifrak, sedentarisation was more gradual and managed by the people themselves, so that the growth of the village and its residential pattern took the form of a number of *ariwan* coming together. Moreover, it was very clear to me during the beginning of this process that the people concerned, from a cognitive perspective, did not see themselves as sedentarising but rather as settling temporarily in their own area, alongside some of their own gardens, while awaiting for rainfall, pasture and the caravan trade to improve. Moreover, and of particular importance to these villages, was the fact that the traditional 'work' of men, with camels, gradually picked up during the 1970s and 1980s in the form of tourism. By the late 1980s, some 10,000 foreign tourists were visiting the region each year.[54] This not only provided considerable employment for many of the men in these villages but ensured their absence from the village for several months of the year, thus partly replicating the labour pattern of the camps. Thus, and as Pandolfi's study of Terhenanet shows, the transition from nomadic to sedentary life was ameliorated and in a sense 'managed' by the people themselves, to the extent that many aspects of 'traditional' culture and social organisation were preserved.

My own view is that major changes in villages such as Terhenanet began to take place in the early 1990s, in the years immediately after Pandolfi had finished his fieldwork there. These changes, comparable in their severity to those experienced in the 1960s in the wake of Algerian independence, were associated directly with the onset of Algeria's political 'crisis' in the north of the country.[55] The three major implications of Algeria's 'crisis' for the extreme south of the country were the complete cessation of tourism, the growth of Tamanrasset into a major administrative and garrison town, and the movement to Tamanrasset of northern Algerians, often with their families, seeking to avoid the violence that enveloped the north of the country. Although the official census shows only a doubling of Tamanrasset's population between the late 1980s and 1998, the actual population growth between the late 1980s and the beginning of the twenty-first century has been at least threefold,[56] from some 40,000 to well over 100,000.[57]

The End of the Matriline?

Tourism provided the Kel Ahaggar and the Kel Ajjer with their place in the modern world: it was 'their industry'. Tuareg saw it as an extension of their traditional camel economy, as expressed in their saying that: 'without nomadism there is no tourism; and without tourism there is no nomadism'.[58] Its immediate and complete cessation around 1992 dealt them a catastrophic blow, particularly the men for whom 'tourism' enabled them to fulfil their traditional roles, or *'travail'* as they called it, as cameleers, guides, drivers of 4WDs and so forth. As tourism 'boomed' during the 1980s, men from villages such as Terhenanet, Tagmart, Azernen and elsewhere spent much of their time away from their homes – analogously to being away on caravan or raiding. With tourism's sudden cessation, these villages became transformed from a group of sedentarised *ariwan* (that is, a *tawsit* section) living together in huts and mud-brick houses rather than tents, to depressed communities in which disgruntled men meddled increasingly in village (women's) affairs while whiling away their 'unemployment'. The loss of male dignity was compounded by the local government effectively offering many of these men 'employment' as *'guardiens'* of the Ahaggar National Park.[59] Being a Park guard involved no real work other than 'sitting around', while the money, approximately £70pm, was regarded as nothing more than a government hand-out: a 'social pension'. Several older men refused to accept this 'offer', saying that it was demeaning.[60]

The Impact of Tamanrasset on Kel Ahaggar Society

Tamanrasset, now a burgeoning administrative centre and frontier garrison town within a day's ride (an hour's drive) of many of these villages, became a magnet and a symbol of modernity for many of these younger men. Some saw it as an opportunity for employment, others as the focus of the 'easy life', 'rich pickings' and adventure in the form of the lucrative trans-Saharan smuggling business – a 'job' in which Tuareg, with their knowledge of the desert, could excel. Although Kel Ahaggar society has always tried to protect itself from the influences of the outside world by categorising Tamanrasset as part of that world, with its social mores and 'goings-on' being conceptualised and classified as outside or beyond their own cultural and social practices, such a separation has become increasingly blurred over the last decade, as Kel Ahaggar men have found themselves being drawn more frequently into Tamanrasset and as the town's (city's) urban sprawl and electricity network has effectively turned the once-small cultivation centres of Tagmart, Otoul, Tit, Amsel, Terhenanet and others into little more than dormitory villages in which television has ousted the hearth as the focal point in social life.

The impact of Tamanrasset on Kel Ahaggar society, notably the surrounding villages, has been profound. Whereas Tamanrasset was once seen by Kel Ahaggar as 'external' to their socio-cultural domain, young Tuareg men, aspiring to the modernity that it offers, have pulled down its cultural drawbridge. Arabism, the contradictions inherent in the national strands of secularisation and Islamisation, the Internet, the cell phone, 'state controlled' television and other such powerful symbols of modernity[61] are being transplanted from the kaleidoscopic cultural 'mish-mash' of Tamanrasset into the heart of Kel Ahaggar society. But, for the most part, the transplantation is seemingly without discernment or comprehension, reducing the virtues of both Arabic and Islamic cultures to little more than a depraved parody, a cruel caricature, of an Islamo-Arabism which advocates the seclusion of women and, albeit more often in jest, the virtues of polygyny over monogamy.

During my enquiries into present-day lifestyles in some of these predominantly Tuareg villages I was struck by certain middle-aged to elderly French-speaking Tuareg describing the general social behaviour of certain villages as 'debauched' (*débauché*) and certain individuals as 'depraved' (*corrompu*). These are strong admonishments, which are difficult for a social scientist to investigate at the best of times. It is even more difficult, and one has to be even more careful, in such a socially and politically sensitive climate, especially when the enquirer is a man and the main subjects of enquiry, the presumed victims of such 'debauchery', are women. Therefore, both my following general comments and illustrative case study should be treated circumspectly, although they are based on accurate genealogical and more qualitative data given to me by reliable informants, who are themselves concerned by many aspects of such increasingly common behaviour.

Changes in Social Behaviour since Sedentarisation

The most immediately noticeable changes in social behaviour since the sedentarisation of most Kel Ahaggar in the 1960s, and particularly since the beginning of the 1990s, especially in regard to marriage practices and the general position of women, are as follows.

First, girls are tending to marry at a much earlier age. As mentioned earlier, in 'traditional' times girls tended to marry in their early twenties. Today, girls are marrying much earlier, frequently as soon as they are nubile around the age of fourteen or even younger.[62]

Second, while some of these young girls are marrying young men, just as many are marrying men very much older then themselves. In fact, there has been a noticeable trend in recent years for extremely young girls to marry very much older men. For example, when Pandolfi was at the village of Tagmart in the summer of 1992, he recorded four marriages involving young girls. One was barely 13, while another, aged 15–16, was married to a man in his sixties.[63] Over the last few years, I have come across several such marriages, with informants assuring me that it is an increasing trend. Kel Ahaggar told Pandolfi that it was a symptom of the increasing Arabisation of their society.[64] This has also been confirmed to me in all my discussions with Kel Ahaggar on the same subject, usually with the rider that the 'Algerianisation' of Ahaggar has led to the Kel Ahaggar adopting all the worst features of Islamo-Arabism.[65]

Third, and related to the previous point, an increasing number of marriages are promised or arranged years in advance. This feature was also noted by Pandolfi in the early 1990s[66] and, from the way in which Kel Ahaggar have explained it to me, it seems to have become even more common since then.

Fourth, with so many girls now marrying at very young ages, and with so many of their marriages having been arranged by their parents several years beforehand, there is even more parental and societal pressure on young girls to go along with such arrangements. A consequence of this, as recognised by the Kel Ahaggar themselves, is that more marriages are ending in divorce, with many of them even ending before the *azalay*.[67]

Fifth, divorces are now very much more common than in 'traditional' times.[68] There are many reasons for this. One is a consequence of girls marrying at a much earlier age and with most such marriages being arranged many years beforehand. A second reason is the result of a practice which is becoming increasingly prevalent in Tamanrasset, and possibly also in the larger villages. This is for girls to get married with the intention of getting divorced as soon as possible, and especially before having a child, so that they can free themselves from the restrictive and onerous pressures of the family, as enshrined in both Islamo-Arabic cultural practice and associated legal statutes, and thus acquire some measure of independence and control over their own lives. Attempts to free themselves from the constraints of Islamo-Arabic cultural practice are not limited to young women. On the contrary, there is a noticeable trend amongst old women to divorce themselves from their husbands so that they will not have to endure the period of seclusion, as required by Islamic law and as encoded in the 'Family Code', which lasts for four months and ten days following the death of their husband.

Further reasons are more complex and relate to a number of factors amongst which one would point to a general decline in respect for women *per se*, associated with sedentarisation, Arabisation and the decline in importance of the matriline; the manipulation and abuse by men of Islamic divorce procedures;[69] and the absence of traditional authority structures. These factors

The Lesser Gods of the Sahara

are perhaps the most pernicious and tend to lie at the heart of most accusations of debauchery and depravity. They are well illustrated in the following case study (see Figure 1).[70]

During the last few years of the 1960s and the beginning of the 1970s, Shikat's encampment moved intermittently between the mountains of Atakor and the village of Talit, not far from Tamanrasset, before finally settling in the village for good. During that period, Shikat's eldest son, Mohamed, married a distant cousin, Zahara, who came to live with him in Talit. About ten years later, Shikat's second son, El Khunti, married Sherifa, his mother's brother's daughter, who came from section X of *tawsit* Y with whom there had been a long history of exchange marriages. Sherifa also came to live at Talit. A short time later, Shikat's daughter, Fatiya, married a first cousin from her mother's brother's section and left Talit to live with her husband's family amongst section X of *tawsit* Y. It was around the beginning of the 1990s that certain members of the village, which now numbered about 60 people, began engaging in behaviour which many, especially their elder kinsmen, now describe as *débauché* and *corrompu*. It began with El Khunti having an affair with Fadimata, the married daughter of his father's brother (parallel cousin). In the meantime, another of El Khunti's neighbours, a second cousin called Ahmed, began complaining to all who cared to listen that his wife, Hadija, became pregnant every time he slept with her, with the consequent offspring becoming an intolerable financial burden on him. Moreover, he complained that her teeth protruded and he could not be expected to sleep with such an ugly woman! He and El Khunti cooked up a plan: El Khunti would divorce Sherifa, as she was now past childbearing age (and not so ugly), and pass her over to Ahmed, who could 'get rid' of Hadija and sleep instead with Sherifa without fear of any more children. The plan was put into effect, with Fadimata leaving her husband and moving in with El Khunti, while Sherifa moved in with Ahmed. Hadija and her four children moved back to her father's village, which was nearby. In the meantime, Ahmed's brother, Mostafa, who was well past middle age, said that he too would like a new wife. El Khunti accordingly arranged for him to marry his thirteen-year-old daughter, Mariama. This meant that Ahmed's wife (Sherifa) was his brother's wife's mother! Mostafa and Mariama have since had five children, four of whom have died. At about the same time as these dramas commenced, Mohamed's wife, Zahara, died and he married Lalla, a cousin from section X of *tawsit* Y, which was seen as an exchange for the marriage of his sister Fatiya. Lalla's ten or so years of married life have been ones of almost perpetual pregnancy, although three of the ten children to whom she has given birth died in infancy. Mohamed's granddaughter by his first wife also died in infancy.

FIGURE 1

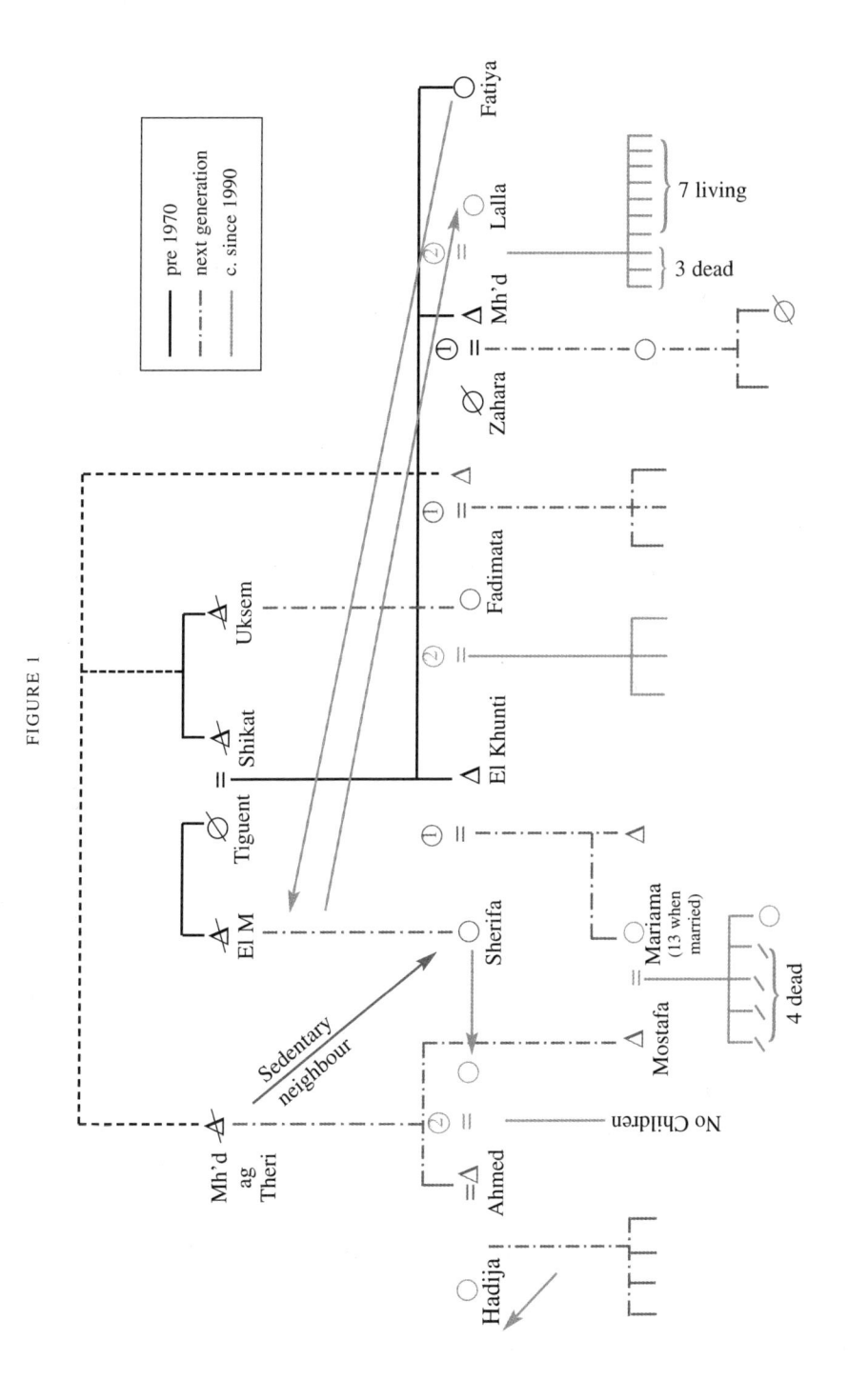

The key point that comes out of this story is the ease and frequency of divorce. Indeed, one might well ask how this is possible legally and how other members of society view it. The first point to make is that most of these 'divorces' have a highly questionable legal basis. The state's laws on divorce, and the 'getting rid' of a first wife to take another are quite strict in that the first wife must sign a document in court agreeing to the taking of the second wife. This, in fact, is rarely done, as men tend to rely on women's ignorance of the law. Moreover, the second marriage is hardly ever registered, but merely undertaken before a *taleb*.[71] In other words, not only is the supposed divorce illegal, but also the second marriage does not exist in terms of national law, as it was never registered. This means that the second wife has no inheritance or other rights on the death of the husband. The net outcome of this situation, to paraphrase female informants, is that there is a lot of 'messing around' by men, many of whom joke, and perhaps imagine, that they can have up to four wives as and how they please.

This situation has led to what several women, in their ignorance of the law, have described to me as a 'fear of Islam'. They believe and fear that the new Islamo-Arabic order gives men the right to get rid of them and take another wife as and when they want. Since my return to the region four years ago, many women have told me that one reason why they are so frequently pregnant, when forms of birth control are readily available, is to demonstrate that they are still young and fertile and consequently still attractive to their husbands (see Hadija, Mostafa's wife and Lalla in Figure 1). A high number of closely spaced pregnancies raises questions about their effect on the health of women. In traditional times, women rarely had more than four children, with births usually being fairly well spaced.[72] In contrast, the five 'second generation' married women (excluding Zahara who died while still of child-bearing age) recorded in Figure 1, have borne an average of 4.8 children. While these women cannot necessarily be taken as representative of society as a whole, they do reflect what I have witnessed throughout the region since my return there four years ago. Indeed, in one small settlement in northern Ahaggar, I counted some 45 children between the ages of birth and about 12 and only five women of childbearing age. There are, of course, other reasons for this increased birth rate, notably a more assured food supply and better medical facilities. Even so, while both those factors play a contributory role, the reason for the high birth rate given to me most frequently by female informants is the belief that proof of fertility, and hence youth, is their safeguard against being cast aside.

However, there are two further significant points which should be made. The first is that nearly all men with whom I have discussed this situation claim that they do not want so many children as it imposes an intolerable financial burden on them. Indeed, one reason why Ahmed 'divorced' Hadija was because 'she was always getting pregnant'. The second point concerns the apparently high incidence of infant mortality. Of the 26 children in generations 3–4 in Figure 1, eight died in infancy. Several Kel Ahaggar have suggested to me that infant mortality is now higher than in earlier times. We should, of course, be wary of such suggestions as we have no firm knowledge of infant mortality rates in earlier times. In traditional times, women used many forms of birth control to space births, and there is considerable evidence in many of the earlier ethnographies to suggest that they used several means for inducing abortions and even practiced infanticide to get rid of unwanted children. There is also the fact that many children who died early in life have simply been 'forgotten' and omitted from the genealogical record. Thus, while there seems little doubt that we have an under-recording of infant mortality in traditional times, I am fairly certain that current infant mortality rates are higher than when I was with the Kel Ahaggar in the 1960s. A summary survey, undertaken in 2003, of Dag Rali births over the last ten or so years, revealed that 52 out of 301 children had died at birth or in infancy. This is a death rate of 17 per cent.[73] It should, however, be emphasised that no more detailed research has yet been undertaken on infant mortality amongst the Kel Ahaggar. Nevertheless, it is a subject on which several of my informants have expressed concern, with some of the better informed amongst them questioning whether the exceptionally high rate and intensity of endogamy has contributed to genetic weaknesses or disorders. In similar vein, a few better-educated Kel Ahaggar are now questioning whether the increasing prevalence of sexually transmitted diseases[74] is a reason why many women now have difficulty in conceiving, and whether such sexually transmitted diseases also contribute to infant mortality. Women who cannot conceive live in fear of being divorced or rejected for another wife. No research has been undertaken into any of these questions, but the fact that some Kel Ahaggar are beginning to raise them is a major step in the right direction.

The reactions of Kel Ahaggar to these changes and trends cannot be summarised in simple terms, as there are many different levels of knowledge, awareness, confusion, ambivalence and consequent attitudes amongst the many social constituencies – old, young, male, female, urban, village, nomad and so on – that comprise Kel Ahaggar society. At the risk of reducing complex social phenomena to meaningless generalisations, there is, not surprisingly, a greater awareness of the more negative aspects of these changes amongst the elder generation and the better-educated, but without there being an outright condemnation of 'modernisation' (a euphemism for 'Algerianisation', 'Arabisation' and 'Islamisation'), which is perhaps accepted with resignation as being inevitable. As one French-speaking Tuareg sage said to me: '*il faut prendre le bénéfice avec les charges*' (one must take the rough with the smooth)!

I have always been struck by the Tuareg's remarkable ability to cope with adversity and the unknown. One might suggest that their ability to manage and adapt to such difficult situations requires the sort of cultural flexibility which comes from a long history of adversity, survival and adaptation to a hard, frequently changing and potentially hostile environment. This was very apparent when I lived with them in the traumatic years of the 1960s, and it is something which has struck me again most forcibly since my return at the end of the 1990s. It is a cultural defence mechanism which is not easily prised open. When it is, one finds the sadness and regrets: the loss of their nomenclature, the loss of their language, the loss of their history, the loss of knowledge of plants, herbal medicines and fauna, the replacement of camels with 4WDs and so forth. In the same way, a discussion of the merits of modernisation is more likely to proceed with its perceived benefits – the hospitals, cell phones, the Internet, better food supplies and so forth – than its adversities, which are considerable. Prime amongst the adversities are the points that I have raised here: the frequency of divorce and the breakdown of familial (and one might add 'tribal') social structures, and especially the implications for children; the degradation of women and young girls; the 'debauched' behaviour of men such as El Khunti and Mohamed (see Figure 1); and the spread of AIDS and other sexually transmitted diseases.

The Reactions of Women: Independency and Reversion to the Nomadic Milieu

Two responses of women to their new-found positions are particularly interesting. One, explained to me by several elder women, is that they now feel excluded from the juridical and political process, in that they consider that the removal of the traditional political system by the Algerian authorities, notably the offices of *Amenukal* (supreme chief) and *amrar* (*tawsit* chief/headman), has left them with no means of appeal. They believe that the traditional system of political authority would not have allowed the sort of behaviour that I have described above, especially the way in which women's marital rights are now so easily threatened. Without an *Amenukal* or *amrar*, women feel they no longer have any right of appeal other than to the state in the form of the *commune, daira, wilaya* or court, which they see as largely inaccessible and as part of their problem rather than its solution.

Secondly, an increasing number of women are deciding to live 'independently of men' and re-establishing themselves in the nomadic milieu.

The End of the Matriline?

Neither the precise details nor the extent of this phenomenon are yet clear to me. I first stumbled upon it in 1999 when I was travelling alone on foot in a part of Atakor, which had long been vacated by Dag Rali camps, and came across two women sheltering in a cave and accompanied by a goat-herd. At the time I supposed that they had merely taken their goats into the mountains for a few days from either the village of Ilaman or Terhenanet. Later, I learnt that they belonged to one of several groups of Dag Rali women who had left their villages and set up their own encampments in the mountains. Since then I have come across a further seven such camps, six of which are inhabited by Dag Rali women and their children, while one has been established by six former slave-girls of the Dag Rali who have left their village of Ilaman for the same reason. All of these camps comprise women who have been rejected or divorced by their husbands, or who have divorced their husbands. Sometimes they include their children and sometimes their widowed or divorced mothers. Of the three such units that I have been able to investigate so far, one camp contained six women, all of 'marriageable age' and a 12-year-old boy, who was the son of one of them. Another consisted of a woman in her sixties, her divorced daughter and her small child, and the old woman's former slave-girl, who, although legally free, had chosen to remain with her former mistress. The older woman was not legally divorced but had 'kicked out' (her words) her husband several years ago for 'messing around' (her words). The third camp comprised a small matrilineage of five women: the widowed grandmother, her divorced daughter and her three daughters, two of whom were fathered by her husband, while the third was born out of wedlock to a father who is apparently unknown. The other four camps all appear to be of a similar social structure. All of these eight camps had their own goats, and at least two had established their own gardens. However, what seems to make these units economically viable is that all of these women[75] owned camels.[76] The camels were kept in Tamesna, where they were tended by Irregenaten, and brought up to Tamanrasset for sale when they needed additional cash.

The phenomenon of women living alone is certainly not new. In the 1960s I came across many small camps comprising one or two tents which were occupied by old women, either spinsters or widows, sometimes accompanied by grandchildren or, quite frequently, old female slaves who had chosen to remain in the nomadic milieu with their former 'owners'. Several such social units can still be found today. The phenomenon which appears to be quite new and very recent[77] is the situation described above, in which women of childbearing or marriageable age have stated that they want to 'live without men' and have accordingly chosen to leave their villages and live alone, or with other women of similar circumstances, in the nomadic milieu.

However, this phenomenon raises a number of questions which cannot be answered at this stage. For instance, although there are at least eight such encampments amongst the Dag Rali (and their former slaves), I do not yet know how widespread this phenomenon is amongst other *tawsatin*. I have heard of similar situations amongst the Aguh-en-tehle and have recently come across camps alongside the Tefedest, near Ahnet and in the central Tassili region, which appeared to consist solely of women and children, but without having the opportunity to investigate more intensively. Similarly, it is not yet clear to me when this phenomenon began. Although the informants with whom I have discussed it have given me a strong impression that it is a response to the sort of changes which women have experienced particularly over the last decade or so, it is conceivable that such camps are merely the changed social form of what I refer to rather loosely as 'goat camps'. Such camps were temporary arrangements which enabled the goat herds of villages such as Terhenanet, Tagmart, Hirafok and many others, to be taken to better pasture further away from the village as surrounding pasture inevitably becomes overgrazed. Managing the goat herds was traditionally, and still is, women's work. Not surprisingly, therefore, such temporary camps were managed by women, usually older, widowed or single women, young unmarried women and children (usually girls), who between them provided sufficient 'labour' to look after the herd. It is therefore tempting to see these new forms of women's camps as taking on the same economic functions as these temporary 'goat camps', as there has always been a close economic relationship between the nomadic and sedentary milieux. While it may transpire that there are greater economic ties between the villages and these 'women's camps' than I am aware of, or that such ties may develop in the future, the impression that I have at the moment is that the key defining element of these camps is their 'independence'. The women with whom I have spoken have stressed that their whole *raison d'être* is to live independently of men and, by implication, their villages.

This analysis, although admittedly very tentative, raises all sorts of crucial questions for the future. For instance: are these camps a temporary phenomenon, or are they the precursors of a new social movement? What will happen to the children now growing up in these camps when they marry? Will any of these women re-marry and return to a sedentary life, or will men perhaps come and join them? At present, there is a sense of bravado in their tone of speech, possibly for my benefit, that having been rejected by men, they no longer need men in their lives, and that they can live quite easily without them. In short, this is a social phenomenon that needs to be watched closely over the next few years. My initial impression is that these camps certainly have a viable subsistence base and that other women, facing the pressures and fears that I have outlined above, are eyeing them as a possible alternative lifestyle.

Changes and Trends in Marital Patterns

The final question which I raise is whether the dramatic changes that have taken place amongst the Kel Ahaggar since Algerian independence have led to any significant changes in their marriage patterns. For instance, with no obvious political or social benefit to be gained from marrying into the matriline, we might expect the incidence of marriage with the matrilateral parallel cousin (or classificatory) amongst the Kel Rela to have declined. Similarly, we might expect to find that with the end of caravan trade and the diminution of a 'camel economy', the encystment of Kel Ulli sections as minimal corporate lineages is no longer so important. Furthermore, we might expect to find that the modernisation and 'openness' of society has lessened the pressures on endogamy both within the *tawsit* and perhaps also between the traditional social classes of Ihaggaren and Kel Ulli.

The conclusions presented below are derived from a comparison of the marriage patterns amongst the Dag Rali (Kel Ulli) and the Kel Rela (Ihaggaren) in the period up to the '*bouleversement*' of Kel Ahaggar society in the 1960s with the pattern of marriages contracted by members of the same *tawsatin* over the last 35 or so years, that is between the late 1960s[78] and today (2003). Although the data set out below is estimated to cover more than 80 per cent of the marriages contracted within both *tawsatin* since the late 1960s, they should be regarded as provisional as the research is still ongoing.[79] From a purely methodological point of view, the main difficulty in updating these genealogical records relates to the change in the system of nomenclature and the associated 'genealogical amnesia' that I have described above. With most of the new family names being derived from an ancestor of about four generations' antecedence, some of the intervening links between Ego and the named ancestor have been dropped or forgotten. For instance, If Ego (Mohamed) chooses Bouhen as his family name, his new name becomes Mohammed Bouhen, whereas his old name would have been, say, Mohamed ag Fendu ag Hosseyni ag Bouhen. When asked to trace out their names according to traditional nomenclatures I have noticed the increasing tendency to drop one of the intervening ascendants, usually the higher one. Thus, Mohamed Bouhen might refer to himself as Mohamed ag Fendu Bouhen, conflating Fendu and Bouhen into one person and completely omitting Hosseyni. This is particularly frustrating in the updating of these genealogies, as the ancestors that seem to be most frequently dropped or forgotten are those closest in ascendant order to the named ancestor. Today this is usually the third or fourth ascendant ancestor. When I first constructed these genealogies, that ancestor was particularly important as he often bridged the generation between the living and the dead and thus became a 'marker' in the process of genealogical reconstruction. His absence now makes such reconstruction extremely difficult, if not impossible. My impression is that this genealogical foreshortening will become so prevalent over the next generation that it will become almost impossible to construct detailed genealogies for the Kel Ahaggar (and other Tuareg groups), and that these two databases (Dag Rali and Kel Rela) may well become the sole genealogical records of *tawsatin* amongst the Kel Ahaggar and Kel Ajjer. I believe that the genealogical records of all other *tawsatin* are now effectively lost. This is particularly regrettable, as we would ideally like a wider comparative analysis than that provided by the Dag Rali and Kel Rela, especially as the Dag Rali were probably the most endogamous of all *tawsatin*. We can comfort ourselves, however, on the premise that 'beggars can't be choosers', in that 100 per cent historical records of any society are virtually unobtainable, and that in this case we do at least have a valuable, albeit selective, comparative study over a significant period of time.

Before undertaking this research, I was anticipating to find that the incidence of marriage with the matrilateral parallel cousin (real and classificatory) amongst the Kel Rela had declined, as political access to the matriline was no longer so important. I was also expecting to find a weakening of the encystment of the Dag Rali sections as minimal corporate lineages, as well as a lessening, amongst both *tawsatin*, of the pressures which had given rise to such high levels of *tawsit* endogamy. I was also anticipating that another couple of generations of high *tawsit* endogamy, combined with the new naming system, would make it even harder to unravel the multifarious and often ambiguous kin ties beyond cousins of first degree.

As this field research got underway, I was soon aware of the fact that I was once again enmeshed in people's failure to distinguish between 'ideational (cultural) forms and transactional structures or processes',[80] or what Barth later referred to as 'the dialectic between cultural aspects and norms, and social reality'.[81] There is, as we are fully aware, a disparity between what people say they do and what they actually do! To begin with I was under the impression that the marital pattern was little changed from traditional times. People still spoke of the preferred marriage as being with the mother's brother's daughter and the importance of cousin marriages in general. This is something that I was not expecting, and I began to think that the apparent continuity of the traditional system was perhaps a reflection of parents and senior kinsmen arranging more marriages in an attempt to preserve the traditional marriage system and the socio-cultural order which

The End of the Matriline?

they saw as being threatened by the 'modernising' forces that I have outlined above.

While the elder generation of Dag Rali are certainly arranging more marriages for their children at what would appear to be an ever-younger age, and are expressing concern at the social values and practices which they see as enveloping their society, an analysis of the actual marriages contracted reveals a marked distinction between ideational (cultural) forms and social reality.

Social reality is based on an analysis of 118 Dag Rali marriages and 77 Kel Rela marriages contracted between the end of the 1960s and today (2003).[82] An analysis of these marriages reveals marked changes over the last 35 or so years. The two most significant changes amongst the Dag Rali are:

1. A decline in the number of marriages with first cousins. Amongst marriages that are endogamous within the *tawsit*, the decline is from 25 per cent to 12 per cent. Amongst all marriages, including exogamous and unknown marriages, the decline is from 17 per cent to 7 per cent. In both measures, we are seeing a decline of more than 50 per cent in percentage points. Although the split between parallel and cross cousins is equal, seven of the eight first cousin marriages are with paternal cousins, emphasising the importance of paternal kinsmen that was noted amongst the Dag Rali in the 1960s survey.[83]
2. A decline in *tawsit* endogamy amongst known marriages from 93–95 per cent to 78 per cent.[84] Particularly significant, in the light of what I have said about the greater freedom of choice exercised in second marriages, is the different rates of exogamy between first and second marriages: whereas only 15 per cent of first marriages were exogamous, the percentage rose to 30 per cent in the case of second marriages. Similarly, seven of the eight first cousin marriages were first marriages.

I have already suggested that the 'crisis' of the 1990s may have invoked more profound changes amongst the Dag Rali than the '*bouleversement*' of the 1960s. Pandolfi's study, undertaken amongst the Dag Rali at the end of the 1980s and early 1990s, is particularly relevant in this context as it enables us to measure the rates of Dag Rali endogamy at the end of the 1960s, prior to the start of the 1990s crisis, and at the end of the next decade. These three sets of data cannot be compared directly, as Pandolfi considers marriages between the Dag Rali and the Usenden section of the Aguh-en-tehle as being endogamous within the Dag Rali whereas I record them as being exogamous. If we 'standardise' our data by regarding all Usenden marriages as exogamous, we achieve the following set of data:

TABLE 1
PERCENTAGE OF DAG RALI MARRIAGES WHICH ARE ENDOGAMOUS
WITHIN THE *TAWSIT*

At end of 1960s	93–95 *
c.1990	86 **
2003	78 ***

* Keenan (note 7) and idem (note 10).
** Pandolfi (note 7).
*** This study.

The above table shows a change of eight percentage points over the two decades from end-1960s to end-1980s, followed by a further change of eight percentage points over the last decade. While we should perhaps not make too much from such a small set of data, such a conclusion is in keeping with what the Dag Rali are themselves saying about their current social situation, namely that the social and economic upheavals of the 1990s are leading to more people marrying outside the *tawsit*, in spite of the conservative efforts of many of the elder generation.

The changes in marital patterns amongst the Kel Rela, perhaps not surprisingly in view of the political changes since Algerian independence, are even more pronounced. The primary concern of the Kel Rela, as explained earlier, was to ensure the reproduction of the class structure and to retain and limit access to political power by securing their core *agg ettebel* matrilineages as minimal corporate lineages. One might expect to find the effects of Algeria's 'social revolution', notably the abolition of the Kel Rela's traditional political power and all associated economic rights inherent within the traditional class structure, being reflected in changes in their subsequent marital strategies.

The two most significant changes amongst the Kel Rela are:

1. A dramatic decline in the number of marriages with the actual or classificatory matrilineal parallel cousin. In the 1960s, I recorded that 32 per cent of marriages with kinsmen were with the actual or classificatory matrilateral parallel cousin. The 2003 survey revealed that not only had the number of marriages with kinsmen[85] fallen from 67 per cent to somewhere below 41 per cent,[86] but that the number of marriages with the actual or classificatory matrilineal parallel cousin had fallen to 11 per cent.[87] This finding is not in the least surprising: it merely reflects the reduced importance of the matriline over the course of the last 40 or so years.

The End of the Matriline?

2. An even more marked decline in the level of *tawsit* endogamy than that found amongst the Dag Rali, from 70.5 per cent in the 1960s to 41.5 per cent today (2003). An analysis of these exogamous marriages (38) and general discussions with both Kel Rela and members of other *tawsatin* reveals what seems to be a very clear strategy on the part of the Kel Rela, namely their concern to maintain what most of them still regard as their pre-eminent social position in Ahaggar. Although most Kel Rela are still very conscious of their former 'noble' (Ihaggaren) status, they recognise that no formal power or rights are attached any longer to their position as Ihaggaren. Their reaction to the diminution of the political power inherent within their *agg ettebel* matrilineages has been to seek out marital alliances with influential groups and families of similar 'social standing' throughout the Sahara and even further afield. The majority (about 60 per cent) of Kel Rela marriages are now exogamous. Of the 38 exogamous marriages recorded in this survey, nine are with prominent religious groups (5 Iforas, 2 Kel es Souk,[88] 1 Kel Tit/Merabtine and 1 Cheurfa from Adrar-n-Iforas, Mali), nine are with prominent ('noble') Tuareg families from other regions (5 from Mali, 2 from Libya and 2 from Djanet/Kel Ajjer), 13 are with Arabs (2 Chaamba, 3 Rehala from Ahaggar, 2 from Mali and 5 from prominent families in northern Algeria), four are with Europeans (3 Belgians, 1 French), two are with Isekkemaren and one is with an Iklan Taoussit. Twenty-four of these marriages have been contracted by Kel Rela men and 14 by Kel Rela women.

When Kel Rela are asked by outsiders, especially Europeans, to explain their history and position in Ahaggar, many of them will often turn to the analogy with Europe's minor aristocracy. This analogy, which I have heard expressed on many occasions, conjures up mixed feelings amongst other Kel Ahaggar, who tend to regard the Kel Rela's anachronistic preoccupation with their social position with a mixture of deference and ridicule. The ingenuity and ability that the Kel Rela have exercised over some 12 generations in maintaining their 'noble' status is one of the most extraordinary and enduring features of the region's history. Unlike the other noble groups of Ahaggar, namely the Taitok and Tegehe Mellet, the Kel Rela reproduced the fundamental class structure of Kel Ahaggar society, and maintained their position within it, by ensuring that there were no marriages between their women ('it is the stomach which colours the child') and men of subordinate classes. When I left Ahaggar in the early 1970s there had never been such a union. When I returned in 1999, I searched Ahaggar for just one such marriage, but found none! Although one Kel Rela man had married an Iklan Taoussit girl[89] (no threat to the class structure), no Kel Rela woman has yet married a Kel Ulli. The fundamental structure of traditional Ahaggar society, the Kel Rela's *raison d'être*, and now one of the Sahara's most sociologically intriguing historical anachronisms, has been safeguarded. This is not to suggest that Kel Rela are not modern 'men of the world'. On the contrary, at least one has a PhD, at least two have served as *sous-préfets* (*wali*) in other parts of Algeria and many have reached prominent positions in politics, administration, business and commerce. Most of them have travelled in Europe, many extensively. Most hold well-informed and knowledgeable views on the prevailing socio-economic problems of Tamanrasset and Ahaggar society, and many will express shock at the growth of prostitution in Tamanrasset and the emergence of AIDS amongst the Kel Ahaggar. But nothing has shocked them more than the recent behaviour of Tuareg women from Mali. In the 1980s and 1990s many Malian Tuareg sought refuge in Ahaggar from drought and Mali's civil war (the Tuareg uprising). Many of their women married descendants of former Kel Ahaggar slaves and *harratin* in order to acquire Algerian papers that would enable them to stay in Algeria. For the Kel Rela, this was 'beyond the pale'![90]

NOTES

I would like to acknowledge the Economic and Social Research Council (ESRC) for its most generous support.

1. Rene Gardi, *Blue Veils, Red Tents* (London: Hutchinson 1953) pp.162, 194 and 164. For an explanation of veiling, see J. Keenan, 'Dressing for the Occasion: Changes in the Symbolic Meanings of the Tuareg Veil', in this volume, pp.97–120.
2. The *imzad* is the traditional musical instrument of the Tuareg. It is like a one-string violin, with the string being made of horsehair.
3. G.P. Murdock, *Africa: Its Peoples and their Culture History* (New York: McGraw-Hill 1959) p.408f.
4. Most writers on the Tuareg are of the view that matrilineal traits are very ancient. See, for example, J. Nicolaisen, *Ecology and Culture of the Pastoral Tuareg* (Copenhagen: University of Copenhagen 1963); O. Bates, *The Eastern Libyans* (London: 1914); M. Baumann, *Volkerkunde von Afrika* (Essen: 1940). Ibn Batutah, during his travels in the fourteenth century, mentions matrilineal traits among the Tuareg. Ibn Batutah, *Voyages d'Ibn Batoutah*, I–IV, trans. Defrémy and Sanguinetti (Paris: 1853–58).
5. The stomach (*tesa*) symbolises the mother's family and, more specifically, matrilineally related women. The father's family and the patriline are symbolised by the back (*arouri*).
6. These rules are in accordance with Goody's conclusions on the nature of African descent systems, that 'matrilineal systems of succession and inheritance are intrinsically more lateral, and hence more corporate'. J. Goody, 'Sideways or Downwards? Lateral and Vertical Succession, Inheritance and Descent in Africa and Eurasia', *Man* 5/4 (1970) pp.627–38.
7. The ethnographic literature on residency amongst the Kel Ahaggar is confusing. This is because the first detailed published account, by Nicolaisen in 1963 (note 4) p.142–3, stating that 'residency was based on both patrilineal and matrilineal principles', was based on an exceptional situation. His case study illustrated actual marriages between two Kel Ulli *tawsatin*, Dag Rali and Aguh-en-tehle. When I worked amongst the same groups only a few years later, I found that there had been only four marriages between these two groups over

The End of the Matriline?

the preceding three generations and these involved 'exchange' marriages between two families. This particular example was also unusual in that several of the children had in fact been 'adopted'. J. Keenan, *The Tuareg: People of Ahaggar* (London: Allen Lane 1977) p.112 and n14 p.332. Pandolfi, who has published the most authoritative account of residency amongst the Kel Ahaggar, also confirms that Nicolaisen's study is an 'exceptional case' and not the rule. P. Pandolfi, *Les Touaregs de l'Ahaggar* (Paris: Karthala 1998) pp.141–83. However, it should be noted that A. Bourgeot, 'Contribution à l'étude de la parenté touarègue', *Revue de l'Occident Musulman et de la Méditerranée* 21 (1976) pp.9–30, agrees with Nicolaisen in that marriage is followed by a period of matrilocal residency. This, I believe, is incorrect, and that the supposed period of uxorilocal residence was, in fact, one of bilocality (*résidence duolocale*), as confirmed by Pandolfi. Any analysis of residency amongst the Kel Ahaggar, whether in earlier times or today, is complicated by the fact that so many cases are the outcome of seemingly capricious and individual 'exceptional' situations. These merely highlight the fact that the basic principles of residency, both today and in 'traditional' society, as illustrated in Pandolfi's excellent study of the subject, allow for considerable flexibility.

8. A tent usually comprises one nuclear family unit. The word *ehen* also refers to the material contents of a tent (domestic utensils and so on) as well as the people (and their animals) who usually live in it. In this wider sense *ehen* means 'a wife', and by further extension of meaning 'a marriage', for it is the marriage which establishes the nuclear family and the 'tent' as the basic structural unit of society. Thus, when one speaks, for example, of Mohammed's tent (*ehen*), one is referring implicitly to his wife, children, domestics (ex-slaves), the livestock belonging to these people, the domestic utensils such as churning bags, grain bags, pestles, mortars, quern stones, cooking utensils and so forth, and all other people, livestock and things that usually accompany him. Each such 'tent' (that is, nuclear family) is thus a self-contained and self-supporting unit, having as the Kel Ahaggar themselves say, 'its own churning bag and its own millet bag'.
9. Goody (note 6) p.628.
10. This type of relationship between the mother's brother and the sister's son is in fact typical of patrilineal systems, viz. A.R. Radcliffe-Brown, *Structure and Function in Primitive Society* (London: Cohen and West 1952) chs.1, 4 and 5; C. Lévi-Strauss, *Structural Anthropology* (New York: Basic Books 1963) ch.2; and J. Goody, 'The Mother's Brother and the Sister's Son in West Africa', *Journal of the Royal Anthropological Institute* 89 (1959) pp.61–88. Indeed, as I have explained elsewhere, the social organisation of the Kel Ulli, amongst whom this relationship was most significant in view of their pastoralism, was (and is) predominantly patrilineal, see Keenan (note 7) pp.115–26; and J. Keenan, 'Power and Wealth are Cousins: Descent, Class and Marital Strategies among the Kel Ahaggar (Tuareg – Sahara)', *Africa* 47/3 (1977) pp.242–52, and 47/4 (1977) pp.333–42.
11. Most *tawsatin* were divided into a number of sections. The Dag Rali, for example, comprised four such sections: the Kel Terhenanet, Kel Tamanrasset, Kel Tinhart and Kel Hirafok.
12. It is the recognition of this fact that provides the key to the understanding of the social structure and organisation of traditional society, for in the one line – the patriline – we see the transmission of most of the means of production and the reproduction of the domestic unit, and in the other the transmission of 'power' (in the form of descent group membership and succession to political office) and the reproduction of the class structure.
13. Keenan (note 7) pp.107–26; idem (note 10). A particularly good analysis of Kel Ahaggar marriage systems is given by Pandolfi (note 7) pp.295–353 and passim.
14. This was not the case in all Tuareg groups. For example, A. Bourgeot, 'L'agro-pastoralisme des Touaregs Kel-Owey, Au contact Sahara-Sahel', *Au contact Sahara-Sahel: Milieux et sociétés du Niger, Revue de Géographie Alpine* (1994) pp.137–56, has noted that amongst the Kel Ewey of Aïr (Niger) polygamy is a frequent and long established phenomenon.
15. Pandolfi (note 7) p.297.
16. Notably amongst the Dag and Aguh-en-tehle This is not because the Dag Rali and Aguh-en-tehle are necessarily more bigamous than other *tawsatin*! Rather, it is simply because their

histories have been researched more extensively by ethnographers, such as Pandolfi, Bourgeot, Gast and myself.
17. For details see J. Keenan, 'From Tit (1902) to Tahilahi (2002): A Reconsideration of the Impact of and Resistance to French Pacification and Colonial Rule by the Tuareg of Algeria (the Northern Tuareg)', in this volume, pp.27–66.
18. Pandolfi (note 7) p.369.
19. What is more interesting about this particular marriage is that it was replicated in the next generation. Dua's eldest son by Tekadayt married a Dag Rali, then, without divorcing her, took a second wife from amongst the Irregenaten in Tamesna.
20. In all cases known to me, the wife was an Irregenaten.
21. There is now an established community of Irregenaten living in Tamanrasset, several of whose daughters have married Dag Rali men. As far as I am aware, none of these Irregenaten wives have moved to the husband's camp/village. Rather the husband has moved to live with his wife in Tamanrasset. Unfortunately, nearly all research on this subject has been undertaken amongst the Dag Rali and Aguh-en-tehle *tawsatin*. Although such rules and behaviour appear to be the case amongst other *tawsatin* in Ahaggar, we cannot be absolutely certain. We should also be cautious in extending such generalisations to the Kel Ajjer, amongst whom far less sociological research has been undertaken than amongst the Kel Ahaggar.
22. C. de Foucauld, *Poésies touarègues – Dialecte de l'Ahaggar*, vol.1 (Paris: Leroux 1925) p.195.
23. One must be a little wary of statements from old people that confirm this trend, for although they are true, they may be more of a statement of disapproval of the current social order than a reflection of a statistical trend.
24. The key to the understanding of the Kel Ahaggar's social system, highlighted in the failure, which characterises much of the ethnographic literature on the Tuareg, to resolve what Barth referred to as 'the dialectic between cultural aspects and norms, and social reality', or in Scheffler's terms, the failure to distinguish between 'ideational (cultural) forms and transactional structures or processes', lies in the recognition of their class structure. F. Barth, 'Descent and Marriage Reconsidered', in J. Goody (ed.), *The Character of Kinship* (Cambridge: Cambridge University Press 1973) pp.3–19; H.W. Scheffler, 'Ancestor Worship in Anthropology: Or, Observations on Descent and Descent Groups', *Current Anthropology* (1966) pp.541–51. This is particularly well seen in Murphy's analysis of kinship among the southern Tuareg. R.F. Murphy, 'Tuareg Kinship', *American Anthropologist* 69 (1967) pp.163–70. Murphy recognised and tried to explain the lack of fit between the kinship terminology and the social system. Iroquoian terminology, in which parallel cousins are designated by the terms for brother and sister, is congruent with exogamous descent groups in which marriage with the parallel cousin is excluded. However, amongst most Tuareg groups, he found that although the stated marriage preference was with the matrilateral cross-cousin, marriages with parallel cousins were just as common. He based his explanation for the presence of the incongruous kin terminology on a somewhat questionable diffusionist hypothesis, namely that the ancient matrilineal kin groups were once exogamous, so that marriage with the parallel cousin would have been forbidden, and marriage with the cross-cousin permissible. He considered that endogamy may well have been introduced by Islam, with its preference for marriage with the father's brother's daughter, which could have been extended to the mother's sister's daughter through the pressure of Tuareg matrilineal institutions. If this did happen, it probably occurred early in the last millennium when the tribes of Tripolitania came under Arab influence. Murphy's hypothesis to explain the persistence of this kinship nomenclature in the altered social structure beyond the mere question of 'culture lag' is that 'imbalance and dissonance may be the very essence of structure'. However, the problem with both Murphy's analysis and his explanations are that his concern for Tuareg social reality ignored its dominant feature, namely its class structure.
25. This research was undertaken in the late 1960s and early 1970s and published in Keenan (note 7) and idem (note 10). The research raises a number of methodological issues. The main

strength of the analysis is that it was the first (and still the only study amongst the Kel Ahaggar) to analyse marriages on a comparative class basis. Nicolaisen (note 4) p.464, had published a summary table of 44 marriages contracted with kinswomen in Ahaggar without giving any source data on the marriages, thus rendering them useless for analysis. My study was based on the reconstruction of the genealogies of the Kel Rela (Ihaggaren) and Dag Rali (Kel Ulli) *tawsatin* over some 7–8 generations, with the analysis of all 'known' (that is, remembered!) marriages over the preceding 3–4 generations. In going over this research again in 2003, I found no errors in the original data collection, except for the absence of a few families, whose descent group membership was probably suspect. For example, my analysis of the Kel Rela covered 90 marriages, while Marceau Gast's study of the Kel Rela in 1976 recorded 243 Kel Rela marriages. M. Gast, 'Les Kel Rela: historique et essai d'analyse du groupe de commandement des Kel-Ahaggar', *Revue de l'Occident Musulman et de la Méditerranée* 21 (1976) pp.47–66. It seems that Gast's definition of Kel Rela may have been more inclusive than mine, which was based on the strict interpretation of matrilineal descent group membership. For example, I have traced 98 descendants from Bouhen ag Khebbi's unions with two slave-girls (see above). Although these descendants often refer to themselves as Kel Rela, that is not strictly the case, and I have therefore excluded them from my analysis. This may partly explain the different rates of endogamy recorded in our two studies. My higher rate of 63–74 per cent, compared to Gast's 53 per cent, may reflect my exclusion of 'nominal' Kel Rela, such as Bouhen's offspring, who were not *agg ettebel* (in line of succession) and for whom there was therefore little point in marrying 'endogamously' into the matriline to secure access to political power for their offspring, and who sought instead to maintain or increase their 'noble' influence through external alliances. Otherwise, Gast's and my analysis are similar. The most comprehensive single study of one *tawsit* was Pandolfi's study of the Dag Rali in the early 1990s, which recorded 255 marriages compared to my 119. The difference in numbers is partly accounted for by the inclusion of marriages undertaken during the 30 or so intervening years. A methodological weakness in all these studies is that there is no detailed analysis in differences between first and subsequent marriages. The reason for this is because many first marriages that produced no offspring, or which were terminated before the *azalay*, seem to have been simply 'forgotten'. A further problem stems from the high rate of *tawsit* endogamy, which amongst the Dag Rali is around 90 per cent. The result of such endogamy is that paternal and maternal ascendants are often merged, so that individuals may consequently find themselves related through at least two and perhaps even three ties, with the result that classification of marriages based on such relationships can be to some extent arbitrary. However, both Pandolfi and myself classified marriages according to the relationships given by the individuals themselves, so that the data tend to reflect the sociological perception of the individuals concerned.

26. In not prohibiting marriage with any one type of cousin, the Kel Ahaggar, as Pandolfi (note 7) p.343, remarked, were in harmony with Islamic precepts. The Quran, notably in the 4th and 33rd *surah*, does not advocate any preferential union and allows marriage with all types of cousin.
27. For ways in which Tuareg manage this 'confusion', see Keenan (note 1).
28. For details of the Taitok and Tegehe Mellet and their struggle for power with the Kel Rela, see Keenan (note 17).
29. Of the 243 Kel Rela marriages recorded by Gast (note 25), 19 were between Kel Rela men and Kel Ulli women. Of these 19, eight were with the Ait Lowayan; the *tawsatin* of the remainder were not recorded.
30. This 'class endogamy' was not practiced by the Taitok and Tegehe Mellet, the two other noble *tawsatin* in Ahaggar (nor, it seems, the Tegehe-n-ou-Sidi before them). The French noted several marriages between Taitok women and Kel Ahnet (Kel Ulli) on their arrival in the region at the beginning of the twentieth century. Indeed, Bissuel, writing in 1888 on the Taitok and Kel Ahnet specifically, remarked on the 'lessening of the gap' between noble (Ihaggaren) and vassal (Imrad) as families of the two 'castes' became tied together through marriage. H. Bissuel, *Les Touaregs de l'ouest* (Alger: Jourdan 1888).

31. Keenan (note 17).
32. Both *tiwse* and *ehere-n-amadal* consisted of a collective payment by each subordinate *tawsit* of various pastoral products and specific assets such as wild donkeys, barbary sheep (mouflon) and so forth, that were found within their respective territories.
33. This pattern was confirmed by Gast (note 25).
34. See, for example, M. Benhazera, *Six Mois chez les Touareg du Ahaggar* (Alger: Jourdan 1908).
35. Nicolaisen (note 4) p.456f.
36. In traditional times, these were the chiefs (*amraren*) of the Taitok and Tegehe Mellet.
37. Keenan (note 17).
38. This does not mean that women could not own camels. On the contrary, in accordance with Quranic inheritance rules, a woman does inherit from her father, thus enabling women also to own camels. In similar vein, men also own goats. Herd ownership must be distinguished from herd management: goat herds are managed exclusively by women while 'work' with camels is the exclusive domain of men.
39. Keenan (note 17).
40. These two sections are together known as the Imesseliten.
41. M. Bloch, 'The Long Term and the Short Term: The Economic and Political Significance of the Morality of Kinship', in Goody (ed.) (note 24) pp.75–87.
42. The Saharan territories of Algeria were scarcely touched by the Algerian Revolution and firmly under French administrative control. Right up until the signing of the Evian Treaty in 1962, France had been trying to get the Algerians to agree to a partitioning of the country which would allow the Sahara, in which France had recently discovered oil, to remain under French control.
43. I have argued elsewhere that the state did not take a firm grip on the region until 1992. J. Keenan, 'Ethnicity, Regionalism and Political stability in Algeria's *Grand Sud*', in this volume, pp.67–96.
44. This meant that the *foggara*-irrigated gardens, most of which had been worked by *harratin* for the 'Tuareg landowners', were taken over by the *harratin*.
45. Details of these changes are found in Keenan (note 43).
46. See Keenan (note 7) for a detailed account of Ahaggar in the 1960s. See also Keenan (note 43). The best account of the sedentarisation of one specific community is Pandolfi's detailed study of the Dag Rali village of Terhenanet, Pandolfi (note 7).
47. They referred to themselves as *imuhagh ouan aghrem* (*imuhagh*, or Tuareg, of the villages). For further details of this nomenclature, see Keenan (note 43).
48. The last salt caravans from Ahaggar to Niger were in 1969 when the Algerian authorities lifted the embargo. However, by that time the caravans that had almost ceased to exist. In the next couple of years a few Kel Ahaggar travelled south to Niger in the spirit of the caravans, but they were mostly preoccupied in the transhumance aspect of camel pastoralism between Ahaggar and Tamesna. For details of the decline and final termination of this caravan trade, see Keenan (note 7) pp.230f., 246, 282–4 and passim.
49. For details of French colonial rule, see ibid.; and Keenan (note 17).
50. The traditional system consisted simply of a single first or 'given' name being prefaced to the father's name, such as Mohammed *ag* (son of) Ahmadu *ag* ... and so on, or, in the case of women, Fatma *ult* (daughter of) Mohammed. See Keenan (note 43).
51. For the reaction to this move, see ibid.
52. I have come across a number of instances of Tuareg doing this quite deliberately in order to distance themselves from a disliked sibling or other such 'troublesome relatives'.
53. There is no word in the Tuareg language which adequately translates the notion of 'work'.
54. J. Keenan, 'Contested Terrain: Tourism, Environment and Security in Algeria's Extreme South', in this volume, pp.226–65.
55. Keenan (note 43).
56. Much of this growth, although probably not all recorded in the census has come from peoples moving into Tamanrasset from the south. Indeed this 'African' element, as distinct from the

substantial population descended from former slaves, is now a significant component of the town's population. In 1999, the manager of the Central Bank in Tamanrasset informed me that there were now 48 nationalities living in the town. Although, he meant 'ethnic' groups, such as Bambara, Fulani and so on, rather than 'nationalities', it gives a measure of Tamanrasset's recent cosmopolitan make-up as 'Africa's desert cross-roads'.

57. The 1998 census did not count the military and was taken in August when many of the townspeople are away. Local people now (2003) estimate the 'real' population as possibly being as high as 150,000.
58. The impact of tourism on the Kel Ahaggar and Kel Ajjer is discussed in more detail in Keenan (note 43); and idem, 'The Last Nomads: Nomadism amongst the Tuareg of Ahaggar (Algerian Sahara)', in this volume, pp.163–92.
59. For details of the Park's establishment and the 'employment' of Kel Ahaggar and Kel Ajjer as guardians, see Keenan (note 58).
60. Few of the younger men seem to have had such scruples and readily accepted the government's 'hand-out'.
61. Modernity can be regarded as a euphemism for Algerianisation, Arabisation and Islamisation. See Keenan (note 43).
62. The law in Algeria, as expressed in the 'Family Code', states that girls may not marry before 18 and boys 21, except in special circumstances and authorised by a judge.
63. Pandolfi (note 7) p.297.
64. Ibid.
65. Some Kel Ahaggar have humorously pointed to the analogy of the Kel Ahaggar adopting the worst of Islamo-Arabism with the Algerian state adopting many of the worst features of France's *ancien régime*!
66. Pandolfi (note 7) p.299.
67. This trend was also noted by ibid. in the early 1990s.
68. This does not mean that divorce was unheard of. On the contrary, divorce could be initiated by both partners, with adultery perhaps being the most common cause. However, the prevailing thinking of traditional society was that marriage was generally regarded as being 'for life', with a man usually only taking a second wife after the death of the first.
69. In Algeria, these are enshrined within the 'Family Code'.
70. The names of the village and the characters are fictive.
71. *Tolba* (sing. *taleb*) are Quranic teachers, scribes, attached to the *zawiyya*. In earlier times (and to some extent still today) the *tolba* made and sold protective amulets and religious inscriptions at a considerable price. They were especially feared for their mystical power (*ettama*), and the Kel Ahaggar were at their unscrupulous mercy. They were more parasitical and feared than the marabouts (holy men). It is said by both Kel Ahaggar and *harratin* that at harvest time and the return of the caravans the *tolba* and *cheurfa* (descendants of the Prophet) 'would descend on them like crows'.
72. In 'traditional' times, births seemed to have been spaced, as far as possible, in accordance with years of good rainfall and pasturage, and with a sufficient gap between births so that mothers would not be encumbered with more than one small child at the same time.
73. The data was collected from unions which were known to have produced children. In other words, unions with no children or who were not known to have produced children were excluded from the survey. This left 88 Dag Rali who were known to have produced children. Of these 88, the number of children produced by 23 of the unions (but known to have produced children) was not known. The remaining 65 unions had produced 222 children, an average of 3.42 births per union. The 23 unions whose births were not known were ascribed the average of 3.42. The total number of children for the 88 unions thus numbered 301. Of these 301, 52 had died at birth or during infancy. This gives an infant mortality rate of 17.3 per cent. However, more detailed research will probably reveal a higher figure. That is because a number of children who died at childbirth or shortly afterwards were probably 'forgotten' and therefore not included within this data. Moreover, there will also certainly have been some deaths amongst progeny born to the 23 'unknown' unions.

74. In Tamanrasset, with its huge transient and military population and prostitution, the incidence of sexually transmitted diseases is becoming a matter of serious concern. Although the presence of AIDs has been suspected for some time, the first reported case of AIDs amongst the Kel Ahaggar encampments and outlying villages was confirmed in 2002.
75. I could not ascertain if the camp comprising only former slave women had its own camels.
76. Women can inherit camels from their fathers in accordance with Quranic inheritance laws.
77. Pandolfi (note 7), for example, makes no mention of it during his time with the Dag Rali in the late 1980s and early 1990s.
78. It has been published in Keenan (note 7) pp.107–26; and idem (note 10).
79. It is hoped to achieve a figure closer to 100 per cent during the course of 2003–04.
80. Scheffler (note 24) p.543.
81. Barth (note 24).
82. As mentioned above, these marriages are estimated to cover more than 80 per cent of the marriages contracted within both *tawsatin* since the late 1960s.
83. First cousin marriages were as follows: FBD (4), FZD (3), MBD (1).
84. The 21 exogamous Dag Rali marriages are with: Aguh-en-tehle (11), Kel Djanet (3), Irregenaten (1), Merabtine (1), Kel In Amguel (2), Mali Tuareg (1), Taklit (1), unknown origin, living in Tamanrasset (1)
85. These data do not include marriages in which the kin relations of the partners could not be established.
86. This figure cannot be compared directly with that of the 1960s, as it has now become virtually impossible to trace the precise kinship ties in some marriage unions because of the 'genealogical amnesia' associated with the changed naming system. The real figure is therefore considerably less than the 41 per cent, which should be regarded as a theoretical maximum.
87. This percentage comprises only three such marriages, two of which are not *agg ettebel*! The new naming system has made it even more difficult to trace matrilineal genealogical ties. It is therefore possible that there are more marriages with classificatory matrilineal parallel cousins that have not been traced and recorded in this survey. However, the fact that they have not been traced also suggests that they are no longer of any social or political importance.
88. The Kel es Souk are a Tuareg religious tribe, considered by many Tuareg to be a 'very holy tribe'. They originate from Es Souk in the Adrar-n-Iforas (Mali), but are found throughout Niger, Mali and Ahaggar.
89. There have been a handful of marriages over the years between Kel Rela men and Kel Ulli women. Such marriages, because of matrilineal group membership, do not threaten the class structure.
90. In May 2003, the recognised 'head' of the Tuareg in Ahaggar (Hadj Moussa ag Akhemouk) gave an interview to a national newspaper (*El Watan*, 17 May 2003) in the context of 32 European tourists who had been kidnapped and held hostage in the Algerian Sahara. The gist of his interview was to assure the world that no Tuareg would be associated with such an action. Rather it was '*Les Maures, les contrebandiers, les terroristes*' who took such advantage of the state's lack of control over the Sahara. The following day, a leading article expressed regret that such racist views could still be found in Algeria!

The Last Nomads: Nomadism amongst the Tuareg of Ahaggar (Algerian Sahara)

Introduction: The Survival and Transformation of Nomadic Pastoralism in Ahaggar

At the time of Algerian independence in 1962, an estimated 90 per cent of the Kel Ahaggar were living a predominantly nomadic existence.[1] I lived with the Kel Ahaggar for much of that decade, and when I left in 1971 I estimated that as many as half of them had either settled or were in the process of sedentarising. I did not return to Ahaggar again until 1999. When I arrived in Tamanrasset, the region's administrative capital, one of the first things I was told was that there were no more nomads. A few of the older townspeople, who remembered me and guessed that I would want to return to the Dag Rali camps in which I had once spent much time, assured me that the Dag Rali were all now living in town (Tamanrasset) or the surrounding villages. To see for myself, I walked across Atakor, the central mountains of Ahaggar, which was once the home of the Dag Rali and heart of the Kel Ahaggar's domain. A Tuareg, who accompanied me to my departure point, described Atakor as *un terrain abandonné*. He was right. I saw no sign or sound of human life, save for the marks of abandoned campsites and the other telltale signs of former human habitation. It was a sad and moving experience, especially as I repeatedly came across the sites of Dag Rali camps in which I had stayed. Today, the Dag Rali are all settled and living in villages such as Tagmart, Terhenanet, Hirafok and Ifrak.[2] A few live in Tamanrasset itself. If there is good pasture, their goats may be taken up into the mountains for a few days at a time. A few camels are also to be found grazing there. But otherwise, these mountains have become eerily desolate.

Within a few days of my return, Tuareg in Tamanrasset reassured me that although the Dag Rali had all now settled in villages, there were still a few nomads in the region. Over the next four years, I had the opportunity of travelling extensively throughout Ahaggar and most of the Tassili ranges. During these journeys of several thousand miles, I tried to establish how many nomads were living in particular regions. It has been impossible to establish a precise number, partly because many, although regarding themselves as 'nomads', are as good as settled. Even so, it is evident that there are still several Kel Ahaggar, as well as a few Kel Ajjer, who are still entirely nomadic, living in tents and moving throughout the year with their herds in search of pasture. On several occasions I was surprised to find quite large nomadic encampments belonging to descent groups (*tawsatin*) that I had been led to believe were now completely settled. For instance, I once came across 11 tents of Kel Ahnet around two wells to the west of the Ahnet massif. Five Irregenaten tents were pitched at another well about a day's travel away. I also came across several camps of Isekkemaren, Kel Rezzi and Ait Lowayan alongside the Tefedest range and scattered throughout the Tourha Mountains as far north as the Tassili scarps of Ahellakane and the Adrar Hagarhene. A few, I learnt later, had even crossed the Tassili and moved as far north as the Tifernine and Issaouane sand seas. On another occasion I came across several groups of Isekkemaren, numbering well over a hundred persons, strung out over several miles between Ideles and Mertoutek so that their camels and goat herds could take advantage of fresh winter pasture in the area. Elsewhere in Ahaggar I came across a few Aguh-en-tehle camped about a day's ride to the east of Assekrem, as well as several dozen Relaydin and Kel Arefsa further east, especially in and around the *oueds* Tamekkendout and Azrou and throughout much of the Tin Tarabine valley. I also came across camps of Tegehe-n-Efis and Iklan Tawsit to the south-west and south-east of Tamanrasset.

When I returned to the Tassili-n-Ajjer I was also told that all the Kel Ajjer were now settled in Djanet, Illizi, Zaouatallaz (Bordj el Haouas), in the villages of Iherir-Edarène, Tamdjert and Afara, and at a few other places such as the *Oued* Tadjeradjeri. All these villages had grown substantially in size as nomads had settled in them. Nevertheless, I came across several Kel Toberen (Tobra) camped in the Afara depression and the adjoining Aharhar and Tasset regions, as well as several families of Kel In Tunin in the Tamdjert area. My travelling companion at the time, an Ait Lowayan who knew the region well, reckoned that there were as many as a hundred families nomadising within the central Tassili region. I also came across a few Kel Medak families on the plateau east of Djanet, as well as an extended family of Idjeradjeriouène camped in the *Oued* Djerat, and was told that there were a few others nearby.

An attempt to undertake a census of nomads begs the question about what is meant by 'nomad'. E.L. Peters's definition of 'nomadism' in the 1960s is still fitting of the present day. In its common usage, he wrote, the word 'nomadism' is used loosely to refer to people who live a tented life and who may or may not wander in search of pastures. Many tribes in many parts of the world move to and from pastures with the changes in the seasons, but the movements of most are so regularised that the term 'transhumance' is better applied, for this carries the meaning of movement in fairly fixed directions from watering points in the dry season abode to pastures in the rainy season. Nomads, when they wander, do so within generally defined limits, but their movements within their territories are much more haphazard. The significance in this difference lies not so much in the kind of movement itself, but what this implies. Nomadism occurs where the natural resources are not only scarce, but also insecure from year to year, compelling a move to this area one year, and to another the following year. Its practice requires a very large area to support very small numbers of animals and human beings, and it is only to be found in areas that are marginal for human habitation. The direct limitation of the size of the local group by the paucity and instability of the natural resources gives character to the whole range of social relationships. Peters stressed that it was quite wrong to use the term 'nomadism' to apply to any people who live a tented life. Indeed, some peoples who live in tents are virtually sedentary, others are tied to towns, markets or oases, and herd animals only as an economic supplement to their agricultural or commercial activities.[3]

Amongst the Kel Ahaggar, especially since the 1960s, the number of nomads has been dwindling and many of those who remain cannot be called 'nomadic' in the above sense. Today, many Tuareg who would describe themselves as 'nomads' actually live for part, if not all of the year, in *zeribas* (reed huts) or even mud-brick houses. For them 'nomadism' is more of a cultural than a geographical or residential concept: it is more a state of mind. For instance, many of the Dag Rali who are now settled more or less permanently in villages have described themselves to me as 'nomads', using the term almost synonymously with the terms *imuhagh*[4] or Kel Ahaggar. Even so, to most Kel Ahaggar, a loosely accepted definition of 'nomad' would involve living for at least part of the year in a tent while moving in search of grazing for their livestock (goats and camels). But even here, there are still shades of grey: one old Ait Lowayan, for instance, and there are many others who would agree with him, insisted to me that he was a 'nomad' even though he lived more or less permanently in a *zeriba* in a small settlement in the Tefedest. His reasoning was quite simple: he was a Kel Ahaggar, an *imuhagh*, and his preferred 'work' was with camels, not tending a garden (which he did most expertly!).

This definitional problem makes it difficult to assess how many Kel Ahaggar and Kel Ajjer are still living in a predominantly nomadic state. However, based on these extensive journeys and discussions with Tuareg in most of these areas, and using the definition which is acceptable to the Tuareg, namely of living for most of the year in a tent and moving in search of pasture for their livestock (goats and camels), I would estimate that there

The Lesser Gods of the Sahara

are still at least 3,000 Kel Ahaggar and Kel Ajjer living in a wholly or predominantly nomadic state. Tuareg who travelled with me on these journeys, and with whom I discussed this estimate constantly, are inclined to put this figure as high as 4,000. These estimates are interesting in that they conform to the 1987 census for the *wilaya* of Tamanrasset, which put the number of nomads at 4,471. As the *wilaya* includes the region of Tidikelt, this suggests that the number of nomadic Kel Ahaggar at that time was probably between 3,000 and 4,000.

The 1987 census suggests that there has not been a great change in the number of nomads over the last 15 or so years. However, although the absolute number of nomads may have remained fairly constant over the last decade or more, the proportion of Tuareg living as nomads has certainly declined. At the time of Independence (1962), it was around 90 per cent. By 1971 it had fallen to an estimated 50 per cent. Today it is estimated at between 10 and 15 per cent.[5]

Having been led to believe that all Algerian Tuareg were now sedentarised, I was particularly interested in how these last 3–4,000 nomads were surviving. What was the basis of their nomadic economy? What sort of social relationships were at the core of their nomadism? And how were these nomads adapting to and interacting with the modern economy around them? In short, was I witnessing the last remnants of nomadism, a museum society, in Ahaggar and the Tassili, or a culture and way of life whose resilience, flexibility and adaptability might yet ensure its survival for the foreseeable future?

One of the first thoughts that struck me when I began looking into the basis of their current economy was that probably at no time in the history of the region have nomads been able to survive solely on the basis of their pastoralism. Such is the scarcity and insecurity of natural resources in this part of the Sahara that nomadic pastoralism has always been dependent on some form of supplementation. While the essence of pastoralism has changed relatively little over the last few hundred years, the forms of supplementation, one might even use the term 'dependency', have changed enormously from pre-colonial times to the present-day. Many of the ethnographers who described traditional society even alluded to some sort of 'dual' economy, seeing the dualism in the different economic activities of the two main classes, the Ihaggaren (nobles) and Kel Ulli (vassals): the Ihaggaren specialised in warfare and raiding while the Kel Ulli, as their name tells us (Kel Ulli means 'people of the goats'), specialised in goat breeding. Some even saw the notion of 'dualism' being expressed in what they saw as an 'internal' and 'external' economy, referring literally to the production or obtainment of goods either from within or outside the region. Bourgeot put this on a sounder theoretical

The Last Nomads

plane when he spoke of the dominance of a 'pastoral-cum-raiding' mode of production in traditional society.[6] Although this use of the concept of 'mode of production' raises theoretical questions that are not relevant to our concerns here, he is emphasising the essential economic unity of these activities and their associated social relations of production.

Rather than confine this article to an analysis of the present form of nomadic pastoralism and its various forms of supplementation, my aim is to show how the continuity of nomadic pastoralism in Ahaggar-Tassili has been dependent on almost continuous changes in its forms of supplementation – raiding, the caravan trade, slavery, agriculture, hunting, Park wardening, wage labour, tourism, smuggling, camel subsidies and so on – and the social relationships associated with these activities. In short, the survival of nomadic pastoralism in Ahaggar-Tassili today, in its present form, cannot be fully understood without an appreciation of the almost continuous economic and social transformations that it has undergone throughout the contact and pre-colonial periods, the colonial period and the subsequent 40 or so years since Algerian independence.

A 'Pastoral-cum-Raiding' Mode of Production and the *Temazlayt* Relationship

The dominant feature of traditional Tuareg society in Ahaggar and Ajjer was its rigid class division between Ihaggaren and Kel Ulli,[7] a division that probably originates from the immigration into the region of a camel-breeding people at some time in the distant past.[8] The dominance of the Ihaggaren as a specialised warrior class, and the associated class division, were maintained by the Ihaggaren's exclusive control of the camel and certain specialised arms.

Although the camel provided the Ihaggaren with the means of their physical control and military dominance, its contribution to their subsistence was not as great as might be assumed. The nobles' raiding and warfare activities made some contribution to the subsistence base of Ahaggar by enabling them to maintain control over the important trade links with the oases of Tuat and Tidikelt, which supplied them with dates and cereals. Furthermore, their raids were often directed towards the acquisition of camels, which might be taken from neighbouring or quite distant peoples.[9] And their ability to raid outwards from Ahaggar certainly provided the Kel Ahaggar with some level of insurance mechanism in times of hardship and need.[10]

However, it was goats, through their milk products, meat and various material artefacts, that were the primary basis of the Kel Ahaggar's subsistence needs. However, the Ihaggaren, because of the demands of their way of life as a 'warrior aristocracy', were unable to engage extensively in goat breeding and were consequently obliged to secure access to goat products through a combination of political and social relations. The most formal of these relations were expressed in the political structure of the 'drum-group' (*ettebel*),[11] which comprised one noble descent group and a number of politically subordinate Kel Ulli and Isekkemaren descent groups (*tawsatin*). Within the drum-group, the subordination of the Kel Ulli and Isekkemaren was expressed in an annual tributary payment of allegiance to the chief of the drum-group, known as *tiwse*, and an annual 'land-rent' known as *ehere-n-amadal*,[12] which consisted almost entirely of subsistence, and particularly goat products.[13]

Beyond the formal political relations of the drum-group, the most important relationship between the Ihaggaren and the Kel Ulli, and the fundamental social relationship of this 'pastoral-cum-raiding' mode of production was a relationship known as *temazlayt*. This word is virtually unknown amongst Tuareg today. Even in the 1960s, few of them recognised it and fewer still were able to explain it to me. This is because the relationship, for reasons I shall explain shortly, was already under pressure before colonial occupation and disintegrated rapidly after the French arrival at the beginning of the twentieth century.[14]

The word *temazlayt*, according to Foucauld,[15] derives from the root *ezli*, meaning to set aside a special portion or share, and refers specifically to the tribute given to the Ihaggaren by the Kel Ulli for their protection. It was, as Gast noted, a 'contract of protection'.[16]

In early times, probably prior to the second half of the nineteenth century, the Kel Ulli owned few, if any, camels. They were goat breeders, and their goat herds provided both themselves and the Ihaggaren not only with numerous food products (milk, cheese, butter and so on), but the materials used in the manufacture of many essential artefacts (clothes, tents, various types of rope and cord, water bags and so on). The Kel Ulli were the main producers, and as such had to suffer the exactions of the Ihaggaren and other groups within the overall federation (*tegehe*) of Ahaggar, as well as foreign raiders. In the case of the latter it was the responsibility of the *Amenukal*, the overall supreme chief of the *tegehe*, to ensure its defence, but it seems that he was often powerless to settle or prevent raids that went on within Ahaggar. Consequently, the Kel Ulli, without camels and specialised arms (notably the *takuba*: sword), were obliged to turn to the Ihaggaren for their protection. It was for this reason that the Kel Ulli would choose a warrior from among their nobility to protect them personally, in return for which they gave him a special tribute in kind – the *temazlayt*.

It was therefore in the interest of this 'secondary suzerain' to defend the wealth and resources of the Kel Ulli who gave him *temazlayt* in the same way that it was in the *Amenukal*'s interest to defend, with the aid of the nobility, the wealth of Ahaggar against foreign raiders. Each group of Kel Ulli, or productive unit, thus had its protector at the local level, while in the event of large foreign raids all the warriors of the drum-group or *tegehe* would join together, on the command of the *Amenukal*, in what could be regarded as the national defence.

Although the need for protection was undoubtedly great and may well have been the fundamental reason for the original instigation of the *temazlayt*, the relationship was, I believe, more functionally diverse and structurally less *ad hoc* than the foregoing implies. According to Nicolaisen,[17] *temazlayt* relationships were structurally akin to the drum-group in that they were matrilineally organised. By this, he means, if I interpret him correctly, that membership of a *temazlayt* group and succession to its leadership, like descent group (*tawsit*) membership and succession to political office within the drum-group, were determined according to matrilineal principles of descent.[18] The *temazlayt* group, as described by Nicolaisen, seems to have consisted of a small noble matrilineage and a larger matrilineage of Kel Ulli. He also recognised that the noble matrilineage would not necessarily correspond to what he called the 'matrilineal core of a (*tawsit*) section', for in the case of the noble Kel Rela there appear to have been more *temazlayt* leaders than there were *tawsit* sections.[19] The Kel Ulli matrilineage on the other hand may have corresponded to an entire *tawsit* section.

The extent to which nobles' *temazlayt* rights over Kel Ulli were held corporately by the 'small noble matrilineage' to which Nicolaisen refers is questionable. Although *temazlayt* rights over Kel Ulli were vested in an individual, the *temazlayt* leader, it seems that these rights may also have been shared by some of his matrilineal kin. Nicolaisen is not explicit on this point, and we can only conclude that the degree to which these rights were held in any corporate sense by the noble matrilineages concerned must inevitably have contained an element of ambivalence, for the predominance of *tawsit* endogamy, as explained elsewhere in this volume,[20] provides the individual with considerable latitude of choice in the manipulation of his descent and the reckoning of kinship relations. Nicolaisen does, however, state quite specifically that a noble Tuareg who held such rights over certain vassals would be succeeded (as *temazlayt* leader) by a maternal (he presumably means matrilineal) kinsman, and that in a group of vassals rights and obligations would usually be transmitted according to matrilineal rules.

These observations on the structural organisation of *temazlayt* relations must be regarded with caution, as the traditional form of the relationship had disintegrated many years before Nicolaisen worked amongst the Tuareg in the 1950s. When I worked there, roughly a decade later, very few Tuareg were able to give me more than a vague outline of its structure. Nevertheless, they do provide us with a reasonable indication that:

1. The relationship had a clearly defined social structure and organisation;
2. The relationship was of a fairly permanent and lasting nature;
3. The Kel Ulli's 'choice' of a protector, except perhaps in exceptional circumstances, may have centred more on the choice of a successor as *temazlayt* leader from within the specific noble matrilineage.

These observations become particularly significant when we shift our attention from 'protection' and focus instead on the wider dimensions of the social system as a whole, particularly the relations of production between the Ihaggaren and the Kel Ulli.

Goats were the main productive resource of the Kel Ahaggar and without assured access to their products the Ihaggaren could not have maintained themselves as a specialised warrior class. When I first visited this question,[21] I suggested various means by which this access might have been assured:

1. The Ihaggaren could have possessed goat herds of their own;
2. They could have relied on raiding goats from the Kel Ulli;
3. They could have established or gained control over some form of exchange with the Kel Ulli.

The first of these was virtually impossible, as goats require permanent attention and could obviously not have been taken on raiding expeditions. Neither would it have been desirable or practical to leave them in the care of their slaves.

Raiding Kel Ulli, particularly of other drum-groups, seems to have been fairly common, but usually only during feuds between the drum-groups. Raiding within the *tegehe*, however, was an essentially negative process, for even if neither men nor animals were killed, it merely resulted in an overall redistribution of productive resources within the *tegehe*. The long-term result of such continuous action would probably have led to the ultimate dissolution of the *tegehe*.

It is to the third of these alternatives that we must turn our attention. The vassals' various tributary payments were one means whereby the Ihaggaren were able to appropriate a certain measure of the Kel Ulli's produce. However, when we consider the amounts of these payments, it is unlikely that they contributed more than a modest proportion of the Ihaggaren's subsistence needs.

The primary means whereby the Ihaggaren gained control over access to goat products was through the *temazlayt* relationship. The obligation of the *temazlayt* leader to protect the Kel Ulli in his *temazlayt* group, or groups, was, I believe, merely the most overt feature of an institutionalised relationship through which the Ihaggaren were able to appropriate sufficient surplus labour from their vassals to meet their subsistence needs. In this respect the relationship was the fundamental means whereby the diverse economic activities of the two classes were integrated within an overall 'pastoral-cum-raiding' economy.

The form of this appropriation, or rather the unequal exchange basis of the *temazlayt* relationship, can be seen in the nature of the various rights and obligations of the two parties.

The rights of the *temazlayt* leader were quite different from those of the drum-chief. He had no judicial authority over his Kel Ulli, nor could he summon them to war unless they were interested. Furthermore, if the Kel Ulli did undertake raids, either on their own or under the leadership of their *temazlayt* leader, half the booty was given as tribute to the drum-chief. The rights of the *temazlayt* leader were essentially of an economic nature. *Temazlayt* payments provided the nobility with valuable goat-breeding products, while the associated but more generalised institution of *tamekchit*, whereby Ihaggaren could claim food from the Kel Ulli, enabled them to obtain more or less anything they needed for their subsistence. Ihaggaren would consequently camp close to their Kel Ulli, who were obliged to feed and provision them.

The Kel Ulli, however, received certain compensations, not least of which was the assurance of protection. Moreover, as Ihaggaren were frequently away raiding or roaming over distant lands, they kept few livestock in their camps. Instead, they would leave most of their animals in the care of their Kel Ulli, who then had certain usufruct rights over them. The more important of these rights was that they could 'borrow' the Ihaggaren's camels for their own caravan or raiding expeditions, for which they gave a tribute consisting of half of the booty remaining after the drum-chief had received his share.

The extent to which the Ihaggaren could make demands on their Kel Ulli is not altogether clear. Through the *tamekchit* relationship, the Kel Ulli were obliged to afford hospitality to the Ihaggaren in the form of food, while the *temazlayt* seems to have entailed several more generalised obligations, in the form of various 'services', in addition to the actual *temazlayt* payment itself. Duveyrier mentions that when in need of riding camels, the Ihaggaren could freely take them from their Kel Ulli.[22] Nicolaisen also mentions that if Kel Ulli had milk-yielding camels, the Ihaggaren could claim them until the milk-yield stopped.[23] This may have been the case, but it seems more likely, particularly as Kel Ulli owned few, if any, camels in earlier times, that many of these animals were in fact owned by the Ihaggaren, but had been left in the care of their Kel Ulli. Their 'taking' may thus have been only a temporary loss of usufruct rights.[24]

Although the rights of the Ihaggaren appear to have been extensive, it should be emphasised that it was in the interests of the Ihaggaren to ensure that their Kel Ulli were rich and well protected, for they were dependent on them to a very large extent for much of their subsistence, and in the case of persistent or excessive demands, the Kel Ulli always held the right to refuse their requests.

Furthermore, in the case of the individual *temazlayt* group, the over-exploitation of the Kel Ulli would have been disadvantageous to the Ihaggaren, for, bearing in mind the earlier comment about 'choosing' a protector, it is conceivable that the Kel Ulli could have reinforced their right of refusal by turning to another noble for protection.

If we were able to take a bird's-eye view of Ahaggar at this time, we would see this vast mountainous area divided into the territories of the three drum-groups, within which each Kel Ulli *tawsit* held extensive territorial rights over thousands of square miles. Their camps, dotted sparsely over their respective territories, varied in size according to pastoral conditions. If pasture was exceptionally good a whole *tawsit* section, comprising anything up to about 20 tents and 80 individuals, might come together for some time, although under normal conditions most camps (*ariwan*) would consist of about two to seven tents; while in severe conditions camps would split into even smaller units to eke out pasture. Though the size of these camps fluctuated considerably, their movements were relatively small, being confined to their specific *tawsit* territories or sectional sub-areas within that territory, and often being little more than a shift from one major valley to the next. Only in exceptional times of pastoral impoverishment or abundant rainfall in a specific area might they move temporarily out of their own territories.

Ihaggaren, by contrast, with their riding camels and territorial rights over the entire territory of the drum-group, roamed extensively throughout Ahaggar and further afield, and were often away from the territories of their drum-groups for long periods, for a successful warrior enhanced the material wealth of both his own immediate family and *temazlayt* groups, as well as his influence and prestige within the political elite. When they were not away from their drum-groups they tended to camp near their Kel Ulli, particularly those with whom they had *temazlayt* relations, and upon whom they depended largely for food and other supplies. We can assume that their duration of stay with any one group of Kel Ulli was determined largely by the condition of the goat herds and the amount of food available, and may have ranged from a few weeks to an entire season. But it was obviously not in the interests of the Ihaggaren to burden their Kel Ulli excessively, and once they had outstayed

The Last Nomads

their welcome we can picture them moving off to camp alongside other Kel Ulli with whom they had *temazlayt* relations.

From our bird's-eye view we can thus see that the Kel Ulli camps were relatively static, moving from time to time over relatively small distances within their specific *tawsit* territories. Beyond this limited range of movement were the rovings of the Ihaggaren, criss-crossing as it were the entire territory of the drum-group; camping alongside one group of Kel Ulli for a time and then moving on to another.

The Internal Dynamic of Kel Ahaggar Society

This description of the *temazlayt* relationship is not only an idealised abstraction, drawn from a range of historical sources, but presents a static picture of the relationship. The reality of pre-colonial society was that it was inherently dynamic.[25] We know that throughout much of the nineteenth century the balance of power between the Ihaggaren and Kel Ulli, in terms of the Kel Ulli's access to camels and weapons and hence their fighting ability, was undergoing a more or less continuous process of change. I have described elsewhere in this volume how the Kel Ulli acquired both camels and weapons of their own, to the extent that by the time of the French arrival at the beginning of the twentieth century they were camel owners in their own right and equally capable warriors.[26] Throughout much of the latter part of the nineteenth century (and possibly earlier), the Kel Ulli were almost certainly the most powerful element in Ahaggar in terms of their numerical superiority and fighting ability.

This shift in the balance of physical power between the Ihaggaren and Kel Ulli had critical implications for the fundamental basis of noble–vassal relations. The *temazlayt* relationship especially found increasingly less justification. Indeed, we have a considerable amount of evidence from the early French reports and travelogues on the region, as well as oral accounts from Tuareg themselves during the course of the last century, to suggest that the Kel Ulli, during the late nineteenth and early twentieth centuries, were becoming increasingly confident in rejecting the demands of the Ihaggaren and acting increasingly on their own initiative in political and economic matters.

The French encroachment into the Central Sahara and the subsequent pacification of Ahaggar played a major part in accelerating the transformation of noble–vassal relations.[27] It also highlighted, as the French themselves anticipated, how dependent Ahaggar's subsistence base was on external resources. The Kel Ahaggar's trade with the oases of Tuat and Tidikelt and their raiding outside of Ahaggar provided them not merely with a supplement to their internal pastoral economy, but enabled them to overcome, or at least reduce, the consequences of the fairly frequent periods of drought and famine.

France's encroachment into the Central Sahara began to limit this option. Indeed we have evidence of this pressure being felt as early as 1896. In that year, we see members of two Kel Ulli *tawsatin* (the Dag Rali and Aguh-entehle) carrying salt from the salt deposits at Amadror to Damergou in southern Niger to exchange it for millet. This was the first caravan from Ahaggar to trade locally mined salt for foodstuffs. We do not know the precise reasons why these Kel Ulli decided to take this initiative at that particular time. Except for an attack of locusts in 1893 and droughts in both 1897 and 1900, the years 1896–1900 appear to have been ones of relatively good pasture in Ahaggar. One can conjecture that Kel Ulli could already foresee the deprivations that would result from French encroachment and that this was an opportune time to try and establish new markets. It also appears that this action was taken independently of the Ihaggaren, suggesting that these Kel Ulli already felt sufficiently confident to flex their muscles.[28]

The Transition from a 'Pastoral-cum-Raiding' to a 'Pastoral-cum-Trading' Economy

By the 1920s, the Kel Ahaggar's subsistence base and the nature of nomadic pastoralism in Ahaggar had been almost totally transformed. Between the turn of the century and 1920, the social revolution amongst the Kel Ahaggar, which I have touched on above and described in more depth elsewhere in this volume,[29] was complete. French pacification put an end to raiding and warfare, with the result that the *temazlayt* relationship virtually disintegrated as the Kel Ulli, goat breeders and camel owners in their own right, no longer had any need for protection and were no longer prepared to tolerate the demands of their nobility.

By 1926 the salt caravans to Damergou, organised almost exclusively by Kel Ulli and Isekkemaren *tawsatin*, had become an annual affair. The caravans involved an immense mobilisation of labour, which partly explains why it was the Kel Ulli *tawsatin* with the most slaves and camels, notably the Dag Rali and Aguh-en-tehle, who undertook the largest caravans. Preparations for the caravans began around August and September, when Kel Ahaggar, or more often their slaves, would make the journey to the salt mines of Amadror. Solid bars of salt weighing between 50 and 60 kilos were cut from the deposits and loaded onto camels, two bars on either side, making a total load in excess of 200kg. The salt was then taken back to the camps, where the caravans, organised on a *tawsit* section basis,[30] would gradually form before leaving Ahaggar in November or December. The return journey to Damergou lasted for five to six months and involved anything up to 4,000 camels. From Ahaggar the caravans headed south for about a month to the plains of Tamesna in northern Niger and the wells of In Abangerit,[31] where they would rest for a month or so before heading south to Tawa and the other markets of Damergou. They would return to Ahaggar in March–April. During the 1920s and 1930s, one load of salt was exchanged for between 15 and 20 loads of millet. However, from the 1940s onwards, mechanised transport and alternative sources of supply led to a progressive deterioration in the terms of trade.

This transformation of the economy was reflected in two major changes in the social relations of production. The first was that the nobility, now only the Kel Rela in Ahaggar, played a rapidly declining role in this new 'pastoral-cum-trading' economy. With the disintegration of the *temazlayt* relationship, they found it increasingly difficult to maintain themselves in a nomadic lifestyle. Disgruntled by the deterioration of their relations with the Kel Ulli, the Kel Rela gravitated increasingly towards the *Amenukal*'s 'court', finding it politically and economically expedient to attach themselves more permanently to his camp near Abalessa. With the French governing through the existing political structure, the *Amenukal* and his entourage became an important part of the French administrative system. Proximity to the centre of administrative authority enabled the Kel Rela to enhance their waning prestige as nobles. From the 1920s onwards, we thus see the Kel Rela moving into a more sedentary existence, around the *Amenukal*'s camp near Abalessa or in Tamanrasset itself, where many of them took salaried jobs as guides, interpreters and so forth within the administration, thus forming something of a self-styled and self-serving bureaucratic elite. Their primary concern was the maintenance of their status as nobles and their associated rights and privileges, notably the traditional payments of *tiwse* and *ehere-n-amadal*, and certain religious taxes, which although payable to the *Amenukal* himself, became of increasing relative value to them as *temazlayt* relations disintegrated.

The second major change was in the social relations of production within the Kel Ulli *tawsatin*. The Kel Ulli emerged from the period of pacification with greater political influence and representation and almost total economic autonomy. Indeed, some of the more powerful Kel Ulli, such as the Dag Rali and Aguh-en-tehle, were now relatively wealthy in camels and access to new grazing lands in Tamesna,[32] had a relative abundance of slaves[33] and were establishing a major trans-Saharan salt trade. In addition, they still had their traditional goat-herding subsistence base, were now free from the threats of being raided and had thrown off the burden of their nobility. Also, as more and more *harratin* came into the region after pacification, they widened their subsistence base still further by establishing an increasing number of *harratin*-cultivated gardens.[34] In modern parlance, they had 'arrived', and were what might be called the *nouveau riche*, although their richness was only relative to Ahaggar!

The management and operation of these new resources, especially their camels and the caravans, required considerable changes in the social organisation of the *tawsit*. The domestic organisation of Kel Ulli society, notably the size and movement of their camps, the internal division of labour and so forth, had been orientated to their fundamental activity of goat breeding. Now, with the acquisition of large numbers of camels and their initiation and management of a substantial trans-Saharan caravan trade, we see the Kel Ulli having to manage two quite different types of pastoral resource: goats and camels, whose pastoral requirements were very different. The requirements of their goat herds were the same as in former times, with the local state of pasture determining the size and movement of camps within their traditional territories. Camels, however, required a greater range, which was scarcely found within Ahaggar. Thus, with the acquisition of Tamesna, we see the development of a type of long-range nomadism, more akin to transhumance, whereby camels were rotated between Ahaggar and Tamesna so that they could benefit from the richer pastures of the latter. This rotation was largely undertaken during the course of the caravans: weaker animals would be taken to Tamesna where they would be left, sometimes for several seasons, and exchanged for fresher animals. The labour required in managing this camel economy, and the caravans themselves, was more than could be mustered from within the *ariwan* (small camps). Labour for these enterprises therefore tended to be organised on a section-wide basis. We thus see the goat pastoralism being managed on a familial (*ariwan*) basis, with camel pastoralism and the caravan trade being organised on a larger and wider sectional basis. The two forms of pastoralism also entailed a rigid sexual division of labour: goats were predominantly the domain of women,[35] while camels were the domain of men. This sexual division of labour was extended to the slaves: female slaves worked mostly in the camp and with the goat herds while male slaves worked almost exclusively in tending camels and undertaking much of the labour required by the salt caravans. This division of labour was more than just a matter of 'men's work' and 'women's work'. The caravans and tendance of camel herds in Tamesna took men away from the camps for much of the year. If men also accompanied their slaves to Amadror, they might be away from August to the following April. This meant that the management of camps and the entire domestic domain was largely in the control of women. It was more often they who decided on when and where to move, and it was they who were responsible for the management of almost all of the activities and tasks undertaken within the domestic domain. Moreover, many Kel Ulli established camps in Tamesna in such a way that part of the family might live there more or less permanently. This even extended on a number of occasions to men keeping a second wife and family in Tamesna and another wife and family in Ahaggar.[36] So important was Tamesna to the Kel Ahaggar that they even established an *Amenukal* in the region.[37]

Rather as in our bird's-eye view of Ahaggar in traditional times, we once again see what can best be described as two circuits of nomadism. One saw camps moving on a fairly regular basis in search of pasture for their goat herds over relatively small distances within their *tawsit* territories. The other saw a much wider range of movement, both within Ahaggar where camels were often left to graze freely in search of pasture, and between Ahaggar and Tamesna as camels were moved, often via the caravans, to the better pastures further south.

An analysis of marriage patterns amongst one Kel Ulli *tawsit*, the Dag Rali, over the last century or so indicates that their social organisation was well adapted to the management of this new form of pastoralism and the associated caravan trade.[38] There are also indications that there may have been significant changes in marriage patterns and other aspects of social organisation to accommodate and manage this transformation in their resource base. However, our data on marriages in the nineteenth century is not sufficiently accurate for us to be more than suggestive on this last point.

It is debatable whether camel or goat pastoralism was the more important to the Kel Ulli during this period. Listening to men talking about their camels, the rituals associated with them and the *rites de passage* involved in a young man's first caravan, one would be tempted to talk about the primacy of camels. But, as with the 'pastoral-cum-raiding' economy in earlier times, it was the goat rather the camel that provided the Kel Ahaggar with the core of their subsistence goods. However, to suggest that the millet acquired through their caravan trade was only a supplement to their subsistence is to understate its importance, for millet was the staple foodstuff of the Kel Ahaggar from the beginning of the caravan trade in the 1920s until it petered out in the 1960s. Nevertheless, the point is that the production of millet was external to Ahaggar, and its acquisition, like the grain and dates obtained from Tuat and Tidikelt prior to their occupation by the French, was a derivative of their camel pastoralism.

By the 1940s, the terms of trade on the salt caravan had fallen from 15–20:1 to 6–10:1. By the 1950s it had fallen to around 2:1, and by 1961 was 1:1. This deterioration in the salt–millet trade was partially compensated by the expansion of the number of *harratin* gardens during the course of the century. The *harratin* population in Ahaggar had grown from 697 in 1909 to equal the number of Kel Ahaggar by 1962, with the amount of land under cultivation increasing from 188 hectares to 1,000–1,500 hectares.[39]

Nomadic Society in the 1960s

During the last few years of colonial occupation nomadic pastoralism was also supplemented by wage labour, not through the employment of the Kel Ahaggar themselves, as manual work was despised as much as agriculture, but through sending their slaves to the *chantiers* to work on their behalf. By the end of the 1950s some 300 Kel Ahaggar nomads were registered as employed at the French atomic base at In Eker,[40] although I believe that in nearly all these cases it was their slaves who took up the work on their behalf!

During the first few years following Algerian independence in 1962, the nomadic Kel Ulli with whom I stayed spoke fondly of the post-pacification period (that is, post *c.*1920) and especially the caravans as if it was their 'traditional' way of life, when in fact it was a mode of production that lasted scarcely 40 years. It also combined a range of economic activities and complex social relations of production that embraced goat and camel pastoralism, the salt caravans and the movement of camels between northern Niger (Tamesna) and Ahaggar, a substantial expansion of agriculture and the development of wage labour. Slaves made a major contribution to all these economic activities.

Thus, when Kel Ahaggar talk of their 'traditional' nomadic way of life, it is true that goat and camel pastoralism were its basis, but it is doubtful whether nomadic pastoralism within Ahaggar could provide a sufficient subsistence base for their survival without the caravan trade to Niger and the increasing supplementation from gardening, wage-labour and, of course, their slaves.

This conclusion was brought starkly to light in the 1960s, the first decade of Algerian independence. This decade brought a traumatic upheaval of Kel Ahaggar society.[41] In the space of a few years, the salt caravans came to an end as a result of the imposition of frontier controls; most of the *harratin*-cultivated gardens were taken into possession by the *harratin*; slavery was abolished and the main source of wage labour, In Eker, closed down. The impact on the nomadic Kel Ahaggar was catastrophic. The removal of these supplementary forms of subsistence, combined with several years of poor rainfall, brought nomadic pastoralism in Ahaggar to its knees. Most of the nomads had little choice but to consider a more sedentary form of lifestyle, settling in existing villages such as Hirafok, Ideles and Tazrouk, or establishing their own village communities such as Terhenanet, Tagmart and Ifrak. In 1962 an estimated 90 per cent of Kel Ahaggar were living a nomadic existence. When I left the region in 1971, I estimated that this proportion had fallen to 50 per cent. Those that remained in the nomadic environment were heavily dependent on social relations with the sedentary community.

The new relations of production that developed between the sedentary and nomadic communities depended on a multitude of factors, with the result that almost every case had its own unique characteristics based on such things as kinship ties, personal friendships or animosity, the nature of past conflicts – especially between cultivators and nomads. In general, however, those nomads whose relationships with their former *harratin* cultivators had not been mired by serious conflict, and those who had maintained 'friendly' relations with Kel Rela, especially those with whom they had formerly had *temazlayt* relations, were more easily able to develop new relations with the sedentary-agricultural community. During the late 1960s I saw countless examples of small-scale exchange relations developing between the nomadic-pastoral community and the rapidly expanding villages and agricultural centres. In some instances, this exchange went so far as to collaborate in illicit caravan trade! Agriculturalists would provide the nomad with a few camel-loads of wheat from their gardens, which he would transport to Niger (where pasture was better) and exchange it for goats that were brought back to the village. Similarly, the Kel Rela, who were now mostly settled in Tamanrasset, still maintained relations with a number of nomadic families, several of whom were the descendants of old *temazlayt* groups. These nomads would provide the Kel Rela with access to the nomadic milieu by looking after their camels and perhaps providing them with 'weekend nomadism', while the Kel Rela facilitated their access to Tamanrasset in such ways as by acting as brokers with the administration, assisting their children in the boarding school or acting as agents for them in the small but developing tourism business.

It is interesting to note that the Dag Rali, who had a much more confrontational experience with their ex-slaves and former *harratin* during these crucial years, are now all sedentarised, whereas the Aguh-en-tehle, whose pastoral resource base was similar to that of the Dag Rali, but who developed more amicable relations with the sedentary community during these crucial years, have managed to retain a solid foothold in the nomadic milieu.[42]

Our conclusion on this traumatic period is that the nomadic communities that were best able to survive these years where those that developed new relations of production with the sedentary community and thus able to supplement their pastoral resources.

The Survival of Nomadism through the 1990s

After my departure from Ahaggar in 1971, an increasing proportion of Kel Ahaggar abandoned their nomadic way of life, so that I was not entirely surprised to be told on my return in 1999 that all the nomads were now settled. However, as I have already mentioned, that was not quite true. Some 3,000 or more Kel Ahaggar and Kel Ajjer, only 10–15 per cent of their number, are still living in a predominantly nomadic state.

The manner in which nomadism has survived during these years, especially since the cessation of tourism in the early 1990s, is testimony to the resilience and flexibility of nomads in being able to take advantage of new opportunities and markets. It also confirms my fundamental argument that nomadic pastoralism in Ahaggar has always been unsustainable unless supplemented by other forms of income.

I do not have any accurate data on the state of nomadism or the rate of sedentarisation of nomads between the time of my departure from Ahaggar in 1971 and the onset of Algeria's crisis in the early 1990s,[43] other than to cite Pandolfi's valuable study of the Dag Rali at the end of the 1980s,[44] which confirmed that all the Dag Rali had sedentarised by that time. The Kel Ahaggar and Kel Ajjer who persisted in a nomadic way of life through the 1970s and 1980s were certainly dependent on the increasing volume of tourism in the region, which by the end of the 1980s had reached some 15,000 foreign tourists a year.[45] The complete cessation of tourism in 1992 thus begs the question of how they have survived since then.

The short answer is that their survival owed much to the direct and indirect policies of the Algerian government.

The most direct of these policies was the employment of Kel Ahaggar as wardens (guardians) of the Ahaggar National Park. Although the Park was legally established in 1987, it seems that the employment of local people, mostly Kel Ahaggar, as guardians of the Park, became increasingly important through the 1990s. By September 2000 the Park was employing 550 people, mostly Kel Ahaggar, as *agents de conservation* or, to use their own term, *guardiens du parc*. This 'employment', regarded by most Kel Ahaggar as a euphemism for 'social security', involves a negligible amount of 'work'.[46] Indeed, with no tourism, there is effectively no 'work' to do! However, as a political 'social security' policy, it has had three very important implications. The first is that it has played a major role in enabling the nomadic community to survive the collapse of tourism in the region. By my calculations, *guardiens* in 2000 were receiving about DA 7,000 a month,[47] approximately £70. This means that the state has been injecting a cash income of approximately £400,000 per annum into the outlying regions and nomadic community of

Ahaggar. There are very few nomadic encampments that have not felt the direct or indirect benefits of these payments. Second, although most Tuareg joke about their 'work' as *guardiens*, and some have even rejected such employment as demeaning, most of them are not prepared to 'bite the hand that feeds them'. In this sense, the policy has been an astute political move in that it has served to bring the Tuareg closer to the Algerian administration. While the Tuareg would certainly not countenance my referring to them as the 'eyes and ears' of the state in these vast empty spaces, they can probably be relied on to report any unusual activity in the region to the authorities. Third, and as I have explained in more detail elsewhere in this volume,[48] the creation of the two Parks,[49] and the employment of local peoples as *guardiens*, has done much to increase local peoples' awareness of their environmental and cultural heritage.

The second direct policy to assist the nomads was the payment of a subsidy of DA 20,000 (c.£200) for each new-born camel. The actual source of this money was the government of Saudi Arabia, which made a gift to all peoples of the Sahara to encourage and support cameline economies. However, as the administration of the money was handled through the governments of the countries concerned, in Algeria's case through the veterinary departments of the Ministry of Agriculture and the local *wali*, the recipients of the payments were not always entirely sure of the original source of the 'subsidy'.[50]

These payments, like the payment of salaries to the *guardiens du parc*, have injected significant funds into the nomadic economy, the consequences of which I will discuss presently. For the moment, however, it is interesting to place this 'payment' in its chronological and political contexts, as it became one of the Kel Ahaggar's complaints about the Algerian government's poor quality of governance.[51]

The story began in November 1993. There had been several poor seasons of rain with the result that the camels in Ahaggar were in a weak condition. However, good rains had fallen over the high mountains (Atakor) of Ahaggar during the summer of 1993. Atakor was traditionally Dag Rali territory, but in the new order of things old tribal land rights have been abolished, so that the few remaining nomads, although nomadising mostly within their old tribal territories, are free to move their animals more or less anywhere. With good winter pasture in Atakor, camel owners from all over the region moved their animals up into the high mountains. I do not know how many camels were moved into the area: Tuareg have spoken to me of hundreds, if not thousands. But in early November there were further rains in Atakor accompanied by sub-zero temperatures. According to nomads in the region at the time, 'the temperature fell so quickly and so low that the water on the camels froze to

The Lesser Gods of the Sahara

ice. They slid and lost their footing on the ice-covered stones and the slippery clay soil underneath and were not strong enough to get back up again. So they just froze and starved to death'.[52] This was a huge catastrophe for the nomads. Some 200–250 camels died, with some nomads losing all their camels. A woman from Tamanrasset who travelled through Atakor a few days later told me: 'I met a man weeping near Terhenanet. Of the 40 camels he had led into the mountains he had found only two alive'. Following the complete cessation of tourism in 1992, this was the second devastating blow to the nomads within a couple of years.

Following the tragedy, the nomads went to Tamanrasset and asked the government for help. But there was no budget for such an occurrence, and apart from some small payments, mostly in kind, the government was unable to do anything. However, some two years later, around 1996–97, the Kel Ahaggar received news of the DA 20,000 'subsidy' being paid for all new-born camels. It led to a huge political row, the gist of which was that the *wali* refused to hand over the money, accusing the Tuareg of fraud. What lay behind this row was that all new camels, quite understandably, had to be brought to Tamanrasset for veterinary inspection and registration. As Kel Ahaggar keep most of their camels, especially the new-born, in Tamesna, the *wali*, who knew nothing of local husbandry practices, could not understand why so many camels were being brought across the border from Niger. In his ignorance, he assumed that the Tuareg were operating a vast camel-smuggling operation and refused to make the payments. In 1999, the *wali* was replaced, but his successor was equally ignorant of the region he had been sent to govern and also refused to make the payments. The dispute dragged on for some four years, with the last payments being made as recently as 2002. Finally, when the nomads did receive their payments, there were widespread rumours that the *wali* had pocketed some of the payments![53]

The main indirect benefit of government policy, if one can call Algeria's crisis a policy, is that it has contributed to the region's population explosion and thus created a substantial new market for pastoral resources – especially meat.[54] Thanks largely to the designation of Tamanrasset as a *wilaya*, its prioritisation since 1991–92 as a major administrative and garrison town, and the inflow of northerners seeking refuge from the bloody struggle between government forces and Islamists in the north of the country, the town's population has leapt from around 40,000 in the late 1980s to some 100,000 by the end of the 1990s and perhaps as much as 150,000 today. Tamanrasset's growth has given the nomads the assurance that they can now count on a steady demand and good prices for their animals – goats, sheep and camels.

A close examination of those Kel Ahaggar who have managed to maintain themselves in the nomadic milieu during these difficult years reveals the

The Last Nomads

importance of the complex network of social relations that they have developed with key elements of the sedentary community.

The relations fall into several categories. The most widespread and significant, not surprisingly, are with kinsmen. Given the high rate of *tawsit* endogamy,[55] the term kinsman can be extended to include virtually all *tawsit* members, who, with the increased social and geographical mobility of the last two generations, can usually be found in an extensive range of social and geographical environments. These relations are the basis of a complex network of economic interdependence between the nomadic and the gardening-village-urban communities. While they provide the latter with access to the products of the nomadic pastoral economy, they also provide the nomads with a sedentary support network when pastoral conditions become difficult. For example, during 1999 and 2000, a mysterious disease killed most of the camels in the eastern Tefedest region, leaving many of the few dozen nomads in the area without camels. However, because all the nomads along the eastern margins of Tefedest had strong support networks in the local villages such as Mertoutek and Dehine, they spent much of that period living in or close to the villages with a few of the men actually working gardens as if they were long-settled villagers! Two years later the disease had gone and the nomads, who had acquired[56] and bred more camels, returned to their nomadic lifestyle.

A second type of relation, which is now almost essential for most nomadic groups to maintain themselves, is with the 'salaried sector'. This is most likely to be as a *guardien du parc*. However, in most nomadic encampments, one usually finds at least one man away in employment, usually in the main towns of Tamanrasset, Djanet or Illizi, but perhaps even as far away as In Salah. For example, during the time when the above-mentioned camps were experiencing the camel disease, three of their menfolk were away in work. Two were employed nearby at Ideles while one young man had a three-month contract in Illizi. I found a similar dependency on wage employment amongst the Kel In Tunin camps in the Tamdjert area, several of whose menfolk worked as far afield as Illizi, Djanet and Bordj el Haoues (Zaouatallaz). Between them they rented a truck which enabled them to commute on a weekly or monthly basis, and to transport their provisions back to Tamdjert. A similar truck service had been organised by most of the nomads and small village communities in the Tefedest and Tourha regions. The truck, rented from Ideles, made a monthly return trip from Ideles to Tamanrasset, via the camps in the Tourha-Tefedest region. It usually transported small livestock (goats and sheep) for sale to Tamanrasset and returned with basic foodstuffs (wheat, oil, tea, sugar and so on) and other goods (blankets, shoes, clothes, batteries, toiletries, cooking utensils and so on). The truck also served as a bus service, enabling those men in the area who were employed as *guardiens du parc* to collect their salaries from the Park office in Tamanrasset. In the case of this group of camps, it was the Park salaries that provided their main source of cash income.

A numerically small, but functionally very important relationship is that between these remaining nomadic camps and their former slaves. In most cases, such as amongst the Kel Tamanrasset and Kel Terhenanet Dag Rali, the ending of slavery by the Algerian government after independence was associated with conflict and antagonism, with the result that the often amicable relationships with their slaves were severed. In a few cases,[57] however, ex-slaves or their descendants, although now totally free persons, have elected to remain with the families of their former 'owners'. These incidences are few in number, but it is significant that in all the cases with which I am acquainted, the 'extra pair of hands' has played a vital role in providing the camp unit with labour flexibility and adaptability.

The most important relationship now for the survival of many nomadic camps is with local tourism agencies.[58] The agencies need access to camels, cameleers, cooks and guides to arrange camel treks for tourists. They also need registered guides to accompany their 4WD-based tours. A good agency needs to have assured access to such nomadic facilities across the entire region. From the nomads' perspective, access to a good tourism agency can assure them of a few weeks', perhaps more, well-paid work in the tourist season (autumn through to spring).[59] Over the last four years, I have studied closely the network of relations between one agency and the nomadic community. Since the resurgence of tourism in 2000, the agency has developed increasingly friendly and good working relations with a network of nomads across the entire Ahaggar region, from the Kel Ahnet in the north-west, to the Tegehe-n-Efis in the south-west, the Aguh-en-tehle in the south-east and the Ait Lowayan in the north and north-west.

The economic importance of these relations to the nomadic community cannot be overemphasised. Over the last four years, I have traced the flow of some €100,000 in tourism income through this agency, a substantial proportion of which has been distributed into these nomadic families and communities. In most cases, these relations have been predicated on what I would describe as very extended kinship networks. For instance, on one occasion the agency needed a guide who knew a distant section of the northern Tassili. The agent made enquiries amongst Tuareg in Tamanrasset and was put in touch by a distant a cousin with a nomadic family camping near Ideles. From the camp near Ideles, he was directed to the camp of a brother in the Tourha Mountains, who then accompanied the agent to the camp of his cousin which adjoined the Tassili range in question. The exercise took three days of driving, but put the agent in touch with the one nomad who knew that area intimately. The onus on maintaining these relationships lies very much with the nomad. Because of the difficulty of communication (few nomads have satellite phones), the agency advises the nomads concerned to come into their offices in Tamanrasset at regular intervals, so they can find out and make arrangements for any future tours in their areas. Quite apart from the business involved, these relations provide the nomad not only with a friendly 'base' in Tamanrasset, but access, if required, to the town's business, administrative and political sector. For example, if the nomad has a problem regarding, say, his employment with the Park, medical attention for a kinsman, payment of the camel subsidy, or the like, he has a powerful ally in town to take up his case for him.

In many ways the relationship between nomads and *agences de tourisme* is analogous to the more symbiotic elements of the old *temazlayt* relationship. In the 1960s I was able to find a few relationships between Tamanrasset-domiciled Kel Rela and nomads that were based on friendships derived from former *temazlayt* relationships. Today, the word *temazlayt* seems to be virtually unknown amongst the Kel Ahaggar. I would therefore be hesitant in suggesting that one can now find much trace of former *temazlayt* relations. Nevertheless, I believe that I have found two current relationships between tour agencies and nomads that have their roots in old *temazlayt* relations. One involves a Kel Rela who runs a tour agency and keeps a number of his own camels in the care of nomadic families. Although the Kel Rela was able to confirm that the nomads belonged to families with whom his own family had been friendly for several generations, he did not know the word *temazlayt*. The second case concerns a Kel Rela who came to work in partnership with an existing agency. Within a few months he had been approached by a group of almost 50 Aguh-en-tehle nomads living some two days ride to the east of Tamanrasset. The nomads told him that they did not like the modernisation they saw in Tamanrasset,[60] but wanted small groups of tourists to come to them so that they could make money by taking them on camel treks. The agency duly arranged for about two dozen tourists to visit the nomads over a two-year period. Although this is not a large number, it provided vital cash income to the nomads involved. When I began to investigate the social relations between these nomads and the agency, it transpired that the nomads were not simply good friends of the Kel Rela, but that the Kel Rela family had known the Aguh-en-tehle section for several generations and often camped with them around the first decades of the twentieth century. Although the word *temazlayt* was unfamiliar to them, their description of the relationship was typical of the traditional *temazlayt* relationship that I have described.

Change in the Management of Pastoral Resources

One feature about present-day nomadism in Ahaggar-Ajjer is that pastoral resources are no longer managed through the traditional authority structure of the drum-group, but by a rather inchoate combination of regulations relating more to the natural resources of the Park, than pastoralism *per se*, and individual nomads themselves. For example, the pruning of acacia trees to supplement the grazing of goats in drought periods now requires the authorisation of the local commune, which is given under more or less the same conditions as in traditional times. However, with the Algerian government's abolition of traditional tribal authorities and their territorial arrangements, access to pasture areas, wells and other such resources is now left very much to the local nomads themselves. While the remaining nomads still broadly respect traditional territorial rights, they have greater freedom to move their herds much further afield than they might have been able to do in traditional times. The slaughter of camels in Atakor in November 1993 seems to have resulted from what can only be described as a 'free-for-all' in terms of access to the area. In traditional times this would have been authorised and managed by the *Amenukal* working in collaboration with local chiefs and headmen. This has one great advantage in that these small nomadic groups, often no more than a single family, can wander over a far greater range of territory than might have been the case in traditional times.[61] For example, I kept a record of the movements of one such family over the last three years. For the first two years of this period, when pasture was very impoverished, the camp moved over a vast area from the southern parts of Tourha, not far from Ideles, to the eastern Tefedest, across Amadror to the Tihodaine region where they dug a temporary well, and through the northern Tourha and into the Adrar Hagarhene and Ahellakane ranges of the Tassili. At one point, when grazing became particularly bad, the camp moved right across the Tassili into the Tifernine area. The significance of these wanderings was not the extent of their geographical movement, but that they required no authority[62] and that during the course of this period the camp grazed its herds in areas that fell traditionally within the territories of four different *tawsatin*. This greater range and freedom of movement is perhaps another factor that enabled nomads to survive the difficult years of the 1990s.

However, this lack of traditional authority has certain disadvantages. For example, in November–December 2002 I travelled through Tamesna to assess the extent to which Kel Ahaggar were still using the area. There had been good late summer rains and the whole area was a green carpet of young shoots. Camels were scattered, grazing contentedly, in all directions and as far as the eye could see. Milk was abundant. Six months later, I met one of my former travelling companions in Tamanrasset. He had just returned from Burkina Faso, and for something to say, I asked him how things were in Tamesna. 'Terrible', he replied. 'There is no pasture. It is all dry'. The reason, as I suspected, was nothing to do with the climate, but the fact that there is now no longer any tribal authority in the region. In the past, when the Kel Ahaggar had their own *Amenukal* in the region, camels would not have been allowed to graze certain pasture areas until the pasture had been allowed to grow. Now, the free for all, which my travelling companions of the autumn had laughingly referred to as the 'great camel restaurant', had led to immediate overgrazing and impoverishment.

The Revivalism of Nomadism

With the benefit of four years' hindsight, I am inclined to think that the reason why so many people in Tamanrasset told me in 1999 that there were 'no more nomads' was because they had seen that the Dag Rali, along with most of the other nomads in the vicinity of Tamanrasset, had sedentarised and that the nomadic economy as a whole had probably reached an all-time low. What would have happened to these last surviving nomads if it had not been for the Park's salaries to the *guardiens du parc* will remain in the realm of speculation. There is a certain irony, which has not been lost on some of the older and more politically aware Kel Ahaggar, that it has been the policies of the same government that brought nomadism to its knees in the 1960s that have now played the major part in its survival. Indeed, I would even suggest that since 1999 there has been a modest revival in the nomadic economy. This revivalism probably began around 2000, when the bulk of the camel subsidy payments began to be made, and was sustained by the Park's salaries and the gradual pick-up in tourism. In addition, poor rainfall through 1999, 2000 and 2001 gave way in both 2002 and 2003 to some of the best rains in living memory.

Two aspects of this revival are worthy of note. The first is that the continuity of this revival and the future of nomadism in Algeria's extreme south depend very heavily on both the support given to the people of the region by the new World Deserts Foundation, whose President, Cherif Rahmani, is also Algeria's Minister of the Environment, and the introduction and implementation of policies by both the Ministry of Culture and the Ministry of Tourism that are geared to the conservation of the region's heritage and the development of environmentally sustainable forms of tourism. At this precise moment (summer 2003), and as I have concluded in both the introductory and final articles in this volume, the Algerian government is finally recognising the cultural and economic importance of nomadism and is showing all the signs of taking these matters seriously.

Second, and finally, I would conclude by drawing attention to two particularly intriguing aspects of this nomadic revivalism. The first is the social phenomenon, referred to elsewhere in this volume,[63] where women in particular social circumstances are re-establishing themselves in a nomadic state. I am only aware of a few such camps, but am inclined to think that they may represent a new social phenomenon, reacting against many of the more negative aspects of the modernisation that I have also discussed elsewhere in the volume.[64] The significant point about this phenomenon is that the traditional division of labour, combined with the traditional, Quranic inheritance system, which allows women to inherit and own livestock (both goats and camels), provides them with the means to subsist in a nomadic state with relative ease.

The second aspect is less tangible. It is merely that a number of Kel Ahaggar who are either living a nomadic existence, or who have close social relations with nomads, have spoken to me of the merits of remaining in the nomadic milieu in preference to entering school and looking for employment in the 'modern world'. Their argument is that by following the route though school and further education, children do not acquire the skills and knowledge of nomadic pastoralism. They then face the risk of becoming unemployed at young middle age with no knowledge and skills of their traditional way of life in which there is a security on which they could fall back. This view is not one that I heard being expressed in the 1960s and 1970s. It is one that I believe has arisen from their seeing too many people going to school, obtaining seemingly good employment and becoming unemployed, and one that has perhaps been compounded by their experience of the socio-economic problems of Tamanrasset and the country as a whole. One might comment, a little cynically, 'welcome to the post-modernist world'. More positively, I am inclined to think that if this slight revivalism in nomadism receives the support of the new policies being spoken of by the Ministries of Environment, Culture and Tourism, then we may see a resurgence in traditional knowledge and education, perhaps in association with an educational system that is more adapted to the needs of the local economy, the main sectors of which are local administration and commerce, tourism, environmental and heritage conservation and smuggling.[65]

Nomadic pastoralism in Ahaggar-Ajjer, from pre-colonial times to the present, has been an almost continual adaptation to new impediments and

The Last Nomads

opportunities, manifested in the almost continuous search for and acquisition of new resources and means of supplementation and an almost perpetual ongoing transformation of the associated social relations of production.

NOTES

I would like to acknowledge the Economic and Social Research Council (ESRC) and the Leverhulme Trust for their most generous support.

1. I have no comparative figures for the Kel Ajjer. However, with the earlier settlement of the Ajjer Tuareg in Djanet and the few other small villages in the Ajjer region, the percentage of Kel Ajjer living a nomadic existence was certainly smaller than in Ahaggar.
2. Many of these villages now have mains electricity.
3. E.L. Peters, 'Nomads; nomadism', in G.D. Mitchell (ed.), *A Dictionary of Sociology* (London: Routledge & Kegan Paul 1968) p.125. See also F. Barth, *Nomads of South Persia* (London: Allen & Unwin 1961); J. Berque, 'Nomads and Nomadism in the Arid Zone', *International Social Science Journal* XI/4 (1964); D.J. Stenning, *Savannah Nomads* (Oxford: Oxford University Press 1959); UNESCO, *Nomades et Nomadisme au Sahara*, Recherches sur la zone aride – XI (Paris: UNESCO 1963); J. Nicolaisen, *Ecology and Culture of the Pastoral Tuareg* (Copenhagen: University of Copenhagen 1963).
4. See glossary, and J. Keenan, 'Ethnicity, Regionalism and Political Stability in Algeria's Grand Sud', in this volume, pp.67–96.
5. The total population of Kel Ahaggar and Kel Ajjer (i.e. Algerian Tuareg) is now estimated at around 30,000, of whom perhaps 3–4,000 are nomads.
6. A. Bourgeot, 'Idéologies et appellations ethniques: l'exemple twareg. Analyse des catégories sociales', *Cahiers d'Etudes Africaines* XII/48 (1972) pp.553–4.
7. The origin of this division and the meaning of these terms is discussed in J. Keenan, 'From Tit (1902) to Tahilahi (2002): A Reconsideration of the Impact of and Resistance to French Pacification and Colonial Rule by the Tuareg of Algeria (the Northern Tuareg)', in this volume, pp.27–66; and in Keenan (note 4).
8. A more detailed analysis of the origin of this division is given in J. Keenan, *The Tuareg: People of Ahaggar* (London: Allen Lane 1977) p.32ff.
9. A summary account of these raiding activities, as well as internal feuds amongst the Kel Ahaggar themselves, is given in Keenan (note 7). A more detailed account is given in Keenan (note 8).
10. From our rather tenuous and limited knowledge of these earlier times, it appears that raiding expeditions outside Ahaggar increased in incidence following periods of physical conflict among the Kel Ahaggar themselves, or following periods of drought when hardship and famine threatened. For more details, see Keenan (note 8).
11. The political structure of the drum-group, comprising one noble descent group and a number of subordinate Kel Ulli descent groups, is described in Keenan (note 7). For a more detailed analysis, see Keenan (note 8).
12. French-speaking Tuareg translate the term *tiwse* as *impôt* (tax), while *ehere-n-amadal* means literally 'the wealth of the land'.
13. Although the payments were fixed for each group, they tended to fluctuate from year to year depending on the condition of pasture, livestock – especially goats – and other resources. For details of these payments, see Keenan (note 8) p.36ff.
14. Although some of the general features of the relationship were observed and described by most of the first European travellers in the region, notably Henri Duveyrier and Maurice Benhazera, they made no mention of the term *temazlayt* itself. H. Duveyrier, *Les Touareg du Nord* (Paris: Challamel 1864); and M. Benhazera, *Six Mois chez les Touareg du Ahaggar*

(Alger: Jourdan 1908). Prior to my attempt to analyse the vestigial elements of *temazlayt* relationships in the 1960s, the only references I have found to the term have been in Foucauld's dictionary, Marceau Gast's note in the *Encyclopédie Berbère* and the valuable comments of Johannes Nicolaisen. See J. Keenan, 'Some theoretical considerations on the *temazlayt* relationship', *Revue de l'Occident Musulman et de la Méditerranée* 21/1 (1976) pp.33–46 (paper first delivered at the Colloque on L'Organisation Sociale des Touareg, at Senanque, France, June 1974); Keenan (note 8) p.44ff.; C. de Foucauld, *Dictionnaire Touareg–Français, dialecte de l'Ahaggar*, 4 vols. (Paris: Imprimerie nationale de France 1951–52) Vol.IV, p.1965; M. Gast, 'Temazlayt (Contrat de protection chez les Kel Ahaggar)', in *Encyclopédie Berbère*, Cahier 7 (1972) p.2; Nicolaisen (note 3).
15. Foucauld (note 14).
16. Gast (note 14).
17. Nicolaisen (note 3) pp.403–4.
18. The principles of descent are explained in J. Keenan, 'The End of the Matriline? The Changing Roles of Women and Descent amongst the Algerian Tuareg', in this volume, pp.121–62.
19. Nicolaisen based this conclusion on the observations of Benhazera (note 14), which are not at all clear in that they make no reference to the *temazlayt*, as Nicolaisen seems to imply.
20. See Keenan (note 18).
21. See Keenan (note 14).
22. Duveyrier (note 14) p.34.
23. Nicolaisen (note 3) p.404.
24. This summary account of the various rights and obligations of the *temazlayt* owes much to the studies of Nicolaisen (note 3).
25. Keenan (note 7).
26. Ibid.
27. Ibid.
28. We see a similar expedition of Isekkemaren travelling as far as the Fezzan in search of dates. There were further attempts by Kel Ulli to find new markets outside Ahaggar in 1908 when they went to Gao in search of rice and in 1912 when they went to Anderamboukane in search of millet. In 1923 they returned once more to Damergou. It appears that all these expeditions were made on their own initiative, using their own camels and independently of the Ihaggaren.
29. Keenan (note 7).
30. For details of the social organisation of *tawsit* sections in the context of the caravan trade, see Keenan (note 18).
31. Tamesna was effectively annexed by the Kel Ahaggar in 1917 after they had helped the French defeat the Kel Aïr. Since that time the Kel Ahaggar have kept the bulk of their camels in Tamesna. Most of the important wells in the region were dug by the Kel Ahaggar – the wells of In-Abangerit being the work of the Irregenaten. Laarmech, their chief who was responsible for this work, died in 1954.
32. Tamesna was ceded from the Kel Aïr to the Kel Ahaggar in 1917 following Moussa ag Amastane's assistance to the French in defeating the Sanussi leader Kaoucen. For details see Keenan (note 7).
33. Statistics for 1949 reveal that the Dag Rali had more slaves than any other *tawsit*, including the Kel Rela; see Keenan (note 8) p.356.
34. For details of the contractual relationships between *harratin* and Kel Ahaggar, and the contribution of the *harratin* to the Kel Ahaggar's economy, see Keenan (note 8) pp.167–8 and passim. Malaurie calculated that in 1946, 375 tonnes of salt were exchanged for 720 tonnes of millet, which was augmented by 179 tonnes of grain from the *harratin*-cultivated gardens. This contribution comprised 20 per cent of the Kel Ahaggar's grain consumption, or perhaps even 25 per cent if we include the exactions of hospitality. J. Malaurie, 'Touareg

The Last Nomads

et noirs du Hoggar: aspects de la situation actuelle', *Annales Economies, Sociétés, Civilisations* VIII/3 (1953) pp.338–46.
35. Men were responsible for certain aspects of the preparation and cooking of meat.
36. For details, see Keenan (note 18).
37. This was at In Gal.
38. See Keenan (note 18); see also Keenan (note 8) pp.107–26; and J. Keenan, 'Power and Wealth are Cousins: Descent, Class and Marital Strategies among the Kel Ahaggar (Tuareg – Sahara)', *Africa* 47/3 (1977) pp.242–52, and 47/4 (1977) pp.333–42.
39. Keenan (note 8) p.144.
40. Ibid. p.185.
41. See Keenan (note 18).
42. This is also true of some other *tawsatin*, such as the Ait Lowayan.
43. In 1992, after a number of years of political and economic instability, Algeria held general elections that were won by the *Front Islamique du Salut* (FIS) and would have brought to power the world's first elected Islamist government. However, the army stepped in and annulled the elections, an action that led to the outbreak of militant and terrorist activity by certain Islamist groups. The spiral of violence that took hold of the country in the ensuing years has seen an estimated 100–150,000 people killed.
44. P. Pandolfi, *Les Touaregs de l'Ahaggar* (Paris: Karthala 1998).
45. For details of tourism in Ahaggar-Ajjer, see J. Keenan, 'Contested Terrain: Tourism, Environment and Security in Algeria's Extreme South', in this volume, pp.226–65.
46. For example, the *chef de poste* at Mertoutek, which is typical of the Park as a whole, recorded not a single tourist between the end of 1993 and December 1999! A few Kel Ahaggar have refused to accept such 'employment' on the grounds that it is demeaning.
47. Algerian Dinars.
48. See Keenan (note 45).
49. The Tassili-n-Ajjer Park was established in 1984 and designated as a UNESCO world heritage site. The Hoggar (Ahaggar) National Park was established in 1987.
50. Further government assistance to nomads has taken the form of issuing all nomadic families with a large tent, while the local administration has on occasion given small amounts of assistance, such as when some 250 camels were killed in the winter of 1993 by icy conditions in the high mountains of Atakor.
51. For details of these complaints, see Keenan (note 45).
52. In winter, temperatures regularly drop below zero. During the night of the millennium, for example, a herd of 40 sheep froze to death near Silet.
53. For details of these complaints, see Keenan (note 45).
54. Because of the huge movement of population into the region since the early 1990s, it is difficult to differentiate between the natural population growth within the region and immigration. For details, see Keenan (note 4). My own estimate is that the local population has increased between three and fourfold since the 1960s. This may be even greater amongst the ex-slave and former *harratin* communities. This internal population growth, alongside increasing sedentarisation, has resulted in many of the larger villages, such as In Amguel, Ideles and Tazrouk becoming small towns with populations of 5,000 or more.
55. For details, see Keenan (note 18).
56. Many from Tamesna.
57. Such as amongst many of the Kel Hirafok, some of the Aguh-en-tehle of the Relaydin and Kel Arefsa sections, the Ait Lowayan in the Tourha and Tefedest regions, and amongst certain Kel Rezzi/Merabtines.
58. *Agences des Voyages* are mostly Tuareg-owned. There are approximately 150 agencies in the two *wilayat* of Tamanrasset and Illizi, although only about a dozen can offer a really professional service.
59. See Keenan (note 45).

60. See Keenan (note 18).
61. With fewer nomads, the pressure on natural resources is less, thus making it easier for nomads to wander more freely.
62. Many of the decisions to move were made solely by the wife, as in traditional times, as her husband was away working with tourists for much of the time. On one occasion, he spent a whole day in a borrowed 4WD and with binoculars trying to find her!
63. See Keenan (note 18).
64. See ibid.
65. For the importance of these sectors, see Keenan (note 45).

The Lesser Gods of the Sahara

Introduction

It is timely – given the increased attention now being paid by archaeologists, ethnologists, auction houses, national museums and governments to the UNIDROIT Convention on Stolen or Illegally Exported Cultural Objects, the UN Draft Declaration on the Rights of Indigenous Peoples and the fact that we are approaching the end of the UN Decade of Indigenous Peoples[1] – to question a number of practices undertaken by France in her former colony, Algeria, regarding both the discovery and recording of prehistoric rock art and the excavation, collection and removal of cultural objects, especially from regions within Algeria which have long been recognised and are now designated by the UN as belonging to 'indigenous peoples'. The intervention is made more urgent by France's seeming determination to undermine both the UNIDROIT Convention[2] and the Declaration on the Rights of Indigenous Peoples;[3] the intransigence being shown within France towards the continuation of a number of long-accepted but nevertheless regrettable practices regarding illegally exported cultural objects;[4] the elevation to cult status of certain personages[5] associated with such practices; and the question of restitution being raised by both Algerians and – perhaps more importantly – the indigenous peoples, namely the Tuareg,[6] from whom this cultural heritage has been expropriated.[7]

The 'Discovery' of the Tassili Frescoes

The mid-1950s saw the 'discovery'[8] of one of the world's greatest archaeological finds, the prehistoric rock paintings of the Central Saharan mountains of the Tassili-n-Ajjer (see map).[9] Amidst widespread media coverage the Tassili Frescoes, as they became known, were presented as 'the greatest museum of prehistoric art in the whole world'. The 'discovery' was attributed almost entirely to the French prehistorian, Henri Lhote, whose 16 months of work in the Tassili, from the beginning of 1956 to early summer 1957, culminated in 1958 in the publication of one of the world's best-known and best-selling books on archaeological discovery: Henri Lhote's *A La Découverte des Fresques du Tassili*.[10]

The immediate impact of Lhote's publication on the wider public was one of admiration for the discoverer and wonder at what he had discovered. Not

The Lesser Gods of the Sahara

FIGURE 1
MAP OF NORTH AFRICA WITH INSERT DETAILING SOUTHERN ALGERIAN
REGION OF TASSILI-N-AJJER AND AHAGGAR

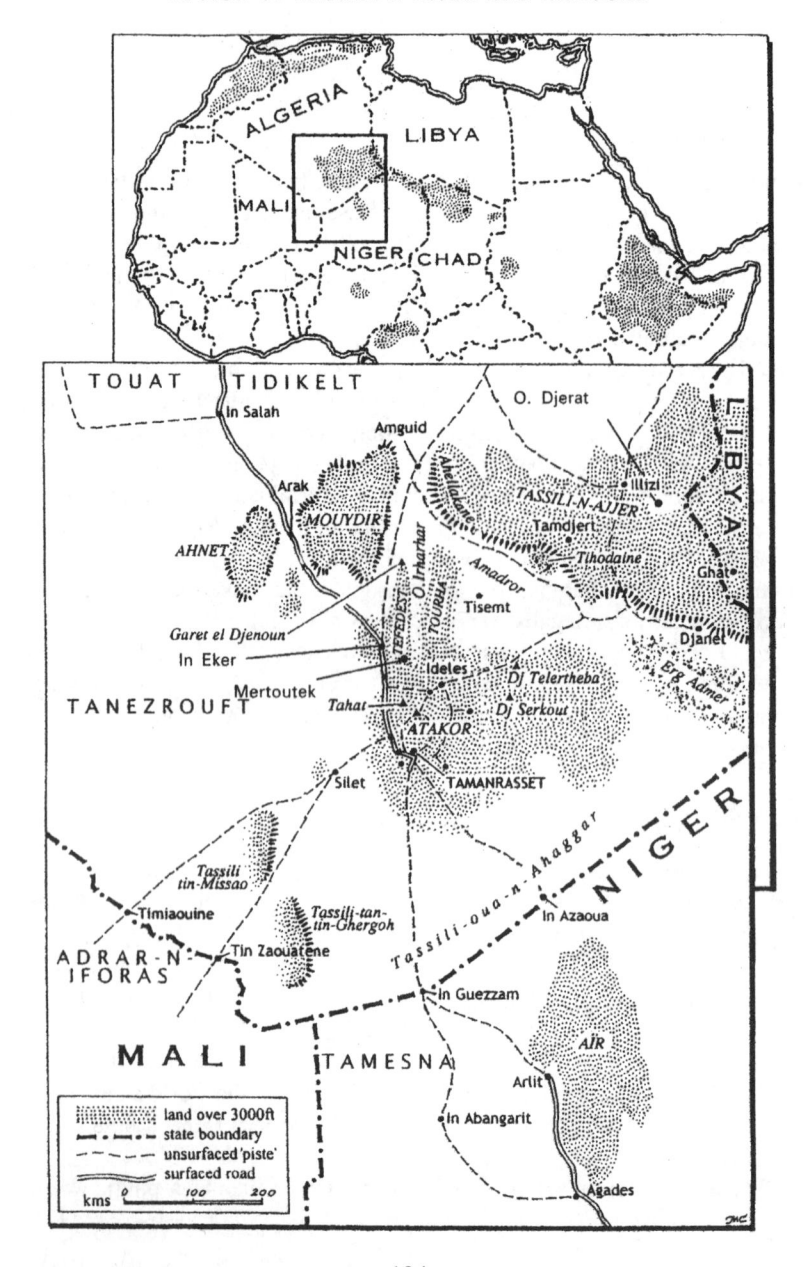

only were the copies of the paintings and engravings that Lhote brought back to France and exhibited to the public splendid in their artistry, colour, naturalism, symbolism and scale, but they gave a huge impetus to the nascent field of enquiry about earlier peoples, climates and conditions in the Sahara.[11] I was fortunate in being able to see many of these paintings when I worked as an anthropologist amongst the Tuareg in the 1960s, less than ten years after their 'discovery'.[12] Like almost everyone else who saw them at that time, I was overawed by their magnificence and exhilarated by the prospect of what they could tell us about the prehistory of the Sahara.

When I returned – some 35 years later – I was more shocked than awed by what I saw.[13] Many of the paintings have faded to the point where they are barely visible at all, and the state of many rock faces has deteriorated, probably as a result of the extensive 'washing' to which many paintings have been subjected by photographers. Vandalism, in the form of graffiti and even the physical looting of paintings, is also widespread. Moreover, the region is almost entirely devoid of portable artefacts – pottery, arrowheads, axes, grinding stones and so on. It is as if the land has been vacuumed, leaving this most important of archaeological landscapes – a UNESCO World Heritage site[14] – completely sterilised.

The way my Tuareg travelling companions, the indigenous peoples who inhabit this part of the Sahara,[15] spoke to me about the rock art was also very different. In the past their attitude seemed close to indifference: it had belonged to other, earlier occupants of the region and was of little direct significance to most of them. Now, an increasing number of Tuareg are beginning to understand the nature and importance of this heritage and want to know more about it. More importantly, they are aware of the consequences of the damage that has been recently inflicted on their heritage, particularly as it will affect their future livelihoods. I was also told disquieting stories, couched in a language that comes close to being a demand for restitution, about Henri Lhote and the removal of important cultural objects from the region.

It is these concerns, expressed by the Tuareg themselves, which have led me to undertake this review of the 'discovery' of the Tassili Frescoes.

A New Perspective on the 'Discovery' of the Tassili Frescoes

Questions raised by a re-examination of Lhote's 'discovery' of the Tassili Frescoes focus on:

1. Lhote's claims regarding the 'discovery' of the Tassili Frescoes.
2. The political, intellectual and cultural context of the 'discoveries'.

3. The authenticity of many of the paintings.
4. The methodology and scientific value of Lhote's research.
5. The denial of access to other academics, especially those of other countries.
6. Lhote's views on and relationship with the Tuareg.
7. The implications of Lhote's research for current researchers; liability and the moral responsibility for restitution.

Claims of 'Discovery'

One might suppose that a work entitled *The Search for the Tassili Frescoes*, subtitled *The Story of the Prehistoric Rock-Paintings of the Sahara*, written under the tutelage of the Abbé Breuil, sponsored by the French *Musée de L'Homme* and financed by France's *Centre National de la Recherche Scientifique* (CNRS) and the Algiers-based *Institut de Recherches Sahariennes* (IRS), would give a fairly detailed, well-chronicled and well-referenced account of the history of the discovery of the rock art of the Tassili. The work does no such thing. Not only is it without indexation, but the text is frustratingly lacking, to the point of intellectual dishonesty, in the names and dates of the discoveries made by earlier prehistorians. Although Lhote's team did 'discover' several hitherto unrecorded sites and paintings, the reader of *The Search for the Tassili Frescoes* is left with an overriding impression that the Tassili Frescoes were largely unknown and undiscovered before Lhote's 16-month expedition. That was not the case.

The first discovery of rock art in the Central Sahara was made by the German explorer, Heinrich Barth, in 1850 in the region of Ghat in south-eastern Libya on his way to Aïr.[16] A decade or so later the young French geographer Henri Duveyrier noted the existence of 'important rock sculptures, evidence of a lost civilisation' in the Tadrart Acacus immediately to the east of the Tassili-n-Ajjer, although he was not actually able to see them for himself.[17] Several other explorers in the late nineteenth century, notably Nachtigal, Erwin de Bary and Fernand Foureau, saw examples of rock art. In the published notes of his 1892–93 explorations, Foureau says, 'I was told that some big, strange rock sculptures exist in the Upper Tassili ...'.[18] Although he did not see them himself, Foureau was also given information by a Tuareg guide about the engravings in the *Oued* Djerat.

These early discoveries were isolated and largely incidental to the main objectives of these explorers. Not until the Tuareg were conquered by the French in 1902 and French military patrols became commonplace throughout the regions of Ahaggar and Tassili, did the French begin to get an appreciation of the immensity and beauty of the rock art that lay within the region. The

The Lesser Gods of the Sahara

rock art in the Ahnet region was fairly well known by 1908; in 1909 Captain Cortier noticed the first painting of the Tassili in the *Oued* Assouf Mellen near Fort Polignac (now Illizi); Lieutenant Gardel noted the paintings at In Ezzan in 1914 and the geologist Conrad Killian came across several significant sites in 1927–28.

By 1932 the existence of prehistoric rock art in the Central Saharan regions of Ahaggar and Tassili was well established.[19] In that year one of France's leading prehistorians, Professor Maurice Reygasse, Director of the Bardo Museum of Ethnography and Prehistory in Algiers, wrote, 'The epic period of the great explorations is now over. Thanks to the preliminary work carried out by the innovators we can now settle down to a period of calm, detailed research'.[20]

Detailed research rather than calmness was more the order of the day as stunning discoveries continued to be made. The greatest of these was that made in 1933 by Lieutenant (later Lieutenant Colonel) Brenans, a camel corps officer, who ventured deep into the gorge of the *Oued* Djerat to the south-east of Illizi. In front of him, stretching for 30km on either side of the *Oued*, were thousands of prehistoric rock engravings. Brenans made sketches of some of the animals and sent them to the Bardo Museum in Algiers. France's leading experts in the field, such as Professors Gautier, Reygasse and Perret, rushed to the scene. Henri Lhote accompanied one of these expeditions.[21]

If there is any one European, other than Lhote, whose name should be associated with the Tassili paintings, it is Brenans, who from 1932 to 1940, and as military commandant at Djanet, never left the Tassili. When Brenans took the scientists to *Oued* Djerat he told them about the paintings he had found on the plateau above Djanet.[22] Between then (1933) and 1940 he discovered many of the most important sites on the plateau, including Jabbaren, Iddo, Tin Bedjedj, Assadjen, Tissougaï, Oua Mellen and Tachekalaout. Until Brenans's explorations, the rock art in the Tassili and Ahaggar was being discovered and, it seems, conceptualised on an almost isolated site-by-site basis. Malika Hachid has suggested, probably correctly, that 'this lonely, passionate man was probably the first to sense the existence not simply of a series of isolated sites but of a whole world of Saharan art. He probably understood that an isolated image might well belong to a bigger ensemble which needed to be detected'.[23]

Brenans's passion was expressed in his artistic ability. He never travelled without his sketchbook and during these years he made hundreds of superb sketches of his discoveries. Realising the importance and value of his findings to the scientific community, Brenans forwarded his notes, sketches and reports to Maurice Reygasse at the Bardo Museum in Algiers. Precisely what happened to them thereafter is not altogether clear, except that they reached

The Lesser Gods of the Sahara

the *Musée de L'Homme* in Paris just before the outbreak of the Second World War, from where they were forwarded to the Abbé Breuil, the leading specialist on rock art. The war put an end to any hope of publishing what was evidently a voluminous report. Some of Brenans's pictures of the rock art began to appear after the war, but it was not until the Second Pan-African Congress on Prehistory, held in Algiers in September–October 1952, that his work was presented to the scientific community.[24]

Meanwhile, in 1950 and 1951, almost two years before the Algiers conference, Yolande Tschudi, a Swiss ethnologist working for the Neuchâtel Museum of Ethnography, travelled quite extensively through the Assakao and Meddak groups of rock paintings above Djanet, notably at Tachekelaout, Ouan Bender, Assadjen oua Mellen, Tin Tazarift, Tin Bedjedj and Oua Moulin. Tschudi made sketches, took photographs and made colour gouache copies of the paintings, which she published in a monograph in 1955.[25]

The extraordinary thing about Lhote's *A La Découverte des Fresques du Tassili* is that there are no references to any of these discoveries other than some rather imprecise references to Brenans and Lhote's 'friendship' with him. At the outset of the book, Lhote writes:

> The Saharan rock-paintings and engravings could not, of course, fail to excite my curiosity; so, after important discoveries of painted rocks had been made in the Tassili by a camel-corps officer, Lieutenant Brenans, I visited these sites with several specialists in Saharan geography and archaeology. Then came the 1939 war and the interruption of all my work. It was not until 1956 that I was able, with the encouragement and support of my revered teacher the Abbé Breuil, to organize a large expedition to copy the known paintings and explore systematically the Tassili massif ... I made discovery after discovery, while, at the same time, we prepared, at each site, faithful copies of the frescoes.[26]

Lhote makes no reference to any discovery or knowledge of Saharan rock art before Brenans's discoveries. Moreover, the impression given by Lhote in this passage, and throughout the remainder of the book, is that very little exploration and discovery took place between Brenans's discovery of the *Oued* Djerat in 1933 and Lhote's expedition of 1956. Again, that was not the case. Brenans was, in fact, based continuously in the Tassili between 1932 and 1940 and spent a great deal of his time travelling on the plateau, discovering rock art sites and recording his findings.

As I have mentioned, Brenans dutifully passed on his many hundreds of sketches to Reygasse at the Bardo Museum in Algiers. His discoveries were clearly known to Lhote, who accompanied Brenans on some of these journeys, notably in 1934 and 1938, when Brenans took Lhote to both Tamrit

The Lesser Gods of the Sahara

and Jabbaren.[27] Lhote's account of these trips is a little curious, underplaying and perhaps even belittling Brenans's enormous contribution. Indeed, from reading *A La Découverte*, one is left with the impression that it was Lhote who played the lead part in these discoveries. He writes:

> Oued Djerat was a decisive experience for me. The engravings and paintings had given me a glimpse of the great importance such unexpected artistic creations would have for archaeology. The beauty of the pictures, their aesthetic value, had aroused in me, also, an enthusiasm which was to increase with the passing of time. Next, I carried on my investigations in the region to the north of Djanet where Brenans had told me that he had seen rock-shelters with paintings. For months I wandered about all over the Tassili and saw so many pictures that my supply of drawing paper was soon exhausted. Brenans himself was an excellent draughtsman, but the copies we made were only poor, small-scale sketches which gave but an indifferent idea of what we had seen.[28]

While Brenans's contribution is at least recognised, there are no references to the work of Tschudi, Frobenius or the many others, such as Cortier, Killian, Monod, Coche, Chasseloup-Laubat, Dubief, Le Poitevin, *et al.*, who had made significant discoveries or contributions to the developing corpus of knowledge of Saharan rock art.[29]

At a recent gathering of Saharan rock art specialists, I asked one of Lhote's 'followers' why he had failed to acknowledge Yolande Tschudi's work. He replied that it was probably because either Lhote thought her work unimportant or he was unaware of it. Tschudi's work was certainly not unimportant: it was not only the first collection of watercolours and photos of the Tassili paintings, but also, in spite of some imperfections, the first attempt at their chronological classification.[30] Lhote was certainly aware of Tschudi's work, for in the immediate post-war years he was employed as an assistant at the *Musée de l'Homme* where he was charged, amongst other things, with compiling an inventory and bibliography of all African rock art north of the Equator. This work was published as part of the Abbé Breuil's publication of Brenans's Tassili recordings at the Pan-African Prehistory Congress in Algiers in 1952.[31] Lhote's scholarly inventory is inclusive of all known discoveries and publications on Saharan rock art at that time. It records accurately the early work of Yolande Tschudi, the work of Leo Frobenius, Le Poitevin, Dubief and others, as well as all sites recorded by Brenans.[32] Moreover, Tschudi presented a summary of her 1950–51 exploration and findings, with maps and photos, at the 1952 Pan-African Congress in Algiers, and in the same section of the Congress in which Lhote himself submitted three papers.[33]

The Political, Intellectual and Cultural Context of the 'Discoveries'

It is something of a mystery why Lhote should show such apparent intellectual dishonesty in *A La Découverte des Fresques du Tassili*, when this trait is not apparent in his earlier work, notably his many contributions to the 1952 Congress in Algiers. Indeed, in his contribution to the publication of Brenans's work at the 1952 Congress he gives an accurate outline of the history of the discovery of the Tassilian rock art as well as full recognition to Brenans's own discoveries and recordings. That, no doubt, is precisely the point that will be made by Lhote's defenders. They will argue that *A La Découverte* is a popular book, not a scholarly work, in which there is no place for the finer points of scholarship. That is to some extent true, but it is popular books, rather than obscure, scholarly works,[34] that tend to colour the public image. In the case of *A La Découverte*, the inclusion of one short paragraph would have done much to set the record straight. Rather, the question to be asked is: what happened to both Lhote and the state of discovery of Saharan rock art between 1952 and 1956?

The main purpose of Lhote's 1956 expedition was not, as the title *A La Découverte des Fresques du Tassili* might suggest, to 'discover' the Tassili Frescoes. That was already largely accomplished: as Jean Dubief remarked several years earlier, 'there are very many paintings, and any company officer can discover one if he just bothers to take the trouble'.[35] Rather, the purpose of the expedition was to bring the frescoes to the attention of the wider public by making a series of colour, life-size copies of them. According to Malika Hachid, who cites Jean-Dominique Lajoux, the photographer attached to Lhote's team, this idea came from Brenans, who may well have been frustrated by the fact that his own small black and white sketches in no way covered the majesty, grandeur and beauty of what he had seen, and that his discoveries would only be known to a few specialists unless they were published on a much larger scale.[36] Lhote put the project into practice after Brenans died in 1955 of a sudden heart attack a month before the expedition set out. Lhote would have been aware of the imminent publication of Yolande Tschudi's collection of watercolour paintings of the Tassili Frescoes, which, as Hachid suggests, 'conveyed much more clearly the grandeur of the paintings'.[37]

However, I believe that there is more to the intellectual dishonesty of *A La Découverte* than the mere 'foibles of men'. Lhote's expedition and the ensuing publication, *A La Découverte*, need to be understood in their wider political, intellectual and cultural contexts.

The Algerian Revolution

Lhote's 16-month expedition to the Tassili, from early 1956 to early summer 1957, coincided with some of the most intense fighting and worst atrocities of the Algerian Revolution. The 'rebellion', as the French called it, which had begun in 1954, intensified and escalated throughout 1955 and into 1956, reaching one of its turning points in the first week of February 1956, when French authority in Algeria gave way to the Algiers mob. The background to this was supplied by elections in France,[38] which had resulted in a government headed by the socialist, Guy Mollet. During the elections there had been much socialist pressure for negotiations with the rebels, and the European community in Algeria feared that Mollet's appointment of a new governor general in Algeria was the first step in that direction. General Georges Catroux's appointment made them cherish his predecessor, Jacques Soustelle, whose departure[39] saw massive demonstrations on the streets of Algiers in which the vociferous crowd blocked Soustelle's official *cortège* and threatened to keep him in Algiers by force. For the first time Soustelle found himself being feted as a hero.[40] But his farewell reception was to have serious consequences, galvanising his increasingly firm belief in a French Algeria, to the extent that on his return to France he was to become the leading spokesman, in Paris, for the European community in Algiers.

Within a month of Lhote's arrival in the Tassili, Algiers was experiencing the first outbreak of urban terrorism, while by the end of the year terror and torture had become the order of the day in the Battle of Algiers. While thousands of Algerians were being tortured to death or summarily executed without the semblance of a trial, Lhote was beavering away in the rock shelters of the Tassili.

The fact that *A La Découverte* makes no reference to these events or the political context in which the expedition was undertaken does not mean that the expedition was an apolitical event. On the contrary, not only had Lhote managed to convince the President of the French Republic[41] of the necessity of the expedition, but he had secured the support of the *Musée de l'Homme*, the financial backing of the CNRS and the IRS and the patronage of the governor general of Algeria. The expedition was no simple archaeological jaunt into the Sahara: it had the full backing of the French political and intellectual/scientific establishment, with both military and civil authorities in Algeria being placed at its disposal.

With such strong backing from the French state and its establishment, Lhote was probably obliged to make no comment on the prevailing political climate in Algeria. After all, the purpose of the expedition was to publicise the great art treasures of the French Sahara, not to draw attention to France's problems in Algeria. Nevertheless, it is surprising that he makes no comment on the events in Algiers at the time of his arrival,[42] not least because the man at the centre of all the commotion, Jacques Soustelle, was none other than the expedition's patron![43]

The expedition's close association with Soustelle[44] raises a number of intriguing political questions, not the least of which relates to the fact that by the time of his patronage of Lhote's expedition he had come to show an uncompromising hostility to Algerian nationalism and had become the political and intellectual standard-bearer of an *Algérie Française*. Following his departure from Algiers, he became the main political and intellectual spokesman for the integration of Algeria with France, becoming a leader of the May 1958 rebellion in Algeria and a major force behind the abortive military uprising (the 'Generals' Revolt') in Algeria in 1961. In between these two radical actions he was appointed to the seemingly bizarre but not entirely dissociated portfolio of Minister for the Sahara and for Atomic Affairs, a position to which I shall return later.

Whether Lhote shared Soustelle's aim of a French Algeria must remain something of an open question, but the fact that he continued to acknowledge publicly Soustelle's patronage when Soustelle became the recognised leader in Paris of the blindly conservative European community in Algiers would suggest that he was certainly not strongly opposed to it.[45]

Lhote's personal views on the Algerian situation are largely irrelevant. What is important is the part played by his expedition and his subsequent writings in these tumultuous events. There is no doubt that Lhote's expedition came at a most opportune time for the integrationists. Lhote's press conference on his arrival in Algiers, at which he revealed to the general public 'the greatest centre of prehistoric art in the world', gave the European community in Algeria just the sort of fillip that it needed.[46] The publicity that his expedition gave to the Tassili paintings, less than a year after the discovery of oil in the Sahara,[47] provided them with a cultural fig leaf in which to wrap their vehemently conservative, imperialist and often racist calls for a French Algeria. The publication of *A La Découverte* in 1958 simply reinforced the 'Frenchness' of the 'discovery' and France's 'cultural rights' over this great artistic and cultural treasure-trove by highlighting its all-French *provenance*: Brenans–Breuil–Lhote. There is no mention of the German, Leo Frobenius, or Switzerland's Yolande Tschudi, while the contribution of the indigenous population (see below) – the Tuareg – is mentioned disparagingly.

Whereas an *Algérie Française*, associated increasingly with the disaffected European community in Algiers and more right-wing elements in France, became more unlikely as the war progressed, the idea of *Le Sahara Français* was much more realistic. Throughout the years of fighting, the

Algerians and the French never ceased to probe for a possible peaceful solution. At all these talks, right up until August 1961, the French had held out for a partition of Algeria in which the Sahara, with its oil and gas, would remain French. France's Saharan interests were not limited to oil and gas: with the United States and Britain denying France access to the atomic bomb, de Gaulle decided that France would develop its own atomic device unilaterally, using bases in the Algerian Sahara to conduct the experiments.[48] The man appointed by de Gaulle in January 1959 as Minister for the Sahara and Atomic Affairs was none other than Jacques Soustelle. By strange coincidence, Soustelle's appointment coincided with the exhibition of the Tassili Frescoes in the *Musée des Arts Decoratifs* in the Pavillon de Marsan of the Louvre in Paris. From a purely political perspective, the timing could not have been better. The worldwide acclaim given to the exhibition and to *A La Découverte*, which was already being published in most languages, not only made Lhote famous throughout the world, but added a massive 'cultural' dimension to the oil and military claims that France was staking out in the Algerian Sahara.[49]

The Abbé Breuil and the Namibian Connection

Another question one must ask relates to the part played by the Abbé Henri Breuil in the initiation of the expedition, on the interpretation of its findings and on Lhote's own views on and interpretation of Saharan rock art. The answer to all three components is: a great deal.

Breuil, at that time, was the undisputed world authority on prehistoric rock art and there is every reason to believe that the idea of the expedition was as much his as Lhote's or Brenans's. Indeed, Malika Hachid remarks that 'Abbé Breuil was now too old to climb the Tassili and *delegated* [emphasis added] the task to Henri Lhote',[50] implying that Breuil would himself have led the expedition if he had been younger. In fact, Breuil promised Lhote that he would come to Africa and spend several weeks with the expedition. Although his age prohibited him from fulfilling this promise, his influence on the expedition was enormous. He was not only Lhote's 'revered teacher', but kept in constant communication with Lhote during the course of the expedition.[51]

Breuil's direct involvement in the expedition gave it massive intellectual respectability. But his association with both the expedition and Lhote's tutelage is particularly disturbing as the Abbé Breuil was the arch-advocate of foreign influence in African rock art.[52] Today, many of his views would be regarded as 'racist'.

The scene of the Abbé Breuil's most outrageous pronouncements was not the Sahara but Namibia, where the prospect of the Bushmen's extinction, following their appalling treatment at the hands of white settlers and their racist administrations,[53] was already provoking concern among a number of scientists. Breuil visited Namibia in 1947, having received a crude pencil sketch of a painting discovered in a small rock shelter in the Tsisab Ravine in 1917.[54] Based largely on the flimsy evidence of this one site and the sketch, Breuil made the outlandish claim that the Bushman paintings owed more to the influences of Classical antiquity than to the beliefs of African hunter-gatherers.[55] 'Thus arose the myth of the White Lady, rejected by every archaeologist of repute, but sustained by colonial settler fantasies and an apparent need to deny the Bushmen their own cultural history'.[56] The Abbé Breuil's contribution to the preposterous cultural baggage of South Africa's apartheid regime was not inconsiderable.

Breuil's outrageous claim, published in his *The White Lady of the Brandberg* (1955),[57] was hot off the press while Lhote was preparing his expedition to the Tassili. It clearly made a big impact on Lhote who, on discovering what he described as 'the most finished and the most *original* [emphasis added] picture we had found among those executed by the *Round-Headed Men*', wrote: 'First of all we called her the "Horned Goddess" but, later on, by a comparison with the famous "White Lady" of Brandberg, so dear to the Abbé Breuil – a comparison which, of course, must be taken as referring only to artistic quality – we called her the "White Lady" of Aouanrhet'.[58]

What Lhote meant by 'artistic quality' goes beyond the mere physical attributes of the painting, which he describes as follows:

> On the damp rock-surface[59] stood out the gracious silhouette of a woman running. One of her legs, slightly flexed, just touched the ground, while the other was raised in the air as high as it would normally go. From the knees, the belt and the widely outstretched arms fell fine fringes. From either side of the head and above two horns that spread out horizontally was an extensive dotted area resembling a cloud of grain falling from a wheat field. Although the whole assemblage was skilfully and carefully composed there was something free and easy about it, something that was especially marked in the thin filaments depending from the hand coverings, and in the arm-band fringes waving, you would [*sic* trans.] say, in the wind ... The body of the woman, delicately painted in yellow ochre and outlined in white, is covered from the shoulders to the belly, at the base of the back and on the breasts with curious decorative designs, parallel rows of white spots enlivened with red lines. I have no doubt that this fine painting belongs to the style of the Round-Headed Men. The rounded belly, the convex, curved buttocks, the breasts like goat's udders all bear witness to a

The Lesser Gods of the Sahara

> relationship with the old Negroid stock whose characteristic features we had already encountered in many of the paintings at Tan-Zoumiatak and other places. The dotted lines must represent scarifications such as are still practiced by the peoples of West Africa. Still, it seemed to me that in this Aouanrhet painting I could make out another artistic influence to which, for the moment, I did not dare put a name.[60]

Two paragraphs further on, Lhote puts the name:

> In other paintings found a few days later in the same massif we were able to discern, from some characteristic features, an indication of Egyptian influence. Such features are, no doubt not very marked in our 'White Lady'; still, all the same, some details such as the curve of the breasts, led us to think that the picture may have been executed at a time when Egyptian traditions were beginning to be felt in the Tassili. And when one thinks of Egypt one is reminded at once of Isis, who, with Osiris, was credited with having introduced agriculture into the Nile Valley ... but we must leave such matters for Egyptologists to deal with. And moreover, it is not the 'White Lady' alone that presents such problems. Other figures, indeed, are to be seen on the same rock-face: a kneeling woman, a man blowing a trumpet, a number of agile little people climbing up a tree and, finally, here is the prize piece ... A big stylised fish displaying decoration identical with that on an Egyptian vase recovered from El Amarna and dating from the time of the Middle Kingdom.

Lhote goes on to say much more about supposed Egyptian influence, for which he set an enduring fashion and which has done much to hamper more meaningful interpretation of Saharan rock art, but for which there is very little evidence. Indeed, we now know that the paintings of the 'Round-Head' period date from much earlier than Lhote supposed, probably from prior to 8,000 BP and possibly as early as $c.12,000$ BP (Before Present),[61] more than just a few years before the Middle Kingdom of $c.2050$ BC. Also, we now have confirmation that some of the most representative of Lhote's 'Egyptian' paintings were faked by his team (see below). This, alongside his serious methodological shortcomings (see below), effectively repudiates much of his interpretation of Tassilian rock art and that of many of his followers.

Even so, the Breuil-Lhote 'White Lady' provided the same sort of shot in the arm for agents of white settler interests in North Africa as it had done in southern Africa, perhaps even more so given the prevailing political context of Algeria. Like his mentor, Lhote had succeeded not only in linking (wrongly) the earliest of the Central Saharan rock art (the Round-Head period) to Egyptian-Classical influences, but had also managed to superimpose 'European' cultural values on both sites and paintings by anointing them with good Classical-European sounding names, such as 'The Great God' (*Le Grand Dieu*), 'Round Heads', the 'Martians', the 'Great Martian God', the 'White Lady', the 'Black Lady', 'Antinea', the 'Egyptian Boat', the 'Two Venuses', the 'Little Devils', the 'Judges', 'The Bird-Headed Goddesses', the 'Marathon Race', the 'Greek Warrior', the 'Amazons', the 'White Men' and so on. Such naming is for the most part quite harmless. Indeed, it is often suitably descriptive and even amusing (itself a cultural value), but it is nevertheless all part of the process of value superimposition.

The Authenticity of Many of the Paintings

It has long been suspected that Lhote's team was responsible for making a number of 'fakes'. This was confirmed publicly in 1998 when Malika Hachid, former Director of the Tassili Park, published the fact that 'unknown to Henri Lhote the people who worked with him made a number of "fakes"'.[62] These people were not 'native labourers' playing jokes or bearing grudges, but members of Lhote's own team of French professionals. The most spectacular of the forgeries is the painting which Lhote entitled 'The Bird-Headed Goddesses: Egyptian influence (18th dynasty?)'. Significantly, this painting[63] adorns the back of the dust jacket of *A La Découverte*.[64]

There is perhaps a sense of *Schadenfreude* in reading now what Lhote had to say on the subject of forgeries. He wrote:

> several people who saw our copies made reserves [*sic* trans., presumably 'had reservations'] about some of the figures whose style seemed so modern that the authenticity of the copies aroused doubts. Such doubts, I hasten to add, were not made in any malicious spirit but in a laudable attempt at constructive criticism. But, alas for these over-zealous critics, we shall not have our Rouffignac, or our Glozel, or our Piltdown or our Moulin-Quignon, all names celebrated in the stormy annals of prehistory. And the reason is that there is not a single forgery – intentional or unintentional – in the paintings and copies we brought back from the Tassili.[65]

The two most serious questions raised by this revelation are: how many other paintings are fakes? And, did Lhote know that his team were making fakes? The answers to both questions are uncertain, but I will deal with each of them in turn (see Postscript).

First, how many paintings are fakes? The answer is that we do not know. Malika Hachid's confirmation that 'The Bird-Headed Goddesses' is a fake comes as no surprise, in that it has generally been regarded as a 'fake' since

The Lesser Gods of the Sahara

it was first exhibited. The first published confirmation of the faking of paintings by Lhote's expedition was made some five years after the expedition's return, when Jean-Dominique Lajoux, the photographer who accompanied Lhote's expedition, published his own excellent corpus of work on the Tassili Rock Paintings. Lajoux wrote:

> There can be no doubt of the authenticity of every single one of the records shown here, although there is the precedent of a work in which a number of completely apocryphal paintings were reproduced; two of these were held to belong to Egyptian art. We have examined them. Five years after their discovery nothing remains of them, except the memory of a joke perpetrated by one of the artists employed to make the copies.[66]

Alfred Muzzolini, who has undertaken a major study of Saharan rock art, suggested that at least four paintings (including the Egyptian goddesses) were fakes. He wrote:

> *Or cette scène d'offrande*[67] *est un faux. A ce propos, signalons aussi dans les faux notoires (oeuvres des rapins des expéditions Lhote, de 1956 à 1959, où les distractions étaient rares...) les quatres fameuses 'déesses à tête d'oiseau', si souvent reproduites dans la literature de vulgarisation (y compris dans le gros dictionnaire Larousse!), et deux autres 'oeuvres' rupestres, vraiment 'trop belles pour êtres vraies' (simple appréciation personelle). D'abord quatre prétendus 'danseurs' Têtes Rondes de Ti-n-Tazarift,*[68] *en fait des femmes, publiées seulement en 'relevé', jamais en photo. Egyptianisées à outrance, elles éclatent de fauseté, et l'on ne relève nulle part ailleurs de telles attitudes ni de telles coiffures. Ensuite, une délicieuse étude anatomique de décomposition du mouvement chez les Caballins, publiée, elle, en photo,*[69] *étude trop parfaite, qu'on dirait droit issue d'une académie de Montparnasse. Seul le premier personnage à droite est peut-être authentique: ce serait un personnage du style de Sefar-Ozanéaré, négroïde. Les trois autres personnages, des Caballins, ne peuvent absolument pas aller avec lui, en outre leurs attitudes, fantaisistes, ne se relèvent jamais chez les innombrables Caballins du Tassili. Ils ont sûrement été ajoutés très récemment.*[70]

At a recent meeting, Malika Hachid confirmed to me that the painting Lhote has called 'Antinea'[71] is also a fake and that the source of the information was the faker himself. When I asked her why she had not also published this revelation, she replied that the faker only made his confession to her (through an intermediary) when he saw her book.[72]

We are thus confronted by perhaps at least five fakes: 'The Bird-Headed Goddesses' (Jabbaren), 'Antinea' (Jabarren), 'The Scene of Offerings'

(Jabbaren), 'The Dancers' (Ti-n-Tazarift) and 'Les Caballins' (Sefar).[73] There are possibly more: Hachid herself refers to there being 'a number of fakes painted by some of the copiers' (see Postscript).[74]

Before turning to the question of whether Lhote knew about the fakes, there is another point which I should try to clarify. This is whether the fakes were actually made on the rock walls or manufactured, as has been suggested to me, on the artists' tracing papers or in their notebooks, as if the latter is a 'lesser crime'. It is true that most of the supposed fakes have never been physically relocated, suggesting that they were manufactured on paper. That may well have been the case. However, Lajoux's comment (see above), that 'Five years after their discovery nothing remains of them', suggests that they once did exist. Harder evidence that at least some of the supposed fakes were painted on the rock walls is provided by Hachid's photograph of 'Antinea'.[75] This was published before she received information that it was a fake. Given the supposed motives for painting these fakes (see below), it seems likely that at least some of the supposed fakes were painted on the rock walls, perhaps deliberately using materials that would soon fade away. This would explain both Lajoux's comment and the faded state of the 'Antinea' photograph (see Postscript).

Did Lhote know about the forgeries? And, what was the motive for making these fakes? One has the impression that they were made by members of Lhote's team to mock him, as he was reputedly a hard taskmaster. Given the team's confined working conditions and the work involved in making such fakes, it is very difficult to believe that Lhote was not aware of what was going on around him. More likely, on learning of what may have begun as nothing more than a prank – or what Lajoux refers to as a 'joke',[76] Lhote actually wanted to believe that they were 'real': they fitted his 'thesis' regarding Egyptian influence. It also defies credibility that Lhote could not have differentiated between a several-thousand-years-old painting and one on which the paint was scarcely dry.

Hachid states in her book that Lhote did not know about the fakes. When I suggested to her that it was highly unlikely that Lhote did not know what was going on, she suggested that 'he might well have wanted to believe [in the fakes]!' In the case of 'The Bird-Headed Goddesses' at Jabbaren, which have never been found and which we know conclusively to be a fake, Lhote describes their 'discovery' in the following terms:

> While he was swabbing down a wall Claude brought to light four little figures of women with birds' heads, figures which were identical with some of those which are to be seen on ancient Egyptian monuments. The figures were, indeed, so characteristic that we expected to find a hieroglyphic inscription explaining the scene, but our hopes were in

vain. We found nothing of the kind, despite repeated washing of the surface.[77]

If the fakes, as some have suggested, were only painted on paper, then Lhote's description is a complete fabrication. If they were painted on the rock wall, then his spurious account of their discovery suggests that he was party to the fraud. Either way, his account is fraudulent. The same applies to 'Antinea': either his written account of the discovery is a complete fabrication, or he was party to the fraud, for he writes:

> While Claude was enriching our collection with these ravishing little bird-headed goddesses [these are the fakes referred to above], Le Poitevin's team cleaned the walls of the Aard-Vark cavern. Here a dark patch had attracted our attention, but it was so shapeless that at first it was thought the thing was one of those paintings which are so much destroyed as to be practically unrecognisable. But once again swabbing produced marvellous results. At the third washing [see below for comments on damage] there appeared in all its beauty the large figure of a kneeling woman, nearly six feet in height. Her head was leaning against her flexed arm. Her face, with its elongated eyes, had a classical purity of line that recalled classical Greek art. The diadem that surrounded her head suggested that she was a personage of high position, maybe even a Libyan goddess. The features, in any case, were those of a woman of Mediterranean type.[78]

The above account of 'Antinea' is significant for its Breuil-like views. But it does give the impression that Lhote was 'on the spot' and personally observing the washing of the wall and the discovery of the painting, which we now know could not have happened.

In addition to the 'fake' paintings, there are other serious 'falsifications' which only someone with intimate knowledge of the originals could identify. These relate to the fact that:

> Lhote and his team copied the finest of the figures but excluded many that were on the same panel on the grounds that they were less attractive.[79] In other words these copies were not scientifically obtained, are far from exact and are today considered 'poetic' copies. Moreover, if the copies are compared with the increasingly indistinct originals on the rock [see below], a number of glaring errors become immediately obvious. An example is one of the copies reproduced in the handsome German book *Sahara: 10,000 Years of Art and History*, where two scenes which in reality come from two different sites are presented side by side as though forming part of the same composition.[80]

The Methodology and Scientific Value of Lhote's Research

The publication of *The Archaeology of Rock-Art* provided probably the best review of the state of rock art knowledge and research at the end of the millennium.[81] Its 19 papers cover most parts of the world: the Americas, the Pacific, Europe, Central Asia, Australasia and southern Africa. There is one noticeable exception: the Sahara. This is extraordinary when barely 40 years earlier the Tassili had been proclaimed as 'the greatest centre of prehistoric rock art in the world'.[82]

What has happened in 40 years? When I put this question to one of the editors of the above-mentioned book, his answer was terse: 'the Sahara has contributed virtually nothing to furthering our knowledge of rock art'. This is a harsh judgement but, with the exception of a small number of researchers, probably true.[83] Malika Hachid, at the forefront of this small number, has concluded that 'the only way to establish a relatively precise chronology once and for all is to organise a second series of copies, this time using more appropriate methods'.[84]

The reason for Hachid's seemingly draconian remedy is because the copies of the Tassili paintings made by Lhote and his team, for the reasons outlined above, are of little scientific value.[85] But to undertake a second copying campaign, as Hachid advocates, would now be extremely difficult, if not impossible. Quite apart from financial considerations, the rock art of the Tassili, along with most other Saharan sites, has been so damaged over the last 40 or so years as to render much of it almost indecipherable.

The major cause of this damage has been the 'washing' of the paintings, a method strongly advocated by Lhote and his team. Lhote's basic method of copying the paintings was to wash the rock face with water in order to 'restore' the original colour of the paintings, which were then traced and copied onto large sheets of paper. His book gives countless descriptions of such 'washings'.[86] But, as we now know only too well, the moistening of paintings upsets the physical, chemical and biological balance of both the images and the supporting rock. Repeatedly washing paintings in such a dry environment has caused severe damage. Visitors to the Tassili looking for the frescoes reproduced by Lhote now find that several are nothing more than a pale reflection of their former glory, while others have disappeared altogether.

Damage to the Tassili paintings soon became apparent, and in 1978 UNESCO convened a major gathering of experts – chemists, biologists, geologists, archaeologists and prehistorians – to examine the paintings. They concluded that Lhote's team had 'severely modified' the paintings. Lhote was the guest of honour at the conference. His response to such criticism was to assure the audience that it was only by moistening the paintings that they

The Lesser Gods of the Sahara

could be seen in all their splendour. To prove his point he sprayed one of the paintings with water from his water-bottle![87] While Lhote had succeeded in bringing the Tassili paintings to the attention of the world, he had also delivered a fatal blow to many of them.

In addition to the damage caused by Lhote's own expedition, further irreversible damage has been caused by tourists, collectors, 'researchers', photographers and other such visitors doing precisely what Lhote advocated.[88] Many paintings and rock art sites have also been severely damaged by graffiti, daubing of paint, tar and other substances, pencil tracings, the chiselling out of 'souvenirs' of rock art from shelters and rock faces, and other forms of human damage.[89]

The method of Lhote's copying, which we would now regard as most unscientific, combined with the damage to many of the paintings, has made it difficult, if not impossible in some cases, to establish clear relative chronologies. The scientific value of Lhote's 'research' is further negated by the almost complete absence of stratigraphy that might have come from sound archaeological excavation. Animal bones, especially, and human skeletal remains are in particularly short supply. This is not because they did not exist or have not been found. Rather, it is because the results of most of the many sites excavated by Lhote,[90] both on the plateau and piedmont areas, have not been published, in spite of many promises 'to make a general study of all the Tassilian sites and the enormous number of remains that were collected during our different expeditions',[91] and the extensive remains have not been made available for analysis.[92]

One reason why is because the enormous number of remains were, quite simply, looted. As the respected rock art specialist, Francois Soleilhavoup, noted at the time of the UNESCO conference:

> There is no doubt that during the exploration of the Sahara precious little care was taken to protect and preserve the fragile evidence of its prestigious past. The important thing was to discover, to dig things up, to tell the world about the finds and thus accumulate honours and glory for having made 'sensational'; discoveries from 'far off' countries.[93]

Lhote wrote quite unashamedly about collecting cultural objects. In describing a passage south of the Ténéré, he wrote: 'scattered about this prehistoric charnel-house was an abundant and magnificent stock of stone implements, many of which I collected ... delicate arrow-heads in flint, gauges [sic] for fishing nets and also superb bone harpoons'.[94] While in the Tassili, he admits to encouraging Tuareg children to look around for arrowheads and other such objects for him. The result of this activity is that almost the entire landscape has been sterilised of its past. Lhote himself made one of the largest personal collections. As another *'saharien'* once remarked: 'What wasn't paid for by the *Musée de l'Homme* went to Lhote's own private collection'.[95]

The cultural objects looted from the region were not without cultural significance and importance to the Tuareg who live there today (see below). Several Tuareg whom I have met in the last couple of years have spoken with considerable anger about the way in which many of these items were taken from their land. One story, in particular, has become a bit of a cause célèbre and epitomises how Tuareg are beginning to demand the return of some of these objects. Malika Hachid recounts it as follows:

> In the thirties[96] the Ajjer Tuareg, (the) Idjeradjeriouène, used to pray in the little mosque (*mihrab*) of Wadi Djerat where a white quartzite millstone lay in front of the *mihrab*. The stone, which was thought to have the power of making rain, was coated with black soot, a colour which evoked clouds full of rain. Henri Lhote subsequently sent the millstone to the *Musée de l'Homme*[97] in Paris and no rain fell for 25 years. This was immediately interpreted as an evil portent by the Tuareg who were very displeased that the object had been taken from them and worse still that it had been removed from its sacred place.[98]

There is much more that could be said about Lhote's methodology in the course of his 'exploration' of the Sahara, but it does not make edifying reading. Suffice it to say that what took place in the Tassili and its piedmont during this period was not just a disgraceful episode in the history of archaeology; it was a tragedy.

The Denial of Access to Other Academics, Especially Those of Other Countries

After Lhote's popularisation of the region, one might have expected it to have become the focus of major research. After all, the great art gallery of the Sahara was, and still is, the biggest museum in the world. But that did not happen. As Marceau Gast remarked, 'The intense general interest provoked by the media soon died down and gave way to some poorly financed research and to popular and often damaging tourism to the area'.[99]

The independence of Algeria in 1962 may have had something to do with this.[100] But the major reason, I believe, was that Lhote used his enormous influence to stop other academics, especially those from other countries, visiting the region. A prime example of this was the combined Cambridge and Sheffield Universities expedition to the Sahara in 1961. One of its members wrote to Lhote expressing a desire to visit the Tassili – following the recent 'discovery' of the frescoes – and requesting a letter of introduction to the

French military authorities in charge of the region. Lhote's reply was an extraordinary document in which he explained that since he, Henri Lhote, had discovered everything that there was to be discovered in the Tassili, there was no point in other academics visiting the area. The expedition[101] duly went to Tibesti instead.

One can only surmise why Lhote acted in this way. Perhaps he did not want his 'discoveries' scrutinised too closely by other academics. Quite apart from all the methodological shortcomings outlined above, visiting researchers might have found that the paint on the 'fakes' was barely dry.[102]

Lhote's Views on and Relationship with the Tuareg

If I have given the impression that Lhote's expedition did not discover much that was new, that is not true. Although many of the frescoes copied by the expedition had been discovered by Brenans, Lhote's expedition did discover several new ones, such as those at Aouanrhet. But the credit for most of these discoveries lay not with Lhote, but with Jebrine ag Mohammed, a Tuareg of the nomadic Idjeradjeriouène Kel Meddak. Jebrine had been the official guide for almost every French expedition that had set foot there. Indeed, by the time Lhote's expedition reached the Tassili, Jebrine was already responsible, through his services as guide to several scientific expeditions, for a number of scientific publications. By the time Jebrine began working for Lhote, he was an old man of over 60 and suffering from rheumatism. And yet he worked continuously for Lhote throughout his time on the plateau (he lived to be about 90, dying in 1981).[103] Jebrine's contribution to Lhote's expedition was incalculable. It is therefore sad, as Hachid has also remarked, that Lhote 'had not always been flattering about Jebrine in his writings'.[104]

Nor do his comments on the Tuareg in general make pleasant reading. For a man who had spent so much time in their company and had been so dependent on them, he might be expected to have understood both them and their culture. Anyone who knows the Tuareg well would not recognise the characteristics he attributes to them. He describes them as 'greedy', 'vain', 'begging', 'cunning', 'wretched' and 'lacking in gratitude'.[105] As for their social organisation, which is immensely complex, fine-tuned and well adapted to surviving in one of the world's harshest environments, he simply likens the Tuareg to wolves and their laws to those of the forest or the jungle. His comments are entirely misplaced, offensive and racist, a view shared by all Tuareg I have met who have read his book.

The Implications of Lhote's Research for Current Researchers: Liability and the Moral Responsibility for Restitution

The result of Lhote's activities in the Sahara is that later researchers cannot be sure what is faked and what is original; what has been washed away; the extent to which the landscape has been 'sterilised' by what appears to have been an almost systematic 'looting' of cultural objects; and what has been excavated and left unpublished, lost or looted. Moreover, his strong advocacy of both washing paintings and collecting cultural objects has led to literally thousands of 'tourists', probably in all innocence, following his example.

Those who do not like hearing what I have said will argue, quite correctly, that I have been selective. They will say that Jacques Soustelle accomplished great and honourable deeds before his 'conversion' in Algeria; that the Abbé Breuil will be remembered for much more than his refusal to accept that the paintings of South Africa were the work of the ancestors of the Bushmen who today inhabit Namibia; and that Lhote has written much else on the Sahara which is of ethnological interest and value.[106]

Others will put forward arguments that will no doubt be considered in some circles as explaining, and perhaps even legitimising Lhote's behaviour and activities in the Sahara. These alternative arguments, with which I do not wholly agree, are that Lhote was by no means unusual in archaeology for taking credit for the discoveries of others or at least giving only minimal credit to his predecessors; that he did not set out deliberately to damage the art, nor to incite the public to do the same, in that it was standard procedure in those days to 'wash' rock paintings, as nobody knew any better, and that even if they had known of the potential damage, they would doubtless still have argued that it was worthwhile and necessary to wet the paintings just once in order to make the best possible copy; and that Lhote was a collector, not an archaeologist or intellectual, whose amassing of a huge abundance of artefacts from the Sahara was by no means unusual but something that still goes on. In short, it may be argued that although Lhote had many faults, he was no worse than many other people of the time. Indeed, in his arrogance, self-aggrandisement, territoriality about his 'finds', his non-publication of excavations, and his collecting, he was fairly typical of his kind.[107]

When I recently confronted one of Lhote's followers with some of these facts, notably his racist comments about the Tuareg, he replied, 'Yes, of course, but what do you expect? He was a colonialist'. Yet there were many French who worked and lived in the Sahara during the colonial period who did not hold such racist views and who were held in great affection by the Tuareg and other local peoples. Several of them are still alive today and are still remembered with affection and respect.[108]

Why then, it may be asked, have I dragged up the past in this way? One reason is because many people are still unaware of what was done in Algeria in their name.[109] Another is that Algerians themselves, notably the Tuareg, the indigenous peoples of the region, are now suffering, and will continue to suffer, from the loss of this heritage. Indeed, it is simply not true that these objects had no significance and meaning to present-day Tuareg,[110] nor that they would be better conserved in Europe. Most of the cultural objects that were 'looted' are not in the *Musée de l'Homme* or other national/public museums: they are, or were, in private collections, with many now being sold to unknown buyers or simply dispersed as a new and uninterested generation comes across boxes of old stones and bones in the attics of forebears who once served in the Sahara.

The question is: where does the blame lie? Is the answer to be found in Lhote's desire for acclaim and fame; in France's centralised state control over the direction and funding of 'research'; in Euro- or perhaps Franco-centric attitudes to the appropriation of foreign cultural heritage;[111] or within France's political agenda for the Sahara at that time? When it comes to the question of restitution, the answers to these questions are important. Much as it may have seemed that the French Sahara was Lhote's own personal fiefdom, we should not lose sight of the fact that he did not operate in the Sahara entirely as a 'free individual'. At nearly all times in his long career as a *'saharien'*, he was either employed, sponsored, financed or provided with support services, by arms of the French state. These arms included, at one time or another, the President of the French Republic, the governor general of Algeria, the *Musée de l'Homme*, the CNRS, the IRS, many of France's leading universities and other learned and scientific institutions, and the services of the French civil and defence forces. At any time, these institutions could have (and should have) intervened in what was being done in the Sahara under their auspices. The French state therefore bears a strong moral responsibility for the appalling state of affairs that I have outlined here. It must therefore take moral and financial responsibility for restitution.

In a strictly legal sense, France can argue that such responsibilities fell away with the Evian agreements that led to Algeria's independence, or that these incidents occurred before the cut-off dates of current international laws and conventions, such as the UNIDROIT Convention on Stolen or Illegally Exported Cultural Objects,[112] or the UN's current Declaration on the Rights of Indigenous Peoples, on which France is one of the major prevaricators.[113] If France does adopt such standpoints, this more unpalatable history of France's damage to the cultural heritage of the Sahara cannot and will not be laid to rest.

The form such restitution should take is something that France should be negotiating with the Algerian government and representatives of the Tuareg themselves,[114] perhaps through various international bodies. But, to end on a positive note, one possible suggestion could be made here. In January 2001 a *Partenariat* agreement was signed between the French and Algerian governments, the aim of which is to assist the development of tourism in the Algerian Sahara. Rather than France provide financial assistance towards the construction of hotels, the facilitation of charter flights and so on, all of which are regarded by the 'indigenous peoples' themselves as potentially highly damaging to their environmental and cultural heritage,[115] let France use its willingness to assist in such development by making restitution in the manner which it holds dearest to its own heart: the promotion and conservation of culture. Given Algeria's own current concerns about the conservation of the Sahara's fragile environment, its unique cultural heritage and the needs and demands of tourism in the area, now is an appropriate time for France to make good the damage of the past by providing the finances, not simply for hotels and cheap flights, but for major museum and associated conservation facilities in places such as Djanet, and perhaps also Illizi and Tamanrasset and, equally important, the long-term financial means for the urgently needed training of local museum and rock-art conservation specialists. Such financial assistance could also be used to purchase back and return to Algeria many of the cultural objects that have been acquired, legally or otherwise, by both public and private collections in France. It would also be appropriate, given the importance of Mertoutek as a significant centre of rock art, if such restitution were also to encompass the reparation still not paid to the people of Mertoutek (and environs) who died as a result of France's atomic tests.[116]

Postscript (August 2003)

This article was written at the end of 2001, re-edited in early 2002 and first published in late 2002 in *Public Archaeology* 2/3 (2002) pp.131–50. In republishing it here, no changes have been made, other than some small grammatical improvements and the addition of and slight modification to footnotes – mostly to facilitate cross-referencing to other articles in this volume. However, this article is now the subject of a two-part documentary film entitled *The Lesser Gods of the Sahara*. During the course of making this film, especially through interviewing certain members of Lhote's original team, the Algerian authorities, French archaeologists and the staff at some of France's museums, notably the *Musée de l'Homme*, further information has come to light. This will be published in full in *Public Archaeology*, probably in 2004. The main points of this new information are as follows.

We have received confirmation that there were at least eight fakes. That is more than the five fakes recorded in this article, but in line with the suggestion that there were probably more. These were all painted on rock faces and not on paper or in notebooks as some people have suggested. Members of Lhote's team also re-confirmed what was already widely suspected, namely that Lhote's tracings and recordings of the real paintings were not only highly 'selective' but often grossly inaccurate and consequently of little or no scientific value.

It has been re-confirmed to us that members of the team did not make the fakes in order to falsify the archaeological record, but simply as a 'joke' against Lhote because he was so unpopular with them. Members of Lhote's expedition have also confirmed that Lhote was fully aware that the fakes had been painted. According to them, his stubbornness was such that he refused, even to his death in 1991, to admit that fakes had been made. This confirms that many of his descriptions of their discovery, which I have quoted in this article, are indeed completely fraudulent. In other words, Lhote, through his publication of *A La Découverte des Fresques du Tassili*, not his team, was responsible for this very serious falsification of the archaeological record. His statement on page 179 of *A La Découverte* (see article), that 'there is not a single forgery, intentional or unintentional, in the paintings and copies we brought back from the Tassili', was knowingly untrue.

According to statements given by members of the team, there is evidence, including court records, to indicate that Lhote subsequently destroyed many of Brenans's original notes and drawings.

This later claim seems to be confirmed by the fact that we have so far not been able to find the original documents at the *Musée de l'Homme*, where they are apparently officially housed. Nor have we been able to find many of the other artefacts reputedly removed from the Sahara to the *Musée de l'Homme*. This may simply be because of the poor state of many of the museum's holdings. It should be noted that the holdings that were left in the Bardo Museum (Algiers) after the French departure are, by contrast, well-displayed and in excellent order. However, we do appear to have located the sacred white quartzite millstone removed by Lhote from the *Oued* Djerat. This is still subject to verification, but if it is the same stone, it is hoped that the relevant French authorities will return it to its rightful owners.

We have also received confirmation from the Algerian authorities that the seriously damaged rock art panel at Jabbaren (see J. Keenan, 'The theft of Saharan rock art', *Antiquity* 74 (2000) pp.287–8) was the result of Lhote himself trying to remove the panel with a chisel-like implement. Finally, we have received confirmation from the Algerian authorities that discussions with France over the matter of restitution (see note 7) are fairly advanced.

The Lesser Gods of the Sahara

ACKNOWLEDGEMENTS

I am gratefully indebted to the British Academy and the Leverhulme Trust for their most generous support. I would also like to thank Neal Ascherson, Mokhtar Bahedi, Christopher Chippindale, Malika Hachid, Tim Schadla-Hall, Alberto Larocca, Kevin MacDonald, Alfred Muzzolini, Peter Ucko and Claudio Vita-Finzi for their much appreciated comments, assistance and encouragement. This essay is a tribute to two Algerians of different generations: Machar Jebrine ag Mohammed and Malika Hachid, whose names will always be associated with the Tassili and the indigenous peoples of the Sahara.

NOTES

1. The decade began in December 1994 and ends in December 2004. The question of the rights of indigenous peoples in the case of the Tuareg is discussed in some depth in J. Keenan, 'Introduction: Indigenous Rights and a Future Politic amongst Algeria's Tuareg after Forty Years of Independence', in this volume, pp.1–26.
2. Although France is an original signatory to the Convention, she has not yet ratified the Convention and is therefore not yet bound by it. However, as a signatory, France does have an obligation (in terms of art. 18 of the 1969 Vienna Convention on the Law of Treaties) not to defeat the object and purpose of the treaty/convention prior to its entry into force, unless it has made its intention clear not to become a party to the treaty. On 24 January 2001, after favourable opinion of the *Conseil d'Etat*, the *Conseil des Ministres* decided to ratify the Convention. The draft law was accordingly sent to the *Assemblée Nationale (Commission des affaires étrangères)*. UNIDROIT sees this as a demonstration of France's clear intention to become a party to the Treaty. Indeed, according to UNIDROIT, the French ministries of foreign affairs and justice both strongly support the ratification of the Treaty. UNIDROIT sees absolutely no reluctance from the French government in meeting the Convention's principles. However, since the draft law was sent to the *Assemblée Nationale*, the *Syndicat des Antiquaires* (which fears the provision of the Convention which obliges the purchaser to inquire into the provenance of the object) has mounted a strong campaign in opposition to the Convention. This opposition succeeded in delaying the deposition of the report of the *Rapporteur* of the *Commission des affaires étrangères*. The *Rapporteur* has since moved to the Senate. Although a new *Rapporteur* has been appointed, the sensitivity of the issue is such that it will almost certainly be set on one side at least until after the French elections in the spring of 2002. (Source: UNIDROIT, Rome).
3. France is not the only country obstructing the UN Declaration on the Rights of Indigenous Peoples. The Declaration will give indigenous peoples collective rights, territorial rights and, above all, rights of self-determination. Many countries, including most EU members, the United States, Brazil and Australia are not keen that indigenous peoples acquire rights of self-determination. As France has no indigenous peoples, one can only suppose that her obstruction is on behalf of her former colonies. In the case of the Tuareg, these are Algeria, Niger and Mali.
4. See note 111.
5. See note 109.
6. The Tuareg of the Tassili-n-Ajjer region are Algerian citizens. However, Tuareg of Mali, Niger and Libya are also beginning to raise questions about the violation of their cultural heritage.
7. Although there have been calls from time to time within Algeria for restitution from France, no official demand for restitution, as far as I am aware, has been made by the Algerian government. Nevertheless, the question of restitution is being raised, albeit informally at this stage, by a number of individuals and groups within Algeria, notably the Tuareg, the indigenous peoples of the Tassili-n-Ajjer, amongst whom there has been a

The Lesser Gods of the Sahara

marked increase in patrimonial awareness of their cultural heritage in the last few years. Although such claims may have a strong moral basis, they have little legal foundation, in that such 'looting' would be regarded as falling within the framework of 'colonial archaeology' (where finds were taken to the mother country) and as predating any possible violation of UNIDROIT, or any other convention. Indeed, France might well try and argue that Algeria was not even a colonial territory, but part of Metropolitan France!

8. This is the term used by Henri Lhote himself in the title of his work, *A la Découverte des Fresques du Tassili* (Paris: Arthaud 1958, 1973); translated as *The Search for the Tassili Frescoes: The Story of the Prehistoric Rock-Paintings of the Sahara* (London: Hutchinson 1959). I use it advisedly in that it is questionable, as this essay argues, whether his 1956–57 expedition made many significant 'discoveries'. What he did succeed in doing was to draw the attention of a much wider public and academic audience to the diversity and wealth of the Sahara's prehistory.

9. The Tassili-n-Ajjer is located in southern Algeria. The Tassili, which means plateau in the native language of the Tuareg tribesmen, who are the indigenous peoples of this region, form a more or less continuous series of uplifted plateaux and scarps around the Central Saharan massif of Ahaggar (Hoggar). The Tassili-n-Ajjer, which stretches around the north-eastern periphery of Ahaggar, is located mostly within the Algerian *wilaya* of Illizi. The nearest town/oasis to the main body of the Tassili Frescoes 'discovered' by Lhote is Djanet.

10. Lhote, *A la Découverte* (note 8).

11. This field was not new. Work on Saharan palaeoclimates and archaeology had been ongoing since the 1920s (see, for example, the work of T. Monod), long before Lhote went to the Sahara. However, the immense 'global' publicity given to Lhote's expedition and his 'discoveries' brought wide attention to what, in the case of the Sahara, had hitherto been a narrow and somewhat insular field of enquiry.

12. J. Keenan, *The Tuareg: People of Ahaggar* (London: Allen Lane 1977; reprinted London: Sickle Moon Books 2002).

13. J. Keenan, *Sahara Man: Travelling with the Tuareg* (London: John Murray 2001). The question of damage and looting is discussed in J. Keenan, 'Contested Terrain: Tourism, Environment and Security in Algeria's Extreme South', in this volume, pp.226–65.

14. The Tassili-n-Ajjer was recognised by UNESCO as a World Heritage site in 1984.

15. The Tuareg are officially listed by the UN as the indigenous peoples of this part of Africa.

16. These first discoveries were made in the Wadi (*Oued*) Tel Issaghen, the Tannezzouft valley and Mount Idinen, near Ghat. H. Barth, *Voyages et Découvertes dans l'Afrique septentrionale et central pendant les années 1849 à 1855*, 4 vols. (Paris: A. Bohne 1860–61).

17. H. Duveyrier, *Les Touareg du Nord* (Paris: Challamel 1864).

18. F. Foureau, *Rapport sur ma mission au Sahara et chez les Touareg Azdjer* (Paris: A. Challamel 1894).

19. In the late 1920s and early 1930s many of the more important sites on the Tassili plateau, notably Tamadjert (Capitaine Duprez discovered amazing paintings of 'Garamantes' chariots in 1932), Dider, Aharhar and *Oued* Tarat were discovered and recorded. The German ethnologist Leo Frobenius also sent a team to the Tassili in 1932 to record the paintings, notably at Addo and Azaka n'Emiren. L. Frobenius, *Ekade Ektab Die Felsbilder Fezzans* (Leipzig: Otto Harrassowitz 1937).

20. M. Reygasse, *Contribution á l'étude des gravures rupestres et inscriptions tifinagh du Sahara Central* (Alger: Jourdan 1932). See also M. Reygasse, 'Gravures et peintures rupestres du Tassili des Ajjers', *L'Anthroplogie* XLV/5–6 (1935) pp.553–71.

21. Lhote, *Search for the Tassili Frescoes* (note 8) p.25, writes, 'Of course, the experts in Paris and Algiers were informed of the discoveries and four months later I myself was on the spot at the same time as Professors Gautier, Reygasse and Perret'.

22. Reference to 'the plateau above Djanet' is to the most famous rock art sites in the regions of Tamrit, Assakao, Meddak and *Oued* Amazzar, which include such well-known sites as

Jabbaren, Sefar, Tin Bedjedj, Tan Zoumiatak, Tin Tazarift, Ouan Bender, Ala-n-Edoument, Aouanrhet, Adjefou and Ouan-Abou.

23. M. Hachid, *Le Tassili des Ajjer* (Paris: Alger et Editions Paris-Méditerranée 1998) p.174; translated as *The Tassili of the Ajjer* (Paris: Alger et Editions Paris-Méditerranée 2000).
24. The First Congress was held in Nairobi in 1947. The work of the Second Congress was published as Congrès Panafricain de Préhistoire, *Actes de la IIe Session*, Alger 1952 (Paris: Arts et Métiers Graphiques 1955). Brenans's work, which takes up 154 pages of the publication (pp.65–219), was introduced and presented by the Abbé Breuil under the title 'Les Roches Peintes du Tassili-n-Ajjer'. The work comprises an introduction written by Breuil, in which full tribute is paid to Brenans, and five chapters, three written by Henri Lhote and two (the main ones) by Breuil. In addition, 144 of Brenans's sketches are reproduced in full detail. Together they comprise approximately 1,000 human and animal figures.
25. Y. Tschudi, *Nordafrikanische Felsmalereien* (Firenze: Sansoni 1955), translated as *Les Peintures rupestres du Tassili-N-Ajjer* (Neuchâtel: 1956).
26. Lhote, *Search for the Tassili Frescoes* (note 8) p.11.
27. Ibid.
28. Ibid. pp.28–9.
29. Tschudi (note 25); Frobenius (note 19); Captain Cortier, *Notes de préhistoire saharienne* (Paris: Larose 1914); C. Killian, 'Quelques observations et découvertes de ma mission de 1927–1928 aux confines Imouhar-Téda dans le Sahara Central et Oriental', *Compte Rendu de l'Académie des Inscriptions et Belles-Lettres* (1929) pp.318–25; T. Monod, *L'Adrar Ahnet* (Paris: Institut d'Ethnologie 1932); R. Coche, 'Les Figurations rupestres du Mertoutek (Sahara Central)', *Journal des Savants* (Nov.–Dec. 1935); F. de Chasseloup-Laubat, *Art rupestre au Hoggar* (Paris: Plon 1938); J. Dubief, 'Découvertes, préhistoriques et archéologiques dans le Sahara central', *Travaux de l'Institut de Recherches Sahariennes* IV (1947) pp.189–91; G. Le Poitevin, 'Avec nos ancêtres les artistes du Tassili', *Algeria* (April 1950) pp.39–45. Le Poitevin, who was a member of Lhote's team, discovered the significant shelter of Tadjelahine (known as 'Tahilahi') in 1950. In 1957 Lhote sent two of his team to copy the paintings of Tahilahi, but makes no mention of the fact that their discovery seven years earlier had been made by one of his own team.
30. Hachid, *Tassili des Ajjer* (note 23) p.174.
31. H. Lhote, 'Inventaire et Références Bibliographiques des Peintures Rupestres de l'Afrique nord-équatoriale', ch.5 of 'Les Roches Peintes du Tassili-n-Ajjer: d'après les relevés du Colonel Brenans', in Congrès Panafricain de Préhistoire (note 24) pp.153–62; H. Breuil, 'Les Roches Peintes du Tassili-n-Ajjer: d'après les relevés du Colonel Brenans', in ibid. pp.165–219.
32. J. Tschudi, 'Die Felsmalereien im Edjeri, Tamrit, Assakao, Meddak (Tassili-n-Ajjer)', in Congrès Panafricain de Préhistoire (note 24) pp.761–7 (at the Congress her initial is published as J., not Y.); Frobenius (note 19); Le Poitevin (note 29); Dubief (note 29).
33. Tschudi (note 32).
34. In this case, Congrès Panafricain de Préhistoire (note 24).
35. Dubief (note 29).
36. Hachid, *Tassili des Ajjer* (note 23) p.175. Lhote, *Search for the Tassili Frescoes* (note 8) p.22, himself states that the first idea of the expedition dates back to 1933 when Lieutenant Brenans ventured into the *Oued* Djerat. This suggests that Brenans may already have had the idea of copying the paintings in this way. However, Lhote, *A La Découverte* (note 8) p.30, refers to the project as 'my scheme'.
37. Hachid, *Tassili des Ajjer* (note 23) p.176.
38. These were held on 2 January, having been brought forward by six months.
39. Soustelle left Algiers on 2 February. His successor, Catroux, arrived on 6 February.
40. By the time of his departure, Soustelle was beginning to be seen by the European community in Algiers as supporting and representing their desires for a 'French Algeria'. On 12 January he had given a broadcast in which he stated that 'Algeria must become an

integral part of France'. When making his farewell speech, he demanded silence and then shouted, 'If you want me to defend French Algeria ... [cries of 'yes, yes']... then let me leave'. See E. Behr, *The Algerian Problem* (London: Penguin 1961) pp.88–9.
41. Hachid, *Tassili des Ajjer* (note 23) p.176, wrote, 'Through his determination and perseverance ... Lhote managed to convince a number of institutions and people, including the President of the French Republic, of the need to organise a series of expeditions into the desert to make the copies ...'.
42. His description of his arrival could not be more bland. Lhote, *Search for the Tassili Frescoes* (note 8) p.33, writes, 'At the end of January 1956 we all left Paris and a few days later I disembarked at Algiers. While our three tons of baggage were being hoisted on to an army truck, a DC3 from the Maison-Blanche air base was put at our disposal by M. Max Lejeune (then under-secretary of state for defence) and took us all in one hop to Djanet'.
43. Ibid. p.33.
44. He was an anthropologist of international reputation, a former assistant director of the *Musée de l'Homme* and a university professor.
45. Lhote, *Search for the Tassili Frescoes* (note 8) p.33.
46. The headline in the *Echo d'Oran* (Feb. 1956) read, 'Le centre préhistorique le plus riche du monde est découvert au Tassili'.
47. The first oil discoveries in the Algerian Sahara were made in 1956.
48. France established two atomic test sites in the Sahara, one at Reganne in Tidikelt and the other at In Eker, 100 miles north of Tamanrasset. The first test was conducted at Reganne with the main device being detonated at In Eker in 1963. An accident occurred in the In Eker test resulting in the escape of radioactivity which resulted in the death of several residents of Mertoutek, a village 50 miles to the east, Keenan (note 13). Mertoutek is the site of significant rock paintings, first discovered in 1935 and the subject of several publications, including H. Lhote, 'Notes sur les peintures rupestres de Mertoutek', *Journ. Soc. Afric.* XII (1942) pp.259–60. French military files on the matter remain closed.
49. A further 'cultural' dimension was provided in 1956 with the reconstruction (begun in 1954) of the hermitage built on Mount Assekrem in Ahaggar by the French priest Charles de Foucauld in 1910 so that he could be nearer to the Tuareg. Following his murder (in the Sanussi revolt) in 1916 his hermitage fell into ruin.
50. Hachid, *Tassili des Ajjer* (note 23) p.174.
51. Lhote, *Search for the Tassili Frescoes* (note 8) p.30. Breuil's influence on Lhote's approach to Saharan rock art is also the reason for the rigid classification, strictly in chronological order, which Lhote proposed. Lhote not only defined very monolithic styles, but also did not allow for the possible contemporaneity of two or more classes.
52. J. Kinahan, 'Traumland Südwest: Two Moments in the History of German Archaeological Inquiry in Namibia', in H. Härke (ed.), *Archaeology, Ideology and Society: The German Experience*, vol.7 of 'Gesellschaften und Staaten im Epochenwandel' (Frankfurt am Main: Peter Lang 2000) pp.353–74.
53. For example, legislation promulgated by the German administration in 1911 amounted, in effect, to a warrant for genocide. See R.J. Gordon, *The Bushman Myth: The Making of a Namibian Underclass* (Boulder, CO: Westview 1992); Kinahan (note 52).
54. The sketch was made by Reinhard Maack; R. Maack, 'Über die Buschleute und ihre Feisenbilder in Suedwest-Afrika', unpublished typescript, National Library of Namibia (1921), is appraised by Kinahan (note 52).
55. Breuil (note 31).
56. Kinahan (note 52) p.364.
57. H. Breuil, *The White Lady of the Brandberg* (Paris: Trianon Press 1955). Subsequent anatomical analysis of The White 'Lady' clearly shows 'her' to be a male.
58. Lhote, *Search for the Tassili Frescoes* (note 8) p.81.
59. The rock surface is damp because Lhote has just washed it, contributing to its subsequent destruction.
60. Lhote, *Search for the Tassili Frescoes* (note 8) p.81.

61. Saharan rock art is notoriously 'thin' on firm dates. With the exception of F. Mori, *Le grandi civiltà del Sahara antico* (Torino: Bollati Boringhieri 2000) (see below), no pigments have yet been successfully dated. However, there are now more than 50 dates for the Neolithic in the Tassili, mostly derived from archaeological deposits situated at the foot of paintings or in the immediate environment, with the oldest going back to the tenth and ninth millennia. Sites in Aïr are dated as far back as 11,000 BP. These dates, along with associated geomorphological, palaeoclimatic, palaeoethnological and palaeoanthropic data, indicate that the Holocene began much earlier in certain parts of the Sahara, perhaps around 13,000–12,000 years ago, than the generally accepted date of 10,000 BP. A number of researchers are inclined to think that the early 'Round-Head' paintings, which were the main focus of Lhote's work, may date from the beginning of the Holocene, perhaps as early as 12,000 or even 13,000 years ago, while Fabrizio Mori, *Tadrart Acacus: Arte rupestre e culture del Sahara preistorico* (Torino: Einaudi 1965), as long ago as 1965, was claiming that the origins of Saharan art were firmly rooted in the Pleistocene. At Uan Tabu in the Acacus, Mori, *Le grandi civiltà*, dated dotted wavy line pottery found with grinding stones with strong traces of pigments –14C from charcoal 8,800 +- 100 BP. At Uan Ufada, organic material from painting dated 14C AMS 6,145 +- 70 BP. Study of patina by M. Cremaschi, 'Le paléoenvironnement du Tertiare tardif à l'Holocène', *Art rupestre du Sahara. Les pasteurs-chasseurs du Messak libyen. Les Dossiers de l'Archéologie*, No.197 (Oct. 1994) pp.4–13, would suggest Pleistocene origins for the earliest engravings, but the method is questionable and contested by many, including A. Muzzolini, *Les Images Rupestres du Sahara* (Toulouse: Alfred Muzzolini 1995).
62. Hachid, *Tassili des Ajjer* (note 23) p.187.
63. Lhote's account of the discovery of this 'fake' and his interpretation of it is given in Lhote, *Search for the Tassili Frescoes* (note 8) pp.71–2. A colour plate faces page 97.
64. Hachid's information was given to her by the forgers themselves who, in their old age, apparently wanted to make a clean breast of their activities.
65. Lhote, *Search for the Tassili Frescoes* (note 8) p.179.
66. J.-D. Lajoux, *Merveilles du Tassili n'Ajjer* (Paris: Ed. Du Chêne 1962) p.38, translated as *The Rock Paintings of Tassili* (London: Thames and Hudson 1963).
67. The scene referred to by A. Muzzolini, 'Masques et théromorphes dans l'art rupestre du Sahara central', *Archéo-Nil* 1 (1991) pp.17–42, is Lhote's 'Scene of Offerings: Egyptian Influence (18th dynasty?)'. Lhote records this scene as being at Jabbaren. It can be seen as figure 26 in *Search for the Tassili Frescoes* (note 8), and as figure 23 in the second French edition of *A la Découverte* (note 8).
68. There would appear to be a transposition of plate and figure numbers in the various editions and translations of *A La Découverte*. Plate 1 in the 1973 edition is, in fact, the 'Egyptian Goddesses'. The 'Tin-n-Tazarift Dancers' are figure 48 (1959 edition).
69. In the English translation, Lajoux, *The Rock Paintings of Tassili* (note 66), this photo is on pp.176–7.
70. Muzzolini (note 61) p.240; Muzzolini (note 67).
71. See Lhote, *Search for the Tassili Frescoes* (note 8) photo 33 and p.73, for his very questionable (see text) description of the discovery.
72. Personal communications. The intermediary is known personally by both myself and Malika Hachid. He is one of the most highly respected experts on the Sahara.
73. The figure and page numbers of these paintings varies between editions. In Lhote, *Search for the Tassili Frescoes* (note 8) they are, respectively, plate 1, figure 33, figure 26, figure 24. 'Les Caballins' of Sefar is found in Lajoux, *Merveilles du Tassili n'Ajjer* (note 66) p.172; and idem, *The Rock Paintings of Tassili* (note 66) pp.176–7.
74. Hachid, *Tassili des Ajjer* (note 23) p.187.
75. Ibid. p.185.
76. Lajoux, *Merveilles du Tassili n'Ajjer* (note 66) p.38.
77. Lhote, *Search for the Tassili Frescoes* (note 8) pp.71–2.
78. Ibid. p.73.

79. 'Lhote affirmed that there were so many paintings and engravings that it would have been impossible to record them all. Thus, he decided to reproduce only some of the motifs', J.-L. Le Quellec, *Symbolisme et art rupestre au Sahara* (Paris: L'Harmattan 1993) p.638. 'Furthermore, although aware of the limits of freehand drawing, Lhote often relied exclusively on the work of his team of artists, not making systematic use of photography and tracing. In fact, he affirmed that rock art should be recorded mainly with freehand drawing because: "Selon 'expression de L'Abbé Breuil, l'essentiel est de garder l'esprit de l'original" [H. Lhote, *Vers d'autres Tassili: Nouvelles découvertes au Sahara* (Paris: Arthaud, col. Clefs du savoir 1976]. In the words of the Abbé Breuil, the essential is to keep the spirit of the original', A. Larocca, 'Rock Art Recording in the Jebel Bani, Southern Morocco', unpublished MA thesis, Institute of Archaeology, University College London, 2001.
80. This brilliant piece of detection was accomplished by Malika Hachid herself, *Tassili des Ajjer* (note 23) p.187. She identified the left part as coming from Eheren (Tadjelahine plateau) and the right part from Tissoukai. *Sahara: 10,000 Jahre Zwichen Weïde und Wuste* (no date) pp.250–1.
81. C. Chippindale and P.S.C. Taçon, *The Archaeology of Rock-Art* (Cambridge: Cambridge University Press 1998).
82. Lhote, *Search for the Tassili Frescoes* (note 8).
83. Exceptions would include the enormous corpus of work by Alfred Muzzolini (although perhaps not adding greatly to our theoretical knowledge), and in terms of their theoretical contributions: J.-L Le Quellec, Christian Dupuy and M. Cremaschi.
84. Hachid, *Tassili des Ajjer* (note 23) p.187.
85. Lajoux, *Merveilles du Tassili n'Ajjer* (note 66) has at least given us a valuable photographic record of many of the paintings recorded by the Lhote expedition.
86. A question which Lhote never satisfactorily answered is why he did not make photographic back-ups. Lajoux, *Merveilles du Tassili n'Ajjer* (note 66) has provided us with the best photographic record made at that time.
87. Hachid, *Tassili des Ajjer* (note 23) p.187. With perhaps a suggestion of regret at the restrictions subsequently placed on moistening the paintings, H. Lhote, 'Oasis of Art in the Sahara', *National Geographic* 172/2 (Aug. 1987) later wrote, 'As we washed the paintings – a practice now forbidden – we were stunned by the vivid colours'.
88. For a description of much of this damage, see J. Keenan, 'The Theft of Saharan Rock-Art', *Antiquity* 74 (July 2000) pp.287–8; and idem (note 13). In the last few years an increasing amount of damage, notably graffiti and general daubing, has been caused by people (*les gens du nord*) from the north visiting or moving into the region. Caution should be exercised before attributing such damage to the 'indigenous' population. In Algeria, this is currently the major cause of damage and is described in J. Keenan, 'The Sahara's Indigenous Peoples, the Tuareg, Fear Environmental Catastrophe', *Indigenous Affairs* 1 (2002); and idem, 'Ethnicity, Regionalism and Political Stability in Algeria's *Grand Sud*', in this volume, pp.67–96.
89. Some paintings (believed to be about six), notably the 'Great God' at Sefar, were damaged in the 1960s by conservationists applying a synthetic resin, a kind of 'fixative' (Paraloid B72). Why such 'experiments' were undertaken on one of the most important paintings is still a mystery.
90. Lhote, *A la Découverte* (note 8) p.18, says that he has 'identified some 80 prehistoric sites in the Hoggar region'. It is not clear from the context whether he has excavated or 'collected' materials from all these sites.
91. H. Alimen, F. Beucher and H. Lhote (with the collaboration of G. Delibrias), 'Les gisements néolithiques de Tan-Tartraït et d'In-Itinen, Tassili-n-Ajjer', *Bulletin de la Société préhistorique française* LXV (1968) pp.421–56. See also Hachid, *Tassili des Ajjer* (note 23) pp.118, 277: 'We also have no information on the results obtained from the excavations carried out at the Ambassadors' Shelter near Djanet, at Tasigmet and other shelters in Wadi Djerat, or about the important deposits of the plateaux of Wadi Tadjelahine and Wadi

The Lesser Gods of the Sahara

Eheren'.
92. Hachid, *Tassili des Ajjer* (note 23) p.120, remarked:

> Henri Lhote noted a great profusion of cattle, sheep and goat bones in all the excavations he conducted on the plateau and the piedmont. It would be very useful today to find these bones and study them, for such an analysis would help us date the domestication of animals in the Central Sahara, and also help identify the species of cattle* and goats that existed in the region.

> * In the French version these are described as *bovines*, but is mistranslated as 'bovids' in *The Tassili of the Ajjer* (note 23).

93. F. Soleilhavoup, 'Les oeuvres rupestres sahariennes sont-elles menacées?', *Publication de l'Office du Parc national du Tassili* (1978). In 1990, Francois Soleilhavoup was arrested by the Algerian authorities and ordered to return geological specimens and artefacts which he had allegedly removed illegally from the country.
94. Lhote, *Search for the Tassili Frescoes* (note 8) p.17.
95. Personal communication.
96. Lhote visited Djerat in 1934.
97. An archaeologist colleague, who has seen the collections of Saharan cultural objects in both the *Musée de l'Homme* and Lhote's private house, told me that when he enquired in the latter about what he took to be original items, notably some stone carved human and animals figurines, he was told that they were replicas and that the originals were at the *Musée de l'Homme*! (personal communication)
98. Hachid, *Tassili des Ajjer* (note 23) p.152.
99. M. Gast, 'Foreword', in Hachid, *Tassili des Ajjer* (note 23).
100. French interests in these parts of the Sahara continued for a few more years after Independence, while Algeria, as far as I am aware, has never discouraged research in this field. Indeed, it has been an Algerian, Malika Hachid, scientist, researcher and Director of the Tassili National Park, who has done most to restore the credibility of the Tassili as a centre of major scientific research.
101. It should be noted that Kennedy thanked Lhote for showing him pictures of the Tassili frescoes in the new *Department d'Art Rupestre*. C. Vita-Finzi and R.A. Kennedy, 'Seven Saharan Sites', *Journal of the Royal Anthropological Institute* 95 (1965) pp.195–213.
102. Or, in the case of 'fakes' manufactured in 'notebooks', that they did not exist at all.
103. Hachid, *Tassili des Ajjer* (note 23) pp.176–8, has told the story of Jebrine's remarkable life and work. There are strong moves afoot to ensure that his name is forever associated with the Tassili Park.
104. Ibid. p.178.
105. Lhote, *Search for the Tassili Frescoes* (note 8).
106. Lhote's extensive publications on the Sahara span some 50 years. Some of his ethnographic publications are of value. Of his work on rock art, his survey of the engravings of the Oued Djerat is an important contribution. See H. Lhote, *Les gravures rupestres de l'Oued Djereat (Tassili-n-Ajjer)* (Paris: Mémoires du CRAPE XXV 1975–76). His extensive work on the petroglyphs of Niger is generally regarded as being of lesser quality.
107. I am grateful to one particularly prominent but anonymous referee of this article for presenting these arguments to me.
108. Of the names cited in this text, I mention especially that of Marceau Gast, who has played a major part in 'righting the wrongs of the past'.
109. Lhote's name and contribution to Sahara rock art is still the subject of *Festschrifts* and other such academic accolades. See for example, Lettre de l'Association des Amis de l'Art Rupestre Saharien (AARS), 'Numéro spécial en mémoire de Henri Lhote' 20/2 (2001), published privately by the AARS.
110. See, for example, general comments made by Hachid, *Tassili des Ajjer* (note 23) on this subject.
111. For example, in 2000 France's new museum of primitive art (*La Musée des Arts Premiers*)

was opened in the Louvre (later to be housed at Le Quai Branley), with a quite unashamed display of three looted artefacts (stolen Nok sculptures from Nigeria), in which the country's President, Jacques Chirac, himself a renowned 'collector', was directly incriminated.
112. Rome 1995.
113. France is one of the countries that have contributed to the delaying tactics used for more than a decade in discussions of a UN declaration on indigenous peoples. Whereas native communities demand to be referred to as 'indigenous peoples', France has proposed that this reference be replaced with 'indigenous populations', a term rejected by the peoples concerned on the grounds that it reduces them to mere groups of persons and denies them recognition as national communities. France, along with most of the EU, the United States, Australia and others, is afraid that the Declaration will give indigenous peoples the right of self-determination.
114. The Tuareg, in terms of the Draft UN Declaration on the Rights of Indigenous Peoples are officially listed as an 'indigenous people'. Given that the UN's current Decade of Indigenous Peoples comes to an end in 2004, it would be a timely and opportune moment for France to agree restitution.
115. Keenan (note 88).
116. See note 48.

Contested Terrain: Tourism, Environment and Security in Algeria's Extreme South

Introduction

Cynics (realists) among both the Tuareg and others of the local populace of Algeria's extreme south, that is the *wilayat*[1] of Tamanrasset and Illizi, say that the region has only two industries, tourism and smuggling (banditry), and that the latter is doing the better of the two. Until March 2003, these two 'industries' were neither mutually exclusive nor in competition with each other. On the contrary, the redevelopment of tourism in the Algerian Sahara over the last four years, from the autumn of 1999 to the spring of 2003, following the effective closure of the Algerian Sahara in the wake of the violence that engulfed Algeria after the army's annulment of the 1992 general election, was more or less oblivious of and inconsequential to the expansion of the trans-Saharan smuggling business over this same period. During the course of this three–four year period, the main issue for many of the Tuareg involved in the tourism business has been the struggle between the increasing number of them who fear an imminent environmental catastrophe throughout much of the Central Sahara and the various and predominantly external interests that have wanted to expand the tourism business regardless of its impact on the environment and the region's rich cultural heritage. The former, whom I refer to as the 'environmentalists', are struggling to develop an alternative and more environmentally sustainable form of tourism. This struggle, which I shall describe and analyse in detail presently, is what I once described as the 'the last significant battle of the Central Sahara'.[2] If this article had been written a few months earlier, it would have described the political ascendancy of the 'environmentalists' in what might have been the determining moment in this struggle, namely their highly successful intervention in a government-organised conference in Djanet in March 2003. Four months further on (July 2003), following the kidnapping of 32 tourists in the *wilayat* of Tamanrasset and Illizi, both tourism and smuggling, as well as the role and effectiveness of 'the state' in the Central Sahara, and in the Algerian Sahara especially, are in a state of crisis. But this is a crisis that presents the Tuareg, along with other elements of the local populace, with their best and perhaps final opportunity to take control of the management of the Sahara's tourism industry and so develop a form of environmentally sustainable tourism that will safeguard both their heritage and their future livelihoods. It also presents the Algerian state with an opportunity to re-establish itself in a far more positive, constructive and mutually respectful partnership with the local peoples of the extreme south.[3]

The Tourism Product and Its Potential

The Central Sahara, and southern Algeria in particular, has long been recognised as a tourism destination with immense potential for growth and development. This potential stems from its unique tourism product and proximity to Europe, the world's largest tourism market. The regions of Ahaggar and the Tassili-n-Ajjer, which comprise an area the size of France, offer the tourist unparalleled desert landscapes of rugged volcanic mountains, deeply eroded sandstone plateaux, massive gorges, sand seas and almost every other conceivable form of desert landscape.[4] The region also has a rich archaeological heritage, with the Tassili-n-Ajjer being described as a museum containing 'the world's greatest collection of Prehistoric Art'.[5] The region's many mountain ranges are not only well-known to rock-climbers but offer the adventure-traveller an almost infinite variety of mountain trekking (on foot and/or camel) through a region of diverse geology and landforms and an extraordinary range of flora and fauna. Moreover, the Tuareg, the legendary blue-veiled warriors of the Sahara, have become a tourist attraction in their own right, especially within the context of their nomadic lifestyle. In short, Ahaggar and the Tassili-n-Ajjer are not only considered to be the most splendid of all the Sahara's many regions, but they can also be counted on a world scale alongside a mere handful of other such uniquely endowed regions.

The Five Phases of Tourism in Southern Algeria

Tourism in the Algerian Sahara has fallen into five distinct phases:

The French Era, Prior to Algerian Independence in 1962. Prior to Independence, much of the Sahara, including the Algerian Sahara, was regarded as a French preserve in which adventure travel and exploration, rather than 'tourism' in the modern sense of the word, were associated predominantly with mountaineering and camel-trekking, motor car rallies[6] and, especially after the publication of Henri Lhote's account of the Tassili Frescoes[7] in the late 1950s, the search for 'unrecorded' rock art. However, the scale of travel and tourism in this era was small, largely because of Algeria's war of independence from 1954 to 1962, and of comparatively little consequence to the Tuareg.

The 1960s and Early 1970s. Following Algerian independence in 1962, a small stream of foreign travellers, many traversing the Sahara en route to other destinations in Africa, visited the region. In addition, a few European travel companies, mostly small and private, ran adventure-type holidays to both Ahaggar and the Tassili-n-Ajjer, either as tours in their own right or as part of larger trans-Africa tours.[8] Although the number of tourists passing through the region in the 1960s and early 1970s was small, being counted in the early years in the hundreds rather than thousands, and of little significance to the country in terms of foreign exchange earnings, it was absolutely critical to the local people, notably the Tuareg, of the region.

The reason why this trickle of tourists was so important to the local Tuareg nomads, especially the Kel Ahaggar, was because they were subjected to great stress in the first years of Algeria's independence as most of the pillars of their traditional economy collapsed.[9] Algeria's independent government immediately abolished slavery and declared that the land was 'free' to those who worked it, thus denying Tuareg access to most of their former *harratin-*cultivated gardens. The imposition of border controls effectively ended the caravan trade to Niger which exchanged locally mined salt for millet, the basic foodstuff of the Tuareg at that time, while the closure of the French atomic base at In Eker in 1966 more or less put an end to wage-earning opportunities. Alongside these disasters, the onset of drought conditions in the mid-1960s brought pastoralism to its knees. The small numbers of tourists who found their way to Ahaggar at that time provided the struggling nomadic camps with a vital trickle of cash. Although this was not enough to prevent most nomads moving towards a more sedentary existence, it provided a lifeline that enabled many Kel Ahaggar to preserve some semblance of their nomadic lifestyle.

From the Early 1970s to the End of the 1980s. In terms of numbers, the 'high point' of tourism in the region was the late 1980s, when an average of some 15,000 foreign tourists visited the Ahaggar-Tassili region each year. However, the key feature of this third phase was that by the late 1980s some of the worst manifestations of 'mass tourism', notably serious environmental degradation, including significant and irreversible damage to rock art sites, were becoming apparent.

Algeria's Crisis and the Cessation of Tourism. In 1992, after a number of years of political and economic instability, Algeria held general elections that were won by the *Front Islamique du Salut* (FIS) and would have brought to power the world's first elected Islamist government. However, the army stepped in and annulled the elections, an action that led to the outbreak of militant and terrorist activity by certain Islamist groups. The spiral of violence that took hold of the country in the ensuing years has seen an estimated 100–150,000 people killed. Although the south of the country was not caught up directly in this violence, tourism came to an abrupt and complete cessation. This isolation was compounded by the closure of Libya to foreign tourists and the Tuareg revolts in Niger and Mali. For eight years, from 1992 to the end of 1999, southern Algeria was effectively cut off from the outside world.

The Regeneration of Tourism: Autumn 1999–March 2003. Abdelaziz Bouteflika's unopposed election as the country's new President[10] on 15 April 1999 was met with a sense of cautious optimism that the country's 'crisis' might soon be resolved. This more optimistic mood was reflected in the number of foreign visitors to Tamanrasset reaching 900 by the end of 1999, of whom about half came through Djanet as part of the Tassili circuit. The following year saw a further slight increase in the number of tourists, although the claim by official sources that the number of tourists passing through Tamanrasset had reached 2,000 by the end of July was probably on the high side. Further statistics provided by official sources, although almost certainly exaggerated,[11] indicate that the number of foreign tourists/visitors to the region reached almost 8,000 in the tourist season October 2000–April 2001. However, the impact of the destruction of the World Trade Center's Twin Towers in New York on 11 September 2001, the US's ensuing 'War on Terror' and the build-up to the Iraq war during the winter of 2002–03 put a dampener on the anticipated expansion of tourism in the region. During February–March 2003, 32 European tourists went missing, later to be discovered as kidnapped, in the region. As the ensuing 'hostage crisis' developed, it soon became apparent that tourism to the region had once again come to an almost complete cessation.

Relationship between Tourism and Nomadism

There is an extremely close, almost intimate, relationship between tourism and nomadism in many Tuareg regions of the Sahara, notably Ahaggar and Tassili-n-Ajjer in Algeria, and the region of Aïr in Niger. From a purely economic perspective, tourism is now a major pillar of the nomadic-pastoral economy. It provides nomads with a rent for their camels and employment for themselves as cameleers, guides, cooks and so forth. Moreover, in the Four-Wheel-Drive (4WD) market, which has boomed in the Sahara since the early

1980s, many Tuareg are employed as drivers or even as owners of their own vehicles, which they sub-contract to tourist agencies.[12] From the Tuareg's perspective, the relationship between tourism and nomadism is much more personal and symbolic. There are several reasons for and levels of perception of this relationship. On the one hand, many Kel Ahaggar still remember how the development of small-scale tourism in the 1960s played such an integral role in the survival of the nomadic community during those difficult years. Although that contribution was small in purely economic terms, it cannot be overestimated, for it is the memory of those years as much as the recognition of the importance of tourism to their present-day economy, that makes tourists so welcome amongst Algeria's Tuareg. But there is a stronger sentiment towards tourism, which is rooted in a sense of ownership, patrimony and the Tuareg's own 'sense of place' or 'insertion' in the modern world. Tuareg believe that tourism is 'their industry' and even refer to it as 'our work'. There are several strands of reasoning to this perception. First, they see tourism as an activity that takes place on their land and therefore as something over which they have certain territorial rights. In this sense, it is an 'industry' which belongs to them, in a territorial sense, rather than to outsiders. Second, they are fully aware of the fact that their cultural heritage, both past and living, is a central component of the tourism product. They know that tourists come to the region to see 'Tuareg', not their ex-slaves, *harratin* or other dependent classes, the town-folk of Tamanrasset, nor the recent immigrants from the north (*les gens du nord*), who together make up the overwhelming majority of the population.[13] Third, they know that it is the one type of work – as cameleers, guides and so forth – in which they are incomparably skilled and through which they can insert themselves into the modern, global economy. They see tourism as 'their industry', and as providing them with 'their place in the world'. They thus see tourism as playing a fundamental role, as being an essential cog, in the maintenance and future development of what remains of their nomadic culture. They have a saying, which has taken on increasing political content and meaning since the regeneration of tourism four years ago, that 'without tourism there is no nomadism; and without nomadism there is no tourism'.

The Differential Impact of Tourism in Ahaggar and Tassili-n-Ajjer

An important feature that must not be ignored in any analysis of Algeria's extreme south, is that throughout the post-Independence history of Algeria, from the 1960s to the present, the impact of tourism, like many other external agents, has not been uniform across the entire region. For instance, the socio-economic impact of tourism on the two 'sides' of the region, that is

Djanet/Tassili (the *wilaya* of Illizi) and Tamanrasset/Ahaggar (the *wilaya* of Tamanrasset), in the 1960s and 1970s was very different. The reason for this stems from significant differences in the two regions' historical backgrounds. The traditional economic bases of the two regions were very different. Although both the Kel Ahaggar and the Kel Ajjer were essentially nomadic pastoralists, the Kel Ajjer had greater agricultural and commercial resources and were consequently much less dependent on pastoralism than the Kel Ahaggar. Both Ghat and Djanet were fertile oases. Djanet, in particular, which in 1914 supported a population of 1,200,[14] enabled the Kel Ajjer to develop a significant agricultural economy. In Ahaggar, by contrast, there were no significant settlements and little agricultural development until after French pacification.[15] Indeed, at the time of the French arrival, Tamanrasset consisted of nothing more than a handful of *zeribas* (huts) and a few *harratin*-cultivated gardens on the banks of the *Oued* Amanrassa. When the French left 60 years later, Tamanrasset was still a small, dusty administrative centre of just over 4,000 inhabitants. In addition to its agricultural base, Djanet was also an important commercial centre strategically positioned on the three trans-Saharan trade routes that ran from Kanem-Bornu, through Damergou, Aïr, Djanet and up to Tripoli; between Iferouane in Aïr and Ghat; and from Kano, through Zinder, Agades and Djanet up to Tripoli.[16] This commercial traffic enabled Djanet to earn revenue from the supply of camels and other related services and to exchange dates, salt and medicinal plants for millet, livestock and manufactured goods. By comparison, relatively little caravan trade passed through the territory of the Kel Ahaggar,[17] who always envied the Kel Ajjer for their control over this trade.[18]

One consequence of the Kel Ajjer's greater agricultural base and commercial orientation is that they had stronger ties than the Kel Ahaggar with an urban centre, namely the town of Djanet. Unlike the Kel Ahaggar, many Kel Ajjer had consequently sedentarised earlier and more readily in Djanet and a few other small village centres such as Tamdjert, Iherir and later Illizi (Fort Polignac). The Kel Ajjer's earlier and more ready acceptance of sedentary life meant that they were less affected than the Kel Ahaggar by the radical changes wrought by the newly independent government in the 1960s. The result of this differential pattern of sedentarisation between the Kel Ajjer and Kel Ahaggar meant that it was the nomadic Kel Ahaggar, more than the Kel Ajjer, who felt the positive socio-economic benefits of tourism in the late 1960s and early 1970s. The redistribution of tourism revenues through the Kel Ahaggar's camps was critical to their nomadic survival. It might therefore be argued that the hinterland of Tamanrasset benefited more from tourism during this period than the hinterland of Djanet. However, the impact of tourism on the two towns, as distinct from their hinterlands, was quite different. Because of the proximity of the recently 'discovered' Tassili 'frescoes' to Djanet, it became a more important 'tourist town' than Tamanrasset, making it more prone economically than Tamanrasset to the vicissitudes of tourism.

In the same way that tourism impacted differentially on the populations of the two regions in the years immediately following Independence, so too did the cessation of tourism in the 1990s have very different impacts on the two regions. By 1992, Djanet had become a booming tourist town, with a population of some 10,000 and a relatively scant surrounding nomadic population. The complete cessation of tourism thus had a catastrophic impact on the town and its commercial sector. The impact on Tamanrasset was less catastrophic simply because the town's economy was less dependent on tourism. During the 1990s, Tamanrasset burgeoned into a large administrative and garrison town, whose population more than doubled from around 40,000 at the end of the 1980s, to around 100,000 or more at the end of the 1990s.[19] This huge growth generated considerable economic and commercial activity in its own right, which partially mitigated the loss of revenues from tourism. Djanet, by contrast, did not experience such a frenetic growth.[20] Furthermore, although those involved in the tourism business in Ahaggar, mostly Tuareg, experienced a collapse in tourism revenue, the effects of this collapse on the nomadic element, in particular, were mitigated by the government's policy of employing several hundred 'nomads' as *'agents de conservation'* (known colloquially as *guardiens du parc*[21]) in the newly created Ahaggar (Hoggar) National Park.[22] The 'compensatory' effect of this policy seems to have been greater in Ahaggar than Ajjer, where some 80 Park wardens lost their jobs during the 1990s.

I am under the strong impression that this almost total collapse of the tourist economy in Djanet led to many people leaving the region and looking for work elsewhere, especially around the administrative centre of Illizi some 450km to the north, and still further north in the oil and gas fields of In Amenas and Hassi Messaoud. Several Kel Ajjer also appear to have moved across the border to Ghat and environs in Libya where tourism began redeveloping around 1995. This same trend was noticeable in Ahaggar, although perhaps on a smaller scale. For example, a few Kel Ahaggar who had been involved in the tourism business prior to its collapse sought work in Mali, a move which was facilitated by the fact that the Kel Ahaggar had given sanctuary to Malian Tuareg during the uprising of Mali Tuareg in the early 1990s.

Realising the Need for 'Sustainable' Tourism: The Tamanrasset Conference

By the late 1980s, with some 15,000 visitors a year, Ahaggar and Tassili were beginning to experience some of the worst manifestations of 'mass' tourism, notably serious environmental degradation, including significant and irreversible damage to rock art and other archaeological and cultural sites. The first people to appreciate the nature and extent of this environmental damage and to try and take action to reverse it were a number of Tuareg tourism agencies (*agences de tourisme*) in Tamanrasset. Although they were the main financial beneficiaries of this booming tourism market, they were sufficiently knowledgeable and perceptive to realise that the continuation of tourism in its present form would lead to the degradation and possibly irreversible destruction of their natural environment and cultural heritage. On 2 February 1989, after much deliberation, they formed an association – the *Association des Agences de Tourisme Wilaya de Tamanrasset* (ATAWT) – whose published objectives were:

- *Le regroupement pour la défense d'intérêt commun des agences de tourisme et de voyage de la wilaya de Tamanrasset.*
- *La contribution au développement touristique de la wilaya de Tamanrasset.*
- *La contribution à la protection et à la sauvegarde des sites touristiques et du patrimoine historique et naturel de la wilaya de Tamanrasset.*
- *La création d'emploi.*
- *La promotion touristique dans son ensemble, tourisme alternatif responsable, développement de l'artisanat local.*

The ATAWT's initiative led to a major international conference being held in Tamanrasset in November 1989 under the aegis of the World Tourism Organisation (WTO). The purpose of the conference, which was attended by 75 participants from 16 countries, was to formulate policies and draw up plans for an alternative, environmentally sustainable form of tourism. Indeed, one of its proposals was to establish in Tamanrasset an international centre for sustainable and responsible tourism.

The conference's ideas, driven largely by a small number of Tuareg in Tamanrasset, soon spread across the Algerian Sahara and led to the creation in 1991 of a national union of agencies: the *Union Nationale des Associations des Agences de Tourisme Alternatif* (UNATA), which brought together almost every agency in the Algerian Sahara into a potentially powerful lobby group.[23]

Although their vision remains, the ambitious and farsighted plans of ATAWT, UNATA and the Tamanrasset Conference remain stillborn. Even before UNATA had been created, the Gulf War, along with strikes and disturbances in Algeria, were deterring tourists from visiting Algeria. The onset of the 'crisis' following the annulment of the 1992 elections brought tourism in Algeria to a complete cessation.

The eight years during which the Algerian Sahara's tourism agencies were without clients was a salutary period, during which they were able to reflect on both the economic damage they were suffering as well as the damage that 'mass' tourism had begun to inflict on the region. With their businesses mothballed, the small number of Tuareg agents who clung to the hope that tourists would one day return to their corner of the Sahara, knew that the cessation of tourism had effectively saved their region from an environmental catastrophe. They were determined that the principles and ideals proposed at the Tamanrasset Conference should provide the basis for any future redevelopment of tourism in the region.

Thus, when the first few tourists trickled back to the region in the latter part of 1999 and the first few months of 2000, the driving figures in UNATA and ATAWT were more determined than ever that tourism should be established on an environmentally sustainable basis. Their main goal was, *'de protéger le patrimoine historique, culturel et naturel du pays, les sites touristiques, la bio-diversité et l'environnement'*.[24] The statistical high-point of tourism in Ahaggar-Tassili in the late 1980s had shown them that unregulated, 'mass' tourism had brought the region to the brink of an environmental catastrophe. They had seen the warning lights and were determined that such a situation should never again be allowed to develop. Accordingly, in July 2000, UNATA and ATAWT published a six-page 'action manifesto'.[25] Its key points regarding the relationship between tourism and the nomadic environment and its directions for environmental protection are reproduced in Appendix I.

The Struggle for an Environmentally Sustainable Tourism

The subsequent three years, from the time of the publication of the UNATA and ATAWT Manifesto in July 2000 to the summer of 2003, has been a struggle between a number of forces to determine what sort of tourism industry would redevelop in the region. The various forces engaged in this struggle have been:

- the small, but increasingly growing number of local people – mostly Tuareg tourism agencies who were the leading players in both UNATA and ATAWT – who were becoming increasingly concerned about the damage to their heritage and realised that the region faced an environmental catastrophe if tourism was allowed to re-develop in the same mode as in the 1980s;
- local 'opportunists' who saw the redevelopment of tourism as an opportunity to make a 'fast buck' or recoup some of the lost business of the previous decade;

- European air charter tour companies;
- the government and various local government agencies, such as the *walis*,[26] directors of tourism, directors of the national parks and so on;
- tourism investment interests in neighbouring countries, notably Tunisia and Morocco;
- 'independent' European travellers; and
- trans-Saharan smugglers and more phantasmatic 'bandit/terrorist' elements who did not become a relevant force until 2003.

I will summarise the positions and interests of each of these forces.

Local, Predominantly Tuareg, 'Environmentalists'

In 1999, as the first few tourists trickled back into the region, this group comprised little more than a handful of Tuareg travel agents who had been involved in the foundation of ATAWT and UNATA and the Tamanrasset Conference and who understood the consequences of 'mass' tourism being allowed to redevelop in the same manner as in the 1980s. However, over the next three years, this 'group' became more of a 'movement' as it became more widespread in numbers and increasingly more conscious of the importance of the region's natural and cultural heritage and the threats that it was facing. This increase in consciousness was based on a number of incidents and experiences, amongst which I would single out the following:

a) In 1999 and 2000 a number of Tuareg agents from Tamanrasset travelled extensively throughout much of Ahaggar and Tassili for the first time in several years. Some of these trips were with clients; most were reconnoitring new trips in preparation for the possible return of tourists. One such journey, involving seven Tuareg and ranging over 5,000km, was undertaken specifically to assess the extent of damage that had been inflicted on a number of rock art and other archaeological sites over the previous years.[27] Even though the seven were seeing many of these sites for the first time, they were shocked and enraged by the extent of the graffiti and despoliation that had been inflicted on a number of sites and the surrounding landscape. During the course of the journey there were constant discussions about who was responsible for inflicting such damage and who should be responsible for protecting the sites, with frequent reference to 'our land' and 'our heritage', as well as persistent enquiries about the 'meaning' of some of the art, its age and its initiators. Indeed, the language of these conservationists was something that I had not experienced when I had travelled with Tuareg to these same sites 30 years earlier. In those days, most Tuareg showed relatively little interest in the rock art, except for the more recent depictions of camels and *tifinagh* script[28] with which they identified, saying that it belonged to the 'Issebeten'[29] or people 'before them'. News of their journey, and the nature of the rock art they had seen,[30] soon spread amongst friends and relatives.

b) The above-mentioned journey coincided with disturbing reports about the redevelopment of tourism in the neighbouring Acacus Mountains in Libya. A small number of tourists had been allowed in Libya from about 1995 onwards. However, a number of Italian tour operators saw the millennium as an opportunity 'to make a killing' by taking hundreds of parties of Italians to the Acacus and Mesak regions of the Fezzan. Some 45,000 tourists, three times the maximum that ever visited the entire Ahaggar-Tassili in a full year, are estimated to have visited the region between December 1999 and April 2000.[31] The damage inflicted on the rock art of the region was immense: some 40 rock art shelters are estimated to have been severely and irreversibly damaged in this orgiastic catastrophe. The rumours of this 'incident' that crept across the border gave further credence to the environmentalists who were already warning of the dangers of such mass tourism in Ahaggar and Tassili.

c) With the return of tourists, there was an increasing realisation amongst the Kel Ahaggar and Kel Ajjer that their heritage, especially the region's prehistoric rock art, was not merely an asset, but their most valuable economic resource for their future. They began increasingly to realise that a secured livelihood for their descendants from a viable and sustainable tourism industry required the long-term protection and conservation of the rock art and associated archaeological sites and landscapes.

d) There is now a far greater awareness amongst local people of the wealth and importance of the region's natural and cultural heritage. Although this new perception is something which I have seen increase enormously in the three years since 1999, it seems to have been triggered a few years earlier by the publicity and general awareness surrounding the establishment of the Tassili-n-Ajjer and Ahaggar as National Parks in 1984 and 1987 respectively, with the former being designated as a World Heritage Site, and the subsequent work that has been undertaken, particularly by the Office of the Tassili Park. More especially, I think that the research and publications undertaken by the Park's first Director, Malika Hachid, engendered a re-awakening of interest amongst local people in the Park and their heritage. Her name is now widely known in the region. On one occasion, when I was asking an elderly man of the Idjeradjeriouène descent group (*tawsit*), who lived near the *Oued* Djerat, if he knew the story of the 'rain-stone' (see below) which had been taken (stolen) from the *Oued* by the French ethnologist Henri Lhote in the 1930s or shortly after,[32] he immediately told me that 'he had read the text'. Although he could not read, he was referring to Malika Hachid's book on the Tassili-n-Ajjer[33] in which she describes the theft of the 'rain stone'. Thanks to her work, growing numbers of Tuareg are being reminded or informed about this theft and a number of other such incidents.

e) In the 1930s the Ajjer Tuareg, the Idjeradjeriouène, used to pray in the little mosque (*mihrab*) in the *Oued* Djerat where a white quartzite millstone lay in front of the *mihrab*. The stone, which was thought to have the power of making rain, was coated with black soot, a colour that evoked clouds full of rain. Henri Lhote[34] subsequently sent the millstone to the *Musée de l'Homme* in Paris and, according to local mythology, no rain fell for 25 years. This was immediately interpreted as an evil portent by the Tuareg, who were very displeased that the object had been taken from them and worse still that it had been removed from its sacred place.[35] I have no recollection of hearing this story when I was with the Algerian Tuareg in the 1960s and early 1970s. Now, with this increased awareness of their heritage, the Djerat 'rain-stone' has become a cause célèbre with a number of Tuareg demanding its return, along with some of the other objects that were taken from them in colonial times (and more recently).

f) Amongst the Tuareg, as with many indigenous peoples, the environment is perceived as a socio-cultural and not simply a physical entity. Not only is the physical environment associated intimately with their histories and mythologies, but it reflects their social order. Features of the land, such as river valleys (*oueds*) and mountains are markers of traditional tribal land rights and so forth, and are often associated with the names of ancestors, real or imaginary, while many mountains and other features of the landscape take on human qualities such as marrying, divorcing, quarrelling and so forth, in a way which reflects the social order, values and lifestyle of traditional society. For example, Mount Tahat is the wife of Ilaman, the highest and best known 'male'[36] lava plug, but their marriage has not been devoid of jealousies and upheavals. Mount Amjer once quarrelled with Ilaman over Tahat and struck him a heavy blow with his sword (*takouba*), which resulted in Ilaman's 'shoulder' and the eruption of a spring beneath it. But while Amjer wooed Tahat to be his wife, Mount Tioueyin was in love with Amjer. In a fit of jealousy over Amjer's refusal to leave his place close to Tahat, Tioueyin flounced off in the direction of Mali, only coming to stop in her present position alongside the *Oued* Amded near Silet, about 150km to the south-west. Mount Iherhé followed Tioueyin, leaving a depression to mark his former proximity to Ilaman, and on arriving in the *Oued* Amded region began to court her; the small crater to the north of the Silet track known as Tegit-n-Iherhé being the mark left by Iherhé before he finally settled in his present position just behind Tioueyin.

Although many of these mythological stories and associations are being lost, especially amongst the younger generation, I have been aware over the last three or four years of a conscious revivalism amongst many Kel Ahaggar, both nomads and sedentarists, of the symbolic and cultural association of their physical environment and cultural heritage. While this is partly associated with the revival of nomadism and 'camel culture'[37] in the last few years, it is also associated with the increased awareness of the essential relationship between nomadism and tourism. In a similar way as the Tuareg revolts in Niger and Mali provoked a strong sense of cultural revivalism amongst Tuareg in those countries, so, in a less dramatic manner, it seems that the threats posed by tourism to the environment and cultural heritage of Ahaggar and the surrounding Tassili is generating a similar response amongst the Tuareg of these regions. The Kel Ahaggar's and Kel Ajjer's increased awareness of the 'value' of their nomadic-Tuareg culture as a real economic resource, within the context of a redeveloping tourism industry, is provoking a renewed sense of patrimonial awareness, proprietorship and custodianship.

g) The one 'incident' that has galvanised the 'environmentalists', widened their support and lifted their 'campaign' to a new political level, was confirmation, in April 2002, that European operators were systematically looting the Sahara of prehistoric artefacts. Although there had been rumours in most Saharan countries of European, mostly German, tour operators looting such artefacts, no hard proof had been found. In 2001, however, the Internet came to Tamanrasset and Tuareg began scouring the web for clues that might help them identify and put an end to this activity. In April 2002, they discovered a website belonging to the German, Munich-based, tour operator, 'Rolling Rover', run by Helmut Arzmüller. The website advertised the illegal commercial sale of hundreds of prehistoric artefacts that the 'Rolling Rover' team had looted from the Sahara. The full details of Arzmüller's operation were downloaded, copied and stored in a number of European and North African sites so that they could be used in the event of future legal proceedings against him. Shortly afterwards, the sites of two other German operators were discovered, downloaded and stored for safe-keeping. The Tuareg's discovery of the German operators not only confirmed the existence and scale of the looting and destruction of their cultural heritage, which had been suspected for a long time, but it has also been the 'driver' behind a number of subsequent critical events, which are discussed presently, that have led to the current state of crisis in Saharan and especially Algerian Saharan tourism.

238

h) Two further elements have hardened the determination of the 'environmentalists'. These are that elements within the central government, as well as business interests, especially those which have moved into the region from the north, have been trying to exploit the post-1999 resurgence in tourism for short-term political and commercial gain, and secondly that the 'environmentalists', represented by ATAWT and UNATA, have received little government support, at least in Tamanrasset, through either the office of the *wali* or the local directors of tourism and the Park.

Local Business 'Opportunists'
With the return of tourists from 1999 onwards, a number of local businessmen, especially in Tamanrasset, saw an opportunity to make a 'fast buck' or recoup some of the lost business of the previous decade with little or no concern for the general principles of environmental sustainability advocated by UNATA and the Tamanrasset Conference. They provided an ideal local infrastructure for a number of European air charter operators (see below), who saw the same potential for profitable business in the reopening of Ahaggar and the Tassili-n-Ajjer as their Italian counterparts had seen in the Acacus and Mesak in 1999–2000. However, with the resurgence of tourism being checked by the impact of 11 September,[38] the invasion of Afghanistan, the Iraq war and the Algerian hostage crisis of 2003 (see below), most of the rapidly built camp sites and other such enterprises have remained empty or closed.

European Air Charter Tour Companies
Between 2000 and 2003, a number of European air charter tour companies have run an increasing number of 'low-cost' package tours into the region with serious implications for the environment. On occasion, as many as four plane-loads of tourists have been known to arrive in Djanet or Tamanrasset on the same day. Such 'invasions' cannot be managed within the limitations of local infrastructural facilities. Not only do they put pressure on the resources of the two towns, but by tending to follow similar routes and visiting the same sites on a rushed, improperly managed basis, they are causing rapid degradation of a number of environmentally fragile sites. Not only is the resurgence of such 'mass' tourism causing the same sort of environmental damage as in the late 1980s, but the associated downward pressure on local costs means that there is little if any economic benefit to the local community. UNATA and other local organisations are currently demanding that the government limit the number, and stagger the arrivals and departures, of such operations.

Government and Government Agencies

The realisation of Algeria's huge tourism potential is precluded by her internal security problems. Most of the country's very limited tourism is restricted to its southern regions. It is therefore not surprising that the central government does not have an established tourism policy. Indeed, many Algerian analysts would argue that the government is divided as to whether the country should or should not be encouraging tourism. Many local people in the extreme south believe that the central government, based as it is in the north of the country, is jealous of the fact that the extreme south is the only part of the country able to attract tourists in the current climate of insecurity, and for that reason is disinclined to listen to their concerns or promote their interests. In fact, the central government's policy towards the Sahara has been limited to three overriding concerns: the hydrocarbons industry and security, political relations with its neighbours, and international economic projects such as the trans-Saharan highway (still far from developed) and the proposed Nigerian–Algerian pipeline. Until now, only minimal consideration has been given to either tourism or the value of the Sahara's rich cultural heritage. The slight resurgence in tourism in the extreme south since 1999 has been encouraged by the central government only in as much as it can be used to show that Algeria is a 'normal country' and that the security issue has been largely resolved.[39] Local 'environmentalists' have thus tended to see the central government as being broadly supportive of the interests of European 'package tour' operators, which are a threat to both the environment and the economic interests of local people. For example, in January 2001 the French and Algerian governments signed a *Partenariat* agreement, the stated aim of which is to assist the development of tourism in the Algerian Sahara. However, local people, especially the 'environmentalists', fear that France's role will be limited to the provision of financial assistance for the construction of hotels, the facilitation of charter flights and so forth, all of which are potentially injurious to their environmental and cultural heritage.

However, 2002 saw the government beginning to take a more enlightened stance on the Sahara. In January,[40] Algiers hosted an international seminar on 'Sustainable Development of Ecotourism in Desert Areas', at which several prominent Algerians, including the Directors of the Tassili and Ahaggar Parks, presented papers. Later in the year, Cherif Rahmani, the Algerian Minister for the Environment and himself a 'man of the desert', established the World Deserts Foundation,[41] with himself as president. Both of these events, followed by further significant initiatives in early 2003 (see below) suggest that the government is becoming more aware of the environmental problems of the Sahara and especially the demands of local people for an environmentally sustainable tourism industry.

The position and role of government agencies in the region is more complex in that the two *wilayat* have experienced very different performances from their respective *walis* and other government appointed functionaries since the middle of 2001, which has led to different perceptions of and responses to government from the local populations in the two *wilayat*. Prior to the summer of 2001, there was growing dissatisfaction amongst local (predominantly Tuareg) citizens in both *wilayat*. This dissatisfaction was based primarily on the performance of their *walis*,[42] the lack of consultation with local people on issues of concern to them, especially the way in which tourism was redeveloping, and the appointment to key local government positions and directorships (such as Parks, Tourism and so on) of people from the north who were often perceived as being disinterested and even hostile to their concerns. Within a year of President Bouteflika's appointment, the 'Citizens of Tamanrasset' wrote an open letter (Appendix II) to him complaining about the *wali*'s behaviour, warning the President that if he did not intervene there was likely to be an explosion of popular anger, the outcome of which could not be predicted. Protests in Djanet and Illizi were more vocal. When the President visited the two towns in the summer of 2001, he was presented with a signed petition demanding the *wali*'s removal from office,[43] and on the streets by a mixture of respect and ribald chanting, the message of which was quite clear: 'If he (the North) didn't want the South to be part of Algeria, he was just to let them know!' The President noted the mood and, on his return to Algiers, the *wali* was duly dismissed.

Since that action, two years ago, the government and its agencies have been viewed rather differently in the two *wilayat*. In Tamanrasset, the *wali* has not been replaced and has continued to invoke the ire of a large proportion of the local population, especially the Tuareg. Nor do local people feel that they have been well served by a number of other government administrators, such as the *wilaya*'s Director of Tourism, although in the case of the Park, they are becoming aware that its shortcomings stem from the need to change the law, and hence its structure, rather than the personal qualities of the director.

Political dissatisfaction in Tamanrasset with the *wali* and other government functionaries rumbled on until reaching a crisis in October 2002, to which I will return presently. In Djanet, by contrast, the appointment of a new *wali* of the highest calibre, alongside a much more professional Park management, led to an almost immediate transformation of the political mood of the *wilaya*. This marked divergence in the political trajectories of the two *wilayat* came to a head, and was to a large extent resolved, at a watershed conference on the future of tourism in both the Tassili and Ahaggar that was organised by the *wali* of Illizi and held in Djanet in March 2003 and to which I shall return in a moment.

The Lesser Gods of the Sahara

Tourism Investment Interests in Neighbouring Countries

The extent to which tourism investment interests in Algeria's neighbours, Morocco and Tunisia, have played a role in shaping tourism in the Algerian Sahara will probably never be fully established. However, two related fears have been widely rumoured throughout the Algerian Sahara. The first has been the fear amongst the 'environmentalists' that Algeria might itself encourage 'mass tourism', through facilitating cheap charter flights and so on in a bid to undercut the major tourism markets of Morocco and Tunisia. The second rumour, albeit rather fanciful, has been that the kidnapping of the 32 European tourists (see below) in the Algerian Sahara in February–March 2003 was masterminded by tourism interests in one or both of Algeria's neighbours to prevent the emergence of a competitive market in the Algerian Sahara.

'Independent' European Travellers

Independent travellers are those who travel in the Tassili and Ahaggar in their own vehicles (or bikes) without a registered guide and without having sought an arrangement with a local travel agency. This form of travel is now referred to locally as *'tourisme sauvage'*. Although many tourists have visited the region in this way, and have always been welcomed, *tourisme sauvage* has been incurring the resentment of local people, especially local agencies, for two reasons. First, such tourism brings virtually no economic benefit to the region and its peoples. Indeed, a small number of Europeans have been trying, some successfully, to set up travel businesses, using their own vehicles and so on, in direct competition to local (mostly Tuareg) agencies. Such operations are almost certainly illegal for a number of reasons, but have never been investigated by local government authorities, which, in spite of repeated protests from local agencies, have given the appearance of favouring such foreign operators in preference to local agencies. Second, there has been a growing awareness, confirmed with the discovery of Helmut Arzmüller's 'Rolling Rover' and other German-based operations, that independent travellers have been responsible for much of the looting of the region's heritage. There are some half-a-dozen European-based websites run by and advocating such *tourisme sauvage* in the Sahara. An analysis of their 'chat-rooms' reveals an increasing (often manifestly racist) antagonism towards local Saharan (Algerian) authorities and local (for example, Tuareg) travel agencies, whom they see as impeding what they regard arrogantly as their 'right' to travel more or less how and as they please in the Sahara, and as merely 'trying to make money from us'. Several of these websites, and their accompanying guide publications, directly encourage the breaking of local laws as well as the looting of artefacts.[44]

Smugglers, 'Bandits' and 'Terrorists'[45]

The Sahara has always been regarded as a sea[46] across which trade, both 'legal' and 'clandestine', has been carried since the earliest of times. Little has changed over the years except the nature of the goods and the technologies used in their transportation. After the hydrocarbons industry, clandestine trade, in one form or another, is now almost certainly the Sahara's biggest economic activity in value terms. Indeed, one of its most extraordinary accomplishments is how it (as distinct from local 'banditry') has managed to operate without encroaching significantly on the Sahara's tourism industry – at least until the beginning of 2003.

Although smuggling across Algeria's southern frontiers is as old as the frontier itself, the present phase of trans-Saharan smuggling, along with the more 'phantasmatic' (see below) 'bandit/terrorist' elements that are associated with it, emerged as a major force in the region around 1998–99. That date is a little arbitrary, but it relates to two, and perhaps three, specific events that have changed fundamentally the socio-political map and nature of much of the Central and Algerian Sahara.

The first of these events was the termination in June 1999 of Mali's UNHCR-funded refugee returnee assistance programme,[47] which signalled to the outside world that the refugee problem was now resolved and the region 'back to normal'. In Niger, a corresponding resettlement programme had been hampered by the overthrow of democratic rule, which, like the UNHCR withdrawal from Mali, also served to divert the eyes of the international community from this remote corner of the world. The net effect was that large swathes of this ill-defined region, especially much of northern Mali and northern Niger (and debatably the frontier regions of southern Algeria) became, once again, increasingly marginalised and beyond the effective reach of the state.

The second key event was that, in the same way as nature abhors a vacuum, the withdrawal of international and state elements from these regions was met by their almost synchronic occupancy by a number of 'outlaw' elements, notably Algeria's infamous Mokhtar Ben Mokhtar (many aliases), a Metlilli Chaamba, now in his early thirties, whose family had long been involved in clandestine trading activities and who, following a stint in Afghanistan, had allied himself with Hassan Hattab, who, in turn, had broken from the Armed Islamic Group (GIA) to form the *Groupe salafiste pour le predication et le combat* (GSPC) in September 1998.

During 1997 and 1998, Ben Mokhtar wrought havoc in much of the Algerian Sahara, attacking *gendarmerie* and military posts, oil companies and the main arterial roads. The route from In Salah to Tamanrasset, for example, was effectively closed during this period except for convoys under military escort. By 1999, the Algerian military had seized the initiative, forcing Ben Mokhtar to operate from the vast area south of Algeria's border stretching from Aïr in northern Niger, across Tamesna and the extensive ramifications of the Azaouagh valley, through the region stretching from Gourma-Rharous and Kidal to the Mali–Algerian border and on up into Mauritania; a zone in which 'bandits', outlaws and other such elements have been able to operate with relative impunity.

The third event, which seems to have been directly associated with the establishment of such local 'warlords' as Ben Mokhtar in the region, is the huge expansion since 1996 of the trans-Saharan clandestine cigarette trade.[48] Major international brands, notably Marlboro, Gauloises and so on, are either shipped into West Africa, or manufactured in counterfeit plants in Mali, Niger and Mauritania, and then trucked across the Sahel,[49] for trans-shipment by 'smugglers'[50] across the Algerian Sahara to further trans-shipment points in the northern Algerian Sahara, for distribution into the huge North African market, as well as across the Mediterranean by speed-boats to networks operating from southern Spain and Italy. The scale of this trade, now mixed with arms trafficking, electronics and illegal narcotics (cannabis and heroin), is enormous. For example, the Algerian security forces seized 356,521 cartons in 2002,[51] with an open market price of around €3.5m. This seizure could amount to anything from 10 per cent to one per cent of the total entering the country, suggesting that the total street value (Algerian prices) of the counterfeit cigarette trade alone is worth somewhere between €35m and €350m.

Ben Mokhtar has been reported dead at least six times, leading many inhabitants of Algeria's *Grand Sud*[52] to suggest that his life is that of a 'phantom', rumours and speculation about which play a convenient role in legitimising certain government actions in the south. For example, the latest report of his arrest at Adrar in southern Algeria in March 2003, following a reported raid on a public works base north of In Guezzam on 18 December 2002 and the capture of 17 Toyota 4x4WDs belonging to a Western oil company near Illizi on 24 December, was denounced by Mohammed Jai, chief of police in El Golea, as unfounded and simply a rumour. Phantom or real, the 'bandit/terrorist' network that has become established in this vast tract of the Sahara, with its links to the GSPC in north-eastern Algeria, has created and is fuelling an increasingly complex situation. This situation includes a number of 'copycat' elements, most of whom appear to be nothing more than simple 'criminals', often disaffected *ishumar*.[53] In Niger, especially, a number of these characters, such as Aboubacar Alambo, a former Tuareg rebel who was incorporated into the Niger army before 'absconding' and undertaking a series of 'hold-ups' during 2002,[54] have taken to raiding passing traffic, especially tourists.[55] More serious, however, is that since 11 September, a number of Islamic fundamentalist elements, mostly from Pakistan and Afghanistan, have moved into the region, attracting the attention of the CIA and other Western and North African security agencies, who have been very ready to draw attention to the presence of *al-Qaeda*. Indeed, the Algerian security forces have shown almost unseemly haste, perhaps for the benefit of their new allies in the Pentagon, in publicising the names of Osama bin Laden's supposed representatives in Algeria and elsewhere in the region; details of *al-Qaeda*'s developing network and co-ordinating role amongst 'terrorist' groups in Algeria and neighbouring countries; the bin Laden relationship with known GSPC 'terrorists' such as Hassan Hattab, Amari Said (alias Abderrazak Lamari, El-Para) and Mokhtar Ben Mokhtar (also known as Belmokhtar and Laouer[56]); along with details of the expansion of *al-Qaeda*-associated terrorist networks in the border regions of Niger, Mali and Mauritania.[57]

While the scale of arms, cigarette and drugs trafficking across the Sahara, especially the Algerian part of it, is undoubtedly enormous, the precise nature of *al-Qaeda*'s presence and the extent of 'terrorist' networks across the region is less clear and still subject to elements of speculation. What is extraordinary is that these two 'industries', tourism and smuggling/'terrorism', have developed over the last four years in harmonious co-existence. Indeed, until the end of 2002 and early 2003, southern Algeria was statistically the 'safest place in the Sahara' for tourists.

Accusations of Sabotage Levelled at the State: The October 2002 Crisis

On 1 November, 2002, the President of the ATAWT wrote to the Prime Minister,[58] accusing the government of sabotaging tourism in the Sahara (Appendix III). Although the grievances listed in the letter might be seen as merely an expression of continued frustration with the quality of the *wali*'s governance, it was motivated by two particular incidents, which occurred more or less synchronously and which have a major bearing on our understanding of the dramatic events that have unfolded so far in the course of this year (2003).

The first incident involved the hijacking of four Swiss tourists on 18 October 2002, at the height of the tourist season, in the Arak gorges where the main tarmac road between In Salah and Tamanrasset had been washed away as a result of heavy and persistent rains. The professional travel agencies in Tamanrasset, who, along with the military, *gendarmerie* and police, are also responsible for the safety of tourists in the region, received no official notification of the incident. The first they heard about it was when they read Swiss newspaper reports on the Internet! The precise details of the incident are not clear. It appears that the four Swiss, along with 17 Algerians, of whom no mention had been made, were hijacked by a group of men purporting to be Islamic fundamentalists, but that they were either set free or managed to free themselves within a day or two. The reason for the official silence might have been that the authorities did not want news of the incident to damage tourism in the region. But local people knew that was most unlikely, as the *wali* in Tamanrasset had spent the past three years putting one impediment after another in the way of local agents (see below). Local people became particularly anxious when it was rumoured that the *Gendarmerie Nationale* had caught the hostage-takers but had been ordered to release them.[59] Suggestions began to circulate that the incident had been contrived to create the impression that Islamic fundamentalists (terrorists) were now operating in the south of the country. This would provide the political justification for a greater military presence in the south, as well as making an even stronger case for further US assistance.[60]

The second incident was also related to the damaged road at Arak. Since his appointment to Tamanrasset in 1999, the *wali* had made it extremely difficult for local travel agencies to run their businesses effectively by limiting each of their vehicles to 200 litres of fuel, which was only obtainable after submitting a dossier to the *Commissariat Central de la Police* and receiving a permit which was then valid for only 48 hours.[61] With the temporary flood damage at Arak, the *wali* immediately and unnecessarily[62] imposed a daily ration of 6,000 litres of fuel for the whole town, thus making it even more difficult for travel agencies, and many other local people, to conduct their business. The 'fuel crisis' that enveloped the town for several weeks was finally resolved when the Prime Minister, in response to ATAWT's letter of complaint, sent a senior government representative to Tamanrasset to instruct the *wali* that fuel distribution and the filling stations were run by commercial companies (Sonatrach and Naftal) over which he had no such authority.

Why had the *wali* acted in this way? As far as the members of ATAWT were concerned, the *wali* had always been a major impediment to the development of their businesses. He was, in their own words, 'not just frightened of them, but also of his own shadow'. This was not simply jocular talk: for two years the *wali* had in fact made his intentions clear to them by refusing to recognise the new board of ATAWT, thus denying the Association proper legal status. If many of these local Tuareg travel agencies are to be believed, and as the insinuations in their letter (Appendix III) imply, one answer for the *wali*'s behaviour might be found to reside in the ease with which fuel is smuggled across the southern frontiers[63] and cigarette and other traffickers consistently manage to avoid the frontier security imposed by the army, customs, *gendarmerie* and police. A more serious suggestion, believed by a number of prominent Tuareg, was that the *wali*'s actions were designed to 'provoke a reaction' from them. This interpretation, when considered in the same context as the 'rumours' relating to the release of the kidnappers of the Swiss tourists, created an eerie anticipation in Tamanrasset that the *wali*, whether acting at the behest of the government or on his own initiative,[64] was trying to justify some form of state or military intervention in the region. The Tuareg and other local people decided that they would provide the *wali* with no such opportunity and accordingly tried to maintain calm and order in the potentially explosive atmosphere that for several weeks surrounded the town's two filling stations.

The Djanet Conference, 10–12 March 2003

One complaint that ATAWT did not mention in its letter of 1 November 2002 was that the authorities appeared to have taken no action against the German 'looters', in spite of having been informed about them six months earlier. From surveillance of their websites, ATAWT members noted that at least two of the German travel companies engaged in such looting had undertaken autumn tours in Libya and were now, once more, planning at least two tours through Algeria in January–February and March 2003. Accordingly, in December 2002, one of ATAWT's members, *Agence Tarahist*, wrote (Appendix IV) to the appropriate government and regional authorities,[65] urging that they take action to arrest these professional looters as a matter of urgency in the country's struggle against the theft of its heritage.

In Libya, where the same looters had also been operating with impunity, the transfer of information to government agencies in December led to the imposition of new travel regulations.[66] While these measures effectively precluded the operation of looters in Libya, they merely batted the problem into Algeria's court, where no action was taken against the looters in either January or February. The only action taken by the Algerians was to organise a seemingly innocuous and low-key conference (*Journées d'Etude*) on 'Tourism in the Tassili and Ahaggar' in Djanet on 10–12 March 2003. The conference was organised by the *wilaya* of Illizi,[67] with the support of the Ministry of Culture and Communication and with both the World Tourism Organisation and the UNDP (United Nations Development Programme) making major contributions.

The Djanet Conference, as it will probably become known, is already being regarded by some of the attendees as the most significant 'political' meeting yet held in Algeria's extreme south. To understand why the meeting was so important, it is necessary to understand the prevailing political issues and agendas at the time the conference was arranged. These were:

The Lesser Gods of the Sahara

a) A growing concern amongst local people, notably tourism agencies, park officials and other 'professionals', that the two Parks were being subjected to increasing environmental degradation, especially by unregulated forms of tourism (*tourisme sauvage*).
b) In addition to the above, a small but growing number of people, notably UNATA members and government officials, were aware of the professional looting of prehistoric artefacts being undertaken by European, mostly German, tour operators (see Appendix IV).
c) Growing political tension in Tamanrasset, stemming from the increasing complaints against the *wali* and a number of regional officials, including the Directors of Tourism and the Ahaggar National Park (see Appendices II and III).
d) An increasing anxiety by members of ATAWT and UNATA, especially in the *wilaya* of Tamanrasset, that the government, both national and regional (that is, through the *wali*), was opposed to the development of Saharan tourism (see Appendix III), especially the sort of environmentally sustainable tourism which they were advocating. For example, for two years the *wali* of Tamanrasset had refused to recognise the new board of ATAWT, thus denying the organisation its registration and hence its existence as a legally constituted association.[68]

The main feature of the conference was the complete unanimity between all delegates and attendees in the tabling and adoption of a huge number of proposals promoting measures to ensure the conservation of the region's heritage, along with a range of suggested policies aimed at putting an end to *tourisme sauvage* and promoting environmentally sustainable forms of tourism. The conference was a sweeping victory for the 'environmentalists', sweetened by the UNDP's announcement of $22m support for the two Parks' future conservation programmes.[69]

There were two other remarkable features of the conference. The first was that there were no attendees from Tamanrasset except for the President of UNATA, who happens to live in Tamanrasset, and a representative from ATAWT. The three most important officials of the *wilaya* of Tamanrasset, namely the *wali*, the Director of Tourism and the Director of the Ahaggar National Park, who had all been specifically invited to the conference, were all noticeable by their absence. In contrast, their counterparts from Illizi and Djanet impressed the attendees by their professional competence and commitment to the aims of the conference. The difference in the calibre of governance between the two *wilayat* was cruelly exposed.

The second remarkable feature was the reaction of attendees to the presentation to the conference of the dossier on 'looting'. In addition to copies of letters that had been sent by *Agence Tarahist* to national and regional authorities (see Appendix IV), the dossier contained material downloaded from the 'Rolling Rover' website, including photographs of prehistoric artefacts they had looted from the area and were advertising for sale on the Internet. The presentation explained to attendees the *modus operandi* and the scale of activity of 'Rolling Rover' and other German tour companies that were also looting the Sahara, and stressed the importance of arresting them with maximum international publicity.[70] The presentation of the dossier was greeted at first with incredulity, which, when its implications had been considered, turned to an anger that played a major part in unifying the conference in its determination to put a stop to such activities.

The story of the looting of the Sahara's heritage was given immediate and prominent coverage in the national media. During the week following the conference, a number of meetings were held between responsible officials in Tamanrasset (UNATA, ATAWT, police, customs, military and so on) and members of the appropriate ministries in Algiers, to discuss the arrest of the looters.

The Hostage Crisis

No looters were arrested. The reason for this was because while the means of their arrest were still being discussed, a far greater and more tragic drama was beginning to unfold in the Algerian Sahara. During the second week of March, while the Djanet Conference was in progress, Tuareg travel agencies in Tamanrasset and Illizi received the first of many phone-calls from friends and relatives of European tourists who appeared to be 'missing' while travelling in the Algerian Sahara. On 17 March, three separate groups, comprising six Germans, one Dutch and four Swiss, who had last been heard of on 22 February, were officially reported as missing. Over the next three weeks, a further four groups were reported missing, until by the end of March the number had reached 29. On 11 April, two more Austrians were reported missing, bringing the number to 31. Finally, a German, allegedly sent by the German intelligence services to get 'caught' by what was now known to be a group or groups of hostage-takers, brought the number to 32. Although the nationalities appeared diverse (16 Germans, 10 Austrians, four Swiss, one Dutch and one Swede), they were all German-speakers. They were all also travelling off piste in their own vehicles or bikes, without guides or any arrangements with local agencies in the sector between Erg Tifernine and Illizi, an area along the northern fringe of the dip slopes of the Tamelrik and Fadnoun plateaux regions of the northern Tassili, which is known by locals and Saharan 'experts' to be exceptionally dangerous as it is intersected by major trans-Saharan smuggling routes.

For the first few weeks following the disappearances, the Algerian media and government spokesmen offered a series of mostly ludicrous suggestions as to what had happened to the travellers, ranging from errors in GPS systems caused by satellite modifications in the run-up to the Iraq war to the claim that the missing tourists had 'staged their own disappearance'.[71] As the weeks went by, with little or no definitive information about the fate of the missing tourists, it became increasingly evident that they had been kidnapped and were being held in two groups, one probably in the Tamelrik region, 150km south-west of Illizi,[72] and another somewhere to the west of Amguid.

But who were the kidnappers and what were their motives? Almost immediately, local and foreign press reports, based on speculation, ignorance of the Sahara, minimal intelligence and a stream of highly questionable statements from 'official' sources, began painting an alarming picture of the Algerian and neighbouring Saharan regions. I have already summarised the 'security' situation in this part of the Sahara at the time of the kidnapping of these tourists (see Smugglers, 'Bandits' and 'Terrorists', above). It was one that was already causing consternation in US intelligence circles, which believed that the arrival of Pakistan and Afghan Islamists in north-west Niger and northern Mali[73] after the invasion of Afghanistan was proof of the establishment of an *al-Qaeda* network running across the Sahel into Niger, Mali and Mauritania and linking with Islamist militants ('terrorists') such as Hassan Hattab's GSPC in north-east Algeria.

The missing link in this network, namely southern Algeria, was soon filled in by both local and foreign press agencies, who gave seemingly authoritative accounts of Islamic fundamentalists operating in Algeria's extreme south, with Mokhtar ben Mokhtar being singled out as the GSPC's *emir* in this region. While this picture was very much in keeping with the image of the world being presented by a US administration still searching for reliable handles in its 'War on Terror', and wanting to establish a more effective intelligence and military presence in the central-western Sahara that would enable it to straddle North and West Africa,[74] it lacked credibility on three counts.

First, Islamic fundamentalism has found little support amongst the peoples of the Algerian Sahara, least of all amongst the Tuareg, who are not only indifferent to it on ideological grounds but regard it as responsible for the cessation of tourism in the 1990s and their consequent loss of income. The growth of any Islamist movement in southern Algeria would almost certainly require the presence of external activists, such as the Afghans and Pakistanis in Mali or Algeria's own Islamists from the north of the country, all of whom would be easily noted by Algeria's security forces.

Second, the kidnappings did not appear to be in keeping with Mokhtar ben Mokhtar's known *modus operandi*. Apart from his opposition to gratuitous killing, the success of his smuggling operations and his professed war against the Algerian state were heavily dependent on his not incurring the wrath of the local populations, especially in Algeria, whose vast southern territory poses difficult 'transit' problems both in terms of its geographical barriers in the form of the Tassili ranges[75] and the necessity to establish fuel and supply caches. It has therefore been imperative for Mokhtar ben Mokhtar to ensure that the Tuareg's tourism business has not been disrupted. Indeed, it is significant that there has not been a single 'bandit incident' affecting tourists in the Tamanrasset and Illizi *wilayat* from the resumption of tourism in 1999[76] until October 2002 (see below).

Third, many local people now believe that the hijack of four Swiss tourists near Arak in October 2002 (see above) was a failed attempt by 'elements from the north' to achieve what they succeeded in doing in February–March 2003, or merely to give the impression that Islamic fundamentalist 'terrorists' were operating in the region.[77]

On 13 May 2003, the Algerian army attacked and freed one of the two groups of hostages. Reports of this incident by the freed hostages, along with their accounts of their experience, confirmed that their abductors were a GSPC cell from the north of the country and that their leader was almost certainly Abderrazak Lamari (El Para), although their use of food caches in the region also confirmed the cell had access to resources put in place by support groups in Mali, possibly Mokhtar ben Mokhtar's network. The freed hostages' accounts of their abduction and the subsequent movement of the second group of hostages to Mali also fuelled the suspicions that had been aired by several members of the media and on the Internet that there was a degree of complicity between the abductors and elements of the Algerian security forces.

The answer to many of the questions surrounding the incident will probably never come to light. And it is certainly too early to attempt an analysis of the event here, as the outcome of the 14 remaining hostages, now being held in Mali, is still awaited.[78] Nevertheless, a number of implications are already becoming clear.

First, the hostage crisis has drawn widespread international attention to both the problems being caused by *tourisme sauvage* and the looting of prehistoric artefacts. This was partly the result of the fact that all the hostages were German-speaking and that their abduction coincided with the widespread media publicity being given to 'German looters' in the wake of the Djanet Conference. Indeed, there were fears in some quarters that the abductions may have been the result of local people, enraged by the reports of the looting, taking the law into their own hands. Also, the Algerian authorities gave much prominence to the fact that all the groups abducted had been travelling 'illegally' in the region. The Algerian authorities were also aware that many

German-speaking travellers were using a well-known German guidebook that encouraged travellers to break Algerian laws by travelling off piste, and without guides, in areas where such travel is forbidden.[79] Within a few days, Algeria introduced radical changes to visa requirements more or less directly in line with the recommendations of the Djanet Conference. Travel in the region is now prohibited unless arranged through a local travel agency or, if travelling in their own vehicles, accompanied by a registered guide provided by an agency. This measure, as in Libya, should bring an end to *tourisme sauvage* and make it almost impossible for looters to operate in the region.

The second implication of the crisis is that it has drawn international attention to what Tuareg have known for some time, namely that the Central Sahara consists of vast spaces over which the three governments involved (Algeria, Mali and Niger) have little or no effective control. This stark fact was more or less admitted in July 2003 when the Malian government suggested, on becoming the recipient of the hostages and their captors, that this sector of the Sahara was now effectively beyond the control of the states and that the three countries should consider the creation of some sort of joint security zone.[80]

The third implication is that the hostage crisis, like Algeria's overall political crisis, has been enormously damaging to Tuareg interests. In the same way that Algeria's Islamist crisis in the 1990s brought tourism in Algeria to a standstill and substantially reduced tourism in the adjoining desert regions of Niger and Mali,[81] so the current hostage crisis is having the same damaging effects.

The fourth implication is that the Tuareg are acutely aware that the hostage-takers are a by-product of Algeria's political crisis, and that like most of the more prominent contraband traffickers, such as Mokhtar ben Mokhtar, they have moved into their traditional lands from northern Algeria. Moreover, as it has become increasingly apparent from the information released to the media that elements of the Algerian security forces may have been complicit in the affair, a sense of betrayal has spread amongst Algerian Tuareg. Thus, not only do they see this incident as a further intrusion of the country's ongoing Islamist crisis into their domain, but there is also a possibility, depending on what is revealed in the aftermath of the incident, that they may come to hold elements within the state responsible for the damage that it has caused them.

A Terrain Contested

The notion of a 'contested terrain' struck me very forcibly soon after my return to Ahaggar in 1999. Initially, I was seeing this contest, which I described at that time as 'the last significant battle of the Central Sahara',[82] in the struggle of a small number of Tuareg to save the region from what they saw as an imminent environmental catastrophe. This battle is being waged against the financially powerful interests of mass tourism, *tourisme sauvage* and looters by a small number of Tuareg, members of UNATA and ATAWT, not only on behalf of their two organisations, but also on behalf of the long-term interests of Tuareg whom these two organisations, for lack of adequate political representation, have taken upon themselves to represent.

However, during the course of these four years, another struggle was becoming increasingly apparent. It is the struggle for sheer physical control over this vast terrain and is being fought out between the forces of the state, smugglers and bandits of various kinds and, if some of the intelligence services are to be believed, perhaps *al-Qaeda* itself. During the course of 2003, in the events surrounding the Djanet Conference and the abduction of the 32 European tourists, these two levels of struggle have been fused.

I believe that this strange coincidence of events, which, if it were not for the editors of JNAS, would quite possibly have gone unrecorded, has led to the possibility of a new Saharan politic and the potential development of Tuareg regions along the lines that I suggested in the Introduction to this volume.[83]

Postscript

The remaining 14 hostages were released in northern Mali during the course of 17–18 August 2003. The precise conditions and circumstances of their release are not yet clear, and probably never will be.

On 18 May 2003, the President of UNATA wrote to Cherif Rahmani, Algeria's Minister for the Environment and the Founding President of the World Deserts Foundation, requesting that Dr Jeremy Keenan, in his capacity as a Founder Board Member of the Foundation and Director of the Saharan Studies Programme at the University of East Anglia (UK), be commissioned to make a full and detailed report on tourism in Ahaggar and the Tassili-n-Ajjer in order to establish the scientific basis for the development of an intelligent and environmentally sustainable tourism policy for the benefit of the *Grand Sud* and all Algeria. This request has been agreed and it is anticipated that the report will be submitted to UNATA, the World Deserts Foundation and the Algerian government in the early part of 2004.

The Lesser Gods of the Sahara

APPENDICES

Appendix I

Extracts from UNATA's and ATAWT's 'Rapport d'activité et Programme d'action pour redynamiser le secteur du tourisme', July 2000

C'est grace au tourisme dans nos regions que les nomads ont été fixés sur leurs terrains et que le méhari a été sauvegardé ...

Sous l'égide de notre association, les personnels des agences de voyages sont formés pour protéger leur environnement. En effet, il y a un style de la mise en place et l'installation du campement, une méthodologie du ramassage du bois, la mise en place du feu et sa destruction après usage, l'utilisation rationelle de l'eau, le rejet des eaux usées (hors des Oued, loin des points d'eau), le nettoyage du lieu du bivouac au moment du départ (il est même fourni aux participants des allumettes pour brûler leurs 'papiers' personnels). Le premier geste après l'installation du campement est l'installation d'une poubelle mobile. Tous les detritus sont brûlés sur place; les restes solides (conserves, plastiques, aluminium, etc. ...) sont ramassés dans des sacs spéciaux et ramenés à Tamanrasset quelle que soit la durée du voyage. Le personnel d'encadrement des agences veille à ce que les peintures ne soient pas dégradées. A la fin de chaque saison touristiques, en été, notre association réunit ses adherents pour organiser des tournées dans les sites afin de procéder à un dernier nettoyage d'ensemble (pour palier aux insuffisances de contrôle de chacun durant la saison). Tant il est vrai que tout le monde n'est pas parfait ...

Notre association n'a pas ménagé ses peines auprès de tous responsables (walis, chefs de Daira, directeurs ...) pour dénoncer les destructions des tombeaux préhistoriques dont les pierres ont été utilisées pour le bâtiment et les stations de concassage, l'abattage des arbres (acacias), la multiplicité des puits dans les lits d'oueds ce qui a siphonné les reserves naturelles constituées par les gueltas. Les diverses carriers illicites; les sables des oueds, les gravillons des plateaux, les rochers des collines; tout a été emportés par des norias de camions de travaux publics ...

De même, notre association n'a pas cessé de tirer la sonette d'alarme en ce qui concerne les poubelles sauvages qui ceinturent les villes, les villages et les hameaux du désert, ainsi que l'invasion des sacs en plastique non dégradable qui couvrent tous les acacias, tous les arbustes, tous les buissons, empoisonnant les puits, les sources et les gueltas et par voie de conséquence tuent les animaux ...

Nous rappelons ici la nécessité d'interdire l'utilisation des sacs en plastique sur les marchés et dans le commerce saharien (notre association a demandé à plusieurs reprises à des walis de faire des arêtés en ce sens) et de créer des unités de production des sacs en papiers bio-dégradable (de couleur de sable) au soleil et au vent ...

Par sa remise à l'honneur comme moyen de transport le chameau a été sauvé par notre forme de tourisme. Sous la pression de notre poids économique, nous avons obtenu de nos bouchers de ne plus abattre des chamelles et des jeunes chameaux. Et, malgré la quasi-inertie du tourisme durant cette dernière décennie, nous avons pu maintenir ces idées écologiques, ce respect de la nature et des hommes à travers la permanence et la vigilance de notre association auprès des populations aussi bien qu les administrations.

Contested Terrain

Appendix II

Letter to Algeria's President from the Citizens of Tamanrasset

LETTRE OUVERTE A MONSIEUR LE PRESIDENT DE LA REPUBLIQUE ABDELAZIZ BOUTEFLIKA

Monsieur le Président,

Vos citoyens de la Wilaya de Tamanrasset vous appellent au secours. Les pauvres, les riches, les nomades, les citadins, les commerçants, les entrepreneurs, les hommes, les femmes, les enfants ... Ainsi que les traditions et la culture dans notre region vivent un cauchemar depuis un an.

En effet, les diverses couches de la société civile de la région subissent un véritable joug par le fait de 'prince', en l'occurrence Monsieur Messaoud JARI, le nouveau wali installé depuis une année à Tamanrasset. Pendant toute cette période, ce monsieur n'a pas montré le moindre signe de respect pour la population, ni la volonté d'essayer de comprendre la situation et les habitudes particulières du grand sud.[84] Nous subissons un régime dictatorial de répression et de démonstration ou de lutte de pouvoir.

Dès son arrivée, la ville a changé de couleur: tous les bâtiments de l'administration sont peints en laque jaune moutarde. Nous voyons notre ville, rouge depuis la construction des premières maisons vers 1910, devenir une sorte de Disneyland de classe inférieure ... Cela malgré l'existence d'un arête municipal datant de 1963 confirmant juridiquement le style de l'habitat traditionnel du Hoggar, à savoir façades recouvertes d'un enduit ocre (de l'argile locale) strié de rayures verticals, méthode spécialement conçue et éprouvée pour lutter contre la chaleur.

A quoi bon cette débauche de couleurs vives, ce maquillage pompeux si la pourriture continue à se putréfier en dessous? Que de dépenses monstrueuses! Alors que la population s'enfonce dans la pauvreté et dans la misère. Le nombre de mendiants augmente tous les jours. N'y aurait-il pas une sérieuse action sociale à mettre en place au lieu de ce gaspillage de prestige? Les services de la santé n'en ont que le nom: ils sont dépassés et scandaleusement démunis. Un seul exemple très parlant: pas un seul gynécologue pour une population d'environ 80,000 habitants!!!

Au printemps dernier, une lubie traversait l'esprit de Monsieur le Wali pour tester la population et les services hospitaliers en cas d'accident d'avion! Il y eut donc simulation d'un crash du vol d'air Algérie en provenance d'Oran. Tout l'hôpital est mis en alerte et les malades hospitalisés vidés de leurs lits et renvoyés chez eux, valides ou non, pour libérer leurs places. La population est sous le choc. Des centaines de citoyens attendent leurs proches à l'aéroport et paniquant ... Sommes-nous des humains ou des animaux qu'on mène à la baguette?

Suite à un mauvais article de journaliste en voyage à Tamanrasset et en mal de scoop, Monsieur le Wali décide l'interdiction du port du chèche pour les chauffeurs de taxis touaregs! S'il savait à quoi il touche lorsqu'il veut décoiffer ces 'Hommes Bleus', justement à la dignité de tout un people qu'il refuse d'approcher et de connaître. Demander à un targui de circuler en public sans son chèche, c'est comme si on demandait à Monsieur le Wali d'aller au bureau sans sa culotte.

Chaque quartier avait son marché de fruits et légumes. Monsieur le Wali les a supprimés pour les centraliser dans un seul hangar insalubre et suffoquant, au centre-ville certes, mais éloigné de plusieurs kilometres de toutes les zones où est concentrée la population urbaine.

A présent, à l'aube de la reprise des activités touristiques – veritable moteur économique de la région – les professionnels de ce secteur, déjà entravés par Air Algérie qui ne semble pas vouloir acheminer les touristes européens vers leur but, Tamanrasset ou Djanet, en une journée, recontrent d'autres obstacles imposés par Monsieur le Wali duquel ils pourraient plutôt espérer une aide ou un encouragement:

- Fermiture de l'hôtel Tahat (hotel de l'état) sous prétexte d'insalubrité et tous les clients, nationaux ou étrangers, sont classés de leurs chambres manu militari par la police. Il s'avère

que c'est la Wilaya qui refuse de payer ses arriérés, sommes paralysant la gestion de cet établissement. La justice a pu trancher et faire rouvrir l'hôtel.
- Il exige des agences de voyages qu'ils délivrent des listes portant noms, prénoms, nationalité, numéros de passeports, professions … de leurs touristes, et les déposent 72 heures minimum avant l'arrivée du groupe de 7 instances locales, la première étant son propre cabinet de wilaya, alors qu'il a une Direction du Tourisme à trois pas de là qui reçoit naturellement aussi cette liste … Monsieur le Wali a-t-il réellement besoin de savoir combien de coiffeuses belges ont visités le Hoggar?
- Ces agencies de voyages, comme chacun sait, ont besoin de carburant pour parcourir le désert. Eh bien pour l'obtenir, c'est un véritable parcours du combattant à travers les administrations qui demandent des tas de photocopies de cartes grises, permis de conduire … etc … et remittent enfin au chaffeur un bon pour aller à la station.

En 1999, le Ministère de l'Agriculture, par sa Direction de la wilaya de Tamanrasset, a enjoint aux éleveurs de camelins de recenser leur cheptel. Une commission de wilaya est constituée à cet effet pour immatriculer tous les chamelons nés dans l'année car une prime de 20,000 DA sera allouée pour chaque bébé chameau à son propriétaire. Rendez-vous a été pris, et obligation a été faite aux éleveurs de rassembler leurs troupeaux pour ce contrôle. Ce furent de longues et pénibles transhumances, parfois sur plus de 500 kilomètres, mais les pauvres éleveurs ont obtempéré, et tout le cheptel de la wilaya fut recensé et marqué.

Bien plus tard, lorsque les sommes promises sont arrivées, pour encore humilier et rabaisser ces braves gens, Monsieur le Wali n'a rien trouvé de mieux que d'inventer de nouvelles tracasseries bureaucratiques malhonnêtes pour ne pas payer cette prime tant attendue … Pour détourner ces sommes vers quelles destinations???

La majorité des entreprises de bâtiments et travaux publics sont soumises depuis un an à de telles tracasseries bureaucratiques, des situations jamais réglées, des signatures de marchés reportées indéfiniment … que la survie leur est impossible; elles déménagent ou s'étiolent et ferment.

Enfin, la dernière en date: le commerce du troc entre la wilaya de Tamanrasset et les départments frontaliers du Niger et du Mali connaît ces derniers jours les foudres de Monsieur le Wali.

Notre petit dictateur local s'impose encore une fois et décide d'effacer d'un trait de crayon toute l'histoire commerciale de ces régions, le mode de vie de nos ancêtres perpétué jusque là de génération en génération.

Ainsi, en une année d'exercice, notre actuel wali a réduit à néant les quatre secteurs principaux de l'économie de sa région. Que cherche Monsieur le Wali? Nous ne le savons pas! Par contre, ce qu'il risque de trouver très vite, si vous n'intervenez pas, Monsieur le Président, c'est l'explosion d'une juste colère populaire générale … dont nul ne peut prévoir les dramatiques conséquences. *Nous vous en supplions, Monsieur le Président, évitez-nous cela.*

Car cet énergumène, pourtant chargé de vous représenter auprès de votre peuple, n'incarne ni votre sagesse, ni votre écoute, ni votre éducation, ni votre érudition, ni votre humanisme, ni votre charisme … Quant à votre message politique …!

Citoyens de Tamanrasset

Contested Terrain

Appendix III

Letter to Algeria's Prime Minister from Tamanrasset's Association of Travel Agencies

Association des Agences
de Voyages et de Tourisme
de la Wilaya de Tamanrasset

                                    Monsieur le Premier Ministre
                                    Palais du Gouvernement
                                                 ALGER

Monsieur le Premier Ministre,

Depuis la reprise du tourisme, soit depuis 3 saisons (2000/2001, 2001/2002 et 2002/2003), ce qui coincide avec l'installation de l'actuel Wali, les agencies de Tourisme de la Wilaya de Tamanrasset, et leurs clients n'en peuvent plus: ils subissent des contraintes, qui surgissent brusquement à chaque début des périodes touristiques (octobre/novembre, décembre/janvier, février/mars, et enfin avril, lorsqu' arrivent les groupes de visiteurs), à savoir:

1 – LE CARBURANT: depuis 3 ans, les agencies de voyages sont tenues, à chaque départ et pour chaque voiture, de présenter un dossier au Commissariat Central de la Police, pour avoir seulement une autorisation d'un maximum de 200 litres de carburant par voiture (quota bien souvent insuffisant pour les circuits un peu longs!). Cette autorisation n'est valable que 48 heures, et sans ce papier, les pompes Naftal n'ont pas le droit de servir les agencies de voyages.

Ces orders, d'après la Police et d'après les services de Naftal, émanent de Monsieur le Wali de Tamanrasset, en raison, paraît-il de l'éventuelle fuite de carburant vers les pays frontaliers! Mais, en quoi cela concerne-t-il les Agences de Voyages, les frontières sont bien gardées par l'armée, les douanes, la gendarmerie, la police ... et les fraudeurs facilement repérables!

Conséquences malheureuses: nos chaffeurs et nous-mêmes passons parfois plus de 24 heures à attendre dans la chaine interminable et honteuse de voiture, 4x4, camions ...

Tamanrasset étant le miroir de l'Afrique sub-saharienne, cette ville, capitale de la région la plus touristique de l'Algérie, ne pourrait-elle pas être mieux administrée?

Si ce n'est pas du SABOTAGE, Monsieur le Ministre, qu'est-ce donc que ces agissements?

Et qu'on ne nous dise pas que le carburant n'arrive pas suite aux pluies et aux routes défoncées! Monsieur le Wali n'autorise au dépôt de Naftal, qu'une livraison journalière de 6,000 litres de carburant pour une ville de 100,000 habitants, à vocation touristique et commerciale de surcroît, et pour la wilaya la plus vaste d'Algérie. Nous signalons au passage que notre grande ville ne possède que 2 pompes à carburants.

2 – LES LIAISONS AERIENNES: la plus grande piste d'atterrissage d'Algérie vient d'être terminée et inaugurée à Tamanrasset. Or dès le début de la saison toristiques, les vols réguliers sont annulés ou retournés à Alger sans se poser sous prétexte de mauvaise météorologie sur le Hoggar. Il s'avère qu'on emmène les étrangers dans les hôtels de haut standing, et qu'ils sont obligés de payer leur hébergement que la compagnie Air Algérie ne prend pas en charge.

On sait qu'il a toujours plu et venté au Hoggar et que des avions beaucoup moins perfectionnés que ceux d'aujourd'hui y ont toujours atterri et que les appareils électroniques de guidage (ILS) dont est doté notre aéroport international. Nous en concluons que c'est une volonté de faire remplir les hôtels de la capitale et créer ainsi des obstacles au bon déroulement du tourisme saharien.

Si ce n'est pas du SABOTAGE, Monsieur le Ministre, qu'est-ce donc que ces agissements?

3 – LA SECURITE: Nous nous référons à l'incident du 18.10.2002 à Arak: c'est par la rumeur publique que nous apprenons la prise d'otage de 4 Suisses dans les gorges d'Arak. Aucun communiqué official, ni des autorités, ni de notre direction, ni de personne, ne nous est parvenu

pour éclaircir cet événement et mettre en garde les professionnels. C'est par la presse étrangère (Internet) que nous apprenons les détails exacts. C'est par ce canal aussi que nous apprenons que 17 autres otages étaient algériens, mais on n'en parle pas! Nous sommes perplexes devant cette attitude de désinformation voulue, car il nous semble que nous devrions être les premiers concernés et les premiers informés afin de pouvoir assurer la sécurité des voyageurs don't nous sommes responsables en toute connaissance de cause.

Coment peut-on appeler ces agissements sinon du SABOTAGE?

4 – CONTROLES DOUANIERS: Nous vous informons que notre clientèle ce plaint d'abus de pouvoir de la part des douaniers de l'aéroport d'Alger, notamment des confiscations de jumelles et de G.P.S.

- Un touriste anglais se voit obligé de laisser ses jumelles, avec en plus un paiement de 8,000 DA (huit mille dinars!), jusqu' à ce qu'il menace de rédiger un rapport à Monsieur le Président de la République.
- Un autre voyageur, américain, se voit confisquer son G.P.S. par les douanes d'Alger. Alors qu'il précise qu'il poursuivra son voyage par le Niger sans revenir à Alger!
- De même, à la sortie du territoire algérien à In Guezzam, les voyageurs étrangers sont soumis à un interrogatoire de une à deux heures par les douaniers, sous le prétexte que leur profession n'apparaît pas dans leur passeport. Le dernier acte de ce genre vient de se produire les 27 et 28 octobre 2002.

Il nous semble bien que chacun fait sa loi ... ou sa collection!

Est-ce que vous trouvez cela normal alors que ces visiteurs ont obtenu leur visa pour l'Algérie auprès des représentations consulaires algériennes à l'étranger. Ce visa n'est-il pas la garantie de l'état Algérien pour que ces visiteurs circulent librement et soient débarrassés de toute contrainte durant leur séjour en Algérie???

5 – LA LOURDEUR ADMINISTRATIVE: A chaque groupe de touristes qui nous arrive, nous croulons sous le fardeau de tracasseries administratives inutiles et fastidieuses:

- Fournir en 7 exemplaires les listes des participants à nos voyages, précisant: nom, prénom, date et lieu de naissance, numéro de passeport et date de délivrance, profession ... Etc ...
- Les dossiers auprès de la police pour obtenir les autorisations d'acheter le carburant nécessaire.
- Les ordres de missions des chauffeurs, guides et chameliers, pour les circuits en voitures, à chameux, à pied, acceptés ou non par les contrôles volants (gendarmerie, douane, police).
- Les statistiques mensuelles, trimestrielles et annuelles du nombre des voyageurs classés par nationalité, profession ou destination de voyage ... Déclarations qui font double emploi avec les fameuses listes précédemment fournies ... ETC ...

Par contre, des agencies ou de simples clandestins nationaux ou étrangers viennent travailler sur notre territoire, équipés de tout le matériel de navigation moderne et sophistiqué dernier cri (qu'on ne leur a pas confisqué à la frontière!). Ils ne présentent ni listes, ni ordre de mission, ni ne paient des impôts ou une redevance au Parc National de l'Ahaggar. Ils ne sont pas responsables des saletés laissées sur les sites, du labourage des dunes, ou des destructions du patrimoine national ... Ceux-ci ne sont ni contrôlés, ni inquiétés par personne, malgré nos avertissements répétés aux administrations concernées ... Alors que tout un chacun sait pertinemment que ces richesses archéologiques sont vendues dans le monde entier par le biais d'internet.

Or, la réglementation du Parc National de l'Ahaggar est bien claire en ce domaine: tout visiteur étranger ne peut circuler dans ce Parc National qu'accompagné par une agence algérienne dûment agréée.

Nos remarques et suggestions pourraient durer encore ... mais arrêtons-nous là! Ces sujets ont été maintes fois abordés et rabâchés.

Contested Terrain

Aujourd'hui, nous, agences de Voyages agrées par Le Ministère du Tourisme et motivées par notre profession, avons besoin de connaître la vérité:

EST-CE QUE L'ALGERIE VEUT DE CE TOURISME SAHARIEN OU NON????

Si oui, Monsieur le Premier Ministre, donnez-nous des signes de soutien, au moins d'écoute, et passez l'information jusqu'à nos administrations locales auprès desquelles nous ne rencontrons que des obstacles et des barrages. Administrations dont il faudrait sérieusement choisir les dirigeants. Ceux-ci devraient être de véritables gestionnaires et non des intégristes déguisés:

- L'actuel Wali vient de donner ordre de fermer le seul débit de boissons de la Wilaya, à l'hotel Tahat, parce que ce lieu attire 'les mécréants consommateurs d'alcool et mangeurs de porc' …!!
- Nous avons vu disparaître les panneaux indicateurs de signalisation et apparaître d'autres uniquement en letters arabes … Tamanrasset accueille annuellement des ressortissants de plus de 40 pays étrangers dont aucun ne lit les letters arabes.

Nous rappelons encore une fois le tourisme est la véritable locomotive de l'économie régionale. Et sans le tourisme, il y a longtemps que les populations de l'Extrême-Sud, oubliées et livrées a elles-mêmes, auraient entendu une autre sirène … Et les conséquences politiques et économiques auraient pu être désastreuses pour le pays. Nous n'en citons pour exemple que le modèle des pays riverains (Mali et Niger).

Monsieur le Premier Ministre, ce n'est ni la première fois, ni la dixième fois (nombreux couriers au Ministère du Tourisme) que nous dénonçons cet situation de délabrement qui s'aggrave avec le temps. Nous voulons que notre profession soit reconnue et respectée, et que nos administrateurs soient dignes de ce nom, efficaces et représentatifs de notre pays et de sa politique.

Monsieur le Chef du Gouvernement, dans l'attente d'un signe de votre part montrant un peu d'intérêt pour notre région et ses populations, recevez nos plus respectueuses salutations.

Fait à Tamanrasset, le 01 novembre 2002

Le Président de l'Association

Copie pour information à:
- Monsieur le Ministre de l'Intérieur,
- Monsieur le Ministre du Tourisme,
- Monsieur le Ministre des Transports,
- Monsieur le Ministre des Energies.

The Lesser Gods of the Sahara

Appendix IV

Letter from *Agence Tarahist* (Tamanrasset) to Government Ministers and Regional Authorities

TARAHIST
Agence de Voyages et de Tourisme
Tamanrasset

Madame
La Ministre de la Culture, Alger
Messieurs
Le Ministre du Tourisme, Alger
Le Directeur du Tourisme, Tamanrasset
Le Directeur Regional des Douanes, Tamanrasset
Le Directeur du Parc National de l'Ahaggar, Tamanrasset

Tamanrasset, le 14 Decembre 2002

Madame, Messieurs,

Dans le cadre de la lutte contre le pillage de notre patrimoine culturel préhistorique nous vous adressons ce courier.

Ce n'est pas le première fois que nous attirons votre attention sur le pillage des sites préhistoriques dans nos parc nationaux du Sahara, notamment le Parc National de l'Ahaggar et le Parc National du Tassili n'Ajjer. Nous savons que ce sont surtout des organisations de voyages étrangères qui programment des circuit de pillage professionel avec leurs propres véhicules dans les zones archéologiques du Grand Sud algérien. Nous ne comprenons pas pourquoi ces agences étrangères puissant exercer librement depuis des années (voir copie de l'article dans le Wiesbadener Kurier du 12.06.1990) avec leur personnel, véhicules et matériel étrangers sans licences algériennes ni représentation dans notre pays. Non seulement leur chiffre d'affaire est déclaré, taxé et investi dans leur pays mais toutes les facilités et priorités leur sont accordés. Il nous semble évident que l'arret immédiat de ce genre de tourisme clandestine serait le premier pas dans la lutte contre le pillage de notre patrimoine.

En navigant sur Internet l'été passée nous tombons par hazard sur une organisation allemande nommée *The Rolling Rover* et son site web. Trouvez-en ci-joint une copie. Avec Prof. Jeremy Keenan, notre ami, correspondant, scientifique et membre fondateur de la fondation algérienne 'Fondation Déserts du Monde' nous avons enregistré tous le matériel d'évidence du pillage et de la vente professionel d'outils néolithiques ramassés dans notre pays par cette organisation.

L'urgence de notre souci se prononce du fait que le 11 décembre 2002 *The Rolling Rover* nous adresse une demande de certificat d'hébergement pour un de leur clients. Dates de voyages en Algérie: 14.01 – 04.02.03. Pour l'instant ce n'est pas clair si ce client fait parti d'un groupe ou pas. Par contre comme vous voyez dans le programme des voyages ci-joint, *The Rolling Rover* prévoit ses prochains voyages en Algérie du 02.03 – 28.03.03 Tassili n'Ajjer / Tassili du Hoggar et du 30.03 – 25.04.03 à Adrar n'Ahnet.

Nous sommes persuadés qu'avec toutes les données et toutes les évidences ci-jointes ainsi qu'une stratégie intelligente nos Services des Douanes et le Parc National de l'Ahaggar devraient attraper ses pilleurs professionals en flagrant délit. Un couvrage médiatique aidera certainement à la prévention de ces actes criminals.

Madame, Messieurs, trouvez ci-joint aussi une letter de Prof. Jeremy Keenan pour démontrer l'importance de la protection de ce patrimoine universel et la responsabilité qui nous revient face à toute l'humanité.

Nous comtons sur votre compréhension et votre soutien.

Veuillez agréer, Messieurs, de nos salutations distinguées.

AGENCE TARAHIST.

Contested Terrain

NOTES

I would like to acknowledge the Economic and Social Research Council (ESRC), the British Academy and the Leverhulme Trust for their most generous support.

1. *Wilaya* is an administrative region, equivalent to a French *département*. During the War of Independence the FLN (*Front de Libération Nationale*) divided Algeria into six military regions, known as *wilaya*. Plural of *wilaya* is *wilayat*. The administrative head of a *wilaya*, appointed by the President, is the *wali*.
2. J. Keenan, 'Thirty years of change and continuity in Ahaggar (1971–2002)', *The Tuareg: People of Ahaggar* (London: Sickle Moon Books 2002) new preface, p.xxvi.
3. The background to the relationship between the state and the people of the region is described in more detail in J. Keenan, 'Ethnicity, Regionalism and Political Stability in Algeria's *Grand Sud*', in this volume, pp.67–96.
4. This article is restricted to Ahaggar and the Tassili-n-Ajjer, the Tuareg regions of Algeria. From a more pan-Saharan and industry-wide perspective, one would include within the potential tourism regions of the Central Sahara, the adjoining Acacus, Oubari and Mesak regions of Libya's Fezzan, the Aïr, Ténéré, Djado and Kawar regions of Niger, and, if and when the security situation ever improves, many parts of both northern Chad and northern Mali.
5. H. Lhote, *A la Découverte des Fresques du Tassili* (Paris: Arthaud 1958, 1973); translated as *The Search for the Tassili Frescoes: The Story of the Prehistoric Rock-Paintings of the Sahara* (London: Hutchinson 1959).
6. For example, the Citroen rallies and Berliet expedition.
7. See note 5. Lhote's discovery and its wider implications are discussed in J. Keenan, 'The Lesser Gods of the Sahara', in this volume, pp.193–225.
8. The best known of these in the UK was probably Minitrek.
9. The details of these changing economic circumstances are discussed in more detail in J. Keenan, *The Tuareg: People of Ahaggar* (London: Allen Lane 1977); see also Keenan (note 3); and J. Keenan, 'The End of the Matriline? The Changing Roles of Women and Descent amongst the Algerian Tuareg', in this volume, pp.121–62.
10. On 27 April 1999, General Liamine Zeroual voluntarily relinquished the presidency in advance of the end of his five-year term following his election in November 1995.
11. Algeria's official statistics on tourism are highly questionable. Neither the precise source of these statistics nor their method of compilation is clear. The country has inherited and retained much of what was bad about the 'ancient' French system of administration, particularly its bureaucratic obsession with *chiffres*. In Tamanrasset, as many as five sets of statistics are compiled for different branches of the administration. Local tourist agencies place little faith in 'official' figures, believing them to be a crude form of double or triple accounting to give a more favourable impression of what is happening in the country. For example, according to local agencies, Tamanrasset received 880 tourists between October and the end of the year 2000. If we assume that the two new charter flight services which ran weekly and fortnightly from December 2000 and February 2001 respectively carried approximately 100 passengers per flight, then we can estimate some 2,200 more arrivals between January and April (the end of the tourism season). If we accept the official figure of nearly 8,000, then it means that some 5,000 visitors must either have travelled overland or by scheduled Air Algérie flights in the first four months of the year. That was almost certainly not the case. Having been in the region twice during those four months, I would be more inclined to agree with the local tourism agencies who put the number of tourists for the season at around 2,500–3,000, roughly a third of the 'official' figure.
12. For details of the nomadic economy, see J. Keenan, 'The Last Nomads: Nomadism amongst the Tuareg of Ahaggar (Algerian Sahara)', in this volume, pp.163–92.
13. For demographic details, see Keenan (note 3).
14. M. Museur and R. Pirson, 'Une problématique de passage chez les populations du Hoggar-

261

Tassili: du nomadisme à la sedentarité', *Civilisations* 26/1–2 (1976) p.67.
15. The Tuareg had attempted some diffident gardening, using their slaves, in the vicinity of Ideles around 1840, but they proved unsatisfactory and it was not until 1861 that renewed efforts were made at both Ideles and Tazrouk.
16. Museur and Pirson (note 14) p.68.
17. The most important market in Ahaggar was at Abalessa, where merchants came from Tidikelt each spring to sell leather goods, riding camels and above all slaves. Abalessa was also a staging post for caravans journeying from the Sudan to Tidikelt. See C. de Foucauld, 'Chez les Touaregs: Taitoq, Iforas, Hoggar – Journal de voyage de Père Charles de Foucauld, mars–septembre 1904', *Bulletin de Liaison Saharienne* 3 (1951) pp.20–30, and 4 (1951) pp.19–32.
18. Indeed, the importance of this trade to the Kel Ajjer was such that one of the demands of their chief, Brahim ag Abakada, on finally submitting to the French in 1919, was that all supply caravans in the Tassili-n-Ajjer should be reserved for them. Maurice Vacher, 'L'Amghar des Ajjers: Brahim ag Abakada', *Le Saharien* 80 (1982) pp.4–5.
19. Tamanrasset's growth was fuelled by its expansion as an administrative and garrison centre, the immigration of refuges from Mali and Niger (who were not counted in the town's official census) and the immigration of people from the north seeking safety for themselves and their families. The 1988 census recorded Tamanrasset's population as 82,000. However, as the census was taken in August, when many people are away on holiday, and also excludes the military, the real population of Tamanrasset was probably around 100,000. Some estimates now (2003) place it as approaching 150,000.
20. Two reasons for this are because Djanet is neither a *wilaya*, but falls under Illizi, nor a major garrison town.
21. See comments on impact of this employment amongst the Kel Ahaggar in Keenan 'The End of the Matriline?' (note 9).
22. See Keenan (note 12).
23. UNATA has approximately 180 members.
24. UNATA's 'mission statement'. UNATA's two other main goals are: '*de contribuer au développement et à la promotion touristique du pays*'; and '*de promouvoir l'activité culturelle et artisanale, de créer des emplois et lutter contre la pauvreté*'.
25. 'Rapport d'activité & Programme d'action pour redynamiser le secteur du tourisme', UNATA and ATAWT, Tamanrasset, July 2000.
26. See note 1.
27. These travels were undertaken as part of a British Academy research project to assess the extent and nature of damage to Saharan rock art.
28. *Tifinagh* is the script of the Tuareg's language, Tamahak (or Tamashek in the south).
29. The Dag Rali, some Kel Ahnet and Ait Lowayen (all Kel Ulli descent groups) consider that they descend from the Issebeten, who they believe were the earliest inhabitants of Ahaggar. Most other Tuareg tend to be less specific with regard to tribal descent and affiliation, referring to the Issebeten in almost mythological terms as the peoples who lived in Ahaggar, at some unspecified time in the past, before the present-day Tuareg.
30. One reason why this journey was widely talked about was because most of the seven Tuareg were travelling in areas that they would not normally visit. The places and the art they saw, as well as the damage, were consequently of special interest.
31. G. Anag, M. Cremaschi, S. Di Lernia and M. Liverani, 'Environment, Archaeology, and Oil: The Messak Settafet Rescue Operations (Libyan Sahara)', *African Archaeological Review* 19/2 (June 2002) pp.67–73.
32. See Keenan (note 7).
33. M. Hachid, *Le Tassili Des Ajjer* (Paris: Alger et Editions Paris-Méditerranée 1998).
34. Lhote visited Djerat in 1934.
35. See Keenan (note 7); and Hachid (note 33).
36. The more softly-shaped lava volcanoes are female, and accordingly have female names, often beginning and ending with 't' – like Tahat; while the phallic lava plugs, like Ilaman, perhaps not surprisingly, are male.

Contested Terrain

37. See Keenan (note 12).
38. This was the terrorist attack on the Twin Towers of the World Trade Center in New York and the Pentagon in Washington DC, and the downing of another flight in Pennsylvania.
39. It is for this reason that official tourism statistics for the extreme south are unreliable, being subject to a certain amount of 'massage'.
40. The seminar was organised by the World Tourism Organisation as one of its activities to mark 2002 as the International Year of Ecotourism.
41. The Foundation's head office is in Ghardaia.
42. The *walis* at this time for Tamanrasset and Illizi were Messaoud Jari and Mohammed Oubah, respectively. The former is still (June 2003) in his post, despite numerous calls for his removal, but is expected to be replaced soon. The latter was dismissed in the summer of 2001 following public demonstrations of protest.
43. The *wali*, Mohammed Oubah, was well known to the local Tuareg population, as he had incurred their wrath during his period of office as *sous-préfet* at Tamanrasset in the 1980s. Following his dismissal, his office was investigated by the procurator-fiscal following allegations of embezzlement of funds.
44. The following text was written by and appeared on the English-language website of the publisher of a number of English-language Saharan travel-tour guides. It was published on 9 April 2003, shortly after seven groups (32 individuals) of European tourists 'disappeared' (were kidnapped). The route on which most of them were travelling is called 'A5' by the publisher concerned: 'I can tell you that GPS is not essential along A5 where the first 3 groups went missing, (tho it helps at a couple of places). Wee [sic] first did it in 89 just working it out. Also we did the far side of Tifernine and I did Afara in December (where the other 3 are thought to have disappeared) also without GPS (although I logged it for the next book of course. I was busy chipping out rock pictures for a Sotheby's auction at the time.). It looks like the Alg [sic] travel agencies are winning the protaganda [sic] war - but not for long! CS.'
45. The term 'terrorist' does not appear to have been used noticeably in the media and other public statements within the Saharan context until the post-11 September 2001 era, and perhaps not even until certain activities in 2002 and the hostage kidnapping in the Algerian Sahara in February–March 2003.
46. The word *sahel* means 'shore'.
47. This followed the Tuareg revolts in Mali and Niger in the early 1990s. For summary details, see J. Keenan, 'The Situation of the Tuareg people in North and West Africa', in *The Indigenous World 2001–2002* (Copenhagen: International Working Group for Indigenous Affairs 2002) pp.353–64.
48. This is ascertained primarily from reports of Algeria's customs and excise services.
49. I have personally seen seven large trucks, fully laden with cigarettes, under army protection close to the northern Niger border post at Assamakka while awaiting trans-shipment into Algeria. A colleague witnessed 40 such trucks in Agades.
50. Smugglers are often known as *'trabandistes'*, from the French word *contrebandier*.
51. *L'Expression*, 5 April 2003. Between 1996 and 2002, 1,055,198 cartons have been seized, representing a street value of approximately €10.5m. Statistics provided by the *gendarmerie nationale*.
52. For an understanding of the concept of *Le Grand Sud*, see Keenan (note 3).
53. This word is the berberisation of the French word *chômeur* meaning 'unemployed'. These were the young men, disillusioned by the repression of their own governments and forced by the droughts of the 1970s and 1980s to search further afield for means to support their families, who sought work elsewhere in North Africa. Some went to Algeria, but most finished up in Libya, where they received military training and came under the influence of Islamic radicals and Colonel Qadhafi's ideas of equality and revolution. Some were incorporated into Libya's regular forces; more entered the Libyan-sponsored 'Islamic Legion' and were despatched as Islamic militants to Lebanon, Palestine and Afghanistan. The collapse of the oil price in 1985 led to hundreds of Tuareg being dismissed from the oil

fields and returning home unemployed and resentful. They were joined in the following year by those released from Libya's armed forces after Qadhafi's humiliating failure to annex Chad. Finally, the dissolution of the Islamic legion and the Soviet evacuation of Afghanistan led to a further wave of unemployed and restless young men with considerable military experience returning to their home areas. Their Qadhafi-inspired ideas of equality and justice merely added to the further dislocation of traditional society. Many of them played prominent roles in the Tuareg revolts in Niger and Mali in the 1990s. Many of them subsequently found it hard to settle down and have drifted into the world of smuggling and 'banditry'. They are often referred to as Kel Ishumar.

54. For example, Alambo undertook a number of 'hijacks' in 2002, including an attack on local security forces in Aïr in July 2002 in which three policemen were killed.
55. In Niger, a number of attacks on tourists, usually denied by the authorities, may have been the work of Alambo or one of a number of such 'bandits' operating in this extensive region. For example, in November 2002, four vehicles driven by French tourists were hijacked near Chirfa (Djado region of north-east Niger). The women were raped, the men beaten up and the vehicles stolen. The attackers have not been caught.
56. *Laouer* is Arabic, meaning 'one-eyed' (French *Le borgne*). This results from his having reputedly lost an eye while fighting the Russians in Afghanistan.
57. Approximately 100 articles have appeared in the main Algerian newspapers and press agencies in the last quarter of 2002 and the first half of 2003.
58. Copies were sent to the Ministers of the Interior, Tourism, Transport and Energy.
59. The tracks of the hostage-takers indicated that they were not well acquainted with the desert, thus enabling the *gendarmes* to catch up with them at Tin Gherour, some 600km due south. Two hours after telephoning news of the capture to Tamanrasset, the *gendarmes* apparently received orders to release them.
60. Since 11 September 2001, American intelligence services (FBI, CIA and NSA) have intensified their links with Algeria's security services in their 'War on Terror'. The American services have shown particular interest in the GIA and especially the GSPC. They are also interested in establishing listening bases in southern Algeria so that they can monitor the activities of Mokhtar ben Mokhtar, whom they see as part of an alleged *al-Qaeda* network that is believed to be entrenching itself across the Sahelian countries of Mali, Niger, Chad and Somalia and becoming a major threat to American regional interests. Although officially 'secret', the developing relationship between US and Algerian intelligence services and personnel is widely reported in the Algerian state-controlled media. See, for example, *Le Quotidien d'Oran*, 10 Feb. 2003.
61. With only two filling stations in towns, drivers were obliged sometimes to queue for 24 hours at the pumps. The 48-hour limitation of validity of the permit meant that travel agencies could not prepare vehicles properly for their clients and would often have to employ additional drivers simply to queue at the pumps.
62. It was unnecessary as the town holds huge strategic reserves and the road was reopened fairly quickly.
63. Fuel is substantially cheaper in Algeria than in Niger and has always been a highly profitable form of contraband.
64. The *wali* came from Batna, a town located between the Hodna and Aures massifs. Many people refer to this region, which is the redoubt of the GSPC, as being in the grip of the 'eastern clans' and their associated 'mafia'. The citizens of Tamanrasset noted that since the appointment of the *wali*, several local business contracts have been awarded to what they refer to as the 'Batna connection'.
65. Copies of the letter, along with all supporting documentation ('the dossier'), were sent to: the Minister of Culture and the Minister of Tourism in Algiers, the Director of Tourism in Tamanrasset, the Regional Director of Customs at Tamanrasset, the Director of the Ahaggar National Park, the *wali* of Tamanrasset, the CTRI and UNESCO's Director of Culture and Heritage in Paris.
66. J. Keenan, 'Tourism, development and conservation: A Saharan perspective', Proceedings of

Contested Terrain

the Conference on Natural Resources and Cultural Heritage of the Libyan Desert, Tripoli, Libya, 14–21 Dec. 2002, *Libyan Studies* 34 (2003, in press).
67. The conference was formally hosted and organised by the President of the *Assemblée Populaire du Wilaya* (APW) of Illizi. The political initiative behind the conference came from the newly appointed *wali*, M. Taft Abdel Haq.
68. The *wali*, possibly politically embarrassed by his failure to attend the Djanet Conference, recognised the new ATAWT board the day after the Djanet Conference ended!
69. *El Watan*, 12 March 2003.
70. Damage to the Sahara's prehistoric heritage has been caused by people, including professional archaeologists and prehistorians, of many nationalities. See Keenan (note 7); and Keenan (note 66). However, at present, most of the known operators looting prehistoric artefacts for commercial sale are based in Germany.
71. This claim was made by Algerian tourism officials on 23 April.
72. Tamelrik is approximately 150km to the south-west of Illizi and not, as nearly all domestic and foreign journalists and government spokesmen reiterated over a period of nearly six months, 150km to the north-east of the town.
73. Several of these elements who moved into southern Algeria at this time were deported by the Algerian authorities. I do not know the exact numbers, but it seems to have been in the dozens.
74. It has been in the interests of both US and Algerian intelligence services to show that Islamic fundamentalist 'terrorists' have been establishing themselves in southern Algeria.
75. Apart from the Djanet–Illizi highway and the Arak and Amguid gorges, which are all guarded by the military, 'bandits' wishing to traverse southern Algeria from north to south are obliged to travel far to the west of Ahaggar or find discrete passages through the Tassili. One such passage cuts through the Tassili at the northern apex of Erg Tihodaine and exits into the region where most of the tourists were kidnapped.
76. Since the resumption of tourism in 1999, tour operators have claimed quite correctly that Algeria's extreme south (the regions of Ahaggar and Tassili-n-Ajjer) is statistically the safest region in the Sahara in terms of hijacks and other such 'attacks' on tourists.
77. See Appendix III and Keenan (note 47) pp.353–4.
78. Seventeen hostages were released in the first group. Of the remaining 15, one died before being moved to Mali.
79. The book, *Algerische Sahara*, is produced by Gerhard Göttler, Erika Därr and Klaus Därr (Hrsg.). The latest edition, produced in 2002, has been updated by Gerhard Göttler, who is well known in the German-speaking world for his work on the Tuareg (*Die Tuareg*) published in 1989.
80. See 'Introduction: Indigenous Rights and a Future Politic amongst Algeria's Tuareg after Forty Years of Independence', in this volume, pp.1–26.
81. Although it is true that Algeria's crisis had a 'knock-on' effect on tourism in Mali and Niger, the primary reason for the collapse of tourism in those two countries was the Tuareg rebellions.
82. See Keenan (note 2); and also J. Keenan, 'The Sahara's Indigenous People, the Tuareg, fear Environmental Catastrophe', *Indigenous Affairs* 1 (2002) pp.50–57.
83. See Keenan (note 80).
84. Note the use of the expression *Le Grand Sud*; see Keenan (note 3).

Bibliography

Abdel Djalil, R.P., 'Aspects intérieurs de l'Islam', *Bulletin de Liaison Saharienne* V/16 (mars 1964).
Abun-Nasr Jamil, M., *History of the Maghreb*, 2nd edn. (Cambridge: Cambridge University Press 1971).
Alimen, H., F. Beucher and H. Lhote (with the collaboration of G. Delibrias), 'Les gisements néolithiques de Tan-Tartraït et d'In-Itinen, Tassili-n-Ajjer', *Bulletin de la Société préhistorique française* LXV (1968) pp.421–56.
Anag, G., M. Cremaschi, S. Di Lerna and M. Liverani, 'Environment, Archaeology, and Oil: The Messak Settafet Rescue operation (Libyan Sahara)', *African Archaeological Review* 19/2 (June 2002) pp.67–73.
Barth, F., *Nomads of South Persia* (London: Allen & Unwin 1961).
Barth, F., 'Descent and Marriage Reconsidered', in J. Goody (ed.), *The Character of Kinship* (Cambridge: Cambridge University Press 1973) pp.3–19.
Barth, H., *Reisen und Entdeckungen in Nord- und Central Afrika in den Jahren 1849 bis 1855*, 4 vols. (Gotha: 1857–58; French trans. Paris: Didot 1863).
Barth, H., *Voyages et Découvertes dans l'Afrique septentrionale et central pendant les années 1849 à 1855*, 4 vols. (Paris: A. Bohne 1860–61).
Bates, O., *The Eastern Libyans* (London: 1914).
Batutah, Ibn, *Voyages d'Ibn Batutah*, I–IV, trans. Detrémy and Sanguinetti (Paris: 1853–58).
Baumann, M., *Volkerkunde von Afrika* (Essen: 1940).
Behr, E., *The Algerian Problem* (London: Penguin 1961).
Bekri, El, *Description de l'Afrique Septentrionale*, trans. MacGuckin de Slane (Paris: 1859).
Benhazera, M., *Six Mois chez les Touareg du Ahaggar* (Alger: Jourdan 1908).
Bernard A., and N. Lacroix, *La pénétration saharienne (1830–1906)* (Alger: Imprimerie algérienne 1906).
Bernus, E., *et al.* (eds.), *Nomades et commandants: Administration et sociétés nomads dans l'ancienne A.O.F* (1993).
Berque, J., 'Nomads and Nomadism in the Arid Zone', *International Social Science Journal* XI/4 (1964).
Bissuel, H., *Les Touaregs de l'ouest* (Alger: Jourdan 1888).

Bibliography

Blanguernon, Claude, *Le Hoggar* (Paris: Arthaud 1955).
Bloch, M., 'The Long Term and the Short Term: The Economic and Political Significance of the Morality of Kinship', in J. Goody (ed.), *The Character of Kinship* (Cambridge: Cambridge University Press 1973) pp.75–87.
Bourgeot, A., 'Le Costume Masculin des Kel Ahaggar', *Libyca* XVII/1 (1969) pp.355–76.
Bourgeot, A., 'Idéologies et appellations ethniques: l'exemple twareg. Analyse des catégories sociales', *Cahiers d'Etudes Africaines* XII/48 (1972).
Bourgeot, A., 'Contribution à l'étude de la parenté touarègue', *Revue de l'Occident Musulman et de la Méditerranée* 21 (1976) pp.9–30.
Bourgeot, A., 'Les échanges transsahariens, la Senoussiya et les révoltes twareg de 1916–1917', *Cahiers d'Etudes Africaines* 18 (1978).
Bourgeot, A., 'Les mouvements de resistance et de collaboration (Algérie) de 1880 à 1920', paper delivered at the Symposium on 'Resistance in Nomadic Societies: The Colonization of the Sahara: 1880–1940', at the 82nd Annual Meeting of the American Anthropological Association, Chicago, 16–20 Nov. 1983, p.11, published in *Annuaire de l'Afrique du Nord* (1984).
Bourgeot, A., 'L'agro-pastoralisme des Touaregs Kel-Owey, Au contact Sahara-Sahel', *Au contact Sahara-Sahel: Milieux et sociétés du Niger, Revue de Géographie Alpine* (1994) pp.137–56.
Brenans, Lieutenant, 'Les Roches Peintes du Tassili-n-Ajjer', Congrès Panafricain de Préhistoire, *Actes de la IIe Session*, Alger 1952 (Paris: Arts et Métiers Graphiques 1955) pp.65–219.
Breuil, H., *The White Lady of the Brandberg* (Paris: Trianon Press 1955).
Breuil, H., 'Les Roches Peintes du Tassili-n-Ajjer: d'après les relevés du Colonel Brenans', in Congrès Panafricain de Préhistoire, *Actes de la IIe Session*, Alger 1952 (Paris: Arts et Métiers Graphiques 1955) pp.165–219.
Charlet, C., 'L'Oasis de Djanet', *Bulletin de la Société de Géographie d'Alger et de l'Afrique du Nord* 17 (1912).
Chippindale, C., and P.S.C. Taçon, *The Archaeology of Rock-Art* (Cambridge: Cambridge University Press 1998).
Coche, R., 'Les Figurations rupestres du Mertoutek (Sahara Central)', *Journal des Savants* (Nov.–Dec. 1935).
Congrès Panafricain de Préhistoire, *Actes de la IIe Session*, Alger 1952 (Paris: Arts et Métiers Graphiques 1955).
Cortier, Captain, *Notes de préhistoire saharienne* (Paris: Larose 1914).
Couret, R., 'L'embuscade de Hassi-Tanezrouft et la mort du Brigadier Paul Bechet au Fezzan (1916–1918)', *Revue Historique de l'Armée* 23/4 (1967) pp.97–109.

Cremaschi, M., 'Le paléoenvironnement du Tertiare tardif à l'Holocène', *Art rupestre du Sahara. Les pasteurs-chasseurs du Messak libyen. Les Dossiers de l'Archéologie*, No.197 (Oct. 1994) pp.4–13.

de Bary, Erwin, *Le dernier rapport d'un européen sur Ghât et les Touareg de l'Aïr (traduit et annoté par H. Schirmer)* (Paris: Libraire Fischbacher 1898).

de Chasseloup-Laubat, F., *Art rupestre au Hoggar* (Paris: Plon 1938).

Dubief, J., 'Découvertes, préhistoriques et archéologiques dans le Sahara central', *Travaux de l'Institut de Recherches Sahariennes* IV (1947).

Dubief, J., 'Les Oûraghen des Kel-Ajjer: Chronologie et nomadism', *TIRS* XIV (1956) pp.85–137.

Duveyrier, H., *Les Touaregs du Nord* (Paris: Challamel 1864).

Ferry, Colonel J., 'Le Sahara dans la Guerre, 1914–1918', *Revue Historique de l'Armée* 23/4 (1967) pp.85–96.

Firth, R., 'Marriage and the classificatory system relationship', *Journal of the Royal Anthropological Institute* 60 (1930) pp.235–68.

Foucauld, C. de, *Poésies touarègues – Dialecte de l'Ahaggar*, vol.1 (Paris: Leroux 1925).

Foucauld, C. de, *Poésies touarègues*, 2 vols. (Paris: Leroux 1930).

Foucauld, C. de, 'Chez les Touaregs: Taitoq, Iforas, Hoggar – Journal de voyage de Père Charles de Foucauld, mars–septembre 1904', *Bulletin de Liaison Saharienne* 3 (1951) pp.20–30, and 4 (1951) pp.19–32.

Foucauld, C. de, *Dictionnaire Touareg–Française, dialecte de l'Ahaggar*, 4 vols. (Paris: Imprimerie nationale de France 1951–52).

Foucauld, C. de, 'Chez les Touaregs (Taitoq, Iforas, Hoggar) mars–septembre 1904', *Bulletin trimestriel des amitiés Charles de Foucauld* 117 (1994–95).

Foureau, F., *Rapport sur ma mission au Sahara et chez les Touareg Azdjer* (Paris: A. Challamel 1894).

Foureau, F., *D'Alger au Congo par le Tchad* (Paris: Masson 1902).

Frobenius, Leo, *Ekade Ektab Die Felsbilder Fezzans* (Leipzig: Otto Harrassowitz 1937).

Fugelstad, F.A., *History of Niger 1850–1960* (Cambridge: Cambridge University Press 1983).

Gardel, V., *Les Touareg Ajjer* (Alger: Baconnier 1961).

Gardi, Rene, *Blue Veils, Red Tents* (London: Hutchinson 1953).

Gast, M., 'Premier résultats d'une mission éthnographique en Ahaggar', *Libyca* XIII (1965) pp.325–32.

Gast, M., *Alimentation des populations de l'Ahaggar* (Paris: Mémoires du CRAPE VIII 1968).

Gast, M., 'Temazlayt (Contrat de protection chez les Kel Ahaggar)', *Encyclopédie Berbère*, Cahier 7 (1972).

Bibliography

Gast, M., 'Les Kel Rela: historique et essai d'analyse du groupe de commandement des Kel-Ahaggar', *Revue de l'Occident Musulman et de la Méditerranée* 21 (1976) pp.47–66.

Gast, M., 'Compléments à la rubrique Attici ag Amellal', *Encyclopédie Berbère*, Cahier 25 (1980).

Gast, M., 'Foreword', in M. Hachid, *Le Tassili des Ajjer* (Paris: Alger et Editions Paris-Méditerranée 1998).

Goffman, E., 'The Nature of Deference and Demeanour', *American Anthropologist* 58 (1956) pp.473–502.

Goffman, E., *The Presentation of Self in Everyday Life* (London: Penguin 1969).

Goody, J., 'The Mother's Brother and the Sister's Son in West Africa', *Journal of the Royal Anthropological Institute* 89 (1959) pp.61–88.

Goody, J., 'Sideways or Downwards? Lateral and Vertical Succession, Inheritance and Descent in Africa and Eurasia', *Man* 5/4 (1970) pp.627–38.

Goody, J. (ed.), *The Character of Kinship* (Cambridge: Cambridge University Press 1973).

Gordon, R.J., *The Bushman Myth: The Making of a Namibian Underclass* (Boulder, CO: Westview 1992).

Graham, T., 'Resistance and Collaboration among the Northern Tuareg, 1900–1920', unpublished MA thesis, SOAS, University of London, 1985.

Hachid, M., *Le Tassili des Ajjer* (Paris: Alger et Editions Paris-Méditerranée 1998); translated as *The Tassili of the Ajjer* (Paris: Alger et Editions Paris-Méditerranée 2000).

Hamet, I., 'Les Kounta', *Revue du Monde Musulman* XV (Sept. 1911).

Keenan, J., 'The Tuareg Veil', *Revue de l'Occident Musulman et de la Méditerranée* 17/1 (1974) pp.107–18.

Keenan, J., 'Some theoretical considerations on the *temazlayt* relationship', *Revue de l'Occident Musulman et de la Méditerranée*, 21/1 (1976) pp.33–46.

Keenan, J., 'Power and Wealth are Cousins: Descent, Class and Marital Strategies among the Kel Ahaggar (Tuareg – Sahara)', *Africa* 47/3 (1977) pp 242–52, and 47/4 (1977) pp.333–42.

Keenan, J., *The Tuareg: People of Ahaggar* (London: Allen Lane 1977; reprinted London: Sickle Moon Books 2002).

Keenan, J., 'The Theft of Saharan Rock-Art', *Antiquity* 74 (July 2000).

Keenan, J., 'The Father's Friend: Returning to the Tuareg as an Elder', *Anthropology Today* 16/4, Royal Anthropological Institute, London (Aug. 2000) pp.7–11.

Keenan, J., *Sahara Man: Travelling with the Tuareg* (London: John Murray 2001).

Keenan, J., 'How and Why the Tuareg Poisoned the French: Some Reflections on *efelehleh* and the Motives of the Tuareg in Massacring the Flatters Expedition of 1881', in Barnaby Rogerson (ed.), *North Africa Travel*, vol.1 (London: Sickle Moon Books 2001).

Keenan, J., 'Thirty years of change and continuity in Ahaggar (1971–2001)', in J. Keenan, *The Tuareg: People of Ahaggar* (London: Sickle Moon Books 2002) new preface.

Keenan, J., 'The Situation of the Tuareg People in North and West Africa', in *The Indigenous World, 2001–2002* (Copenhagen: International Working Group for Indigenous Affairs 2002) pp.353–64.

Keenan, J., 'The Sahara's Indigenous Peoples, the Tuareg, Fear Environmental Catastrophe', *Indigenous Affairs* (Quarterly Journal of the International Working Group for Indigenous Affairs) 1 (2002) pp.50–57.

Keenan, J., 'The Development or Re-development of Tourism in Algeria', in Mohamed Saad (ed.), *Transition and Development: The Algerian Experience* (2002).

Keenan, J., 'Tourism, development and conservation: A Saharan perspective', Proceedings of the Conference on Natural Resources and Cultural Heritage of the Libyan Desert, Tripoli, Libya, 14–21 Dec. 2002, *Libyan Studies* 34 (2003, in press).

Killian, C., 'Quelques observations et découvertes de ma mission de 1927–1928 aux confines Imouhar-Téda dans le Sahara Central et Oriental', *Compte Rendu de l'Académie des Inscriptions et Belles-Lettres* (1929) pp.318–25.

Kinahan, J., 'Traumland Südwest: Two Moments in the History of German Archaeological Inquiry in Namibia', in H. Häerke (ed), *Archaeology, Ideology and Society: The German Experience*, vol.7 of 'Gesellschaften und Staaten im Epochenwandel' (Frankfurt am Main: Peter Lang 2000) pp.353–74.

Lajoux, J.-D., *Merveilles du Tassili n'Ajjer* (Paris: Ed. Du Chêne 1962); translated as *The Rock Paintings of Tassili* (London: Thames and Hudson 1963).

Larocca, A., 'Rock Art Recording in the Jebel Bani, Southern Morocco', unpublished MA thesis, Institute of Archaeology, University College London, 2001.

Lecointre, Captain, 'Les Touareg Hoggar: Petite Société Berbère en face de l'Islam et du monde arabe', *Contre d'etudes sur L'Afrique et l'Asie modernes* 2152 (1953).

Lehuraux, L., *Les Français au Sahara* (Alger: Editions Les territories du Sud 1936).

Le Poitevin, G., 'Avec nos ancêtres les artistes du Tassili', *Algeria* (April 1950) pp.39–45.

Bibliography

Le Quellec, J.-L., *Symbolisme et art rupestre au Sahara* (Paris: L'Harmattan 1993).

Lettre de l'Association des Amis de l'Art Rupestre Saharien (AARS), 'Numéro spécial en mémoire de Henri Lhote' 20/2 (2001), published privately by the AARS.

Lévi-Strauss, C., *Structural Anthropology* (New York: Basic Books 1963).

Lhote, Henri, 'Notes sur les peintures rupestres de Mertoutek', *Journ. Soc. Afric.* XII (1942) pp.259–60.

Lhote, Henri, *Les Touaregs du Hoggar* (Paris: Payot 1944, 1955).

Lhote, Henri, 'Au sujet du Port du Voile chez les Touareg et les Teda', *Notes Africaines* 52 (octobre 1951).

Lhote, Henri, 'Inventaire et Références Bibliographiques des Peintures Rupestres de l'Afrique nord-équatoriale', in Congrès Panafricain de Préhistoire, *Actes de la IIe Session*, Alger 1952 (Paris: Arts et Métiers Graphiques 1955) pp.153–62.

Lhote, Henri, *A la Découverte des Fresques du Tassili* (Paris: Arthaud 1958, 1973); translated as *The Search for the Tassili Frescoes: The Story of the Prehistoric Rock-Paintings of the Sahara* (London: Hutchinson 1959).

Lhote, Henri, *Les gravures rupestres de l'Oued Djereat (Tassili-n-Ajjer)*, 2 vols. (Paris: Mémoires du CRAPE XXV 1975–76).

Lhote, Henri, *Vers d'autres Tassili: Nouvelles découvertes au Sahara* (Paris: Arthaud, col. Clefs du savoir 1976).

Lhote, Henri, 'Oasis of Art in the Sahara', *National Geographic* 172/2 (Aug. 1987).

Maack, R., 'Über die Buschleute und ihre Feisenbilder in Suedwest-Afrika', unpublished typescript, National Library of Namibia, 1921.

Malaurie, J., 'Touareg et noirs du Hoggar: aspects de la situation actuelle', *Annales Economies, Sociétés, Civilisations* VIII/3 (1953) pp.338–46.

Mathieu, M., 'La Mission Afrique Centrale', thèse du 3ème cycle, University of Toulouse-Mirail, 1975.

Merton, R.K., *Social Theory and Social Structure* (Glencoe, IL: Free Press 1957).

Metois, J., *La soumission des Touaregs du Nord* (Paris: Challamel 1906).

Monod, T., *L'Adrar Ahnet* (Paris: Institut d'Ethnologie 1932).

Mori, Fabrizio, *Tadrart Acacus: Arte rupestre e culture del Sahara preistorico* (Torino: Einaudi 1965).

Mori, Fabrizio, *Le grandi civiltà del Sahara antico* (Torino: Bollati Boringhieri 2000).

Murdock, G.P., *Africa: Its Peoples and their Culture History* (New York: McGraw-Hill 1959).

Murphy, R.F., 'Social Distance and the Veil', *American Anthropologist* 66 (1964) pp.1257–74.

Murphy, R.F., 'Tuareg Kinship', *American Anthropologist* 69 (1967) pp.163–70.
Museur, M., and R. Pirson, 'Une problématique de passage chez les populations du Hoggar-Tassili: du nomadisme à la sedentarité', *Civilisations* 26/1–2 (1976).
Muzzolini, A., 'Masques et théromorphes dans l'art rupestre du Sahara central', *Archéo-Nil* 1 (1991) pp.17–42.
Muzzolini, A., *Les Images Rupestres du Sahara* (Toulouse: Alfred Muzzolini 1995).
Nicolaisen, Johannes, 'Essai sur la réligion et la magie touaregues', *Folk* 3 (1961).
Nicolaisen, Johannes, *Ecology and Culture of the Pastoral Tuareg* (Copenhagen: University of Copenhagen 1963).
Nicolas, J., 'Le voilement des Twareg: Contributions à l'étude de l'Air', *Mémoires de l'IFAN* 10 (1950) pp.497–503.
Norris, H.T., *The Tuaregs: Their Islamic Legacy and its Diffusion in the Sahel* (Warminster, Wilts: Aris and Phillips 1975).
Pandolfi, Paul, *Les Touaregs de l'Ahaggar* (Paris: Karthala 1998).
Pandolfi, Paul, 'Tijaniyya et Touaregs du Sahara central à la fin du XIXème siècle: l'exemple de la délégation de 1892', *Islam et sociétés au sud du Sahara* 10 (1996) pp.25–41.
Peters, E.L., 'Nomads; nomadism', in G.D. Mitchell (ed.), *A Dictionary of Sociology* (London: Routledge & Kegan Paul 1968) p.125.
Porch, D., *The Conquest of the Sahara* (London: Cape 1985).
Prasse, K.G., 'L'Origine du mot Amazig', *Acta Orientalia* XXIII/3–4 (1959) pp.197–200.
Prasse, K.G., *Manuel de grammaire touarègue (tahaggart)*, 3 vols. (Copenhagen: Editions de l'Université de Copenhague/Akademisk Forlag 1972–74).
Radcliffe-Brown, A.R., *Structure and Function in Primitive Society* (Glencoe, IL: Free Press and London: Cohen and West 1952).
'Report on the 6th Session of the Commission on Human Rights Working Group on the Declaration on the Rights of Indigenous Peoples', in *The Indigenous World, 2000–2001* (Copenhagen: International Working Group for Indigenous Affairs 2001) pp.414–54.
Reygasse, M., *Contribution á l'étude des gravures rupestres et inscriptions tifinagh du Sahara Central* (Alger: Jourdan 1932).
Reygasse, M., 'Gravures et peintures rupestres du Tassili des Ajjers', *L'Anthroplogie* XLV/5–6 (1935) pp.553–71.
Richer, A., *Les Touaregs du Niger (Région de Tombouctou-Gao): Les Oulliminden* (Paris: Larose 1924).

Bibliography

Roberts, H., *The Battlefield Algeria, 1988–2002* (London: Verso 2003).
Rogerson, Barnaby (ed.), *North Africa Travel*, vol.1 (London: Sickle Moon Books 2001).
Rodd, F., 'The origin of the Tuareg', *Geographical Journal* 67 (1926) pp.27–52.
Sahara: 10,000 Jahre Zwichen Weïde und Wuste (no date).
Scheffler, H.W., 'Ancestor Worship in Anthropology: Or, Observations on Descent and Descent Groups', *Current Anthropology* (1966) pp.541–51.
Soleilhavoup, F., 'Les oeuvres rupestres sahariennes sont-elles menacées?', *Publication de l'Office du Parc national du Tassili* (1978).
Stenning, D.J., *Savannah Nomads* (Oxford: Oxford University Press 1959).
Steward, C.C., with E.K. Stewart, *Islam and Social Order in Mauritania* (Oxford: Clarendon 1973).
Triaud, J.-L., 'Un mauvais départ: 1920, l'Aïr en ruines', in E. Bernus *et al.* (eds.), *Nomades et commandants: Administration et sociétés nomads dans l'ancienne A.O.F* (1993) pp.93–100.
Tschudi, Y., 'Die Felsmalereien im Edjeri, Tamrit, Assakao, Meddak (Tassili-n-Ajjer)', in Congrès Panafricain de Préhistoire, *Actes de la IIe Session*, Alger 1952 (Paris: Arts et Métiers Graphiques 1955) pp.761–7.
Tschudi, Y., *Nordafrikanische Felsmalereien* (Firenze: Sansoni 1955); translated as *Les Peintures rupestres du Tassili-N-Ajjer* (Neuchâtel: 1956).
UNESCO, *Nomades et Nomadisme au Sahara*, Recherches sur la zone aride – XI (Paris: UNESCO 1963).
Vacher, Maurice, 'L'Amghar des Ajjers: Brahim ag Abakada', *Le Saharien* 80 (1982).
Vita-Finzi, C., and R.A. Kennedy, 'Seven Saharan Sites', *Journal of the Royal Anthropological Institute* 95 (1965) pp.195–213.
Westermarck, E., *Ritual and Belief in Morocco*, 2 vols. (London: 1926).

Abstracts

Introduction: Indigenous Rights and a Future Politic amongst Algeria's Tuareg after Forty Years of Independence

The article serves as an introduction to the other seven articles in the volume, by describing the broad geographical, political and demographic situation of the various Tuareg groups and explaining the nature of the relationship between Algeria's Tuareg and the Algerian state over the 40 years of Independence. The article focuses on the question of indigenous rights and concludes that if the two main instruments of indigenous rights legislation, the ILO Convention and the UN's Draft Declaration on the Rights of Indigenous Peoples, were to be enacted in Algeria at this moment, Algeria would be found to be in compliance with the majority of clauses, and far more than neighbouring Tuareg states (Niger and Mali). The article shows that most of the problems facing Algeria's Tuareg today stem from general problems of modernisation, along with the impact on the region of Algeria's 'Islamist problem', rather than any abuse of their human or indigenous rights. Indeed, the major criticism of Algeria is not of its policies towards the Tuareg but rather the quality of its governance. The article concludes by suggesting that the Central Sahara, or at least that part of it which traditionally belonged to the Tuareg, has reached a critical watershed. This is because the key issues underlying the current complex state of affairs in Algeria's extreme south, namely the loss of tourism resulting from Algeria's 'Islamist problem', the 'invasion' of the region by *les gens du nord*, the threats being posed to the region's cultural and environmental heritage, the poor quality of local governance, and the security weaknesses exposed by the recent hostage crisis, have coalesced in a way that will almost certainly herald the development of a new politic, not only in the Algerian Sahara but throughout all Tuareg regions.

From Tit (1902) to Tahilahi (2002): A Reconsideration of the Impact of and Resistance to French Pacification and Colonial Rule by the Tuareg of Algeria (the Northern Tuareg)

This article attempts to capture and analyse key elements of the pre-colonial and early colonial period of Tuareg history before they become lost or fixed forever in what is a predominantly French and imperialistic perspective. This perspective, which provides the sole literary record of this crucial era, has contributed not only to a very distorted notion of the social structure and dynamics of Tuareg society at the time of the French arrival in the Central Sahara, and what is meant by 'traditional' society, but also, because of the Tuareg's own lack of written records, to the Tuareg's own increasingly misconstrued notions of their history. The article shows that the picture of Tuareg society that France presented to the world after the final pacification of the Algerian Sahara in 1920 was a semblance – almost a caricature – of traditional society.

Ethnicity, Regionalism and Political Stability in Algeria's *Grand Sud*

The article analyses changes in the socio-ethnic and political landscape of Algeria's extreme south, notably the Tuareg regions of Ahaggar and Ajjer, since Algerian independence in 1962. It argues that the 'Tuareg problem' of today is not only a conceptually different social construct to the 'Tuareg problem' of the 1960s, but that its continued use as an analytical tool is of questionable value. The article explains how new social and political currents, notably a sense of regionalism and the potentially inflammatory notion of *Le Grand Sud*, are replacing the more traditional ethnic social categories in shaping the region's social and political terrain. Unless more democratically inclusive development policies are adopted in the region, the emergence of these new social and political forces may come to threaten the political stability of this strategically important part of the Sahara.

Dressing for the Occasion: Changes in the Symbolic Meanings of the Tuareg Veil

The veiling of Tuareg men has been their most distinctive custom and the most dominant symbol of 'Tuaregness'. This article describes the many aspects of the veil and veiling and provides a summary review of the literature and the many explanations that have been given for Tuareg veiling. The last such analysis was undertaken in 1971, a decade after Algerian independence. It explained the many values and symbolic meanings that were attached to veiling, especially in relation to changes in both the traditional magico-religious belief systems and aspects of their social organisation. It concluded by saying that the acceleration of the prevailing changes in Ahaggar society may lead to further considerable changes in both the traditional belief systems and social structure of Tuareg society, with the possible disappearance of the veil in its traditional form and meaning. This article examines the changes that have taken place in both the deportment of the veil and its many symbolic meanings and values in the light of the complex changes that have taken place in Tuareg society over the last 30 or more years. The article shows how a dominant and multivocal symbol, such as the Tuareg veil, can act as a society's weathervane, often indicating subtle and sensitive changes taking place in a society's complex array of values and beliefs.

The End of the Matriline? The Changing Roles of Women and Descent amongst the Algerian Tuareg

This article examines the changing roles and significance of descent and matrilineality in the social organisation of the Kel Ahaggar Tuareg from traditional, pre-colonial times to the present, a period in excess of a hundred years. The article explores how changes in the meaning of descent, alongside such radical changes as sedentarisation and various other aspects of modernisation, notably the intrusion of certain Islamo-Arabic influences, have not only 'downgraded' the importance of both descent and the matriline in recent years, but have also resulted in a considerable degradation of the position of women in social life, while posing serious threats to their health and general well-being. The article also includes a detailed analysis of changes in marriage patterns amongst the Kel Ahaggar over the last 40 years. The analysis, based on the comparison of all marriages undertaken since the 1960s by two descent groups belonging to different social classes with marriages undertaken by the two same groups prior to the 1960s, reveals that both groups have adopted a new range of marital strategies to manage and cope with the dramatic changes that these groups, and their society as a whole, have experienced over the last two generations.

The Last Nomads: Nomadism amongst the Tuareg of Ahaggar (Algerian Sahara)

The Tuareg of Algeria, the Kel Ahaggar and Kel Ajjer, were traditionally nomadic pastoralists. In 1962, at the time of Algerian independence, an estimated 90 per cent of them (Kel Ahaggar) were living a predominantly nomadic existence. A decade later, that figure had fallen to an estimated 50 per cent. Today it is estimated at 10–15 per cent. The article explores the nature and survival of nomadism in Ahaggar (and Ajjer) from traditional, pre-colonial times to the present day. It reveals that the fundamental nature of nomadism in Ahaggar has been its almost continuous process of change, through pre-colonial, traditional times, through the colonial period, and again over the 40 or so years of Algerian independence to the present day. This dynamic reflects an almost continual adaptation to new impediments and opportunities, manifested in the almost continuous search for and acquisition of new resources and means of supplementation and an almost perpetual ongoing transformation of the associated social relations of production. Field research over the last four years into the way in which the remaining 3–4,000 nomads are surviving, suggests that we may currently be witnessing a modest revival in the nomadic economy. There is a certain irony, not lost on the Tuareg, that this revival owes much to the current policies of the Algerian government, which only 30 years ago had succeeded in bringing nomadism to its knees.

The Lesser Gods of the Sahara

Following a highly publicised expedition in the 1950s, the Tassili-n-Ajjer mountains of the Central Sahara (Algeria) were presented to the world as 'the greatest museum of prehistoric art in the whole world'. Many of the claims of the expedition's leader, Henri Lhote, were misleading, a number of the paintings were faked, and the copying process was fraught with errors. The 'discovery' can only be understood within the political and cultural context of the time, namely the Algerian Revolution, France's attempt to partition Algeria, and the prevailing views of the Abbé Breuil, the arch-advocate of foreign influence in African rock art. The expedition's methods caused extensive damage to the rock art while the accompanying looting of cultural objects effectively sterilised the archaeological landscape. Any restitution process must necessarily include a full recognition of what was done and the inappropriateness of the values.

Contested Terrain: Tourism, Environment and Security in Algeria's Extreme South

Tourism has for a long time been an integral part of the nomadic economy and the Tuareg's domain, and is seen by them as providing them with their rightful place in the world economy. However, the way in which tourism has developed in the Sahara in recent years has brought the Central Sahara, in the opinion of many Tuareg, to the brink of what they see as an environmental catastrophe. This article examines the struggle over the last four years between a small, but rapidly growing, number of 'enlightened' Tuareg who are battling for an alternative, environmentally sustainable form of tourism and the short-term financial and political interests of mass tourism, unregulated *tourisme sauvage* and professional looters. However, during the course of these four years, another struggle has been waged by the forces of the state, smugglers and bandits of various kinds and, if some of the intelligence services are to be believed, *al-Qaeda* itself, for sheer physical control over this vast terrain. During the course of 2003, through the strange coincidence of a number of events, these two levels of struggle have been fused. The result is the possible development of a new politic, emerging from the fact that local people, notably the Tuareg, now realise that their governments have not only been inept in both safeguarding their regions' cultural and natural heritage and developing an environmentally sustainable tourism industry, but also that they can no longer ensure the region's security.

Index

Abalessa 61n, 64n, 94n, 113, 175, 262n
aballag (tribute) ix, 42
Abdel Djalil 101, 118n, 266
Abdel Khader 28
Abdelessalem (Kaimakam of Ghat) 36
Abidine al-Kunti (nephew of Bay al-Kunti) 47, 55, 65–6n; 'two Sultans with same title' 47, 55
Abun-Nasr Jamil, M. 62n, 266
Acacus, Mts. (Libya) 22, 196, 222n, 236, 238, 261n
Addo 219n
Adjefou 220n
Admer 37
Admer ag Ammou 126
Adrar 244; *wilaya* 89
Adrar Hagarhene 164, 186
Adrar-n-Iforas ix, 21, 23, 34, 37, 47, 54–5, 59n, 63n, 68, 155, 162n
Afara 164, 263n
Afghanistan 25n, 239, 243, 245, 250, 263–4n
Aflan 66n
Aflan ag Doua 126
Africa 30, 60n, 160–61n
African Charter on Human and Peoples' Rights 9
Afrique Occidentale Française (AOF) 59n
Ag Mama 45, 64n
'ag/ult' system of naming ix; abolition of 80–81, 136
Agades 24n, 61–2n, 118n, 231, 263n
Agangan 37
agedellehouf 99; *see also* veil
agg ettebel (in line of succession) ix, 45, 52, 94n, 128–30, 136, 154–5, 159n, 162n
Aguh-en-tehle ix, 87, 93n, 119n, 135, 137, 150, 153, 156–7n, 162n, 164, 174–5, 179, 184–5, 191n; foothold in nomadic milieu 179; case of bigamy 125; salt caravan from Amadror to Damergou (1896) 49, 118n, 174–5; sedentarisation within traditional territories 135; tourist camel treks 185–6; wealth of livestock holdings 132; wealthy in camels and new grazing lands 175; *see also* Kel Ulli, Dag Rali
Ahaggar ix, 5, 23, 24–5n, 31–3, 36–8, 43–50, 52–4, 58–9n, 61–4n, 66n, 67–8, 70–72, 76, 79, 81–3, 85, 87, 91–2n, 98, 100, 102, 108–12, 115, 117–19n, 125–7, 143, 146, 155–6, 159–60n, 162n, 163–8, 172, 175–7, 180, 184, 189–90n, 196–7, 227–9, 232, 235–6, 238, 241, 252–3, 261–2n, 265n, *et passim*; 25,000 Tuareg 68; 25,000 Tamahak-speakers 2, 68; *Amenukal* El Hadj Akhmed (1830–77) 45; anarchic state of affairs (1990s) 82; damage by mass tourism 22, 234; depend on tourism 19; first visit by governor general (1932) 31; French needed suitable leader 50; French pacification 34; *gens du nord* and 89; map 194; no European had entered by (1880) 28; nomadic pastoralism and supplementation 180; refugees from Mali 83, 111; severe drought (1882) 49; shocked by battle of Tit (1902) 29; social and political structure at Independence 70–75; stories of Kalashnikov-wielding Tuareg 83–4; subsistence base at Independence; tourism 81, 86, 227, 229; traditional home of Kel Ahaggar 67; *see also* Kel Ahaggar, Ihaggaren
ahal (social gathering at night) ix, 121
Aharhar 164, 219n
aheg ix, 73
Ahellakane 164, 186
Ahl Azzi (known as Kel Rezzi) ix, 59n, 71–2, 74, 110
Ahl el Litham ix, 98
Ahmed, Si, married Aurélie Picard 53
Ahmoud, Sultan 30, 35–7, 53, 62–3n
Ahnet 150, 164; rock art known in region (1908) 197; severe drought (1882) 49; *see also* Kel Ahnet
AIDS 16, 148, 156, 162n
Ain el Hadhadj 62n
Ain Galakka 62n
Aïr (Niger) ix, 24n, 34, 36, 44, 61–3n, 68, 101–2, 106, 118n, 157n, 196, 231, 244, 261n; agricultural irrigation schemes 21; Sudanese indigo cotton in 100; Taitok sought refuge in 44; tourism 229; *see also* Kel Aïr
Ait Lowayan ix, 62n, 93n, 159n, 164, 184, 191n, 262n; *see also* Kel Ulli

279

Aitarel 45–6, 52; links with Tidjani 54; near-anarchy on death of (1900) 48–9
Ajjer ix; 5,000 Tuareg 68; disrespect for peoples of 89; nobles opposed the French 50; *see also* Kel Ajjer, Tassili-n-Ajjer
Ajjer–Ahaggar war (1875–78) 40–41, 46, 48, 51, 57, 64n; Kel Ulli acquired their own camels 40–41
Akabil 59n
Akarao 63n
Akhemouk ag Ihemma 38, 63n
Aktouf, M. (*sous-préfet* of Tamanrasset) 75, 77–9
al-Qaeda 25n, 95n, 264n; associated networks, Niger, Mali and Mauritania 245, 250; struggle against in Central Sahara 253; *see also* El Para, Mokhtar ben Mokhtar, GSPC
Alambo, Aboubacar (Niger) 244, 264n; *see also ishumar*
alechcho ix, 99–100, 117–18n; *see also* veil
Algeria 21, 30–32, 52, 56, 60n, 62n, 67–8, 87–8, 90, 95–6, 98, 100, 107–8, 113, 116, 120n, 155–6, 162n, 191n, 193, 218n, 252, *et passim*; 1992 before national government controlled Sahara region 69; admonition for abuse of human and indigenous rights 9; Arabisation and 12; attractions across the southern borders 88–90; case for assistance from US 246, 264n; civil and family law (Family Code) 11, 143, 161n; current concerns about conservation of Sahara 216; declared French (1848) 28; difficulty establishing itself in Saharan regions 134; difficulty finding administrators for Sahara 18; general elections (1992) 3–5, 228–9; 'Generals' Revolt (1961) 202; governor of 63n; *Grand Sud* 67–96; Gulf War and disturbances stopped tourists 233; hostage-takers are by-product of political crisis 252; ILO Convention not ratified 11; Islamist crisis (1990s) and tourism 19–20, 252; major national parks 23, 26n, 81; nomads 75; quality of governance 18–19; recognising nomadism as part of cultural heritage 81; security forces 5, 20; tourism potential and internal security problems 240; Tuareg population 68; Tuareg and tourism-transport 113–14; UN 'Draft Declaration on the Rights of Indigenous Peoples' 8–16, 90–91; veil still symbol of 'Tuaregness' 116; visa requirement in line with Djanet conference 252
Algerian army 83, 251; (13 May 2003) freed group of hostages 251; annulment of (1992) general election 5, 82, 226, 229, 233; *see also* ALN
Algerian state, government, authorities 5–8, 10–16, 21, 67, 69–70, 74–7, 79–80, 84–5, 89–90, 97, 117n, 134, 136, 148, 180–81, 184, 186–8, 226–7, 240–41, 251, *et passim*
Algerian independence (1962) 4, 6–7, 14, 18, 67–70, 74, 91–3n, 97, 108, 111–12, 119n, 121, 134–6, 140, 151, 154, 163, 166, 178, 227–8, 232; 90 per cent Tuareg were nomads 166, *et passim*; abolition of slavery after 74–5, 134; census (1966) 92n; decade after traumatic upheaval of Kel Ahaggar society 178; Kel Ahaggar nomadic existence at 163; lack of research on Tassili Frescoes 212; land made free to those who worked it 108, 134, 160n; nomadic Kel Ulli and post-pacification period 178; population of Ahaggar by time of 73; relations between Kel Ahaggar classes since 111; shocks to Kel Ahaggar's economic and political system after 135–6; social revolution of Tuareg society after 108; socialism 75, 78–9; subsistence base of the Kel Ahaggar at 74–5; systems of *métayage* labour abolished 75; Tuareg problem after 67–70; word 'Algerian' synonymous with enemy to Tuareg after 6
Algerian Islamists, kidnapping of 32 European tourists (2003) 19, 22; *see also* hostage crisis, Islamists
Algerian Revolution (War of Independence) 7–8, 24n, 60n, 160n, 201–3, 228
Algerian Sahara 53, 67–9, 85, 92n, 160n, 203, 221n, 226, 233, 243, 250, *et passim*; tourism (1999–2003) 226f, 238, 240, 242, 244; *see also* Sahara, tourism, Ahaggar, Tassili-n-Ajjer
Algerian Tuareg 1–6, 97–8, 100, 107, 113–14, 116, 166, 189n, *et passim*; *bouleversement* of their society 4, 153; *see also* Tuareg, Kel Ahaggar, Kel Ajjer
Algerianisation 6, 25n, 56, 78, 108, 161n; increased Arabisation and Islamisation and 13, 139; initial of the Tuareg 78–80; second state of incorporating the Tuareg (Kel Ahaggar) 80–81; *see also* Arabisation, Islamisation
Algeria's crisis (1990s) 3–8, 19–21, 140, 180, 182, 252; impact on its extreme south 82, 229
Algeria's south, extreme south 5–6, 13–16, 25n, 33, 62n, 67–9, 81–91, 110, 140, 187, 226–7, 229–30, 240, 250–51, 263n, 265n,

Index

et passim; *gens du nord* and 83, 85–6; *see also* Grand Sud
Algerie Française (French Algeria) ix, 202, 221n
Algiers 7, 10, 24n, 32–3, 46, 59n, 61n, 65–6n, 69, 77, 82, 94n, 120n, 197–8, 201–2, 217, 219n, 221n, 240, 249, *et passim*; Battle of 201; seminar on 'Sustainable Development of Ecotourism in Desert Areas' (2002) 240; Tuareg delegation to (1892) 46
Alimen, H. *et al.* 223n, 266
Aloua, 44
ALN (*Armée de Libération Nationale*) 76
amacheg ix, 93n; *see imuhagh*
Amadror 138, 174, 176, 186
amajeg 93n; *see imuhagh*
amaoual-oua-n-afella ix, 99; *see also* veil
amaoual-oua-n-aris 99; *see also* veil
Amanrassa, *Oued* 231
Amastane, *Oued* 62n
Amazzar, *Oued* 219n
Amazon Rain Forests 22
Amazigh, people ix, 9–10; *see also* Berbers
Ambassadors' Shelter (Djanet) 223n
Amded, *Oued* 237
Amenukal (title of supreme chief of the Kel Ahaggar) ix, 30, 35, 38, 44–5, 47–8, 50, 55, 57–8n, 59n, 63–5n, 71–2, 76, 80, 87, 93–4n, 104, 126, 128, 130, 136, 148, 168–9, 175, 177, 186–7; established in Tamesna 177; Hotel 136; Kel Ulli *tawsatin* and dues for 130; post abolished (1975) 136
Americas, the 210
Amguid 265n
Amjer, Mt. 237
Amsel 113, 141
amrar (chief, headman) ix, 50, 58n, 104, 130, 148, 160n
Amr'i ag Mohammed 64n
Anaba ag Amellal, attack on Flatters 46, 63n
Anag, C. *et al.* 262n, 266
anagad x, 97; *see also* veil
Anahaf 37
Anderamboukane 65n, 190n
anet ma (mother's brother) x, 124, 133
animal husbandry 74f; *see also* nomads, camels, goats
Antarctica 22
'Antinea', fake painting 207; Lhote's description of discovery 209; painted on rock wall 208; *see also* rock art
Antiquity 217
Aouanrhet 204–5, 213, 220n

Aoulef 59n
Appendix, *La soumission des Touaregs du Nord* 57–8
Appendix I, extracts from UNATA'S and ATAWT's report 254
Appendix II, letter to Algeria's President from citizens of Tamanrasset 248, 255–6
Appendix III, letter to Algeria's Prime Minister from Tamanrasset's Association of Travel Agencies 245–6, 248, 257–9
Appendix IV, letter from *Agence Tarahist* (Tamanrasset) to government ministers and regional authorities 247, 248–9, 260, 264n
Arabic, language (culture) 6, 27, 58, 69, 72–3, 84, 97, 99, 109–10, 117n
Arabisation 12, 78, 84, 109, 139, 143, 161n; decline of the matriline and 143
'arabism' 142; *chic à la mode* 84, 110
Arabs 43, 61n, 69, 71, 73, 90, 97–9, 101, 117n, 121; nomads 72, 74, 110, 158n
Arak 52, 246, 251, 265n
Archaeology of Rock-Art 210, 223n
ariwan (small camp) x, 123–4, 130–32, 134, 140–41, 172, 176; reed and stone huts beside them 135
Armed Islamic Group (GIA) 85, 243, 264n; *see also* GSPC
Armée de Libération Nationale (ALN) x, 76, 93n
Armée Nationale Populaire (ANP) x, 93n; *see also* Algerian army
arouri (the back), father's family x, 131, 156n
arrem 73
Arzmüller, Helmut, 'Rolling Rover' website 238, 242
Ascherson, N. 218
Asia, Central 210
Assadjen oua Mellen 197–8
Assakao 198, 219n; Col d' 31, 37
Assamakka 263n
Assekrem 164, 221n
'assimilation' 6
Association des Agences de Tourisme Wilaya de Tamanrasset (ATAWT) x, 233–5, 239, 245–9, 262n; anxiety that regional and national government opposed Saharan tourism 248; battle over tourism 253; German looters and 247; letter to Prime Minister 257–9; meetings and 249; President of wrote to the Prime Minister 245–6; Report of 254
Association des Amis de L'Art Rupestre Saharien (AARS) 224n
Atakor x, 149, 163; fate of camels in 181–2;

slaughter of camels (Nov. 1993) 95n, 186, 191n; 'sedentarism' in the region 135; traditionally Dag Rali territory 181; *un terrain abandonné* (1999) 163
Attici ag Amellal, attack on Flatters 46–7, 53, 65–6n
Aures 67, 95n, 264n
Australia (Australasia) 96n, 210, 218n, 225n
Austria (tourists) 249
Azaka n'Emiren 219n
azalay (marriage move) x, 123, 126, 143, 159; *see also* marriages
Azaouagh valley 244
Azernen 141
Azioul ag Ser'ada 30, 47, 59n
Azrou, *Oued* 164

babies and young children, effects of Kel Asouf 107
Bahedi, Mokhtar 218; *see also* Tarahist
Bambara 161n
banditry 3, 16, 243–5; *see also* smugglers, Mokhtar ben Mokhtar
Bardo Museum (Algiers) 197–8, 217
Barruwa 60n
Barth, F. 152, 158n, 162n, 189n, 266
Barth, Heinrich 39, 63n, 152; first discovery of rock art (1850) 196, 219n, 266
Bates, O. 156n, 266
Batna 95n, 264n
Battle of Algiers 201; *see also* Algiers
Battle of Essayen (1913) 30, 35; *see also* Essayen
Battle of Tit (1902) 29–30; *see also* Tit
Batutah, Ibn 97, 117n, 156n, 166
Baumann, M. 156n, 166
Bay ag Akhemouk 136
Bay al-Kunti (1865–1929) 54–5
Bechar 87
Behr, E. 221n, 166
Bekri El (1028–94) 97, 117n, 266
Belgium (Belgians) 155
Belin, M. (commander of *Cercle de Laghouat*) 29, 32, 49
Ben Gardane 61n
Benghazi 62n
Benhazera, M. 54, 61n, 65–6n, 93n, 100, 160n, 189n, 266; *Six Mois chez les Touareg du Ahaggar* 27
Berbers x, 10–11, 19, 24n, 63n, 68–9, 87; disturbances (2001) 19, 87–8, 96n; 'problem' 10
Berket 261n
Bernard, A. 30, 59n, 266
Bernus, E. 63n, 266

Bernus, S. 63n
Berque, J. 189n, 266
Besset, Lieutenant, police visit to Ajjer region (1903) 29–30
Bettu, Hadj (local 'war-lord') xi, 17, 82, 84, 86, 89, 94n, 98, 117n
'bigamous' unions, no communal residency 125; *see also* marriages
Bilma 23
Bio-Diversity, Convention on 9
'Bird-Headed Goddesses', fake painting 206–7; Lhote describes their 'discovery' 208–9; *see also* rock art
Bissuel, H. 59n, 65n, 119n, 159n, 266; *Les Touaregs de l'Ouest* 27
black Tuareg 70, 72
Blair, Tony 4
Blanguernon, C. 92n, 267
Bloch, Maurice 133–4, 160n, 267
Boer Republics 60n
Bordj el Haouas 164, 183
Borku 62n
Bornu 61n, 231
Boudiaf, President Mohammed, assassination (June 1992) 82, 117n
Bouhen ag Khebbi 66n, 126, 138, 159n
bouleversement (of Tuareg society) 4, 48, 134–8f, 153
Boumediènne, Houari, coup (1965) 75
Bourgeot, A. 54, 61–3n, 66n, 102, 117–18n, 157–8n, 166–7, 189n, 267
Bouteflika, President Abdelaziz 10, 13, 18–19, 229; open letter from Citizens of Tamanrasset 241, 255–6; visits to Djanet and Illizi 18–19, 87–8, 241
Brahim ag Abakada 34, 262n
Brandberg (Namibia) 204
Brazil 96n, 218n
Brenans, Lieutenant, discovery of prehistoric rock engravings (1933) 197–8, 200, 202–3, 213, 220n, 267; Lhote destroyed many of his original notes and drawings 217; in the Tassili (1932–40) 198–9; *see also* rock art
Breuil, Abbé Henri 196, 198–9, 202, 209, 214, 220–21n, 223n, 267; Namibian connection and 203–6, 214; outrageous pronouncements in Nambia 203–4; *The White Lady of the Brandberg* (1955) 204; *see also* Lhote, rock art
Britain 60n, 203; colonial policy 31, 60n; Sultan of Morocco and 31
British Academy 24, 218, 261, 262n
Bubekir ag Allegoui 30, 35, 37
Burkina Faso 1, 120n, 187

Index

Bush, George W. 4
Bushmen (of Namibia) 203–4, 214

Caid Andennebi Ben Ali 62n
Caid Baba, 59n
Caillé, René 58n
Cambridge University 212
'camel unit' of *ariwan* 132
camels 71, 73, 94n, 129–30, 132–3, 139, 149, 160n, 162n, 176, 181–2, 187, 191n, 236, 238, 262n, *et passim*; disease killed those in eastern Tefedest region 183; domain of men 140, 176; grazing in mountains 163; importance to men of Kel Ulli 177; nomads would care for Kel Rela 179; pastoralism 74f, 131; problem of increase of Kel Ahaggar's herds 37; provided Ihaggaren with military dominance 167; replaced by 4WDs 148; rotated between Ahaggar and Tamesna 176; subsidy for each new-born 167, 181, 187; tourism and 141, 229 veterinary inspection and registration for subsidy 182; *see also* Tuareg class structure, Tamesna
camp (*ariwan*) 4–5; tents (*ehenen*) 123, 149; *see also ariwan*, goat camps
caravan trading 34–5, 42, 61n, 64–5n, 69, 74–6, 93n, 100, 108, 113, 118n, 130–33, 138–9, 141, 151, 160–61, 174–9, 190n, 228, 231, 262n, *et passim*; end of 151; illicit 94n, 114, 179; management of 176, slave caravans 72, southern border closed to 93n, 134–5; *see also* salt trading, cigarette trade
Catroux, Gen. Georges 201, 220n
Cauvet, Cpt. 29, 32–3, 38, 61n
census (1987) 4,471 nomads in *wilaya* of Tamanrasset 81, 166
Central African Mission 59n
Centre National de la Recherches Scientifique (CNRS) x, 196, 201, 215
Chaamba x, 25n, 58n, 69, 72, 96n, 110, 155, 243
Chad 59–60n, 261n, 264n; civil war 3; Lake 62n
Chanoine 59n
Charlet, Cpt., French garrison at Djanet (1911) 35, 61–2, 267
Chasseloup-Laubat, F. de 199, 220n, 268
chech (veil) x, 86, 98, 100, 115–16; *see also* veil
cheurfa (descendants of Prophet) x, 61n, 72, 155, 161n
China 100
Chinoui/Chnaoui, name given to *les gens du nord* x, 86–7, 95n

Chippindale, C. 218, 223n, 267
Chirac, Jacques (President) 225n
Chirfa 264n
CIA (Central Intelligence Agency) 245, 264n
cigarette trade (illicit) 244–5, 263n; *see also* smuggling
Citroen 261n
'class endogamy', position in the class structure 128; *see also* endogamy, marriages
Coche, R. 267
colonial presence, exacerbated cleavages of traditional society 49
Confedération des Toureg du Nord, La, French misconception x, 33–5, 37
construction of political identities 6
'contested terrain' 10, 15, 17–21, 91; return to Ahaggar (1999) 252
Cortier, Cpt., paintings of the Tassili in *Oued Assouf Mellen* 197, 199, 220n, 267
Cottenest, Lieutenant, punitive raid on Kel Ahaggar (1902) 29, 32–3, 59n, 61
Couret, K. 65n, 267
cousins; *see* marriages
Cremaschi, M. 222–3n, 268
Cultural Diversity, Universal Declaration on (UNESCO 2001) 9
cultural norms and social reality, intervention of social classes 127–8, 152–3, 158n
cultural environment; *see* heritage
Cyrenaica 35

Dag Rali x, 4, 62n, 66n, 72, 87, 111, 113, 119n, 125, 127–33, 137, 139, 149–55, 156–9n, 161–2n, 163, 165, 174–5, 179–81, 184, 187, 190n, 262n; decline in *tawsit* endogamy 111; equate section membership with residency 130; four sections 130; infant mortality, survey (2003) 147, 161n; living in villages today 163; marital strategies 129–34; marriage patterns, pastoralism and caravan trade 177; marriages 153; marriages with cousins of all types 131; most endogamous of all *tawsatin* 152, 154; pastoral resources 132; salt from Amadror to Damergou (1896) 49, 118n, 174–5; sedentarisation of 135, 160n; sedentarised now 179–80, 187; social reality of 118; *tawsit* endogamy in 127–8, 131; wealthy in camels and grazing lands in Tamesna 175; women who left villages and set up camps 149; *see also* Kel Ulli
Damergou 36, 61n, 74, 100, 118n, 174–5, 190n, 231; *see also* Niger

283

Dassine ult Ihemma 56, 66n; marriages of 126
dates 49, 167, 177
de Bary, Erwin 44, 196, 268
de Gaulle, Charles 203
Dehine 183
Depommier, Cpt. 66n
descent 45, 65n, 80–81, 92n, 94n, 112, 121–4, 128–33, 136–8, 151f, 159n, 190n, *et passim*; *see also* matrilineality; groups 109, 113; *see also tawsit*
Dider 219n
Dinaux, Cpt. 30
divorce, family saga of frequent divorce 144–6; *see also* marriages
Djado 261n, 264n
Djalil, Abdel 101
Djanet x, 15, 30–31, 34–8, 44, 50–51, 55, 63n, 81, 95n, 113, 155, 164, 183, 189n, 197–9, 216, 219n, 221n, 229, 231–2, 239, 262n, *et passim*; Algerian Tuareg residents 113; commercial centre 72–3; fertile oasis 34, 231; French should provide museum 216; French withdrawal (1917) 55; important tourist town because of Tassili 'frescoes' 232; letter to President Bouteflika re *wali* 87–8; position on caravan routes 35; recaptured (May 1916) 36; Tuareg donkey handlers 2; visit of President Bouteflika 10, 18–19, 87, 241
Djanet conference (10–12 March 2003) 15, 226, 247, 251–2, 265n, main features of conference 248–9; political issues and agendas 247–8, 253; 'Tourism in the Tassili and Ahaggar' 15, 22–3, 226, 247–9; *wilaya* of Illizi organised 247
djenoun (spirits) x; *see also* Kel Asouf
Djerat, Oued xiii, 196–7, 199, 212, 217, 220n, 223–4n, 236–7, 262n; *see also* rock art, Brenans, Lhote
Djurdjura, Mts. 24n
Dourneaux-Duprée expedition (1874) 28
Dreyfus affair 60n
drought 3, 49, 51, 65n, 75–6, 81, 108, 112, 135, 174, 185, 228, *et passim*; (1970s and 1980s) in Niger and Mali 3, 108, 114
drum (*ettebel*), transfer to the *mairie* of Tamanrasset 80
drum-chief, *aballag* and 42; rights to the land and 41
drum-group(s); *see ettebel*
Dua ag Agg-Iklan, married Dag Rali wife Tekadeyt ult Ebekki 125, 158n; second wife among the Irregenaten *tawsit* in Tamesna 125

Dubief, J. 60n, 65n, 199–200, 220n, 268
Duprez, Cpt. 219n
Dupuy, C. 223n
Duveyrier, H. 58, 61n, 63–4n, 93n, 118n, 171, 189–90n, 219n, 268; black and white cotton veils in Kel Ajjer 100–101; Ihaggaren could take riding camels from Kel Ulli 171; 'important rock sculptures' 196; *imuhagh* 73; Kel Ulli weapons and 39–40; *Les Touareg du Nord* 27; travelled amongst Kel Ajjer (1859) 28

echchach, veil for day-to-day use x, 99–100, 117; *see also* veil
Echo D'Oran 221n
education 77–8, 139, 188; all schooling is in Arabic 109; compulsory for nomadic children 108; women's responsibility for removed by schools 139
efelehleh 58n, 242
Egypt 60n, 205–8
ehen(en), tent(s) x, 123, 157n
ehere-n-amadal (tributary land-rent) x, 41, 64n, 128, 136, 160n, 168, 175, 189n
Eheren 223–4n
Eid Es Rir religious festival xi, 77
ekerhei (headcloth) xi, 97
El Golea 244
El Hadj Akhmed 45, 47, 58; links with Tidjani 54
El Molathemine xi, 98; *see also* veil
El Oued 67
El Para (alias), Amari Said, alias Abderrazak Amari 245, 251
El Watan 162n, 265n
El-Abed, Sidi Mohammed (Sanussi representative for the Fezzan) 35–6, 51, 55, 62n
elmengoudi 97; *see also* veil
endogamy 5, 103, 110–11, 119n, 127–8f, 131–4, 137, 147, 152–5, 159n, 183, *et passim*; *see also* marriages
English, travellers 44, 61n, 263n
environment (protection, conservation of) 7, 16–18, 20–21, 89–91, 188, 226–65, *et passim*; damage to, degradation of 228, 232–4, 248; fear of catastrophe 226, 234, 253
environmentalists 21, 248; Europeans looting Sahara of prehistoric artefacts (2002) 238; *see also* looting; fear that Algeria will encourage 'mass tourism' 86, 242; little support from government 239–40; predominantly Tuareg 235; *see also* tourism agencies

Index

environmentally sustainable tourist industry 23, 89, 187–8, 226–7; struggle for 234–5; *see also* tourism
Es Souk 162n
ESRC (Economic and Social Research Council) 24, 91, 156, 189, 261
Essayen 30, 34
ethnicity 6–7, 9, 13–14, 17–18, 67–96, 108; ethnic groups, identity 8–9, 14, 16, 90, 109, 112–13, 120n; and social categories 70–74, 86–7
Etienne, Eugène 60n
ettama xi, 106, 161; *see also tehot*
ettebel (drum group) xi, 39, 41, 44, 64n, 71, 80, 95n, 123, 128, 168
Europe (EU) 95–6, 98, 114, 156, 210, 215, 218n, 225
European air charter tour companies 235, 239; pressure on Djanet and Tamanrasset from 239
European community in Algiers, Soustelle as leader 202
Europeans 155, 238; tourism and 227, 242, 248–52, 263n
Evian agreements (Treaty) 93n, 160n

Fadnoun 249
female slaves (*taklitin*) 139; *see also* slaves
Feraud, M. 65n
Ferry, J. Col. 62n, 268
Fezzan xi, 23, 35–6, 49, 61–3n, 190n, 236, 261n; drought and famine (1911) 51; state of anarchy 55
Firth, R. 118n, 268
Flamand-Pein expedition (1899) 29, 32
Flatters, Fort 30, 62n
Flatters mission (1881) 2, 24n, 28–9, 33, 45, 58–9n, 64n, 66n; Khyar condemned massacre of 46; supported by Tidjani 53
foggaras 160n
Foreign Aid 76
Foucauld, C. 36, 40, 44, 54, 61–6n, 93n, 100–101, 117–18n, 158n, 190n, 221n, 262n, 268; *temazlayt* and 168
Four-Wheel Drives (4WDs) 141, 148, 229; 17 Toyota captured 244; *see also* tourism, Mokhtar ben Mokhtar
Foureau, F., discovery of rock art 196, 219n, 268
Foureau-Lamy expedition (1900), hindered by Sanussi 35, 66n
France 2, 30–31, 34, 46–7, 53, 56, 60n, 62n, 67, 74, 86, 93n, 96n, 135, 160–61n, 193, 218–19n, 225n, *et passim*; agreement with Kel Ahaggar Tuareg 57–8; capture of Algiers (1830) 28; classification of 'white Tuareg' or 'black Tuareg' 70–71; colonial advance, encroachment into Sahara, 48–9, 51, 53–4, 64, 68, 72; exiled Taitok from Ahaggar 44; installed Moussa ag Amastane ruler of Djanet 37, 63n; *Partenariat* (2001) 240; precarious hold on Saharan territories (1917) 30, 36; preserving 'feudal' elements of pre-colonial society 50, 92n; resistance to 24n, 35–7, 44; restitution with Algerian government and Tuareg 215–16; submission to 50, 52; Taitok sought peace (1901) 29; travellers 44; Tuat conquest (1899–1900) and occupation 31–2, 43–4, 48, 59–60n, 177; wanted Sahara with its oil and gas to remain French 160n, 203; withdrawal 134
Franco-Algerian relations 3, Algerian Revolution 201–3
Franco-centric attitudes, appropriation of foreign cultural heritage 215, 224–5n
freed slaves, classified as Kel Aghrem (people of the gardens) 74; *see also* slaves
French colonial rule, expansion of, pacification 2, 27f; collaboration with 27–8, 46, 52–4, 56, 65n; colonial policy 31–3, 60n; impact of 27–66, 119n, 168, 173–5, 190n, 196, 231; marriages with 155; resistance to 27–66, 46–7, 50–54, 56, *et passim*
French perspectives of Tuareg history, misconceptions 33–9
French West Africa 30, 38; *see also* West Africa, Sudan territories
Frobenius, Leo 199, 202, 219n, 220n, 268
Front de Libération Nationale (FLN) 24n
Front Islamique du Salut (FIS) xi, 94n, 191n, 229
Fugelstad, F.A. 65n, 268
Fulani 161n

gandoura (Arab kaftan) xii, 86, 98, 115–16
Gao 65n, 190
Garamantes 219n
Gardel, Lieutenant, 30, 60–61n, 268; paintings at In Ezzan (1914) 197
Gardi, Rene 121, 156n, 268
Gast, Marceau 41–2, 59n, 63n, 65n, 100, 118n, 158–60n, 168, 190n, 212, 224n, 268
Gautier, Prof. 101–2, 197, 219n
Gavart, Dr 62n
gender (roles, position of women) 132, 138–41; degradation of women 148; *see also* women

285

'genealogical amnesia', system of nomenclature and 80–81, 136–8, 151–2
genetic disorders 5
gens du nord xi, 16–18, 20, 83, 85–6, 89, 95n, 223n, 230
Germany 265n; South West Africa 221n; travellers 44, 238, 242, 247–9, 251–2, 265n
Ghadames 2, 23, 28, 53, 58n
Ghardaia 263n
Ghat xi, 22, 30, 34–6, 48, 53, 55, 61–2n, 65n, 196, 219n, 231–2; Kel Ajjer moved to 232
Glossary ix–xv
Glozel 206
goat and camel pastoralism 74, 132, 165, 167–8, 176, *et passim*; *see also temazlayt*
goats 41–2, 71, 74, 160n, 186, 189n, *et passim*; *ariwan*, an economically viable unit with 130, 132; camps 149–51; breeding 130, 132; core of Kel Ulli subsistence goods 166–8, 175; 177; domain of women 139, 160n, 176
Goffman, E. 119n, 269
Gogo 58n
Goody, J. 123, 156–7n, 160n, 269
Gordon, R.J. 221n, 269
Göttler, G. 265n
Gourma-Rharous 244
Graham, T. 51, 65–6n, 269
grain 167, 177
Grand Sud (Tamanrasset, Illizi, Adrar and Tindouf) xi, 1, 7, 9, 13, 15, 17–18, 21, 67–96, 244, 253, 263n, 265n; towards a new regionalism 86–8, 90–91, 112; *see also* Algeria's extreme south
'Great God' (Sefar) 223n
grievances in the south, emergencies of new 'issues' 84–6
Groupe(s) Islamique(s) Armé(s) (GIA) xi, 95n
Groupe salafiste pour la prédication et le combat; *see* GSPC
GSPC xi, 95n, 243–5, 250, 264n; abductors of hostages 251
guardiens du parc xi, 94n, 141, 161n, 167, 180–81, 183–4, 187, 232; Hoggar National Park 84, 94n, 141, 180–81, 232
Guerara (Gourara) 29, 60n
Guilho-Lohan, Lt, tour through Ahaggar 29

Hachid, Malika 197, 200, 203, 206–8, 210, 212, 218, 220–24n, 262n, 269; Tassili Park director 236–7
Hadj, veil could be divested entirely 106–7
Hamet, I. 64n, 269
haram (forbidden) 66n
harratin (agriculturalists) xi, 49, 58, 72, 73–6, 87, 93–4n, 109, 111–13, 141, 156, 160–61n, 175–6, 179, 190n, 228, 230–31; expansion of gardens 177–8; *harratin* took possession of gardens 178; Kel Ulli and 175–6
Hassi Inifel 58n, 65–6n
Hassi Messaoud 232
Hassi Tanezrouft 62n
Hattab, Hassan 85, 95n, 243, 245, 250
health, problems 16; *see also* infant mortality, AIDS and sexually transmitted diseases
Heguir 45
heritage, cultural 6, 17, 22–3, 81, 187, 193–226, 230, 238, 248
Hirafok 93n, 150, 163, 178
history 55–7
Hodna, Mts. 67, 264n
Hoggar (Ahaggar) National Park xi, 17–18, 20, 26n, 30, 81, 87, 94–5n, 191, 236, 240, 250; people as *guardiens du parc* 84, 94n, 141, 167, 180–81, 187, 232; attitude to employment 141; *see also guardiens du parc*, Ahaggar, Tassili National Park
Holland (tourists), 243, 249
'hostage crisis' (2003) 15, 18, 21, 25–6n, 91, 162n, 226, 229, 242, 249–52, 253; implications of 19–20, 22, 91, 239; international attention to problems of *tourisme sauvage* 251; *see also* tourism
hunting 137, 167
hydrocarbons 5, 240; *see also* oil

Ibettenaten xi, 59n; 'noble' but reduced to vassal status 71
ibubah (male cross-cousin) xi, 127; *see also* cousins, kinship, marriages
Iddo 197
Ideles 29, 61n, 92n, 113, 164, 178, 183–4, 186, 191n, 261n
Idinen, Mt. 219n
Idjeradjeriouène descent group (*tawsit*) xi, 213, 236–7; *see also* Djerat, Oued
Iferouane 61–2n, 231
Iforas 28, 45, 47, 59n, 155
Ifrak 113, 137, 140, 163
Ihaggaren (nobles) xii, 38f, 43f, 70f, 71–3, 92n, 104, 110, 119n, 122, 124, 127–30, 155, 159n, 166–75, 190n, *et passim*; camel breeders 71; class division between and Kel Ulli 167; could claim food from Kel Ulli 171; ensured that Kel Ulli were rich and well protected 172; Kel Ulli provided them with subsistence products 129–30; left camels in care of Kel Ulli 42, 171; ownership of camels and weapons 39–40, 73; raided for dates and cereals for Kel

286

Index

Ulli 167; *temazlayt* relationship with Kel Ulli 168; roamed extensively throughout Ahaggar 172; specialised in warfare and raiding 166; *tawsit* (descent group) membership determined by matrilineal descent 122; versus Kel Ulli ('vassals') 38, 39–43; *see also* Kel Rela, nobility, Tuareg class structure
Ihan, *Oued* 62n
Iherhé, Mt. 237–8
Iherir-Edarène 164, 231
Iheyawen Hada 66n
ihwar 72
Ikaskasen 62n
Ikerremoien 47
Ikhenoukhen 28, 58n, 65n
iklan 87; *see also* slaves
Iklan Tawsit xii, 155, 164
Ilaman, Mt. 237, 262n
Ilaman, *Oued* 62n
Ilaman, village 149
Illizi xii, 18–19, 67, 87–9, 96n, 113, 115, 164, 183, 197, 216, 231–2, 244, 249–50, 262n, 265n; *see also* Polignac, Fort; movement of people from Djanet to 232; visit of President Bouteflika 10, 18–19, 87–8, 241; *wilaya* of 10, 25n, 67, 87, 89, 96n, 136, 191n, 219n, 226, 231, 241, 251
ILO Convention No.169 on Indigenous and Tribal Peoples 9, 11–12, 15–16, 24n
Imanrassaten xii, 44
Imenan 34, 37, 61n
Imesseliten 160n
Imlaoulaouene, graffiti in Arabic 17–18; *see also* environment damage
Immidir; *see* Mouydir
imrad (vassals) 104, 119n, 159n; *see also* Kel Ulli, vassals
imuhagh xii, 73–7, 79–80, 87, 93n, 95n, 160n, 165; 1968 and 'modernisation' of 77; nomadic existence and 76; nomads and 165
imuhagh ouan aghrem 160n
imuhagh and Kel Aghrem, political meaning 79
imzads (musical instruments) xii, 121, 156n
In Abangerit 37, 62n, 175, 190n
In Amenas 96n, 232; and Hassi Messaoud, oil and gas fields 232
In Amguel 113, 191n
In Dalag 93n, 135
In Eker 62n; atomic test base xii, 92–3n, 108, 221n; French withdrew from 134, 178; wage labour 74–6, 178, 228; *see also* wage labour
In Ezzan 197
In Gal 191n
In Guezzam 5, 244
In R'ar 59n
In Salah xii, 24n, 29–30, 32, 37, 45, 52, 57–8, 59–61n, 72, 87, 91–2n, 96n, 112–13, 183, 243, 245
independent European travellers, *'tourisme sauvage'* 235, 242; *see also* tourism
indigenous peoples and rights 8–16, 21, 23, 24n, 90–91, 96n, 193, 218n, 225n, 237
ineden (blacksmiths) 72–3, 87
ineslemen (religious group) xii, 54, 72–3, 87, 92n
infant mortality 5, 146–8, 161n
Inguedazzen 30, 35, 53
Institut de Recherches Sahariennes (IRS) xii, 196, 201, 215
'internal' and 'external' economy 166
International Working Group on Indigenous Affairs; *see* IWGIA
Internet, the 114, 142, 148; Swiss newspaper report of hijacking of four Swiss tourists (18 Oct. 2002) 245–6, 251; (2001) looted Tuareg heritage and 22, 238, 242
Iraq war, build up (2002–03) 229, 239
Irregenaten xii, 37, 71, 125, 149, 158n, 162n, 164, 190n
Isekkemaren xii, 36, 41, 43, 55, 66n, 71–3, 76, 87–8, 104, 155, 168, 174; *imuhagh* 73; marriages 111; in nomadic camps 76, 164; sought dates in Fezzan 49, 190n; Tuareg from Arab men and Tuareg women 71
ishumar 244, 263–4n; *see also* Kel Ishumar
Islam(ic) 64–5n, 107, 110, 129, 146
Islamic fundamentalism, Islamists 18–19, 82, 85, 94n, 109, 182, 191n, 229, 246, 250–52, 263–5n
Islamisation 78, 84, 94n, 109–10, 139, 142, 161n; penetration of values 55
Islamo-Arabisation 142–3, 146, 161n; Algerian Tuareg society and 109–10; degradation of position and roles of women 122, 139; *see also* gender, marriages, women
Issaouane 164
Issebeten 238, 262n
Italy 35, 61–2n; tourists and tour operators 236, 238, 244
IWGIA 8–16
Iwllemmeden xii, 47, 59n
izeggaren (cultivators) xii, 72–3, 87; *see also* harratin

Jabbaren 197, 199, 207–8, 217, 220n, 222n; *see also* rock art

Jebrine ag Mohammed 213, 218, 224n
Jews, Jewish origin 92n
jihad 35–6, 44
joint security zone 20, 26n, 252
Journal of North African Studies 1, 253

Kabyle people xii, 10, 69
Kabylia 24n
Kaimakam xii
Kalashnikov 83
Kanem 61n, 231
Kano 61n, 231
Kaoucen (Muhammad) 24n, 36–7, 55, 62–3n, 190n; suppression of (1917) 50, 125; Taitok's alliance with 44
karem (religious fast) xii, 84, 110; *see also* Ramadan
Kawar 23, 261n
Keenan, Jeremy 24–6n, 58–9n, 61n, 64–6n, 91–6n, 117–20n, 154, 156–62n, 189–92n, 217, 218–19n, 221n, 223n, 225n, 253, 261–5n, 269–70; report on tourism in Ahaggar and the Tassili-n-Ajjer 253
kehal xii, 100; *see also* veil
Keita, President, crushed Tuareg rebellion (1961) 76
Kel Aghrem xii, 73–5, 79–80, 87, 93n
Kel Ahaggar (Tuareg, People of Ahaggar) xii, 4–5, 11, 24n, 29–30, 33–41, 45, 48–9, 51–4, 58–9n, 61–5n, 67, 72, 74–80, 84, 86–7, 89–96n, 97–8, 100, 104, 106, 109–15, 117, 119, 121–7, 133–9, 141–3, 147, 151–2, 155–62n, 163–7, 170, 172–4, 177–8, 180–82, 185–8, 189–91n, 228, 230–31, 238, 262n, *et passim*; (1962) 90 per cent were living nomadic existence 178–9; ages at marriage 126; *bouleversement* of society 134–8; change in marriage patterns 111; change in residential pattern of (1962–2002) 113; changes and trends in marital patterns (1962–2002) 151–6; creation of three drum-groups (1755) 40, 43; decline in descent and kinship 112; endogamy in traditional society 110; few options but to sedentarise 135; fewer nomads (1999) 180; five main pillars of subsistence economy 74; go to Europe to bring in tourists 114; goat products were main subsistence materials 167; great 'shock' 80; infant mortality and 5, 147; internal dynamic of society 173–4; Islamisation and Arabisation since early 1970s 84; lax Moslems 129; marriage systems in 'traditional' times 125–7; more marriages ending in divorce 143; nomadic existence, arguments for 188; nomadic milieu and kinsmen 182–3; number of nomads dwindling since 1960s 165–6; pastoralism decimated by drought 135; questions about sexually transmitted diseases 147, 162n; revisionism of history and 56–7; several still nomadic 164; sought dates as far as Fezzan 49; 'stomach which colours the child' 122, 137; strong matrilineal emphasis 133; tourism and 86, 141, 161n, 180, 230–31; trade with oases of Tuat and Tidikelt 173–4; wars of (1875–78) 35; women no longer had slaves 139
Kel Ahaggar and Kel Ajjer, rock art as asset and economic resource 236
Kel Ahem Mellen xii, 59n
Kel Ahnet xii, 30, 47–8, 59n, 65–6n, 119n, 159n, 164, 184, 262n
Kel Aïr xiii, 2, 37, 63n, 190n; *see also* Aïr
Kel Ajjer xiii, 5, 28–31, 33–9, 44–5, 50–51, 53, 56, 59–61n, 63n, 65n, 67, 86, 90, 91n, 98, 110, 112, 114, 119, 124, 136, 141, 152, 155, 158n, 164–5, 180, 189–90n, 231, 237–8, 262n, *et passim*; agricultural base and commercial orientation 231; attacked French unit and were defeated (1913) 30; called Turks for assistance 48, 65n; decline in descent and kinship 112; fewer nomads (1999) 180; had never fallen under rule of the Kel Ahaggar 38; Kel Ahaggar cleavages 38; repulsed at Tadjemout (July 1917) 36; rivalry amongst 44; still a few nomadic 164, 166; summer in Europe to bring in tourists 114; suppression of by French 50; tourism and 86, 141, 161n, 180; *see also* Tassili-n-Ajjer, tourism
Kel Amadal (people of the earth) xiii, 110
Kel Arefsa xiii, 164, 191n
Kel Asouf (*djenoun* – wicked spirits) xiii, 119n; effect of Islamisation and Arabisation on 108, 110; veil and 106–7
Kel Djanet xiii, 162n; *see also* Djanet
Kel Es Souk 155, 162n
Kel Ewey 157n
Kel Had (people of the night) xiii, 107, 110
Kel Hirafok section of Dag Rali xiii, 130, 133, 157n, 191n
Kel In Amguel xiii, 162n
Kel In R'ar 66n
Kel In Tunin 113, 164, 183
Kel Ishumar 263–4n; *see also* ishumar
Kel Medak 164
Kel Rela xiii, 37–8, 40, 43–50, 52–3, 56,

288

Index

58n, 63n, 66n, 71–2, 76, 93n, 109, 111, 117n, 119n, 125, 127–31, 135, 138, 151–6, 159n, 162n, 175, 179, 185, 190n, *et passim*; bigamy of a noble 125; changes in marriage patterns 154–5; chief held title *Amenukal* (supreme chief) 71, 175; 'class endogamy' and 128; 'cousin marriages' with classificatory matrilateral parallel cousin 129; declining role in 'pastoral-cum-trading' economy 175; drum group 40, 43, 56, 61n, 64n, 151; ensure wealth and dignity of 50; exogamous marriages with Taitok and Tegehe Mellet 128; living in Tamanrasset 135; marital strategies 128–9; men have travelled in Europe 156; more *temazlayt* leaders than *tawsit* sections 169; noble status and 155, 175; political factions and external forces 48; settled in Tamanrasset 76; shock of Mali women who have married slaves and *harratin* 156; slave ownership and 72; social reality of 77 marriages 153; Taitok cleavage exacerbated by French encroachment 48; *tawsit* endogamy 127–8; tourist agencies and 185
Kel Rezzi 111, 164, 191n; *see also* Ahl Azzi
Kel Tagelmoust xiii, 98; *see also* veil
Kel Tagmart xiii, 137
Kel Tamanrasset section of Dag Rali xiii, 130, 133, 135, 137, 157n, 184
Kel Tazulet 66n
Kel Tenere (people of empty places) xiii, 107, 110
Kel Terhenanet section of Dag Rali xiii, 130, 133, 135, 137, 140, 157n, 184
Kel Tinhart section of Dag Rali xiii, 130, 133, 151n
Kel Tit 155
Kel Toberen 164
Kel Ulli xiii, 30, 35–6, 38–49, 52–3, 55, 64–6n, 71–3, 76, 87, 92n, 109–10, 119n, 122–4, 127–34, 139, 151, 157n, 159n, 162n, 166–78, 189–90n, 262n, *et passim*; acquisition of camels 132, 175–6; acquisition of Tamesna and long-range nomadism 176; attached to Algerian administration 44; camps relatively static 173; caravan to Damergou to exchange salt for millet 49, 174; changed marriage patterns 111; 'goat-breeders' 41–2, 71, 130, 132, 166, 168; had to turn to Ihaggaren for protection 168–9; Ihaggaren animals in care of 42, 171; *imuhagh* and 73; nomadic camps and 76; political and economic initiative 49; political rights with Kel Rela and 128; political subordination expressed through tributary payments 129; right to refuse requests of Ihaggaren 43, 172–3; salt caravans to Niger 130, 132; support for Moussa ag Amastane 48–9; *tawsit* (descent group) determined by matrilineal descent 122; *temazlayt* leader had no judicial authority over 42; tenant rights transmitted with political office 123; usufruct rights over Ihaggaren animals 171; veered towards patrilineality 124; 'warriors in their own right' 39, 130; weapons and camels of their own 173, 175
Kel Ulli and Isekkemaren *tawsatin*, deterioration of trade (1940s) 175; salt caravans (1926) 174–5
Kenan ag Tissi ag Rali 66n
Kennedy, R.A. 224n
Khader, Abdel ('resistance leader') 28
khamast (agricultural contract) xiii, 72
khent (further type of veil) xiii, 99–100; *see also* veil
Khyar ag Heguir (stepson of El Hadj Akhmed) 45–8
Kidal 54, 244
kidnapping of tourists; *see* hostage crisis
Killian, Conrad, significant sites (1927–28) 197, 199, 220n, 270
Kinahan, J. 221n, 270
kinship 13, 81, 103–5, 108, 111–14, 131–4, 136, 152f, 154, 158n, 162n, 179, 183–4, *et passim*; *see also* cousins, descent, marriages, *agg ettebel, anet ma*
Kufra 51, 62n
Kunta, the, defeated by Kel Ahaggar (1755) 39, 54, 63–4n

Laarmech (chief of Irregenaten) 63n, 190n
Lacroix, N. 30, 59n, 66n
Laghouat 29
Laing, Gordon 58n
Lajoux, Jean-Dominique (photographer) 200, 207–8, 222–3n, 270
Lamari, Abderrazak 25n, 251; *see also* El Para
land-rents (*ehere-n-amadal*) 128
land rights, held corporately by each *tawsit* 123; transmitted through matriline but redistributed through patrilocal 'sections' 124
land use 21; sustainable development and 15
Laouer 264n; *see also* Mokhtar ben Mokhtar
Laouni 108
Laperrine, Henri 29–30, 32–3, 36–9, 51, 61n, 63n; Aziouel submitted to 47

289

Lapierre (*Maréchal de Logis*), report of famine (1917) 51, 66n
Laporte, M. 77
Larocca, A. 218, 223n, 270
Le Poitevin, 199, 209, 220n, 270
Le Quellec, J.-L. 223n, 270
Lebanon 263n
Lecointre, Cpt. 66n, 270
Lehuraux, L. 62–3n, 270
Lejeune, Max 221n
Lesser Gods of the Sahara, The (film) 216
Levé, Captain Ferdinand 32
Leverhulme Trust 24n, 91n, 117, 189n, 218, 261
Levi-Strauss, C. 157n, 270
Lhote, Henri 39, 63n, 65–6n, 101–3, 118n, 195–7, 201–2, 209, 261–2n, 270–71; *A La Découverte des Fresques du Tassili* (1958) 193, 198–203, 217, 227; 'artistic quality' description 204–5; implications of his research for current researchers 214–16; looting and desire for acclaim and fame 215; methodology and scientific value of his research 210–12; rain-stone stolen from *Oued* Djerat 212, 217, 236–7; reasons for moistening the paintings 210–11; scientific value of research negated by absence of stratigraphy 211; stopped other academics from visiting Tassili 212–13; team responsible for making number of 'fakes' 206, 216–17; Tuareg children to look for arrowheads for him 211–12; views on relationship with the Tuareg 213; 'washing' of paintings and damage 210, 223n; *see also* rock art
Libya 1–2, 21–3, 51, 62n, 69, 90, 96n, 98, 113, 155, 196, 209, 218, 261n, 263–4n; closure to Westerners 3, 229; looters and new travel regulations 247, 252; redevelopment of tourism in Acacus Mountains 236; revival of tourism (1995) 232; tourism and 22; Tuareg in 90; *see also* Fezzan, Qadhafi
litham 117n; *see also* veil
locusts 49, 51, 174
looting of cultural artefacts 18, 22, 26n, 215, 238; hostage crisis drew attention to 251–3; professional 242, 247–9; *see also* rock art
London 92n
Louvre (Museum) 203, 225n; *see also* Musée de L'Homme, Lhote
low turban (*amaoual-oua-n-afella*) 99; *see also* veil

Maack, R. 221n, 271
MacDonald, K. 218
Maghrib 9–10, 24n, 117n; *see also* North Africa
Malaurie, J. 190n, 271
Mali 1, 10, 17, 19–21, 23, 25n, 33, 68–9, 72, 84, 88–91, 95–6n, 99, 111, 113–14, 116, 117n, 120n, 155–6, 162n, 218n, 232, 237, 244–5, 250–53, 261–2n, 264–5n, *et passim*; 14 hostages held in 251; 14 hostages released (17–18 Aug. 2003) 253; Kel Ahaggar sought work in 232; population of 675,000 Tuareg 68; termination of UNHCR-funded refugee returnee assistance programme 243; tourism and 252; Tuareg displaced 2; Tuareg into tourism-transport 113–14; Tuareg revolt (1990s) 2–3, 21, 69, 76, 83, 88, 92n, 112, 114, 116, 156, 229, 238, 263–5n; veil retains levels of meaning 116; women from Mali married *harratin* men 112, 156
marabout (*cheurfa*) religious families xiii, 45, 54–5, 66n, 110; followed French push south 72
Marlboro 952, 244; *see also* cigarette trade
marriages 110–12, 119n, 121, 123–8, 131–4, 137–8, 142–6, 156n, 159n, 162n, *et passim*; changes in patterns 151–6; close cousins and 126–7, 131; *see also* kinship, cousins, descent
Masqueray, M. 66n
Mathieu, M. 59n, 271
matriarchy 2
matrilineality (matriline) 2, 5, 13, 16, 45, 64n, 97, 111–12, 117, 119n, 121–62, 169–70; distinction between Tuareg and Arabs 97; irrelevant now 137
Mauritania 1, 21, 64n, 90, 120n, 244–5, 250
Mecca 62n
Meddak 198, 219n
Mediterranean 60n, 209, 244
meharistes 29, 59n
Merabtine xiii, 155, 162n, 194n; *see also* Ahl Azzi, Kel Rezzi
Merton, R.K. 118n, 271
Mertoutek 93n, 95n, 113, 164, 183, 191n, 221n; reparation for France's atomic tests 216, 221n
Mesak (Libya) 236, 238, 261n
Messaoud, Jari (*wali*) 263n
métayage (agricultural labour) xiii, 13, 75, 94n; *see also* harratin, khamast
Metlilli xiii, 25n, 96n, 243; merchants move south 72

Index

Metois, Cpt., negotiations with Moussa ag Amastane 30, 57–8, 271
Meynier, Lt Col. Octave 36
Middle East 7
Middle Kingdom (Egypt) 205
mihrab (mosque) xiii, 212; *see also* Djerat, Oued
millet 49, 74–6, 93–4n, 174–5, 190n, 228, 231, 237; staple foodstuff of Kel Ahaggar (1920s–60s) 177; *see also* caravans, salt
Ministry of Culture and Communication 15, 23, 247
Minitrek 261n
modernisation 16–18, 75, 77, 79, 108, 110, 116, 142, 151, 188; and Algerianisation, Arabisation and Islamisation 8, 147–8, 161n; negative aspects for women 188
modes of descent (the rules) 122–4; *see also* descent
Mohammed ag Mohammed 44, 64n
Mohammed ag Ourzig 46–7, 53
Mohammed Jai 244
mokadem (holy man) xiii, 54
Mokhtar ben Mokhtar (*contrabandier*, alias Belmokhtar, Laouer) 25n, 85, 89, 95–6n, 243–5, 252, 264n; GSPC's *emir* 250–51; 'Liberation' of *Le Grand Sud* 89–90, 243–4
Mollet, Guy 201
Monod, T. 199, 219–20n, 271
monogamy 125f; *see also* marriages
Moors (Maures) 54, 162n
Mori, F. 222n, 271
Morocco 24n, 58, 60n, 106, 235, 242; Sultan of 31, 60n
Motylinski, Fort (Tarhaouhaout) 30, 92n
Mouadhi Chaamba 56n, 65n
Moulin-Quignon 206
Moussa ag Amstane 24n, 30–31, 35–8, 47, 54–6, 63n, 65–6n, 126, 190n, *et passim*; 'collaboration' and 51–3; doubts about his loyalty to French (1916–17) 55; French gave title of *Amenukal* 50, 59n; negotiated peace in In Salah 30, 57–8; role in Sanussi revolt 36–7; subjected to revisionism 56; support of Kel Ulli 48–9; Taitok placed under command of (1918) 44; warrior against Iwllemmeden Tuareg 47
Moussa, Hadj 87, 93–4n, 95–6n, 136, 162n
mouth, meaning and beliefs about 106; *see also* veil
Mouydir (Immidir) 29, 59n
movable wealth, principles of Quranic law and 123; *see also* descent
Mozabites xiii; merchants move south 72

Munich 238
Murdock, G.P. 122, 156n, 271
Murphy, R.F. 101, 103–4, 107, 118–19n, 158n, 271–2
Murzuk 62n, 65n
Musée de L'Homme xiii, 196, 198–9, 201, 212, 221n, 224, 237; 'looted' cultural objects not in 215; original Brenans documents destroyed 217
Musée des Arts Premiers 224n
Museur, M. 61n, 261–2n, 272
Muzzolini, Alfred, on fake paintings 207, 218, 222–3n, 272

Nachtigal 196
Naftal 246
Namibia, 214; *see also* Breuil
Neuchâtel Museum of Ethnography 198
New York 229
Nicolaisen, Johannes 39, 58n, 63n, 102, 118n, 156–7n, 159–60, 189n, 272; Kel Ulli and milk-yielding camels 171; on *temazlayt* relationship 169, 171, 190n
Nicolas, J. 118n, 272
Niéger, Cpt., mission to Djanet (1909) 35
Niger 1, 10, 17, 19–23, 24–5n, 33–4, 36–7, 50, 59–60n, 62n, 68–9, 72, 82, 84, 88, 90–91, 93–6n, 99, 113–14, 116, 117–18n, 120n, 139, 157n, 162n, 174, 178–9, 182, 218n, 220, 243–5, 250, 252, 261–2n, *et passim*; Aïr Mountains and prehistoric artefacts 22; camel pastures acquired by Kel Ahaggar (1917) 125; cultural revivalism 83; deterioration of terms of trade for millet (1962, 1965–66) 75; millet-salt caravans 74–6, 94n, 130, 138, 160n, 175; million Tuareg today 68; resettlement programme hampered by overthrow of democratic rule 243; salt caravans took men away for months 138; Taitok moved towards (1930s) 44; tourism and 252; traditional salt caravans to were blocked 108, 135, 160n, 178; Tuareg displaced 2; Tuareg into tourism-transport 113–14; Tuareg revolts 2–3, 21, 69, 83, 88, 92n, 114, 116, 229, 238, 263–5n; veil retains many of old levels of meaning 116
Niger Bend country, agro-pastoral initiatives 21, 59n
Nigeria 1, 59n, 225n
Nigerian–Algerian pipeline 6, 240
Nile, River 60n, 205
nobility 35, 38f, 43f, 56, 71f, 100–101, 104, 119n, 122, 124–5, 155, 166, 175; political factions within the 44–8; predominantly

291

matrilineal 124; sovereign rights over territory of drum-group (*ettebel*) 123; *see also* Ihaggaren, Kel Rela
noble–vassal division 38–9, 92n; French encroachment and pacification of Ahaggar 48, 173; fundamental cleavage within Tuareg groups 39; *see also* Ihaggaren, Kel Ulli, *temazlayt*
nobles; *see* Ihaggaren
Nok (sculptures) 225n
nomads, nomadic milieu, number of 68, 73, 76–7, 81, 83, 93–5n, 113–14, 135, 163–92, 191–2n, 220, 238, *et passim*; access to pastures, wells and other resources 186; relationships with local tourism agencies (*agences de tourisme*) 184–5
nomadic economy (nomadic pastoralism) 163–92; in 1960s 178–9; collapse of 75–8; drought 75; importance of 81; old people, women and children 113; organisation of truck transport 183–4; relations with sedentary community 179, 182–3; 'salaried sector' as *guardien du parc* 84, 183–4; survival due to Algerian government policies 180; tourism and 81
nomadism, Algerian government recognising importance of (2003) 188; continual adaptation of and supplementation 188–9; definition 164; relationship between tourism and 141, 229–30; reversion to 148–51; revival of 187–9; supplementation and 166–7; survival of through 1990s 180–86; transition to 'sedentarism' 135
Norris, H.T. 54, 66n, 272
North Africa 7, 10, 63n, 95n, 194 map, 244, 250; white settlers 205
Norway 14
notion of 'we', no single term for 87
nuclear (French tests in Sahara) 60n; *see also* In Eker

oil 60n, 92n, 160n, 203, 221n, 263n; *see also* hydrocarbons
Osama bin Laden 245
Othman, Sheikh 28, 45, 53–4, 58n
Otoul 69, 94n, 113, 141
Oua Mellen 197
Oua Moulin 198
Ouallen 59n
Ouan Abou 220n
Ouan Bender 198, 220n
Ouaou el-Kebir 51
Ouargla 29, 32, 61–2n, 70
Ouarsenis 67
Ouba, Mohammed (*wali* of Djanet) 88–9, 263n

Oubari (sands), Libya 23, 261n
oult ettebel (woman through whom political succession transmitted) xiii, 45, 47

Pacific 210
Pakistan 25n, 245, 250
Palestine 263n
Pan-African Congress on Prehistory (Algiers 1952) 198–200, 220n
Pandolfi, Paul 4, 24n, 58–9n, 63n, 65–6n, 119n, 125, 139–40, 142–3, 153–4, 157–62n, 180, 191n, 272
Paris 36, 60–2n, 66n, 198, 203, 219n, 221n, 237, 264n
Park wardening; *see guardiens du parc*
Parks (national) 91; policy of 84; *see also* Hoggar (Ahaggar) National Park and Tassili National Park
Partenariat agreement (2001), France and Algeria 240
pastoral resources, change in management 186–7
'pastoral-cum-raiding' econmy 73; *temazlayt* relationship and 42, 167–73; transition to 174–8; *see also temazlayt*
Pein, Cpt. Théodore 32–3, 60–61n
Perdriaux, Cpt., report (1917) on misery of drought 51
Perret, Prof. 197, 219n
Peters, E.L., definition of 'nomadism' 164–5, 189n, 272
Philip Morris 95n; *see also* cigarette trade
Picard, Aurélie, 53
Piltdown 206
Pirson, R. 61n, 261–2n
Polignac, Fort (Illizi) 30, 36–7, 62n, 197, 231
political allegiance (*tiwse*) 128; *see also tiwse*
Porch, Douglas 60–61n, 272
Prasse, K.G. 93n, 272
problems of modernisation, invasion of *les gens du nord* and 16–18
Prophet, The 61n, 161n; *see also cheurfa*
Public Archaeology 216–17

Qadhafi, Colonel (Libya) 22, 69, 90, 96n, 263–4n
Qadiriya brotherhood xiv, 53–4
Qiru 62n
Quai Branley 225n
Quran 159n
Quranic law 160n, 162n, 188

racist views 203, 214
Radcliffe-Brown, A.R. 103, 118n, 157n, 272

Index

Rahmani, Cherif (Environment Minister, Algeria) 15, 20–21, 23, 25n, 187, 240; letter from UNATA president (18 May 2003) 253
raiding (and warfare) 42, 49, 167–73, 189n; Ihaggaren specialised in warfare and 166–7; men away for long periods expeditions 138–9, 141; Taitok raids on Arabs under French authority 43–4; within Ahaggar 42–3
Ramadan, observance of *karem* by the nomads 84, 94n, 110, 119n
Regane 21n, 92n
regionalism 7, 9, 13, 17–18, 67–96, 85, 87–8, 112
residency, changes to 137; patrilineal axis 123; *see also* descent
Reygasse, Prof. Maurice, prehistoric rock art and 197–8, 219n, 272
rice 190n
Richer, A. 59n, 272
Roberts, H. 24n, 273
rock art (prehistoric) 17, 22, 193–225; African 203; Antinea 206–9; Bushmen 203–4; copying of 195, 198, 210, 214; damage to 17, 22, 195, 210–11, 223n, 233, 235, 239, 265n; dates, dating 222n; denial of access to 212–13; discovery of 196–202, 217; excavations, archaeological 211, 223n; fakes, forgeries 205–8, 213, 216–17, 224n; looting 195, 211–12, 214–15, 218n, 238, 247–9, 251; portable artefacts and 195; round-heads 204–6, 222n; tourists and 212, 214, 216; washing 195, 210–11, 214, 221n; White Lady 204–5; world's greatest museum of 202, 227; *see also* Breuil, Brenans, Djerat, Hachid, Lhote, *Musée de L'Homme*, Tassili frescoes, Tassili-n-Ajjer
Rodd, Francis 101, 118n, 273
Rogerson, Barnaby 24n, 58n, 273
'Rolling Rover' website 238, 242, 249; *see also* looting
Rome 225n
Rouffignac 206
Round-Headed Men 204–5
Russia 264n

Sahara 3, 5–7, 15, 30–32, 34, 45–6, 48, 54–5, 59–60n, 62n, 66n, 69, 89, 98, 114, 129, 155–6, 173–4, 181, 193–5f, 212, 224n, 226, 229, 240, 243, 245, 252, 261n, 265, *et passim*; 4WD market has boomed since 1980s 229–30; conquest of 27f; discovery of oil in Algerian (1956) 202; French abandoning (1917) 55; history of 2; looting of artefacts 22; rich cultural heritage 6, 240; Sanussi revolt (1914) 30, 35; struggle against smugglers and bandits 253; *et passim; see also* Ahaggar, Algerian Sahara, Tassili-n-Ajjer
Sahara: 10,000 Years of Art and History 209, 273
Saharan Studies Programme (UEA) 253
Saharan Territories 60n
Sahel, the 16, 54, 98, 114, 244, 250, 263n; drought 4
Sahraouis xiv, 17, 86, 89
Salisbury, Lord 60n
salt mines 74–5, 138, 174; *see also* Amadror, salt trade
salt trade 190n; blocked after Algerian independence 108, 135, 220; caravans to Damergou 118n, 174–5, 177, 179; caravans to Niger 93n, 108, 130, 138, 160n, 220; Kel Ahaggar and 74; trans-Saharan 175, 231; *see also* caravans, millet
Sanhaja 64n
Sanussi xiv, 30, 35–7, 51, 53–5, 61–2n, 190n, 221n; Ahaggar Kel Ulli and Isekkemaren joined 55; *jihad* against Italian and French infidels 35, 44; revolt spread across Sahara 30, 36, 53, 55
Sanussiya; *see* Sanussi
Saudi Arabia, gift to people of Sahara for cameline economies 181
Say 60n
Schadla-Hall, T. 218
Scheffler, H.W. 158n, 162n, 273
Search for the Tassili Frescoes 196
sedentarisation 122, 140, 160n, 166, 185, 228, 231, *et passim*; (1971) and onset of Algeria's crisis in 1990s 180; acceptance of new Algerian order 79; changes in social behaviour since 142–8; effect on roles of women 138–9; gradual not such a shock for nomads 140; Kel Ahaggar by (1971) 163; Kel Ajjer early around Djanet 231; not simple for nomads 135
sedentarist and nomad, Kel Aghrem and *imuhagh* distinctions 75
sedentary and nomadic communities, new relations of production 179
Sefar 207, 220n, 223n
September 11th 2001, 25n
sexually transmitted diseases 147–8, 162n
Sheffield University 212
Si Ahmed 53
Sidi ag Keradji (Taitok chief) 29–30, 47–8, 59n

293

Sidi ag Mohammed el Khir 45, 64n
Sidi Ahmed al-Sharif 62n
Sidi Mohammed ag Rotman 66n
Sidi Muhammed al-Kunti 63n
Sidi Muhammad b. 'Ali al-Sanussi 62n
Silet 191n, 237
slaves xii, 1, 13, 49, 56, 61n, 68–70, 72–6, 78, 87, 92n, 94n, 108, 111–13, 121, 126, 134, 138–40, 149–50, 156, 159n, 161–2n, 167, 176, 178–9, 190–91n, 228, 230, 262n, *et passim*; abolished in Algiers 69–70, 75, 80, 134, 178, 184; Dag Rali abundance of 72, 175; female worked within the camp 176; Kel Rela and 72; male worked with camels and salt caravans 176; nomadic camps and 184; *see also iklan*
smugglers 16, 20, 263n, 'bandits' and 'terrorists' 243–5
smuggling 83–5, 141, 167, 188, 226, 243, 245; *see also* trans-Saharan
social change 4, 8, 16–18, *et passim*
social distance, the veil and 103; *see also* veil
social security 84; *see also* Parks
socialism (Algeria as a socialist state) 13
Soleilhavoup, Francois 211, 224n, 273
Somalia 264n
Somme, River 36
Sonarem (national mineral exploration company), jobs on points system 78, 108
Sonatrach 246
Sothebys 263n
Souri ag Chikat 63n
Soustelle, Jacques 201–3, 214, 220n; Minister for Atomic Affairs 202
South, southern Africa 210, 214
'southerners' as Sahraouis or Hadj Bettus 86, 89
Spain 244
Stenning, D.J. 189n, 273
Stewart, C.C. and E.K. 64n, 273
Sudan, civil war 3
Sudanese territories 30, 59n, 61n, 99–100, 262n
sufi xiv, 35
supplementation of nomadic pastoralism 166–7, 180; gardening, wage labour and slaves 178
sustainable development 15, 21–3, 89–91, 187, 240; Conference on 240; *see also* tourism
Sweden (tourists) 249f
Swiss tourists, hijacking of four (Oct. 2002) 245–7

Tabelbalet, *Oued* 62n

Tachekalaout 197–8
Taçon, P.S.C. 223n
Tademait 60n
Tadjelahine ('Tahilahi') 223n
Tadjemout 36, 52, 58
Tadjeradjeri, *Oued* 164
Tadrart Acacus 196; *see also* Acacus
tagelmoust xiv, 99–100, 115; *see also* veil
Tagmart 93n, 113–14, 135, 137, 140–42, 150, 163; *see also* Kel Tagmart
Tahat, Mt. 237, 262n
Tahebert 62n
Tahifet 93n
Tahilahi xiv, 4, 24n, 27, 55–7, 220n
Tahoua (Tawa) 58, 175
Taitok xiv, 29–30, 38, 44, 46–7, 50, 59n, 65n, 119, 128, 155, 159–60n; drum group 36, 40, 43, 53, 56, 61n, 64n, 128; fight with Kel Rela (1935–36) 44; raids on Arabs under French authority (1900) 43–4; respect for today 56; splinter groups 47; stripped of power in Ahaggar 50
Taiwan 86
Tajakanat 64n
taklit (pl. *tiklatin*) xiv, 139, 162n; *see also* slaves
takouba (sword) xiv, 39–40, 73, 168, 237
Talarak 25n
taleb (Quranic teacher) xiv, 146, 161n
Taliban 25n
Tamahak, language in the north 1–2, 6, 24n, 68, 72–3, 84, 91n, 93n, 95n, 262n
Tamanrasset xiv, 6, 14–17, 19, 25n, 29–30, 44, 55, 59n, 67, 69, 73, 75–8, 80–83, 85, 87, 94–6n, 98–100, 108–9, 112–13, 115–17, 117–18n, 120n, 125, 135–6, 142–4, 149, 156, 158n, 160–62n, 163–4, 175, 179, 182–8, 216, 221n, 229–33, 235, 238–9, 241, 243, 245–9, 262–4n, *et passim*; Algerian Tuareg 113; Algerians not in control after Independence 69; *arrondissement* 92n; benefited more from tourism than Djanet 231; *bidonvilles* 75; bigamous and exogamous marriages 125; café society and the veil 116; citizens' letter to President 241, 255–6; commercial centre 72–3, 92n; complaints against the *wali* and regional officials 248; country's sixth military region 82; dropping of the veil around 98, 108; effect of new *wali* and veil 117; French priest Charles de Foucauld murdered (Dec. 1916) 36; French should provide museum 216; growth of population (1980s–1998) 140, 182; growth of prostitution and AIDS 156;

Index

impact on Kel Ahaggar society 141–2; *imuhagh* fear of Algerian administration in 76; invaded by *les gens du nord* 83, 85; Labour Exchange 14, 93n; less dependent on tourism than Djanet 232; major administrative and garrison town, growth of (1990s) 140, 232; Mohammed ag Mohammed gaoled 44; no Berber unrest 87; oil and gas developments 89; open letter to President Bouteflika 241; population growth 16; schools for nomad children 77–8; small dusty administrative centre when French left 231; Tuareg from Niger and Mali 2; *wali* and 'fuel crisis' 246–7, 264n
Tamanrasset Conference (Nov. 1989) 22–3, 232–5, 239
Tamanrasset and Illizi, tourism and smuggling (banditry) 226
Tamanrasset *wilaya* 2, 24–5n, 67–8, 81, 83, 87, 89, 94n, 112, 136, 166, 182, 191n, 226n, 231, 241, 248, 251; 4,471 nomads in *wilaya* (1987 census) 81; 1998 census of 92n, 94n, 112
Tamashek, language in the south xiv, 1, 24n, 262n
Tamazaght 24n
Tamdjert 113, 164, 183, 219n, 231
tamekchit (food given as hospitality) xiv, 41–2, 171
Tamekkendout, *Oued* 164
Tamelrik 249–50, 265n
Tamesna xiv, 2, 24–5n, 44, 62n, 125, 158n, 160n, 175, 177–8, 182, 186–7, 190–91n, 244; bulk of Kel Ahaggar camels in 37, 139; Dag Rali women's camels tended by Irregenaten 149; 'double residency' 125
Tamrit 198, 219n
Tan Zoumiatak 205, 220n
Tanezrouft 58n
Tannezzouft, *Oued* 219n
Tarahist, Agence 247, 249; letter to government 260
Taramut 135
Tarat, *Oued* 219n
Targuis or Hadj Bettus (derogatory terms for Tuareg) xiv, 86, 98
Tarhaouhaout 29–30, 92–3n
Tasigmet 223n
Tasset 164
Tassili Frescoes 193–225, authenticity of many of the paintings 206–9; claims of 'discovery' 196–9, 232; damaged over 40 years by 'washing' of paintings 210; discovery of 193–5; exhibition in *Musée des Arts Decoratifs* (Paris) 203; fake paintings 206–9; 'falsifications' 209; new perspective on the 'discovery' 195–6; political, intellectual and cultural context 200
Tassili-n-Ajjer xiv, 5, 21, 23, 25n, 28–30, 33–6, 39, 49–51, 53, 55–6, 58n, 62n, 67–8, 72, 79, 81, 83, 85, 91n, 150, 164, 166–7, 186, 227–9, 232, 235–9, 241, 249, 253, 261–2n, 265n, *et passim*; 5,000 Tamahak speakers 2; damage by mass tourism 22, 234; donkey handlers 2; drought and famine (1882) 51, 65n; Kel Ajjer all settled 164; map 194; rock art 193–225; stories about 83–4; tourism and 19, 81, 227, 229; traditional home of Kel Ajjer 67
Tassili-n-Ajjer National Park 26n, 81, 94n, 191n, 193–225, 232, 236
Tassili-ouan-Ahaggar 21
tawsit (pl. *tawsatin*) (descent groups) xiv, 37, 39, 40–41, 43, 48, 53, 62n, 64n, 66n, 71–2, 87, 92n, 110, 113, 122–5, 141, 150–60n, 162n, 164, 168–9, 172–7, 183, 186, 190–91n, 236, *et passim*; endogamy within 110–11, 119n, 127–30, 132, 134–7, 139; *see also* marriages
Tazrouk 61n, 113, 178, 191n, 262n
Tefedest 29, 115, 150, 164–5, 183, 186, 191n
tegehe (federation) xiv, 42, 64–5n, 110, 168–70
Tegehe Mellet xiv; drum group 40, 43, 61n, 64n, 119n, 128, 155, 159–60n; Flatters massacre in their territory 46
Tegehe-n-Efis xiv, 164, 184
Tegehe-n-ou-Sidi 64n, 119n, 159n
Tegit-n-Iherhé 237
Tehi-n-Akli 63n
tehot ('evil eye' or 'evil mouth') xiv, 102, 106–7, 110; *see also* ettama
tekerheit (white woollen veil from Tripol) xiv, 99–100; *see also* veil
Teleya 54
Temassinine 30
Temassint 62n
temazlayt relationship (contract of protection between nobles and vassals) xiv, 41–3, 49, 64n, 92n, 167–73, 179, 185–6, 190n; less justification for 173
Tenere 21–2, 62n, 211, 261n
Teniet El-Abed 95n
Terhenanet 93n, 113–14, 135, 139, 141, 149–50, 160n, 163, 182; major changes in villages like (1990s) 140
tesa (the stomach), mother's family xiv, 131, 156n

The Lesser Gods of the Sahara

Théveniault, Cpt. 30
Tibesti 62n, 213
tibubah (female cross-cousin) xiv, 127; *see also* endogamy, marriages
Tidikelt 23, 24n, 29, 43, 47–9, 58–63n, 65–6n, 72, 94n, 100, 138, 166–7, 173, 177, 221n, 262n
Tidjaniya brotherhood xv, 59n; support for French 53–4, 66n
Tifernine 164, 186, 249, 263n
tifinagh (script) xv, 27, 236, 262n
Tiguent, Lella 45
Tihodaine 186, 265n
Timaiouine 30
Timbuktu 32, 45, 58n, 61n, 66n
Timimoun 60n
Ti-n-Esa xv, 55, 59n
Tin Bedjedj 197–8, 220n
Tin Gherour 264n
Tin Hinan, hotel 136
Tin Tarabine 164
Tin Tazarift 198, 207, 220n
Tin Zaouaten 37
Tindouf (*wilaya*) 89
Tinné, Miss (killed) 28
Tioueyin, Mt. 237–8
Tisemt 138
Tissougai (Tissoukai) 199, 223n
Tit 4, 24n, 27, 29–30, 55, 59n, 62n, 92n, 113, 141
tiwse (annual tributary payment) xv, 41, 47, 49, 64n, 93n, 128, 136, 160n, 168, 175, 189n
Tizi Ouzou 24n
Toubou revolt, north-east Niger 3
Touchard, Cpt., submission of Kel Ulli at Djanet 30, 35
Tourha, Mts. 164, 183, 185–6, 191n
tourism 6, 15, 18–20, 86, 89–91, 94–5, 111, 141, 160n, 167, 180, 187, 191n, 216, 226–65, *et passim*; Ahaggar and Tassili and 'mass' (1980s) 228, 232–4; battle against mass, *tourisme sauvage* and looters 248, 251–3; different impact on Djanet/Tassili and Tamanrasset/Ahaggar 230–32; Djanet Conference (March 2003) on 15; employment based on merit 111; environmentally sustainable 22, 226–7, 232–45, 248, 253; European air charters 235, 239; 'get-rich-quick' interests 22, 86, 234; government agencies and policies 235, 240–41; importance of 81, 141; in Mali and Niger 25n; independent travellers (*tourisme sauvage*) 235, 242; investment interests in neighbouring countries 235, 242; isolation and collapse of (1990s) 83–4, 96n, 140, 180, 229; Kel Rela acting as agents 179; lack of government planning 85–6, 91; lands of the Tuareg and 21–2; mass 22; nomads, local tourism agencies and 114–15, 184–5, 191n, 233–5, 242; official statistics 261n; people of the south and 89; relation between nomadism and 229–30; revival of (2000) 187; Sahara and 216; rock art and 212, 214, 216; smugglers and 235, 243–5; state of crisis (2003) 226; Tuareg need to take control of 226–7; Tuareg saw it as traditional camel economy 141; 'work' of men with camels (1970s and 1980s) 140
tourism product, French era prior to Algerian independence 227–8; 1960s and early 1970s 228; from early 1970s to end of 1980s 228; Algeria's crisis and cessation of tourism 228–9; potential 227; regeneration of tourism (autumn 1999–March 2003) 229
'*Tourisme Alternatif et Responsible*' 15, 21, 23; *see also* ATAWT and UNATA
tourisme sauvage 22, 25n, 235, 242, 248, 251
tourists 76, 185, 214, 228–9, 233; illegal 251–2; return of (1999) and local business 'opportunists' 239
traditional society 4, 31–2, 34, 38, 44, 48, 63–4n, 69, 73–4, 76, 79, 83, 98, 103, 107, 110, 119n, 122, 136, 146, 155, 157n, 161n, *et passim*; divorce in 126–7; dynamics of 38–9; façade of 49–50; 'pastoral-cum-raiding' production 167
trans-border international park 23
trans-Saharan caravan routes, nobles and 71
trans-Saharan highway 6, 240
trans-Saharan railway idea 28–9, 31–2
trans-Saharan smuggling 226f, 243–5, 249; arms, electronics and hard drugs 141, 244; and banditry 83–5, 226, 235; cigarettes especially 24, 85, 244; younger men and 141
trans-Saharan trade 61n, 175–6
transhumance 164–5, 176
Treaty of Ghadames (1862) 28
Triaud, J.-L. 63n, 273
Triploi 58, 61n, 199, 231
Tripoli–Bornu/Wadai trade routes, control of
Tripoli–Bornu/Wadai trade routes by Sanussi 35
Tripolitania 35, 62n, 158n
Tschudi, Yolande (Swiss ethnologist) 198–200, 202, 220n, 273
Tsisab Ravine (Namibia) 204

Index

Tuareg xv, 30, 35–6, 38, 60–61n, 83, 90, 95–6n, 97, 99, 101, 103, 105–6, 108–9, 112, 117, 121, 136, 141, 162n, *et passim*; Algeria and Algeria's crisis 3–8; Algerian now live in towns 113; 'Algerianisation' of 56, 78–80, 119n; belief that illness caused by Kel Asouf (*djenoun* – wicked spirits) 106; Berbers not Arabs 69; class structure (social classes) 27–8, 38–50, 70f, 111, 122, 124, 127–8, 155, 157–8n, 167f, *et passim*; classified themselves in terms of lifestyles 74; diaspora 114; disrespect (Sahraouis or Hadj Bettus) 17; dissatisfaction with *walis* 241; government's stance against Islamic fundamentalism 18; hostage crisis damaging to their interests 19–20; as *imuhagh ouan aghrem* (Tuareg of the villages) 80; incident (1963–64) 69–70; indigenous *Amazigh* people ('Berbers') 1, 10; 'indigenous rights' in Algeria 8–16; Islamic fundamentalism not supported by 250; journeys to assess damage to sites (1999 and 2000) 235, 262n; language 1; matrilineality and veiling of their men 2; Lhote and 213; men had first wife in Ahaggar and second in Tamesna 177; mentioned disparagingly in *A La Découverte* 202; never politically unified 23; 'nomads' but live in *zeribas* (reed huts) 165; older people talk of *débauché* behaviour 142; poor governance and 19; problems of modernisation 16; referring to themselves as 'Algerian Tuareg' (1970) 78; renaming taken with good humour 138; role of drought in weakening resistance of 51; role in Sahara and French colonial expansion 2; Sanussi revolt 34–7; stories from the landscape 237–8; story about white quartzite millstone 212, 217, 236; *see* Djerat; suffering from loss of heritage 212, 215; Tassili Frescoes 193, 195; *temazlayt* relationship and 170–71; ties with peoples of Mali and Niger 88; tourism their industry 15, 230; tourism-transport and 113–14; treatment as 'Algerian citizens' 14–15, 136; veiling (*anagad*) of their men 2, 97–120

Tuareg, northern (Algerian) 2–8, 37, *et passim*; France's last military engagement with (27 July 1920) 31; history of 27–8f, 59n, 83, 97f; no written records of history 27; political factions 27–8, 45; structural cleavages and 48; *see also* Kel Ahaggar, Kel Ajjer

'Tuareg problem' 7, 67–70, 81–2, 185; resolution of 70
Tuareg regions, potential development and new Saharan politic 20–24
Tuareg society, 'social externalisation' of 109–10
Tuareg, southern (Niger and Mali) 3, 10, 37, 47, 93n, 101, *et passim*; and revolts 2–4, 10, 21, 25n; *see also* Mali, Niger
Tuareg tourism agencies (*agences de tourisme*) in Tamanrasset 114–15, 184–5, 191n, 233–5, 242; 'mass' tourism and 233
Tuareg–Algerian relations 21
Tuat, xv, 23, 24n, 29, 31–3, 43–4, 47–9, 59–60n, 65n, 72, 87, 100, 138, 167, 173, 177
tugarchet 102
Tunisia 24n, 60–61n, 235, 242
Turkey, Turks 31, 35–6, 48, 60–62n, 65n

Uan Tabu 222n
Uan Ufada 222n
Ucko, P. 218
Ulad Ba Hammu xv, 59n
Ulad Dahane xv, 59n
Ulad Mokhtar xv, 59n
Ulad Yakhia xv, 59n
ult (daughter of) xv; *see also ag*
UN (United Nations) 8
UN Commission on Human Rights (CHR) 9, 85
UN Decade of Indigenous Peoples 9–16, 193, 218n, 225n
UN Draft Declaration on the Rights of Indigenous Peoples 9–11, 14, 15–16, 24n, 85, 90–91, 193, 215, 218n, 225n
UNATA xv, 21–3, 25n, 233–5, 239, 248–9, 262n; aware of professional looting by European tour operators 248; battle of tourism and 253; Report of 254; wrote to Cherif Rahmani 253
UNESCO 189n, 264n, 273; Declaration on Race and Racial Discrimination 9; major gathering of experts (1978) to examine paintings 210; World Heritage site, Tassili Frescoes 26n, 94n, 191n, 195, 219n, 236; *see also* Tassili National Park
UNIDROIT Convention on Stolen or Illegally Exported Cultural objects 193, 215, 218–19n
Union Nationale des Associations des Agences de Tourisme Alternatif; *see* UNATA
United Nations Development Programme (UNDP) 247

297

United States of America 96n, 203, 218n, 225n, 250, 264–5n; invasion of Afghanistan 25n; interests 25n; War on Terror 229, 250, 264n
University of East Anglia 253
Uqba ibn Nafi 63n
Uraren, the 34–5, 44, 51
Usenden, section of Aguh-en-tehle 137, 153

Vacher, M. 61n, 262n, 273
vassals 30, 35, 38–9, 50, 64n, 71f, 92n, 110, 119n, 122, 124, 166; traditionally goat pastoralists 71; *see also* Kel Ulli, *imrad*
veil, the (veiling) 2, 24n, 97–120; communicative symbol in traditional camp environment 114; *elmengoudi* (marking adolescent boy's initiation to adulthood) 97; interpretations and explanations 101–2f; new meanings of 114–17; other uses and beliefs associated with 105–14; physical properties of 99–101; protection in camp situations 108–9; social interaction and 103–5; still symbol of 'Tuaregness' 98, 116; women unveiled 121; worn on festive and ceremonial occasions 115
'veil and trousers are brothers' 106
villages, television has ousted hearth as focal point 141
Vita-Finzi, C. 218, 224n, 273
Voulet 59n

wage labour 74–6, 78, 167, 228; *see also* In Eker
Waldeck-Rousseau (PM of France) 60n
wali xv, 24n, 95n, 156, 181, 261n; and directors of tourism and national parks 235, 248
wali of Illizi 10, 15, 19, 88–9, 241, 263n, 265n
wali of Tamanrasset 96n, 117, 182, 241, 245–8, 263–4n
war-lords (syndrome) 82
'weekend nomadism' 179
West Africa 205, 244, 250
Westermarck, E. 106, 119n, 273

Western Sahara 3, 64n
white quartzite millstone (rain-stone), story of 212, 217, 236–7; *see also* Djerat, Lhote
wilaya (administrative region) xv, 2, 24n, 80; *see also wali*
women, position of, roles; *see* gender; as 'camp managers' 139, 176; in charge while men were away 138–9; 'fear of Islam' and 146; feel excluded by Algerian authorities 148; goats the domain of 176; health 146, living alone 148–51, 162n; living as nomads 'independently of men' 148–51, 188; marriages arranged years in advance 143; marrying younger since sedentarisation 142; prominent roles in social life 121–2; Tamanrasset, divorces for freedom 143; unveiled explained by their impurity in Islam 107; wear a headcloth (*ekerhei*) 97; *see also* gender
Working Group on Indigenous Populations' (WGIP) 'Draft Declaration on the Rights of Indigenous Peoples' 85
World Deserts Foundation (*Fondation Déserts du Monde*) 15, 20, 23, 25n, 187, 240, 253
World Tourism Organisation (WTO) 233, 247, 263n
World Trade Center's Twin Towers 263n; destruction (11 Sept. 2001) 229, 239; Islamic fundamentalists from Pakistan and Afghanistan have moved into region since 245
World War, First 30, 35, 62n
World War, Second 198

Yorkshire Light Infantry 58n
Younes 64n

Zaouatallaz 164, 183
zawiyya (religious lodge) xv, 54, 61n, 161n
zeriba (hut) xv, 165, 231
Zeroual, L. General (President) 261n
Zinder 58n, 61n, 231
Zoua xv
Zurich 5

Other Titles in the Series

Technology, Tradition and Survival

Aspects of Material Culture in the Middle East and Central Asia

Richard Tapper, SOAS, University of London and
Keith McLachlan, formerly of SOAS, University of London

This book seeks to promote a wider knowledge of traditional technologies in the Middle East and Central Asia. The contributors address three related themes: the history, originality, variety and sophistication of traditional science, technology and material culture in these regions; their influence on the history of Europe and the West; and the threat posed by modern Western technologies to the survival of traditional technologies which have continuing value according to late-twentieth-century standards of sustainability and appropriateness to local cultural, social and ecological conditions. There is a clear need for conservation of some artefacts that are under current threat of extinction. Individual chapters focus on specific aspects of technology and material culture: science and medicine; water technologies; vernacular architecture, both fixed buildings and the mobile tents of nomads; looms and weaving; and the structure of bazaars.

224 pages illus 2003
0 7146 4927 9 cloth
0 7146 4487 0 paper
History and Society in the Islamic World Series

FRANK CASS PUBLISHERS
Crown House, 47 Chase Side, Southgate, London N14 5BP
Tel: +44 (0)20 8920 2100 Fax:.+44 (0)20 8447 8548 E-mail: info@frankcass.com
NORTH AMERICA
920 NE 58th Avenue Suite 300, Portland, OR 97213-3786 USA
Tel: 800 944 6190 Fax: 503 280 8832 E-mail: cass@isbs.com
Website: www.frankcass.com

The Walled Arab City in Literature, Architecture and History

The Living Medina in the Maghrib

Susan Slyomovics, Massachusetts Institute of Technology (Ed)

This book offers a multidisciplinary approach to the medina, the traditional walled Arab city of North Africa. The medina becomes a concrete case study for comparative explorations of general questions about the social use of urban space by opening up fields of research at the intersection of history, comparative cultural studies, architecture and anthropology. Essays by American, European and North African scholars demonstrate the variety of new sources and theoretical approaches now being used in writing historical narratives framed within the city space, shed light on recent studies by anthropologists regarding social praxis within the urban context, and analyse the urban experience of the medina and the casbah as they are represented in visual and material culture.

176 pages 2001
0 7146 5177 X cloth
0 7146 8215 2 paper
A special issue of The Journal of North African Studies
History and Society in the Islamic World Series

FRANK CASS PUBLISHERS
Crown House, 47 Chase Side, Southgate, London N14 5BP
Tel: +44 (0)20 8920 2100 Fax: +44 (0)20 8447 8458 E-mail: info@frankcass.com
NORTH AMERICA
920 NE 58th Avenue Suite 300, Portland, OR 97213-3786 USA
Tel: 800 944 6190 Fax: 503 280 8832 E-mail: cass@isbs.com
Website: www.frankcass.com

Nation, Society and Culture in North Africa

James McDougall, St Antony's College, Oxford

The essays in Nation, Society and Culture in North Africa explore the complexities of the relationship between states, social groups, and individuals in contemporary North Africa, as expressed through the politics, culture, and history of nationhood. From Morocco to Libya, from bankers to refugees, from colonialism to globalisation, a range of individual studies examines how North Africans have imagined and made their world in the twentieth century.

200 pages 2003
ISBN 0 7146 5409 4 cloth
ISBN 0 7146 8337 X paper
A special issue of The Journal of North African Studies

FRANK CASS PUBLISHERS
Crown House, 47 Chase Side, Southgate, London N14 5BP
Tel: +44 (0)20 8920 2100 Fax: +44 (0)20 8447 8548 E-mail: info@frankcass.com
NORTH AMERICA
920 NE 58th Avenue Suite 300, Portland, OR 97213-3786 USA
Tel: 800 944 6190 Fax: 503 280 8832 E-mail: cass@isbs.com
Website: www.frankcass.com

Tribe and Society in Rural Morocco

David M Hart

This is an anthropological study of tribal societies in the modern world with particular reference to Morocco and the comparison between Morocco and Pakistan / Afghanistan. All the societies considered are Muslim in nature and the approach taken from the structuralist-functionalist perspective.

224 pages 2000
0 7146 5016 1 cloth
0 7146 8073 7 paper
A special issue of The Journal of North African Studies
History and Society in the Islamic World Series

FRANK CASS PUBLISHERS
Crown House, 47 Chase Side, Southgate, London N14 5BP
Tel: +44 (0)20 8920 2100 Fax: +44 (0)20 8447 8548 E-mail: info@frankcass.com
NORTH AMERICA
920 NE 58th Avenue Suite 300, Portland, OR 97213-3786 USA
Tel: 800 944 6190 Fax: 503 280 8832 E-mail: cass@isbs.com
Website: www.frankcass.com